Pepper, Silk & Ivory

Amazing Stories about
Jews and the Far East

PEPPER,
SILK
&
IVORY

Marvin Tokayer and
Ellen Rodman, PhD

gefen נפן
publishing house בית הוצאה לאור גפן
JERUSALEM ◆ NEW YORK   Est. 1981

Cover concept: Francois Ilnseher and Cynthia Herrli
Typesetting: Raphaël Freeman, Renana Typesetting
Cover layout: Keterpress Enterprises, Jerusalem
Photo of Ellen Rodman by William Heuberger

ISBN: 978-965-229-647-4

1 3 5 7 9 8 6 4 2

Gefen Publishing House Ltd.
6 Hatzvi Street
Jerusalem 94386, Israel
972-2-538-0247
orders@gefenpublishing.com

Gefen Books
11 Edison Place
Springfield, NJ 07081
516-593-1234
orders@gefenpublishing.com

www.gefenpublishing.com

Printed in Israel

Send for our free catalog

LIBRARY OF CONGRESS CATALOGING-IN-PUBLICATION DATA
Tokayer, Marvin, 1936- author.
 Pepper, silk & ivory : amazing stories about Jews
and the Far East / by Rabbi Marvin Tokayer and
Ellen Rodman, PhD.
    pages cm
 Includes index.
 ISBN 978-965-229-647-4
 1. Jews--Japan--History--20th century. 2. Jewish businesspeople--Japan--
History--20th century. 3. Jewish musicians--Japan--History--20th century.
4. Jews--China--History--20th century. 5. Jewish woman--China--History--
20th century. 6. Jews--China--Shanghai--History--20th century. 7. Refugees,
Jewish--China--Shanghai--History--20th century. 8. Jews--India--History--20th
century. 9. Jews--Burma--History--20th century, 10. Jews--Singapore--History--20th
century. I. Rodman, Ellen, author. II. Title. III. Title: Pepper, silk and ivory.
 DS135.J3T65 2014
 950'.0492400922--dc23

2014010983

To my wife Mazal
and our children
Shira, Amiel, Naama and Dan

In memory of Keith Andrew Rodman

Contents

Preface

There is a missing page in Jewish history. We usually assume that Jewish history is in the Middle East, Europe, North Africa and the Americas, not in the Far East. Soon after my arrival to serve as the rabbi of the Jewish community of Japan, I was invited to Australia for a series of lectures in St. Kilda, Melbourne, and I spent a most delightful Sabbath at the home of the Lubofsky family. I was in my early thirties, and this experience changed the focus of my life.

Rabbi Ronald Lubofsky was an erudite and distinguished rabbi who was not only comfortable with the tomes of Jewish learning but also grasped the broad vision of the entire Jewish perspective. He

Rabbi Shimon Shalom Kalish, the Amshinover Rebbe

politely suggested – even urged and encouraged – that I not only serve the Jewish community with diligence and dedication but that I also research, interview, collect, publish and become the repository of the experiences of the Jewish communities in the Far East.

It is to his credit that I published twenty books in Japanese on Jewish subjects, and in this book there are more wonderful stories that I collected, stories that gave Rabbi Lubofsky great pleasure. I think his favorite story was about a Hassidic Rebbe (rabbi), known as the Amshinover Rebbe or Rabbi Shimon Shalom Kalish, who as a refugee in Japan was interrogated by the Japanese military at the very same table where later the attack on Pearl Harbor was planned.

The quick retort by the Hassidic Rebbe, as you will read, helped overcome the heavy Nazi pressure on the Japanese to exterminate the Jews living in their territory during World War II.

The great Hebrew novelist and Nobel Prize winner S.J. Agnon tells the story about when the Baal Shem Tov (the founder of Hassidism, a form of Orthodox Judaism that promotes spirituality and happiness through Jewish mysticism as a fundamental part of Jewish faith) had a difficult task before him, he would go to a certain place in the forest, light a fire and meditate in prayer, and what he had set out to achieve would be accomplished. A generation later, when his successor was faced with a difficult task, he would go to the same place in the forest and say, "We can no longer light the fire, but we can still recite the prayers," and what he wanted to achieve became a reality. A generation later, when his successor had to perform a similarly difficult task, he, too, went to the forest and said, "We can no longer light the fire, nor can we recite the exact prayers and meditations, but we know the exact place in the forest and that must be sufficient," and it was. But when another generation had passed, and the new successor was called upon to perform the task, he sat down in his chair and said, "We do not know the place in the forest, we cannot light the fire, we cannot speak the prayers, but we can tell the story of how it was done." And, Agnon adds, "The story that he told had the same effect as the actions of the other three."

We stand on the shoulders of the historians who write about what their research has found to be true. An Italian proverb, however, says, "If it isn't true, it's a good story." In this book, while all of the stories are true, some may be anecdotal and some may have been embellished in the course of being passed down through the generations, but all of them – whether from ancient, medieval or modern times – are amazing stories that will give you great joy. In many instances I either knew the subjects of these stories or knew their relatives and still am in touch with many of them. In addition, I had access to, and now even possess, personal documents and artifacts relevant to their stories.

Every part of the Far East has a relationship with Jews. The Eastern world did not have a history of anti-Semitism or persecution; it was blessed with the concepts of tolerance and cultural pluralism. The stories in this book tell some of the extraordinary and amazing ways Jews contributed to the countries of the Far East and how the people of the Far East helped the Jews.

Their stories remind us all that four thousand years of Jewish history are far more than the Jewish experience in Europe, the Middle East, and the Holocaust. In the most unexpected and amazing ways, Jewish history also includes the Far East, now such an important part of the world politically and economically.

Acknowledgments

Pepper, Silk & Ivory was forty years in the making and influenced by many people and events in my life during those years. When I was the rabbi in the Far East, each one of my congregants became a "talking book" as they shared with me their memories, photos and diaries. Whether they were refugees in Japan and China during the Holocaust who later became my congregants, or residents of Japan, China, Hong Kong, Singapore, Burma (now Myanmar), Taiwan, the Philippines or India, they all led me as we retraced their steps and relived their experiences.

Congregants at the Cherry Lane Minyan, a modern Orthodox synagogue in Great Neck, New York, where I served as its founding rabbi until my retirement, patiently listened to my stories about Jews and the Far East and encouraged my research, and synagogues where I lectured as a scholar in residence also were very encouraging to me, and I am thankful to all of them.

While reading The Kogan Papers (*aka* The Berton Papers), eight thousand pages of Japanese Foreign Ministry secret documents relating to an intelligence network to determine policy on Jews before and during World War II, I was present vicariously at the highest level cabinet meetings. Subsequently, I searched for the individuals named in the documents, their relatives or their diaries.

Many Japanese and Chinese experts, some anti-Semites and several of those who helped to save Jews, all proved invaluable, and many academics encouraged, guided and corresponded with me and became my very close friends.

Libraries all over the world also were great assets to my research including the Library of Congress in Washington, DC; the Great Neck Library in New York; the Jewish Theological Seminary in New York; Yeshiva University in New York; the New York Public Library; the Columbia University Library in New

York; the Jewish National Library in Jerusalem; the Diet Library in Tokyo; the British Library in London; the Bodleian Library in Oxford, England; Hebrew Union College in Cincinnati, Ohio; and the Southern Methodist University Library in Dallas, Texas.

In addition, library archives aided my research including the archives at the JDC (Joint Distribution Committee) in New York; HIAS (Hebrew Immigrant Aid Society) in New York; the Jewish Welfare Board in New York; YIVO (Institute for Yiddish Research) and the Leo Baeck Institute at the Center for Jewish History in New York; Sino-Judaic Institute; Yad Vashem in Jerusalem, Israel; *Igud Yotsei Sin* (Society of Former Residents of China) in Tel Aviv, Israel; and the World Jewish Congress in New York.

Museum collections were also invaluable including those at the Jewish Museum in New York; the Museum of the Jewish People in Tel Aviv, Israel; the Israel Museum in Jerusalem, Israel; the British Museum in London, England; the Royal Ontario Museum in Toronto, Canada; the Kaifeng Museum in Kaifeng, China; the Shanghai Museum in Shanghai, China; the Shaanxi History Museum in Xian, China; the National Museum in New Delhi, India; the Indian Museum in Calcutta (now Kolkata), India; and the Victoria and Albert Museum in Bombay (now Mumbai), India.

All the countries and places in the Far East, including Thailand (formerly Siam), Hong Kong, Singapore, Myanmar (formerly Burma), Taiwan (formerly Formosa), the Philippines, China, India and Japan, are not only wonderful places to visit, they also are rich in the history of, and stories about, their relationships with the Jews over many centuries, and I am grateful to Lotus Tours for providing me with the opportunity to return to the countries of the Far East each year.

It was on a Lotus Tour to India that I met Ellen Rodman, who not only insisted that I publish my stories and research but also was willing to take her time and talent to cowrite them with me for posterity. She was a dream come true.

Here are some people, whose names are in alphabetical order, whom we wish to thank personally (please note that in China and Japan, family names are given first):

Ezekiel Abraham, Professor Wendy Abraham, Michael Alderton, David and Daniel Avshalomov, Jacob Ballas, Chaplain Louis Barish, Zelig Belokamen, Joshua Benjamin, Siona Benjamin, Irwin Berg, Samuel Bernstein, Professor Peter Berton, Professor Joan Bieder, Rebecca Bitterman, George Bloch, Mary

Goorevich Bloch, Paul C. Blum, Dr. Avrum and Martha Bluming, Harry Z. Bornstein, Kevin Callen, Phil and Millie Campanella, Professor Ruth Cernea, Chan S.J., Walter J. and Judy Citrin, A. Martin Cohen, Dr. Frederick Ira Cohen, Dr. Manley Cohen, Theodore Cohen, Dr. Yahya Cohen, Dr. Abraham J. Cohn, Leah Cooper, Paul Cummins, Eli David, Chaplain Herman Dicker, Professor Al Dien, Hans and Claire (Lala) Diestel, David Dorfman, Robert Dorfman, Solomon Dorfman, Lynn Douek, Professor Irene Eber, Audrey Eig, Shoul N. Eisenberg, Frank Ephraim, Israel Epstein, Professor Marc Epstein, Sam Evans, Professor Nissim Ezekiel, Rhetta Felton, Dr. David and Wendy Fretzin, Professor Walter Fischel, Benjamin Fishoff, Michael and Dr. Yonat Floersheim, Professor Arrigo Foa, Professor Mordechai Friedman, Michael Freund, Joseph Ganger, Michael and Ruth Gerson, Professor S.D. Goitein, Morris and Phyllis Gold, Ellen S. Goldberg, Professor Jonathan Goldstein, Professor David G. Goodman, Beate Sirota Gordon, Jacob Gotlieb, Peter Gravina, Marcel and Sandra Grossman, Nathan Gutwirth, Samuel and Queenie Hallegua, Leo Hanin, Professor Hasegawa R. Shin, Brodie Hefner, Fred Hendeles, Bill Heuberger, Professor Higuchi Ryuichi, Lynn Hollister, Francois Ilnseher, Inuzuka Kyoko, Lieutenant General J.F.R. Jack Jacob, Ralphy Jhirad, Al and Cookie Joseph, Mila Ionis, Mischa Kachanovsky, Caroline Kades, Sir Horace Kadoorie, Lord Lawrence Kadoorie, Professor Gerd Kaminski, Kase Hideaki, Professor Nathan Katz, Teddy Kaufman, Amy Kingston, Professor Kobayashi Masayuki, Samuel Sattu Koder, David and Judi Koffsky, Michael and Asya Kogan, Jac Kolberg, Michael Kong, Professor Kotsuji Setsuzo Abraham, Professor David Kranzler, Paul and Sophie Kraslavsky, Bernard Krisher, Samuel and Marcia Kublanow, Jacob Kurlyandsky, Wolf Ladejinsky, Rabbi Anson Laytner, Professor Donald David Leslie, Dennis Leventhal, Yaacov Liberman, Professor Seymour Liebman, Jennifer Lima, Professor Rudolf Loewenthal, Professor Fery Lorant, Rabbi Ronald and Shirley Lubofsky, Robert M. Lury, Ezekiel Malekar, Rabbi David A. Mandelbaum, Laura Margolis, Chief Minister David Marshall, Jean Marshall, Professor Meron Medzini, Professor Matthias Messmer, Professor Maise Meyer, Yael Meyer, Professor Jeannette Mirsky, Misha Mitsel, Victor Moche, Taarini Mookherjee, Nissim Moses, Reverend Nakada Ugo, Mozelle Nissim, Reverend Otsuki Takeji, Professor Pan Guang, Professor Tudor Parfitt, Professor Shalom Paul, Professor Peggy K. Pearlstein, Teddy Piastunovich, Professor Andrew H. Plaks, Daniel Polin, Michael Pollak, Hans Pringsheim, Kezia Raffel-Pride, Henrietta Reifler, Dorothy Jean Cohen Reiser, Chaplain Elihu H. Rickel, Frank and Helen Risch, Drs. Kenneth X. and

Joyce Robbins, Melissa C. Rodman, Pamela B. Rodman, William B. Rodman, Arthur Rosen, Irving Rosen, Chaplain Milton Rosen, Ann Margaret Rosenfeld-Frija, Professor Joseph Rosenstock, David Rubinson, Professor Sacon Y. Herman, Moses Samuel, Sammy Samuel, Cesar Sassoon, Professor Sato Izumi, John Schiff, Sidney Shapiro, Joshua Shapurkar, Dr. Cyril Sherer, Shi Lei, Shih Hung-mo, Professor Ben-Ami Shillony, Joseph Shimkin, Professor Frank Joseph Shulman, Rabbi Victor Solomon, Solomon Sopher, E.P. Stein, H. Alexander Straus, Sugihara Chiune (Senpo), Professor Sugita Rokuichi, Sun Lixin, Mary S. Swartz, David and Bea Tendler, Reverend Teshima Ikuro, Alex Triguboff, Bernard and Dorothie Valier, Dina Waht, Michael Wallace, Emanuel Warhaftig, Zorach Warhaftig, Michael Wasserman, Karel Weiss, Ruth Weiss, Professor Susan Whitfield, Joe and Rosalie Wise, Professor Xu Buzeng, Professor Xu Xin, Yasue Hiro, Amikam Yechezkely, Professor Moshe Yegar, Yi Brenda, Al Younghem, Jamshid Zar and Professor Zhao Xiangru.

Chapter One
Two-Gun Cohen: A Jewish General in the Chinese Army

Who would believe there was a Jewish general in the Chinese Army? Who would believe that a street in a very fashionable neighborhood in Shanghai is named Cohen Road? Who would believe that a Jewish tombstone in Manchester, England, etched in Hebrew and English, is also etched with signed calligraphy in Chinese from one of the most famous women in China, Vice-Premier Mme Sun Yat-sen, acknowledging her respect for this Jewish general, a hero of China?* And who would believe that at the Canadian embassy in Beijing (formerly Peking), an entire wall is a collage of photos of this legendary hero, frequently cited in the press as the "uncrowned Jewish king of China"?

The legendary Morris Abraham Cohen, born in Radzanow, Poland, on August 3, 1887, was one of many children of a Polish immigrant family who settled in London. Orthodox Judaism was strictly observed in his Yiddish-speaking home, with his mother wearing a *sheitel* (wig) and his father serving as the *shammash* (sexton) of a small synagogue in London's East End. Morris, or Moisha, as he was known, was a tough kid, a truant after only a few days in kindergarten who later became a petty thief, stealing wooden boxes from the docks of London to sell for firewood. Eventually, he started a joint venture with an adult whereby he would smash a window with a rock which his partner then would offer to repair, and they would share the profits. He may have used most of his money, including money that his father gave him for attending Hebrew lessons, to attend vaudeville shows.

---

* Mme Sun Yat-sen was one of the Soong sisters, all of whom were extraordinarily accomplished, well-known women, including Soong May-ling, who was married to Generalissimo Chiang Kai-shek.

1

Two-Gun Cohen, age twenty-six, 1913

At age eight, Moisha was so overweight that people referred to him as "Fat Moisha," and he became an underage boxer, flyweight division, fighting under the name of "Cockney Cohen." His best match was with "Battling Murphy," whose real name was Izzy Fink, but Fat Moisha never entered the ring on Friday night because he was always present at his family's Sabbath table.

The London police classified Moisha Cohen as a truant, petty thief, pickpocket and future criminal and sentenced him to reform school. The Jewish community of London, embarrassed by its juvenile delinquents, created a Jewish reform school called Hayes Industrial School for Delinquent Jewish Boys. It was funded by Lord Rothschild, and Morris Abraham Cohen was registered there in February 1901 as the eighth Jewish delinquent to attend.

We all know that the right teacher with the right student at the right time and place can make a world of difference. Moisha did meet such a teacher, Israel Ellis, who convinced him that he possessed such a commanding presence that if he could speak clearly and correctly, he would have a successful future. Moisha learned to overcome and correct his speech impediments – difficulty saying *g* and *h* and slurring his words – by reciting "he had his hard head hammered" hundreds of times while standing on one foot. On parents' visiting day Shakespeare's *Richard III* was performed. Moisha successfully memorized his part and, with a closed book, recited his entire section to a standing ovation. Moisha had turned the corner.

At age eighteen, Moisha was released from the Jewish reform school and returned home. His father informed him that society now labeled him an ex-con and that he would have absolutely no future in England. Meanwhile his father had corresponded with Abie Hyams, a friend in Canada, who replied that he was very successful, that there was gold in the streets of Canada and that he would take Moisha under his wing. So with five British pounds in his pocket, Moisha was shipped off to Canada to seek his fortune. His father's last words of advice to him were to study Torah regularly, pray daily, be honest, donate to *tzedaka* (charity) and spend money carefully.

Upon arriving in Canada, Moisha Cohen learned that his father's friend actually was a financial failure who could not care for him. So starting in Wapella, Saskatchewan, in the Canadian West, where Cohen was exposed for the first time to the taste of forbidden foods like pork (observant Jews don't eat pork), Cohen worked as a farmhand earning one hundred dollars a year. He continued working as a farmer and then worked as a rancher, dishwasher and shoe shiner. Eventually, however, he became a peddler of fake jewelry and defective watches, which resulted, yet again, in run-ins with the law.

Bobby Clark, a friend, taught Cohen how to master the art of gambling and cheating, which, not surprisingly given his past, Cohen took to exceptionally well. He could detect loaded dice, marked cards, hidden mirrors and every other trick in the book. In short, he could beat anyone and learned that it takes a cheat to cheat a cheat.

The Chinese had traveled to Canada to pan for gold, build the railroad, open restaurants and introduce the Chinese laundry, but in both western Canada and the United States in the early twentieth century, the immigrant Chinese were a disenfranchised minority – unprotected, exploited and robbed, even by the local authorities. They were lynched and expelled, and their neighborhoods were set on fire. If someone had gambled or wasted his salary, for example, one could simply rob a Chinese person, and no one would say a word – no one, that is, except Moisha Cohen.

Cohen identified with the Chinese and realized how much they shared in common. They both came from ancient cultures and they were far from their homelands, were misunderstood, disliked and subjected to hate and discrimination, yet they were proud of their ancestry. The Chinese had their folktales and Confucius; Cohen had the Jewish folktales he had heard at his parents' Sabbath table. Remarkably, Chinese and Jewish folktales are very similar and frequently reflect shared values.

If Cohen saw someone mistreating a Chinese person, he did not hesitate to use his powerful fists. Once, for example, Cohen entered a Chinese restaurant in Saskatoon and realized that the Chinese proprietor was being robbed at gunpoint. The thief already had emptied the cash register and stolen the proprietor's wallet and watch, but he was having difficulty removing a ring from the proprietor's finger. Cohen, without hesitation, delivered a blow with a powerful fist to the thief's head and a powerful knee to his mid-section, leaving the thief unconscious. Cohen then returned the money, watch and wallet to the proprietor. Word spread quickly about what Cohen had done, and the Chinese were surprised and grateful that Cohen defended them, protected

Two-Gun Cohen, wearing white suit and surrounded by the Chinese Army, on July 1, 1926, the first anniversary of the founding of the nationalist government

them, spoke politically on their behalf and even put his own life in danger for them.

Another popular hero of the time in the Chinese community was Dr. Sun Yat-sen, the charismatic leader who dreamed of returning China to its ancient glory by ending the corrupt imperial system and creating a progressive, democratic and proud China. He went to Canada clandestinely to seek support from the Canadian Chinese, and all meetings were held in secret since the emperor had put a price on his head, dead or alive. Cohen was invited to one of those meetings and, surprisingly, was unanimously voted into the Chinese secret society to liberate China, a unique achievement for a foreigner. The Canadian Chinese accepted Cohen as a brother and considered him a fellow exile who had street smarts and could be a useful ally.

Dr. Sun, however, felt otherwise. He said he would not meet with Cohen because he did not trust any foreigner and would meet with only the Chinese. The Chinese argued that Cohen was one of them and succeeded in arranging a private meeting between Cohen and Dr. Sun. When the two made eye contact and Dr. Sun looked deeply into Cohen's blazing green eyes, and when Cohen saw a friendly twinkle in Dr. Sun's eyes and a warm smile on his face, Cohen sensed the old-fashioned manners that reminded him of home. Dr. Sun asked Cohen to join him in China, but Cohen did not think the time was right. He did see a chance to do something right and just, however, and he agreed to serve as Dr. Sun's personal bodyguard in Canada. Their friendship blossomed, and Dr. Sun gave Cohen funds to purchase thousands of rifles, revolvers, spare parts and ammunition which Cohen smuggled into China in boxes labeled "Singer sewing machines." In China, to this day, light machine guns are called "Singer," but no one remembers why.

Cohen, who was making a fortune in real estate speculation by selling what he thought was useless real estate for fifteen dollars per acre, donated a portion of his profit to the Chinese cause. (Today that land is worth a fortune because it contains oil.) At the start of World War I in 1914, Cohen trained 750 Canadian Chinese to serve in the future Chinese Army and also to serve in the existing Canadian Army, but their enlistment was refused by the Canadian military. Eventually, however, when the Canadians were short on labor, they were accepted. Cohen himself volunteered for the army and was sent to France where, not surprisingly, he was later commissioned to head a regiment of a Chinese labor brigade.

Cohen thought that the Chinese dream to be free in one's own land was the greatest dream of all, and after the war, he finally accepted Dr. Sun's persistent invitations to come to China, where, in 1922, he signed a contract with a Canadian firm to construct fifteen hundred miles of railway from Canton (now Guangzhou) to Chongqing. With the rank of colonel, he served as Dr. Sun's personal bodyguard, adviser, friend and arms purchaser. He was a pioneer in creating China's secret service and saved Dr. Sun's life at least twice. Without a doubt Dr. Sun, who was considered both the George Washington and Abraham Lincoln of China, valued Cohen as an indispensable friend and confidant. Cohen was so well known and respected in China that he could enter any store and purchase anything without paying because his face was his bond, and everyone knew he would pay the next day.

Cohen also was very friendly with the Jews who lived in China. His presence in court when a Jew was on trial was very useful. He attended B'nai B'rith (a Jewish fraternal organization) and Zionist meetings, attended synagogue on the holidays and always tried to be helpful. Whenever Cohen was in Hong Kong on Friday night, he went to Hans Diestel's home for Sabbath dinner. Hans was from Germany and was not born Jewish, but he came to China, met a Jewish woman (not a refugee) in Shanghai, fell in love, converted to Judaism and married her. Hans and Claire (known to everyone as Lala) lived in Shanghai until they moved to Hong Kong. My wife and I stayed with them when we were in Hong Kong and we also enjoyed Sabbath dinner at their home. Recently, while I was visiting Hong Kong, I met with Hans Diestel's daughter, who reminisced about Friday night dinners with Cohen, recalling how much he loved her mother's gefilte fish with loads of horseradish, chicken soup with matzah balls, well-done brisket and kugel (a baked pudding or casserole usually made from egg noodles or potatoes, but sometimes made from fruits and vegetables).

Whenever someone asked Cohen why he didn't marry a Chinese girl, his standard reply was, "A good Chinese girl would never marry a foreigner, and a bad Chinese girl I don't want. Besides, I promised my father that I would marry only a Jewish girl." In June 1944, Cohen did marry a Canadian Jewish girl, thirty-eight-year-old Judith Clark, but the marriage ended in divorce after twelve years. They had no children, and although it was an amicable divorce, it was a sad breakup that left Cohen depressed.

Ironically, Cohen, the ex-con, helped raise much-needed funds for the young government of Dr. Sun, and by 1927, Cohen had become so well respected that President Chiang Kai-shek named him to a vital post with the Central Bank of China, responsible for bullion vaults and even empowered to issue new currency. Once, Cohen prevented a run on the bank, an accomplishment that greatly enhanced his reputation. The foreign press, tongue in cheek, cited Cohen as the "Chancellor of the Exchequer."

Cohen wisely advised China's government to seek support and cooperation from the Chinese in Hong Kong, Canada, the United States and Singapore. As an intelligence officer, Cohen was responsible for Hong Kong and kept his eye on foreign powers in China. He purchased, borrowed and begged for all types of arms and military equipment, and he even arranged for the construction of an airplane that was named *Rosmonde*, the name Mme Sun had used as a student in the US, at Wesleyan College for Women in Georgia.

The young republic, nevertheless, was beset with numerous problems and calamities, including the many warlords in the northern part of China who prevented the unification of the country into one China. Suddenly, however, messages were received that a prominent warlord, General Cheung Shih, had serious gambling debts, so for the right offer he could be persuaded to change sides. A few others had tried but failed, and they never came back, probably having lost their lives in their attempts. But who could reach him and talk to him alone person to person? "Moisha," was Dr. Sun's answer. He told Cohen that there was no one else he could turn to for a mission of this importance. He warned Cohen that his life might be at risk but emphasized that so was the future of China. "Don't worry about that *mamzer*" (literally means "bastard," but used here as "wise guy"), Moisha responded. "I'll take care of him for you."

In April 1924, Cohen – camouflaged with baggy pants, a loose jacket and rope-tied slippers – smeared his face with mud and donned a coolie hat. He was provided with maps and everything else he needed for this perilous journey. Mme Sun offered to cook his favorite chicken soup with kreplach (dumplings) and grits upon his safe return. Cohen was amused by her confusion of recipes, just as he had been when he presided over a Passover Seder (the holiday dinner during which Jews celebrate the story of their hasty exodus out of Egypt and slavery) held in the spacious dining room of Dr. Sun's presidential palace and attended by cabinet members, generals and high-ranking officials. They sat with matzah

Two-Gun Cohen, with Generalissimo Chiang Kai-shek; courtesy of Michael Wallace. Mr. Wallace's grandmother, Rose Bernstein, was Two-Gun Cohen's sister.

(unleavened bread) and horseradish, washing it down with sweet Passover wine as Cohen explained the elaborate Passover rituals. At the conclusion, Dr. Sun inquired whether the Seder meal had followed Jewish tradition correctly, to which Cohen replied without missing a beat, "It would have been more Orthodox without the roast pig!"

In any event, Cohen traveled from Canton to Hong Kong where he boarded a commercial junk (small, inexpensive boat with no amenities) that smelled of urine, feces, vomit, chickens and opium. He survived on rice and gruel, and in six days, 930 miles later, he arrived in Shanghai. From there he traveled by train. Trains were frequently hijacked by local warlords for ransom, but he was not discovered because he was not traveling first class, the section of the train where the hijackers made their money. Finally he arrived in the northern city of Beijing and found his way to the compound of General Cheung. There he was captured by two armed sentries, who bound his wrists behind his back and brought him to the general. "*Ni na li?*" (Who are you?), barked the general in Mandarin. Cohen responded in pidgin Cantonese that he had come with a message from Dr. Sun Yat-sen for him.

The general recognized the name, and although he did not understand Cantonese, he did not call for a translator. He had noticed Cohen's size and demeanor, which reminded him of his university days in Hamburg, Germany, where he had lived for four years with a Jewish family. "*Nu, vas toot sich?*"

(What's going on here?), the general asked. Cohen believed he was witnessing a miracle and thought to himself, "He speaks Chinese but I hear Yiddish!" What's going on here indeed! If it were not a miracle, then it was certainly a lucky break. Continuing in Yiddish the two reached an agreement: the general changed sides and joined Dr. Sun Yat-sen, and the two men ended with rice wine, clicking their glasses to *mazel* and *brocha* (good luck and blessings).

Sadly, Dr. Sun Yat-sen died on March 12, 1925, at the age of fifty-nine. Cohen cried only twice in his life: when his father died and when Dr. Sun, his hero, died. Considered family, Cohen was the only foreigner present at the last, most prestigious funeral for the first president of China. Dressed in top hat and tails, Cohen was among the group that led the procession paying final tribute to the George Washington/Abraham Lincoln of China.

Chiang Kai-shek promoted Cohen to the rank of general, for he had high regard for this long-trusted servant of Sun Yat-sen and China. Cohen had helped train Chinese farmers and other citizens to defend China from foreign invaders. He had warned Chiang Kai-shek about the dangerous number of Soviet agents in China's government, and they were subsequently purged. Cohen had stressed early on the danger Japan posed to China, pointing out that Japan was a small country with a large population and no natural resources and had its sights fixed on expansion. Cohen, alerting Chiang Kai-shek that Japan was China's primary enemy, even provided a cylinder of gas as proof that the Japanese were using poison gas during the Second Sino-Japanese War, 1937–1945. And Cohen had saved Dr. Sun's life at least twice.

Within hours of the Japanese attack on Hong Kong, on December 25, 1941, Cohen found a plane and pilot to fly Mme Sun out of Hong Kong, but he stayed on, despite her pleas. In early 1942, Cohen was arrested by the Japanese in Hong Kong and incarcerated in the infamous Stanley Prison, where he was beaten and brutally tortured by the Japanese but refused to reveal any information. On February 2, 1942, Cohen's head was placed on the block next to a table where a shining sword waited. "*Shema Yisrael, Adonai Eloheinu, Adonai Echad*" (Hear O Israel, the Lord our God, the Lord is One), Cohen screamed with all his might. The Japanese returned Cohen to his cell with no explanation.

Cohen was repatriated on the *Gripsholm* in 1943, all skin and bones, eighty pounds lighter with bloodshot eyes. When the ship docked, the Canadians resented all the emphasis on, and questions about, Cohen. They announced, "There was no Canadian general in the Chinese Army," but they later retracted their statement and admitted, "There is a General Cohen in the Chinese Army."

Very few people are aware of the role that "Two-Gun Cohen" played in support of the Zionist movement and the creation of the Jewish homeland. He cooperated in any way he could to ensure a Jewish homeland and encouraged China's vital support as well. On April 24, 1920, Dr. Sun had written, "I express my sympathy to the movement which is one of the greatest movements... All lovers of democracy cannot help but support the movement."

Before the end of World War II, in April 1945, during the formative days of the United Nations, there was a meeting in San Francisco, and the partition of Palestine into a Jewish and Arab state already was on the agenda. Present were the leading Zionist leaders of the United States and representatives of the Jewish community of British Palestine. Security Council members France, the United States and the Soviet Union planned to support the partition, in part to assuage their guilt about the unforgivable Holocaust in Europe and also to push the British away from the rich oil fields in the Middle East.

The Chinese, however, were a major obstacle. The Arab states tried to dissuade them from supporting the United Nations' partition option with the cry of "Asia for the Asians" and their claim that Zionism is colonialism. The Zionist leaders, who were meeting in San Francisco, were desperate to talk with the Chinese delegation but their efforts had failed. Suddenly Rabbi Israel Goldstein, the rabbi of Congregation B'nai Jeshurun in Manhattan, remembered reading about Cohen in the Yiddish press and telephoned him in Montreal, requesting that he fly immediately to San Francisco. Upon his arrival in San Francisco, Cohen met with the Zionist leaders and learned that General Wu Tiecheng was heading the Chinese delegation. Cohen, not surprisingly, knew General Wu very well. General Wu had been mayor of Shanghai, was a fellow general in the Chinese Army and they had participated together in a goodwill mission of China to the Philippines, Malaysia and the Dutch East Indies.

Cohen met with General Wu the next morning, and the rest is history. China did not vote against the partition, and the Jewish state was created after two thousand years of Jewish exile. Indeed it was General Wu who as foreign minister in 1949 offered diplomatic recognition of the new State of Israel.

In 1966, when Cohen visited Israel, Prime Minister Ben-Gurion needed a favor. Palestinian terrorists were planting Chinese-made land mines in the area of schools, causing loss of limbs and other serious injuries to children. Cohen was asked to intercede with China. Cohen met with Zhou Enlai in Geneva, and whether that meeting was the reason or not, suddenly the Palestinians no longer had those Chinese mines.

Tombstone of Two-Gun Cohen in Manchester, England. *Bottom right*, inscription by Mme Sun Yat-sen (Soong Ching Ling) to "Ma-Kun" (Cohen's Chinese name). Ribbons on flower wreaths (*bottom*) represent the People's Republic of China (Beijing) and the Republic of China (Taiwan).

During the throes of China's Civil War that forced Chiang Kai-shek to relocate to Taiwan, leaving Mao Zedong's People's Republic of China in Beijing in control of mainland China, Cohen claimed to be the only person who could fly directly from Taiwan to Beijing. He was trusted by both sides and conveyed top-secret messages and peace "feelers" between the two men. When Cohen died in September 1970, surrounded by his family, since both men revered and were loyal to Sun Yat-sen and his friend "Two-Gun Cohen," it was reported that Cohen's funeral was the only time that representatives of the two Chinas appeared together. They did so peacefully out of respect for this loyal friend of the first president of China, and each of them placed a wreath of flowers on Cohen's grave.

Cohen, described by the *Manchester Guardian* as the "diplomatic and financial force behind modern China," was invited to mainland China as a state guest for the one hundredth anniversary of Dr. Sun Yat-sen's birth and for the tenth and twentieth anniversaries of the People's Republic of China. At the "Double Tenth" state banquet, Zhou Enlai, the popular premier of China, came to Cohen, patted him on the shoulder, raised his glass for a toast and said, "Morris, old friend, so nice to see you, long life." Moisha Cohen, or "Two-Gun Cohen," as he will be known forever, was overcome with emotion upon hearing these tender words on his last visit to China.

It's clear why some called Cohen "Fat Moisha," "Cockney Cohen," and an ex-con, and why some called him the "uncrowned Jewish king of China," the "Chancellor of the Exchequer," and *Mah Kun* or General Cohen. *Mah*, in Chinese, can be translated as mother, curse, linen, strong horse or clenched fist, depending on how it is pronounced, and it was "strong horse" and "clenched fist" that were attributed to Cohen. (In Chinese names, usually the first name is the family name, and the second name is the given name.) But why was Cohen nicknamed "Two-Gun Cohen"?

Cohen had mastered the use of a gun and always remembered to "never point a gun at a friend" and to "do unto others, but do it first." Cohen was quick to severely wound a cowboy when the cowboy dared to call him a "dirty Jew." In 1924, when Cohen received two bullet wounds to his left arm while protecting Dr. Sun from an assassination attempt, he learned the importance of being able to shoot with both hands, which is one of the origins of his being called "Two-Gun Cohen." He also carried both an automatic gun in his shoulder holster and a Smith and Wesson revolver in his hip holster, and in the hot summer one could always see two guns on his hip brace, additional reasons for his nickname.

Chapter Two
The Secret behind One of the World's Most Famous Logos

The reader may be surprised to learn that the world famous shell in the logo of the Shell Oil Company, first used in 1901, has its roots in Japan. Even more surprising, perhaps, is that the name of the company was once the Rising Sun Petroleum Company (1900), with offices in the Japanese cities of Yokohama and Kobe. Marcus Samuel Jr., creator and founder of Shell Oil and creator of the first oil tanker, had a close personal relationship with Japan. I learned this story from two sources.

One of my favorite pastimes when I lived in Tokyo was my frequent visits to Jinbocho, a major street lined with used bookstores, in Kanda (an area in Tokyo near universities). I am always excited by being in used bookstores; I love the smell of the used books and I never know what I might find!

One day while visiting a bookstore that had a foreign book section on the second floor, the proprietor, who recognized me from my frequent visits, stopped me as I started up the stairs. I was both startled and delighted when he said, "I have put aside a book for you." And with the smile of success on his face, he handed me a thick biography of Marcus Samuel Jr., a person with whom I was totally unfamiliar. He wondered aloud how I, with my rabbinic beard, yarmulke (skull cap) and interest in Jewish books did not know who Marcus Samuel was.

He told me that Marcus Samuel Jr. (1853–1927) was Jewish; had maintained an office in Yokohama, Japan; headed companies originally called Samuel Samuel and Company and the Rising Sun Petroleum Company; and had founded Shell Oil. He knew this, he said, because his family was from Yokohama, and his grandfather had worked for Shell Oil. Needless to say, I bought this rare

book, grateful to the bookseller for providing me with one of the monumental
experiences of my life.

A few months later I met someone
from England who worked at Shell Oil
in Japan, and he told me the same story
as the bookstore owner. When I asked
him for his sources, he told me he had
read the story several years earlier in *Shell
Times*, the company newspaper. Sadly, this
in-house newspaper, published in Yokohama, does not exist there or in the company's archives in London but, fortunately,
we can still tell Marcus Samuel Jr.'s amazing story.

Marcus Samuel, 1863–1927, founder
of Shell Oil

Born in 1853 in Whitechapel in the East
End section of London, Marcus was one
of eleven children, nine of whom survived,
the second of three sons born to his parents, Abigail Moss and Marcus Sr.,
immigrants from Bavaria and Holland who married on August 28, 1833. Marcus Sr. came up with the clever and enterprising idea to meet returning ships
on the dock with cash to purchase items the sailors brought back from the
Far East. The most common purchases Marcus Sr. made were coral, mother
of pearl, ivory, and occasionally semi-precious stones. What he wanted most,
though, were exotic seashells, which he would polish and use to adorn boxes,
picture frames, mirrors, needle cases, pin cushions and other trinkets and
souvenirs for sale in the curio shops to the people of Victorian England (who
loved bric-a-brac of all kinds) and to tourists. The family lived over their store
and warehouse, which was near the docks in the East End of London.

From this humble beginning the family expanded their imports from shells
to ostrich feathers, wool, silk, wax, goat skins, gum, tin, coal, pepper, tea, jute
and rice. The family also started exporting manufactured goods and machinery and became the first ones to export to Japan mechanical looms with small
seats that accommodated the petite Japanese women very well. Their most
important items, however, were the exotic and highly fashionable seashells.
Also important was the network of trusted relationships the family built with
trading houses in India, Singapore, Bangkok, Manila, Hong Kong, Burma and

other major ports of the Far East. The family went from poverty to running a relatively successful business.

Marcus Jr. was educated in Jewish schools in London and Brussels before joining the family business when he was sixteen. In 1873, at age nineteen, he set out on his first voyage to the Far East, where he succeeded in chartering fifty thousand tons of shipping capacity to bring surplus rice from Siam (now Thailand) to famine-stricken India. Behind this venture one could already see the simple business principle that would guide all his future commercial decisions, namely to find the nearest supply of a commodity that was needed to fill an urgent local demand. Pretty amazing and daring for a nineteen-year-old! Three years later, in 1876, Marcus took a trip around the world, not so much because he sought adventure but rather because he sought knowledge, experience and new contacts.

When Marcus Sr. died, he left the wish that "his sons should remain united, loving and considerate, and keep the good name of Marcus Samuel from reproach." In 1878 Marcus Jr. and his brother Samuel partnered to create two different companies, M. Samuel and Company based in London and Samuel Samuel and Company based in Yokohama and later also in Kobe, Japan.

By the age of thirty, Marcus already had made a fortune from his Japanese trade. He also was aware that changes were taking place that would affect his business, and all Japanese commerce, as a result of the arrival in 1853 of Commodore Perry who opened up Japan to Western trade. The conversion from sails to steam in shipping, the opening of the Suez Canal and the rapid industrialization of Japan were all factors that offered opportunities to someone with vision.

An example of the seashell-adorned, black-lacquered boxes that launched the Samuel family's successful business

Marcus sensed that the old system of trade was doomed because it was no longer possible for foreign companies to count on purchasing raw material from an undeveloped country in exchange for the industrial machinery and finished products it needed. In keeping with his business principle of finding the nearest supply of a needed commodity to fill an urgent local demand, Marcus looked for a product which was not produced in Japan, was needed by Japan and could find a large market in Japan. His company's traffic in charcoal from Yokohama to Malaya provided him with the answer. Japan was dark because the fuel the Japanese used in their paper lamps was inefficient, and the charcoal they were using to heat their homes also emitted carbon monoxide and led to explosions. He suddenly realized the great need for kerosene in Japan and in the entire area of East Asia.

Years earlier, the worldwide demand for kerosene, distilled from crude oil, for use in lamps had prompted a group of American investors to finance a drilling project designed to find oil. Edwin Drake, a retired railroad conductor, headed the project. He erected an engine house and drill on a farm in Titusville, Pennsylvania, where on August 27, 1859, he struck oil, sparking a boom that continues today. Less than forty years later, the oil industry was dominated by John D. Rockefeller's Standard Oil Company.

Marcus knew that the production, refining, transporting and marketing of kerosene for oil lamps were all in the hands of a few monopolies such as Rockefeller's Standard Oil. He also knew that you could not fight these companies unless you could find some means of reducing costs so dramatically that the oil monopolies would be undersold without a means to retaliate. He created his plan in Yokohama.

To start, Marcus had to find an oil supplier. In 1891 he traveled to Russia, where he found that Robert and Ludwig Nobel, the elder brothers of the inventor and manufacturer Alfred Nobel, along with the Rothschild family, had been firmly entrenched in Russia (since the 1880s) as refiners, transporters and marketers of kerosene and fuel oil in competition with Rockefeller. He also saw the huge, bulky ships designed by the Nobel brothers that were used to transport bulk oil. These ships were known as the "Ships of Death," because the frequent explosions that occurred were deadly. Workers were recruited to sail on them by picking up the drunk, unemployed men who were found around the docks. Marcus delicately managed to negotiate a contract with the Nobel brothers that gave him exclusive rights for nine years to buy and sell their oil east of the Suez Canal.

With a supply of oil now secured, Marcus returned to Japan and met with all the trading houses with which he regularly did business, asking them to join him as partners in a new venture. He wanted to create depots, warehouses, docks, storage tanks, refineries and railroad lines to service the entire area, including India, Siam, Burma, China, Singapore, Malaya, the Dutch East Indies and the Philippines, with Japan as the base. Amazingly, the trading houses had so much confidence in Marcus that they all agreed to participate in and finance his grand design for the shipping, storing and distribution of oil.

Next Marcus focused on the thorny problem of transporting oil. At the time, kerosene was shipped in wooden barrels that were not only bulky but also wasted space. The barrels always leaked, the fumes often led to explosions, the barrels frequently caught fire and they could be used only once in any case. Once the kerosene was emptied, the barrels remained too dirty for anything else to be put in them for the return trip. Genius that he was, Marcus wanted a new type of ship in which kerosene could be shipped in bulk, drastically reducing the cost per gallon of shipping it. He promptly went about finding a company that would build the ship he wanted, to be called a tanker, where the wall of the ship also would be the wall of the container, thereby increasing space by 50 percent and eliminating the problematic wooden barrels. The engine, furthermore, would be far away from the oil to prevent fires.

A British firm, William Gray & Company, accepted the challenge and worked with Marcus on every one of his amazingly brilliant details to build a ship that addressed and solved all the issues of the old ships, the ones used by Rockefeller's Standard Oil Company. Marcus's ship, completed in May 1892, could be steamed clean upon arrival so it could then take on cargo for the return trip. And Marcus's ship met the strict safety requirements of the Suez Canal, which did not allow oil ships through because of the danger they posed from fires and explosions. If ships carrying oil could pass through the Suez Canal en route from the Russian port to the Orient, the trip would be shortened by four thousand miles, thus further reducing costs and increasing Marcus's competitive advantage against the monopoly of Rockefeller's Standard Oil. By 1900, only eight years later, Marcus had thirty tankers.

With the first tanker completed, the British firm asked Marcus to name it. Saying he knew nothing about naming ships, Marcus initially ignored the request, but the firm insisted. It was his concept, his idea, and, if the ship sank, it would be his problem, not theirs, so they insisted he choose a name, even if he simply named it after his mother.

Marcus said, "My father taught me that a Jew lives not only in the present and future but also in the past." His father made a lot of sense. After all, when in a boat one has to row backward to move forward. Marcus continued, "I started by collecting seashells from the beaches in Japan to decorate boxes to sell, then went to Japan and now I am in the oil business. I want to name this pioneering oil tanker the *Murex*." They agreed to the name but had no idea what

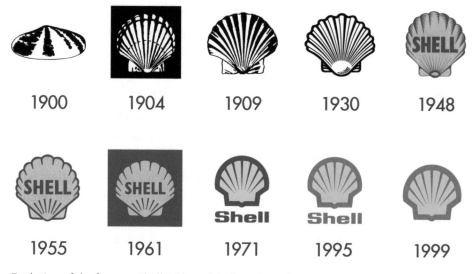

| 1900 | 1904 | 1909 | 1930 | 1948 |

| 1955 | 1961 | 1971 | 1995 | 1999 |

Evolution of the famous Shell Oil logo (Shell trademarks reproduced by permission of Shell Brands International AG)

"murex" meant. Marcus explained that it was the name of a common sea snail found on the beaches of Japan. From that moment on, Marcus named every oil tanker that he built after another one of the seashells commonly found on Japan's beaches. Looking back, he remembered his past with the seashells as he moved forward into the oil industry, just as his father had taught him. The first logo (1901) for Shell Oil was a mussel shell, but by 1904 a scallop shell (or pecten) was used, and it was this design that ultimately became the basis of the company's logo, a logo that many consider the most famous logo of any company in the world.

With the completion of the *Murex*, now filled with Russian oil, Marcus requested permission to use the Suez Canal. After careful consideration of the safety of the *Murex*, the Suez Canal authorities gave permission for it to pass through. Not only did the *Murex* exceed the requirements for passage through the Suez Canal, but also Lloyd's of London gave it an A1 rating. On July 22, 1892, the *Murex* made its maiden voyage to the Far East, where it discharged kerosene in Singapore, Bangkok and then Yokohama. Taken by surprise at the swiftness and boldness with which Marcus had moved, the shocked executives of Standard Oil rushed to the Far East, but they were too late. Marcus's kerosene was everywhere. He had successfully accomplished an amazing coup over the oil industry's most formidable member and was the first one to defeat Rockefeller in oil. Rockefeller mounted a campaign to stop Marcus's tankers from passing through the Suez Canal, and London newspaper articles referred to "the conspiracy of powerful finances and merchants of Hebrew influence." In 1895, Rockefeller offered to buy Marcus out, one of several attempts, but Marcus had no intention of selling then or later.

As mentioned earlier, Marcus received commitments and financing from all the trading houses with which he did business. They became his partners and built docks, depots, bulk storage warehouses, storage tanks, refineries and railroad lines at strategic ports in India, China, Malaysia, Burma, Singapore and Japan. From there, they would ship the oil to other cities where dealers would place the kerosene in smaller drums which they sent to retailers who, in turn, dispensed the product to the customers' own containers. The retailer then would return the empty drums to the depot for refilling.

Each trading house was the expert in its area, allowing Marcus to maintain a small, qualified staff, in an unassuming office in Yokohama with only a world map on the wall, a desk, a telephone and a few chairs. So as not to spread himself too thin by having to be everywhere, Marcus dispatched his nephews Mark and Joseph Abrahams over East Asia to work closely with his trading house partners to find proper storage sites and to supervise construction of the storage tanks.

Marcus expected the Asian customers to bring their own receptacles to be filled with kerosene, but that did not happen. Even though everyone had Standard Oil's five-gallon receptacles, they used these receptacles to build everything from roofing to bird cages to household goods and they were not willing to reuse them to fill with oil. Once again, though, Marcus demonstrated his entrepreneurial genius. He sent out to the Far East a ship loaded with tin plate and instructed his partners in port cities to begin manufacturing tin receptacles similar to those used by Standard Oil when they shipped oil from the United States to Asia. Marcus advised his local partners to establish local factories to make the containers quickly, and soon throughout Asia Marcus's bright, shiny and locally-manufactured red receptacles were competing with Standard Oil's blue cans, which were rusty, battered and chipped after the long voyages halfway around the world from the United States. In addition to the savings in shipping gained by manufacturing the containers locally, costs were further reduced by manufacturing them in Asia where production costs were lower. Marcus's red cans were a much-wanted commodity in Asia, so when the Shell logo was placed on them, the company became well known there. An aside, the word *shell* first appeared in 1891 as the trademark for kerosene being shipped to the Far East by M. Samuel and Company.

Dark clouds began appearing on the horizon, however, when the Russian czar announced without warning that Russian oil could be transported only in Russian ships. Marcus wanted to free himself from dependency on Russian oil and began looking for a new source. Marcus acquired some concessions in the Dutch East Indies, and on October 18, 1897, the word *shell* was elevated to corporate status when he created the Shell Transport and Trading Company.

No one on Marcus's team was an oil engineer or an oil chemist, people with the necessary skills for oil exploration, and another company, Royal Dutch, also in the area, was looking for oil as well. Marcus did not know whether his men would find oil, or, if they did, whether it would be the right kind of oil for his markets. But on April 15, 1898, in the Dutch East Indies (now Indonesia), there was a loud rumbling, the earth shook, and a black column of oil shot high into the air! Marcus's workers did not know how to stop the flow of this great oil find! Demonstrating his loyalty and fairness to all his partners in the Far East, he made each one a partner in his new company, as per his original agreement with them, and since he had invested the most money, he was the majority partner. In 1899, the Shell Company, with its own oil, was on its way to markets throughout the Far East.

Another crisis occurred thousands of miles away in America. In 1901 a group struck oil at Spindletop, an oil drilling site near Beaumont, Texas, and Marcus quickly contracted with them for a twenty-one-year supply and transport deal with the field's owner, making 1901–02 a good year for Shell. Overproduction at Spindletop, however, cut their supplies to a dangerous low in less than a year. Royal Dutch outdid Shell across Asia as half of Marcus's ships remained docked. Marcus had been so busy serving the people in London as a local politician that he had not kept as close a watch on his Shell Company as he should have, and Shell was in serious trouble. In 1907, however, Shell Oil and Royal Dutch merged. Royal Dutch had the supply of oil which Shell Oil could transport, store and distribute, and Shell Oil soon became debt-free and posted a 20 percent dividend.

The oil business faced many other problems. Sometimes there was a glut on the market and prices would fall. When Russia experienced economic problems, the czar would flood the market with his oil, thus reducing world oil prices. And in China there was the Boxer Rebellion (1898–1901) against foreigners, disrupting the nation's economy. Several Shell Oil facilities were destroyed during China's Boxer Rebellion. Then also, the British sailors, who lived on their ships, surprisingly refused to convert from coal to liquid fuel, and it took Marcus fifteen years to convince the British Royal Navy to change. Winston Churchill, who was in charge of the British navy, did not like Marcus – some say because of his Jewish background – and was unwilling to acknowledge his genius. Fear of the German submarines that were appearing, however, finally enabled Marcus to convince the British that liquid fuel provided 40 percent more energy than did a similar weight of coal. In addition, he argued successfully that oil made it easier and faster to reach full speed and that refueling at sea was also much easier and faster and required fewer sailors.

On the bright side, a new vehicle, the automobile, was being developed in Europe and in the United States and offered great opportunities for the oil industry. The demand for gasoline, the fuel required by automobiles, grew by leaps and bounds, and Marcus was among the first entrepreneurs to recognize the importance of this new invention. He had attended the first "horseless carriage exhibition" in England in 1895, after which Parliament passed legislation allowing this new vehicle on public streets. In 1895 there were only 300 cars in all of the United States. By 1914, there were 1.7 million cars, each one with a gas tank, and Shell Oil became the first company to produce gasoline for automobiles in addition to producing kerosene and fuel oil.

Marcus Samuel established his reputation as a brilliant and daring businessman. As he launched more and more oil tankers, each with the name of a shell, he became a very rich man. He owned an estate of more than five hundred acres and sent his children to the finest schools, all of which brought him recognition and status in London but sometimes caused him to ignore Shell. He was elected an alderman in the ward of Portsoken in London (1891–94) and became sheriff of the City of London (1894–1901) before becoming Lord Mayor of London on November 10, 1902, a post he held for one year.

The day he was appointed Lord Mayor was one of the best days of Marcus's life, for he had attained the highest honor to which a London merchant could aspire, all the more remarkable for a working-class Jew from the East End and the son of a seashell merchant. There had been two other Jews who served as Lord Mayor of London, but they came from affluent families.

Marcus never forgot his humble beginnings or that he was Jewish. During his installation ceremony as Lord Mayor, he insisted on diverting the procession to the Jewish section, the slums of the city, and the music for his inauguration as Lord Mayor was provided by an orchestra of Jewish orphans. When he was Lord Mayor, he dined with kings, emperors and heads of state but never with anyone who hated Jews. When he attended London's New Synagogue while he was Lord Mayor, he was accompanied by many city dignitaries. He also wanted to acknowledge his close ties to Japan, so the Japanese ambassador was his principal guest, frequently honored in every way, including riding in the inauguration procession.

In 1913 the *Times of London* attacked Marcus as a Jew. "Sir Marcus Samuel is a typical Jew.... He is a pronounced Jew. You could never take him for anything else. He is stout, swarthy, black haired, black mustached, thick nosed, thick lipped, bulge eyed, in short, he fulfills every expectation that one habitually forms of a prosperous Jew." The reason for the attack was probably the sharp rise in oil prices. Even though the price of oil in England was cheaper than the price of oil in the United States, there were no attacks on Rockefeller. Marcus was attacked because he was a Jew. His response was, "The price of oil is exactly what it will fetch." This means the price is determined by the market.

Those who knew Marcus described him as charming, imaginative, socially ambitious and desirous of performing public service, yet shy, soft-spoken and introverted. His religious faith also was very important to him as was his patriotism to England, because it was a country where Jews were not oppressed, despite the anti-Semitic slur against him in the *Times of London*.

Marcus had the opportunity for more public service and patriotism to England when he announced in August 1914, at the outbreak of World War I, that Shell Oil would make no profit from the war and voluntarily lent seventy tankers to the British Royal Navy for pennies. He also came up with an ingenious plan that helped England solve their shortage of explosives during World War I. Toluol, a chemical extracted from coal, was an essential ingredient in the manufacturing of the explosive TNT. In 1903, a scientist discovered that toluol also could be extracted in significant amounts from the heavy crude oil that Shell Oil was producing in the Dutch East Indies. England was not interested, however, and refused Marcus's offer consistently until 1915, when coal production was in such short supply that the Allies were close to running out of explosives. The Germans, however, had unlimited sources, and England realized that it needed toluol to end the shortage but had no facilities to make it. In January 1915, in the middle of the night, a plant in Rotterdam that made toluol from oil was disassembled, camouflaged, numbered and secretly loaded onto a freighter protected by British destroyers. It was transported to England and, within a few weeks, the transplanted factory was producing toluol for TNT. Marcus was able to provide 80 percent of the British military's TNT explosives. Marcus also converted his London home into a military hospital during World War I. He lived in one small section of the home, visited daily the soldiers recovering in the rest of the house and paid all the expenses of running the military hospital in his home.

Marcus married Fannie Benjamin, the daughter of a tailor, in a ceremony performed by Rabbi Nathan Adler in January 1881. The couple had two sons and two daughters. Marcus adored Fannie and never looked at another woman at a time when a mistress was considered something of a status symbol for a man with money. Marcus sought her advice, deferred to her judgment and found great happiness and pleasure in being with her.

Marcus Samuel had advanced very far during his seventy-three years. Of course, as chairman of Shell Oil from 1897 to 1921, he was very proud of the business he created. At the time of his death on January 17, 1927, less than twenty-four hours after his beloved wife died, Shell Oil was the largest oil enterprise in the world. But for Marcus, his most important achievements were the social services he had given and the social recognition he had earned. His attitude can be summed up by his maxim "Never lend money, but if you can afford to, give it."

Here are some additional facts about Marcus Samuel:

- He was the largest rice exporter from Japan.
- He was involved heavily in coal exporting from Japan.
- He was the first bulk oil importer to Japan.
- During a famine in Japan, he imported rice from Burma to Japan.
- During the Sino-Japanese war of 1894, he supplied Japan with food, oil, raw materials, weapons and other necessary goods. After the war in 1895, China ceded Formosa (now Taiwan) to Japan, and Japan asked Marcus Samuel to manage the camphor deposits of Formosa and also to manage the Japan-owned opium company.
- In 1897–98, when Japan needed £14,500 to change from the silver to the gold standard, government officials asked Marcus Samuel, whose trustworthiness and reliability had earned him everyone's respect, including that of the government of Japan, to float this loan, the first time that Japan floated a gold loan overseas. He was considered an expert on Japanese financial matters by Japan's foreign ministry and by the Japanese ambassador to England and later assisted with other loans.
- Marcus Samuel played a role in encouraging the adoption of the diesel engine and even built a diesel-powered tanker long before any other ship

of this type was built. In 1910, Shell built the first sea-going motor ship called the *Vulcanus*.

Marcus Samuel was the recipient of numerous honors, including the following:

- In 1898 he earned a knighthood for his assistance in salvaging a ship, the HMS *Victorious*, which ran aground in Egypt and was pulled to safety by Shell's tanker, the SS *Pecten*.
- He was the first British citizen to receive Japan's Kiokujitsu-Sho Award, the Imperial Award known also as the Commander of the Rising Sun Award.
- In 1903, he became Baronet Samuel; in 1921 Marcus Samuel became Baronet Bearsted of Maidstone in the county of Kent; and in 1925 he was advanced to the next rank in British nobility when he was named Viscount Bearsted of Maidstone.
- He received an honorary doctorate of law from the University of Sheffield in England.
- Bearsted Memorial Hospital in London is named for him.
- There is a Marcus Samuel Street in London.

Chapter Three
Moe Berg: Baseball Player and Spy

When I served as the rabbi of the Jewish community of Japan, I often visited congregants who were patients at St. Luke's Hospital, a major hospital in Tokyo. Located in the Tsukiji area, the world's largest wholesale fish market, near the Ginza (the "Times Square" of Tokyo), this hospital was often the choice of foreigners because English and other languages besides Japanese were spoken there. One day, a staff member, who assumed I was Jewish from my beard and yarmulke (skull cap), approached me and inquired if I knew the story of the American Jewish baseball player who had spied for the United States from the roof of that very hospital. This was my introduction to Moe Berg. More recently, I met and became friends with one of Moe Berg's cousins, a Harvard-educated attorney who is a supporter of Jewish communities on the periphery of the Diaspora.* He lives on the Upper West Side of Manhattan and owns the largest collection of letters, photographs and memorabilia related to Moe Berg.

Most documents give Moe Berg's birth date as March 2, 1902, and his name as Morris, but the birth certificate Moe's cousin gave us states that Moe's date of birth is May 3, 1902, and his name is Moses. There is only speculation about the reasons for the discrepancies. What we know for certain is that Moe was born in a cold water tenement in Jewish Harlem to Bernard Berg from a *shtetl* (a small, simple village in Eastern Europe comprised of mostly Jews) in the Ukraine and Rose Tasker from a nearby community, and that he was nicknamed "Moe" from birth. We also know that Moe was the best educated man to play major league baseball.

---

* The center of the Jewish Diaspora would be the United States, England, Argentina, France and Russia. Countries like Burma, India, China and Japan are far from the center and are, therefore, on the periphery of the mainstream of Jewish life.

While most sources give Moe Berg's birthday as March 2, 1902, his birth certificate states his birth date as May 3, 1902; courtesy of Irwin M. Berg

Education was a legacy transmitted to Moe by his father. Bernard had been raised in a home where Yiddish was spoken, studied Hebrew in school, and conducted business in Polish, but he was quite worldly and had a gift for languages, so he also knew some French and German. He came to the United States and settled on New York's Lower East Side. It was there that Bernard ironed shirts in a laundry on Ludlow Street and where he and Rose were married in January 1897. Because Bernard wanted to succeed in his new land, he studied English and tried to speak only English.*

Bernard eventually opened his own laundry while studying to be a pharmacist at night school, and people often witnessed him ironing laundry while reading a book he had placed on a stand. He ended up burning so many shirts, however, that his wife finally stopped him from ironing anymore! He

---

* Rose and Bernard had three children: Samuel, who was a graduate of New York University and eventually became a pathologist; Ethel, a difficult person who held grudges forever against almost everyone; and Moe.

graduated from pharmacy school, and in 1906 the family moved from Manhattan's Lower East Side to Harlem, which was a Jewish neighborhood at the time.

Eventually, however, New York – with Yiddish being spoken and the European mentality all around him – troubled Bernard and he moved the family to the Roseville section of Newark, New Jersey, where they lived in an Irish/Italian neighborhood with very few Jews. Bernard opened a pharmacy and the family lived in an apartment above his drugstore. The three children did not have access to a Jewish education, and neither of the two Berg boys had a bar mitzvah (a ceremony in which a thirteen-year-old Jewish boy accepts his responsibility to observe the Jewish way of life), although Bernard personally taught his sons Hebrew. Bernard's religion for his children was study, study, study! And Bernard himself wrote a novel in Yiddish about a cantor who hears the magnificent voice of a woman. While they were sometimes lonely in Roseville, especially during the Christmas season, the Christian neighbors were friendly and respectful. Bernard worked fifteen hours a day, seven days a week and had a good reputation, perhaps because he did not charge poor families who could not afford their medicines. He saved his pennies and eventually brought many of his family members from Europe to the United States.

From the beginning Moe loved to play ball, especially baseball. At the age of five, he would squat behind a manhole cover on the street, local policemen would throw the ball to him, and Moe would catch it every time. "Throw harder, throw faster," Moe would plead, and neighbors watched in amazement as he caught every ball. Moe had such a good reputation as a ballplayer that at age seven he was invited by the local Methodist Church to play on their baseball team, which he did, but only after he changed his Jewish-sounding name to Runt Wolfe.

His father was angry that he had to change his name and also hated that Moe played baseball every minute he could. Playing baseball was not for Jews! Jews, you recall, were supposed to "study, study, study," and he believed a Jew should study as much and as hard as possible and then become a teacher, attorney, businessman, physician or pharmacist, but certainly not a ballplayer. He looked like he wanted to spit whenever he described Moe's playing baseball as a waste of time!

Moe also was a superstar academically in his public school. He was a brilliant student who had perfect grades and was faulted only for singing off key. When Moe came home with a test score of ninety-nine, his father did not compliment him but, instead, asked him who had received a score of one hundred. Moe was frequently called "Christ Killer" at school, on the street and even on the baseball field, but he usually raised his fist in defiance upon hearing anti-Semitic statements.

Upon graduation from high school, Moe spent a year at New York University before applying to Princeton University. It is well known that at that time Princeton and other Ivy League schools sent unconscionable letters to applicants who had sterling recommendations and high academic achievements saying, "We have received your excellent application, but we already have filled our quota of Jews." Princeton usually accepted rich WASPs (White Anglo-Saxon Protestants) who attended exclusive high schools, and Moe was poor, Jewish and had attended a public high school. He was considered a brilliant student and an excellent ballplayer, however, and Princeton accepted him, one of the youngest students in his class. By the end of the year, three hundred of the seven hundred students had dropped out.

Moe's studies at Princeton included Latin, Greek, French, Spanish, Italian, German and Sanskrit, and he excelled in all of them, thanks to his photographic memory. Although he was referred to as a "Hebrew" by his fellow classmates and had no close friends at Princeton, some say that he was invited to join an eating club (a kind of exclusive fraternity) on condition that he not come with any other Jewish students and that Moe declined. Others say that Moe was not invited to join an eating club and felt so slighted by this exclusion that he went home to assuage his hurt feelings at the time the invitations went out. Sometimes he presided over Friday night services with some of his few fellow Jewish classmates at Princeton.

During the summers, Moe worked in the post office to help pay for his college tuition. One summer he also worked at a Jewish summer camp where the rabbi helped him improve his Hebrew. He also played semi-professional baseball during the summer which, if known, would have disqualified him from playing amateur baseball for Princeton, but Moe made Princeton's varsity baseball team (probably the reason he was invited to join an eating club) where he played shortstop. It is said that Princeton's baseball players yelled out signals in Latin, which, of course, was no problem for Moe. He was a clutch hitter, meaning that he got a hit when the team needed it most. He was Princeton's best baseball player ever; in 1923 Princeton won eighteen games in a row and Moe hit for a great average of .337, yet this star player never was named captain of the team.

Moe Berg in catcher's uniform, date and team unknown

Moe was not invited to join Phi Beta Kappa either, although he had an academic record that qualified him, and out of forty-one categories of awards given at graduation, including one for best athlete, sadly Moe did not win even one. In 1923, he graduated *magna cum laude*, twenty-fourth out of the 211 students in his class and in the top 11 percent of his class. He sometimes was scorned by other students, but one professor spoke very highly of him, and after graduation Moe was offered a faculty position in the language department at Princeton, an offer he refused. Instead, in June 1923 Moe accepted a contract for $5,000 to play baseball for the Brooklyn Robins, later renamed the Brooklyn Dodgers.

Moe played baseball for seventeen years, between 1923 and 1940, playing for the Brooklyn Dodgers, Chicago White Sox, Cleveland Indians, Washington Senators and Boston Red Sox. In the 1940–1941 season, Moe was a coach for the Boston Red Sox. Ironically, the last hit of Moe's career was a home run. He was described as a slow runner and poor hitter but a good fielding catcher. Just as he did at Princeton, Moe, the clutch hitter, made most of his hits when men were on base. In 1929, he was nominated as most valuable player in the American League but did not win; in 1933, he was playing for the Washington Senators when they won the pennant, and in 1934 he held the record of playing 117 games without committing any errors. His best batting average was .288. He had a strong and accurate throwing arm and a lifetime batting average of .243. In 106 games, he permitted only five stolen bases.

He started as a shortstop but spent most of his career, surprisingly, as a catcher. One day while Moe was playing for the Chicago White Sox, there was an accident that left both of their catchers injured. The manager yelled, "Get us a catcher quick, even from the Class D minors!" Moe responded, "We have a catcher on the bench." The manager looked at him and told him to "get dressed, get a glove and go behind the plate." This was really an error, since Moe was referring to another player on the bench who had some catching experience.

When he told the manager there was a catcher on the bench, he was not refer-ring to himself. Without any previous experience, however, Moe survived his first day as a catcher and went on to become an exceptionally good one. Wal-ter Johnson, one of the game's greatest pitchers, described Moe as one of the greatest catchers who ever played. Hall of Fame pitcher Ted Lyons said that Moe "was the finest catcher in the game, his signal calling was flawless and he never waved off a sign." The best of the pitchers loved Moe as a catcher.

Sports writers, who often referred to Moe as "mysterious Moe," had a field day with Moe, an intelligent, articulate, cosmopolitan, Ivy League–educated Jewish player. Numerous writers referred to Moe's ability to speak French, Spanish, Latin, Portuguese, Italian, Russian, Japanese, Greek, Sanskrit and Yiddish, the language in which Moe's mother communicated with him. It was sports writer Dave Harris who coined the phrase, "Moe can speak seven lan-guages but can't hit in any of them." During a Washington Senators game when Moe was their catcher, the score was tied and there was a runner on third base. The batter hit a high pop foul ball which Moe circled and caught, then flicked the ball back to the pitcher's mound and trotted off to the dugout. The problem was that there were only two outs, and the other team's runner scored the win-ning run, leading another reporter to say, "Moe can speak a dozen languages but can't count to three!" And Al Schacht, former baseball great known as the "clown prince of baseball," said, "Moe can speak eight languages, has sixteen degrees from universities and can't drive a car."

Sixteen university degrees may be an exaggeration, but off-season Moe attended Columbia University Law School, received his law degree, and passed the bar exam; he then worked for three years during the off-season for Satter-lee and Canfield, a prestigious law firm that hired only graduates of Harvard, Columbia and Yale, but usually not Jews. Moe studied philology at the Sor-bonne for only one year. He wanted to stay longer, so he wrote a letter asking to be excused from spring training, but he received a reply that he could either study at the Sorbonne or play baseball, but he could not do both. Moe chose to attend spring training.

Moe thought there was a kind of "majesty" to the written word and was usually seen with about ten newspapers under his arm, no matter what city he was in and even when he was in the baseball dugout. He read his newspa-pers from the first page to the last, and only after he was finished was anyone allowed to touch or discard them.

In 1938 baseball officials wanted to raise the image of baseball players to be perceived as smart and eloquent people, so Moe became a contestant on the "Information Please" radio program. Moe answered every question posed to him, such as the meaning of *poi* (the Hawaiian word for bread) and the meaning of *loy* (the old French word for law). He knew that Venus was the brightest star and that the Boreau letter was evidence that Captain Alfred Dreyfus was innocent in the famous Dreyfus Affair case. He was, in short, a walking encyclopedia. In 1941 he wrote an article for the *Atlantic Monthly* titled "Pitchers and Catchers," an article many sportswriters consider the best article ever written about baseball by a baseball player. In the article Moe analyzed great hitters like Ty Cobb, Joe DiMaggio, Mel Ott, Babe Ruth and Ted Williams. He explained how the pitcher attempts to fool the hitter and described the "two o'clock hitter" as someone who "knocks down fences in batting practice but cannot hit during the baseball game."

As for the game of baseball, Moe considered it to be a very democratic game where skills alone mattered, not creed or religion. For him, baseball was nirvana. He stayed at the best hotels, ate the best meals, worked two or three hours a day and generally enjoyed life even though baseball players made very little money at the time.

Because of low salaries, baseball players increased their income by playing exhibition games after the season. In the 1930s, selected baseball players went to Japan, where baseball was played only on university campuses, and they served as teachers to the Japanese on the techniques, strategy and psychology of baseball. Moe was among the three American players who went to Japan in 1932, and after the exhibition games in Japan he traveled to the Great Wall of China, Saigon, Angkor Wat in Cambodia, Siam, India and Palestine. He wrote to his family that he had seen rickshaws, watched sumo wrestling, gone drinking and visited the "Red Light" district. Moe's letters made it clear that he loved the Orient!

In October 1934, Moe sailed from Vancouver back to Japan with Babe Ruth, Lou Gehrig and other famous baseball players. Why was Moe included on this team, since he was no longer an all-star player? Why did Moe have in his pocket a letter from Secretary of State Cordell Hull and a US senator introducing him to the American embassy in Tokyo? No other player carried a letter like this. And why did Moe, who had been to Japan two years earlier and had studied Japanese with a tutor, study six books on Japanese grammar and language during this sea voyage? Babe Ruth asked Moe if he could speak Japanese and Moe said "no," but when the ship landed in Japan Moe was reading Japanese signs and speaking Japanese to the Japanese staff. When Babe Ruth reminded Moe that two weeks earlier he had said he could not read or speak Japanese, Moe replied, "That was two weeks ago." Moe had to keep his mission a secret.

In Japan, every all-star American baseball player visited nightclubs, geisha houses, and infamous bordellos, but Moe, who admired Japan's culture, history, progress and adaptability, also visited museums, attended the theater, studied the language and absorbed as much as he could. He lectured at Meiji University and at Tokyo Imperial University, where he tried to teach the Japanese to pronounce the letter "L," a sound that does not exist in their language. He delivered a speech over Radio Tokyo to the United States telling Americans they would be surprised at how the all-American baseball team could foster good relations between the US and Japan and overturn the barriers of race, language, politics and customs.

One day, Moe did not appear at the scheduled baseball game, and other players assumed he was ill. The truth is that he had taken the day off and dressed himself in Japanese clothing, including a kimono and wooden *geta* (sandals) on his feet. He purchased a bouquet of flowers and went to St. Luke's Hospital where he planned to visit American ambassador Joseph Grew's daughter, who had just given birth to a baby there. With seven floors, the hospital was one of the tallest buildings in Tokyo. Buildings were kept low in Tokyo because of the danger to taller buildings from earthquakes and because it was inappropriate to "look down on" the imperial palace of the emperor.

Moe entered the hospital, where they thought he was Japanese, and asked to visit the ambassador's daughter, who was on the seventh floor. He took the elevator up to the seventh floor and then climbed the narrow staircase to the roof, where he took out a Bell and Howell 16-millimeter matchbook spy camera and photographed Tokyo harbor, warships, military installations, factories and other items of military importance. He then hid the camera in his kimono, climbed down the narrow stairs, deposited the flowers in the rubbish, took the elevator to the lobby and left the building without ever seeing the ambassador's daughter. Eight years later, sixteen B-25 bombers had their first raid over Tokyo, and it is said that Moe's photos were used to find targets to bomb in that first raid (known as the Doolittle Raid) by the Americans over Japan. Moe Berg, the catcher, was now Moe Berg, the spy. After that trip to Japan, Moe traveled to Manchuria and took the Trans-Siberian railroad to Russia. He then continued on to Germany, where he saw the troublesome actions of the Nazi government and was horrified by the sight of Nazi officers burning books.

In 1942, Moe made a speech in Japanese to the Japanese people telling them that he admired them and was their friend, but that he was disappointed in their cruel and war-like behavior. He told them that their leaders had betrayed them, that they could not win a war against the US, assured them that Americans and the Japanese could be friends and asked them to seek peace. President Roosevelt thanked Moe for his speech. In 1942 Moe also joined the Office of Strategic Services (OSS) which later became the Central Intelligence Agency (CIA).

In 1944 Moe was chosen for a very special mission. The Americans were concerned that the Nazis were getting closer to producing an atomic bomb. Many of the Americans working on the Manhattan Project were Jewish scientists who had studied with the great German physicist Werner Heisenberg, the recipient of the 1932 Nobel Prize for physics when he was in his early thirties. Uranium was available in Czechoslovakia, and heavy water for an atomic bomb was available in Norway, and both countries were occupied by the Nazis. Should Americans sabotage the German attempt to make an atom bomb? Should they kidnap or kill Heisenberg? Despite the willingness of prominent physicists to do whatever was deemed necessary, the OSS decided that only Moe Berg, who had been briefed on atomic weapons by Albert Einstein, was qualified to get the job done. In preparation for that assignment, Moe told Albert Einstein that he would teach him about baseball, using a picture of a baseball diamond he drew, if Einstein would teach him nuclear physics. Einstein agreed.

A lecture was arranged for Heisenberg at the University of Zurich on December 18, 1944. Moe was sent to this lecture with a gun in one pocket and a poison pill in the other one. Moe's job was to determine from Heisenberg's lecture what the nature of Germany's nuclear research on atomic weapons was and whether the Nazis were close to producing an atomic bomb. If so, Heisenberg was not to walk out of that lecture alive. After the lecture, which was on the S-matrix theory, Moe was invited to a small dinner party given by a Swiss physicist with Heisenberg in attendance. After dinner Moe walked to the hotel with Heisenberg, who thought Moe was a member of the German SS sent to monitor his table talk; no one ever suspected that Moe was American or Jewish. Based on statements Heisenberg made to Moe, which Moe passed on to US intelligence, they determined correctly that German production of an atomic bomb was not imminent and Moe never pulled the trigger. In 1946 Moe was awarded the Medal of Merit, but he rejected it, perhaps because he couldn't tell people what he had done to earn it. Moe, who even parachuted behind Nazi lines once, always managed to evade German counterintelligence agents and was never caught for any of his spy activities.

Moe and his family were eccentric, to put it mildly. Moe's father never saw him play in any major league baseball game, not even once. Neither Moe nor his siblings ever married, and they did not get along with each other. After the war, Moe behaved more strangely than ever, wearing a dark charcoal gray suit, white shirt, thin black tie – and sometimes, a gray hat – every day for more than fifty years. He owned eight identical sets of his drab, daily outfit, which he said he wore because he was "in mourning for the whole world." He bathed daily and washed his underwear every evening, not wanting to have dirty clothes around.

Moe rarely worked after leaving the CIA, lived with his sister or brother or sometimes even in the train station, enjoyed womanizing and maintained his love for baseball, attending fifty to sixty games a year at Shea or Yankee Stadiums, where he sat in the press box. The ball park was his theater. Wherever he sat, he was the head of the table. Whenever anyone asked him what he was doing, he put his index finger to his lips as if to say "a slip of the lip can sink a ship."

Moe Berg died of an aortic aneurism in 1972 at age seventy. It is said that his last words were, "How did the Mets do today?" His brother and sister fought over what to do with Moe's ashes; in the end Ethel prevailed and scattered his ashes in Israel. It is possible that some of the stories about Moe Berg are embellished or even untrue, but what is certain is that Moe Berg was an amazing linguist, whether that meant being fluent in seven, eleven or fifteen languages; that the baseball museum in Cooperstown, New York, has Moe's Medal of Merit (which his sister accepted after his death); that in CIA headquarters (not open to the public) in Langley, VA, there is a small section dedicated to Moe Berg memorabilia; and that Moe Berg was a mediocre ball player, a brilliant man and a perfect spy.

Chapter Four

Beate Sirota Gordon: The Only Woman in the Room

Beate Sirota Gordon (1923–2012) was an amazing woman. A personal friend of mine who lived in New York City, Beate wrote *The Only Woman in the Room* (1997, reissued in 2014), the story of her writing of the historic women's rights section of the Japanese Constitution after World War II.

Beate was the daughter of Russian Jewish musicians. Her father, Leo Sirota, a world-renowned pianist, had moved to Vienna to escape Russian anti-Semitism. It was there that Jascha Horenstein, an orchestral conductor in the city, introduced Leo to his sister Augustine, and Leo and Augustine fell in love and later married. Their daughter Beate was born in Vienna on October 25, 1923, moved with her parents to Tokyo at age five and lived there for ten years before leaving for college. Although Beate's parents intended to go to Japan for only six months, they ended up staying for seventeen years. Leo gave concerts throughout Japan and was invited to become a professor at the Imperial Academy of Music, later known as the National University of Arts. Both Beate's parents also gave private piano lessons. One of Leo's students was the daughter of a prominent Japanese man and, when he became ill, Leo continued teaching his daughter for free. Beate's parents were good role models.

Beate first attended the German school in Tokyo, since her first language was German. With the rise of Nazi Germany, however, her teachers suddenly had to follow the Nazi party line, and each school day started with "Heil Hitler." Wanting to escape from Nazi oppression, Beate then attended the American School in Japan where she learned English. After graduating in 1939 at the age of fifteen, Beate enrolled in Mills College in Oakland, California, where she majored in languages and literature. Having lived in Japan for ten years, Beate was one of only about sixty-five Caucasian Americans in the United States at that time who were fluent in Japanese.

There was a slight problem, however, with her application to Mills College. Beate required a US visa, and the visa application required police clearances from all her places of residency, including her birthplace Vienna, in Nazi-controlled Austria, from which Beate, a Jew, certainly could not get police clearance. Fortunately, however, the former prime minister and foreign minister of Japan, whose family name was Hirota, was a neighbor of the Sirota family, and since their names – Hirota and Sirota – were so similar, the mail often was delivered to the wrong family. The families had become good friends, so when Leo Sirota explained Beate's problem to Prime Minister Hirota, he called the American embassy, vouched for the family, and Beate received her US visa.

After the Japanese attacked Pearl Harbor in December 1941 and the war started, Beate no longer could receive money from her parents in Japan. Since she needed money for college tuition and living expenses, she obtained temporary employment with the CBS listening post, which became the Federal Communication Commission's (FCC) Foreign Broadcast Intelligence Services listening post, translating shortwave radio broadcasts from Japan. While monitoring these shortwave radio broadcasts, Beate heard a report about a Japanese submarine approaching San Francisco, a fact that was not picked up by anyone else. She immediately was offered a permanent position by the FCC, a US government agency, which contacted Mills College requesting that she be excused from attending classes although she would complete all her reading assignments, write all her term papers and take all the exams. The administration at Mills College agreed.

When Beate moved on to the Office of War Information, she had her own radio program and became known as the American Tokyo Rose.* She wrote a daily seven-minute message in Japanese for Japanese shortwave broadcasts, urging the Japanese to surrender, and usually included some modern American music she thought the Japanese would like. She also deciphered a message from Japan that two professors at the Imperial Academy of Music, Leonid Kreutzer and Leo Sirota, had been dismissed because they were Jewish. This was both bad and good news for Beate. On the one hand, after the Japanese

---

* Allied forces in the South Pacific during World War II referred to several English-speaking Japanese female broadcasters of propaganda aimed at American soldiers on Japanese radio as "Tokyo Rose."

attacked Pearl Harbor, Beate could neither return to her family in Japan nor could she have any contact with them. On the other hand, this news of her father's dismissal meant that he was still alive, although she feared for the future.

After Beate graduated *Phi Beta Kappa* from Mills College in 1943 with a bachelor's degree in modern languages, she obtained a position as a researcher at *Time* magazine where there were no female writers. Men were writers, women were researchers, and there was no such policy as equal pay for equal labor. In 1945, Beate became a United States citizen, and later that year when the war ended, the United States occupied Japan and needed translators, interpreters and scholars in every field. Beate applied for translator/interpreter positions with the hope that if she secured a position she would be able to return to Japan and find her parents if they were still alive.

Beate was accepted to serve as an interpreter on General Douglas MacArthur's staff during the Occupation. She became the first female civilian permitted to enter Japan and was able to travel to Japan, when that was almost impossible for US civilians, because she spoke Japanese, Russian, English, German, French and Spanish. And she found her parents! How Leo and Augustine survived during the war is its own story, but survive they did. When Beate saw them for the first time, Leo was skin and bones with hollow cheeks, suffering from malnutrition. Augustine's body was bloated. Leo was able to travel to Tokyo, but Augustine was too ill to leave their summer home in Karuizawa, a resort city in the mountains (at the time, a two-hour train ride from Tokyo), where most foreigners and embassies had relocated during the bombings in Tokyo. It was there that Beate visited her mother who eventually did recuperate. All that remained of her family's house in Tokyo was a burnt column. (Both Beate's parents became US citizens in 1952, and her father became artist in residence at the St. Louis Institute of Music. He died in 1965, and Beate's mother died in 1985.)

After a long and arduous flight from New York City to Japan in 1945, Beate landed at a Japanese naval air station in the suburbs of Tokyo where Japanese soldiers were now working for the Americans. When she saw a Japanese naval officer, she looked down with her hands crossed in front in typical Japanese fashion, but the naval officer bowed deeply to her. That an officer would bow to a young girl was so unbelievable that Beate realized how totally defeated Japan was, and she appreciated being the first female civilian in occupied Japan.

There were so many male soldiers and so few females that Beate recalls being whistled at by many of the men.

Beate worked as one of more than two hundred thousand Americans serving in the Occupation. Many of them and General Douglas MacArthur worked across from the Imperial Palace in the Dai-Ichi Insurance Company building, and Beate was assigned to the Government Section, Political Affairs Division. Many of her coworkers were professors in military uniforms, civil service personnel or legal scholars, all of whom were enthusiastic about creating reform. The goal of the Occupation was to destroy Japan's military,

Beate Sirota in Japan during the Occupation, 1946; courtesy of Beate Sirota Gordon

create a representative government, free political prisoners, liberate farmers, free the labor movement, produce a free economy, abolish police oppression, create a free press, liberalize education and enfranchise women. The two men in charge of implementing General MacArthur's goals were General Courtney Whitney, who met privately with MacArthur every day, and Chief of Staff Colonel Charles Kades, a forty-year-old Jewish military officer with a sharp mind, cordial manner and gift for leadership.

Each day Beate would leave Kanda, the Tokyo neighborhood where she lived, at 7:30 a.m. and walk to work at the Occupation building where she would arrive at 7:55 a.m. On February 4, 1946, when Beate entered the sixth floor where MacArthur's office and her section were located, she was met not with the usual warm "hellos" but with an eerie silence. At 10:00 a.m., about twenty members of the Government Section were invited to a very small conference room with standing room only. General Whitney entered and announced that General MacArthur had given orders for them to draft a new constitution for the Japanese people. The constitution would deal with determining the status of the emperor, abolishing war and ending the feudal system, among other items, and the deadline was February 12, only eight days away. The room became electric. Colonel Kades would head the steering committee, and committees were formed around specific departments. The civil rights committee consisted of Lieutenant Colonel Pieter K. Roest, Professor Harry Emerson Wildes and twenty-two-year-old Beate Sirota, who felt a great sense of mission, especially when Lieutenant Colonel Roest said to her, "You are a woman; why don't you write the women's rights section?"

The status of women in pre-war Japan was not good. The Meiji Constitution of 1889 assumed that women were incompetent. Consequently, women had no power and were treated as chattel. They could not sue anyone; they had no property rights or rights of inheritance; they could not vote; they could receive only minimum education; and they were not accorded equal employment. Men could easily divorce their wives; women often could not marry the man of their choice; and wives walked behind their husbands.

Beate had witnessed the plight of women personally because she had lived in Japan and could speak Japanese. She had seen that women were second-class citizens even in their own homes. When guests were invited to dinner, the wife could not sit at the dinner table with the guests but, instead, had to eat in another area with the children. She had seen that a Japanese man could adopt children he had with another woman without even consulting his wife and that he could bring his mistress into the same house where he lived with his wife. Beate did not believe in male dominance. She believed in equality between the sexes, in cooperation not coercion and in individual dignity.

Determined to improve the plight of Japanese women and children, Beate requisitioned a jeep and a driver, visited many libraries and returned with ten constitutions, including those of France, Scandinavia, the Soviet Union, Weimar Germany and the United States. When she returned to work with these constitutions, everyone wanted to borrow them. Beate favored the 1919 Weimar Germany Constitution as a model for her own ideas. The United States Constitution did not make any specific references to women, and that concerned Beate.

Beate decided to include the status of children born out of wedlock and disabled children, and she wanted free medical care for all children and so much more. Sadly, the powers that be in the Occupation did not include all of Beate's suggestions in the constitution, arguing that they should be included as the basic laws of the country, laws that, for the most part, were never written. Beate and her colleagues worked day and night for eight days to complete the constitution secretly, and the secret was kept despite rumors and speculation.

At the same time the Japanese, it turns out, were writing their own constitution, which was basically the old constitution with minor changes. They were shocked and unhappy to learn that the Americans also had written a constitution, and many meetings followed. While the Japanese ultimately were unable to write a constitution, about twenty members of the Occupation working in nine committees got the job done, believing that they had a responsibility to effect a social revolution in Japan. They wanted to establish democracy in Japan, and they felt no anger, bitterness or need for revenge against Japan. Beate remembered that before the war, when her family invited guests for dinner, the military police would come the next day to collect the place cards to see who had attended. The Occupation wanted to end this type of repression and replace it with democratic principles.

The chief translator/interpreter, Lieutenant Joseph Gordon (whom Beate married in 1948 and with whom she had two children) was Jewish, quick-witted and very capable. When the Americans and the Japanese met together, it was in the same room where each side also convened privately. One day, when the American officials were meeting alone, Lieutenant Gordon saw a pamphlet in Japanese that a Japanese official had left behind in the room after the Japanese had finished their private committee session. The pamphlet was a translation of the Occupation's proposed constitution and seemed to indicate to Gordon that the Japanese had given up on what was a losing battle.

The final meeting of the two sides to review the constitution in detail started at 10:00 a.m. on March 4, 1946, and lasted for thirty-two hours. Beate was the only woman in the room, and it was 2:00 a.m. the next morning when they finally got to the section she had drafted on civil and women's rights. Needless to say, everyone was tired. The Japanese argued strongly that the ideas put forth about rights for women and children went against Japanese culture and customs, although they did not know that they were Beate's ideas. When Colonel Kades explained that Beate had lived in Japan for a long time, knew Japanese women very well and had her heart set on guaranteeing women's and children's rights when she wrote that part of the constitution, the Japanese agreed to accept her wording of the text. It helped that the Japanese thought of Beate as a superb translator and interpreter.

Thanks to Beate, Article 14 of Japan's Constitution says: All of the people are equal under the law and there shall be no discrimination in political, economic or social relations because of race, creed, sex, social status or family origin.

And thanks to Beate, Article 24 of Japan's Constitution says: Marriage shall be based only on the mutual consent of both sexes and it shall be maintained through mutual cooperation with the equal rights of husband and wife as

Beate Sirota Gordon during her years working for the Japan Society and the Asia Society in New York

a basis. With regard to choice of spouse, property rights, inheritance, choice of domicile, divorce and other matters pertaining to marriage and the family, laws shall be enacted from the standpoint of individual dignity and the essential equality of the sexes.

Beate cried when the committee did not include everything she hoped would be in the constitution, but the extent of what her efforts had accomplished became evident on October 10, 1946, when Japan held its first postwar general election. Not only did many women of all ages rush to vote, but also thirty-nine women were elected to parliament, and all of them met General MacArthur personally. The new constitution took effect in 1947.

The Japanese government may not have been too happy, but many Japanese people, especially the women, were grateful to Beate for all she had done on their behalf. General MacArthur said in his reminiscences, "Of all the reforms accomplished by the Occupation in Japan, none was more heartwarming to me than the change in the status of women." The cornerstone of a new, democratic and peaceful Japan was the liberation of women, initiated by Beate, and that, in turn, contributed to the success of the demilitarization policy of the Occupation. During the Korean War, when MacArthur wanted Japan to rearm, it was the women who said "no."

Beate faced other challenges besides the resistance of some Japanese to her reforms. One member of the Occupation, General Charles A. Willoughby, was viewed as a Prussian by the others. He believed in the superiority of the white race, thought Jews were a foreign and domestic problem, and considered the Jews to be Communists and a threat to the United States. According to author Joseph Bendersky, *The Jewish Threat: Anti-Semitic Politics in the U.S. Army* (Basic Books, 2001), Willoughby made the following accusations against Beate:

> Her English is initially the kind that is spoken in a foreign household.... [She is] certainly not American; and her familiarity with American standards,

thoughts and ideals are those hastily acquired.... [Her] parents are stateless persons.... They are Jewish. Nevertheless, they appear in Japan... [which] has never been a haven of refuge for foreigners.... At this time, we run into a small Jewish clique.... One Jew recommends the other; so here we find strange characters drift into Tokyo... where they work mysteriously and precariously... [later] we find the "expert" [daughter] almost psychopathic in her hatred of the [Japanese] police and authority... able to vent her fury [by] purging neighborhood Japanese officials.... [A] stateless Jewess, a hastily acquired citizenship, wielding the power of the United States and the prestige of General MacArthur.

Fortunately, everyone ignored Willoughby.

Beate returned to the United States with her parents in 1947 and resumed her deep interest in the performing arts. She had studied modern dance with Marian Van Tuyl at Mills College and had studied Japanese and modern dance in Tokyo with Forrest Garnett (former member of the Anna Pavlova troupe and eventually Beate's dancing partner). Beate also had studied modern dance with Gertrude Bodenweiser of the Vienna Academy. After her return to the US, Beate studied Spanish dance with Elena Imaz (former prima ballerina of the Argentine Ballet). In 1954 Beate became the director of student programs at the Japan Society in New York and also began introducing many Japanese artists to the West. In 1958 Beate was appointed the Japan Society's director of the performing arts. In 1960 she became a consultant to the Asia Society's performing arts program, expanding her work to countries in Asia besides Japan, and in 1970 Beate was appointed director of the performing arts program of the Asia Society. Finally, Beate served as the Asia Society's director of performances, films and lectures from 1987 until her retirement in 1991.

No matter what else Beate was doing, whenever it was necessary she returned to Japan to defend the rights of Japan's women and children as stated in Articles 14 and 24 and also to defend Article 9 of Japan's Constitution in which Japan renounces war and embraces peace. In 2005, for example, Beate traveled to Japan to fight off a movement by some Japanese politicians to undo the gains she had made to preserve peace and provide rights for Japanese women and children. These politicians argued that Beate's Western sensibilities were the cause of Japan's deteriorating society and the weakening of the family unit in Japan. For decades, until her memoir was published, Beate remained silent about her role in the fight to gain rights for women and children in Japan's Constitution, not only because the work was confidential, but also because she did not want her young age, Jewish religion and/or US citizenship to lead Japanese conservatives to react exactly as they did at times, including in 2005.

Beate received numerous awards and honorary degrees during her life, including the John D. Rockefeller Award from the Asian Cultural Council in 1997 for her "extraordinary contributions in introducing American scholars, artists and general audiences to the performing arts of Asia and in increasing the American understanding and appreciation of Asian dance, theater and music traditions"; and the Order of the Sacred Treasure for "her long-term service to Japan," presented to her in 1998 by the Japanese government. In 2004 a Japanese film entitled *The Gift from Beate* was shown in Japan. Beate died in December 2012, four months after her husband. She was a spirited, idealistic, cosmopolitan woman who was sensitive to repression and persecution and wanted Japan to remain peaceful, and her work on Japan's Constitution changed not only the lives of Japanese women and children but also changed the course of history.

Chapter Five
Jewish Chaplains from Iwo Jima to the Bridge on the River Kwai

I served from 1962 to 1964 as a Jewish chaplain in the US Air Force, assigned to Itazuke air base in southern Japan, on the island of Kyushu, one hundred miles from Nagasaki. From there, I covered additional assignments on the Air Force bases in Korea one week per month for twenty-four months and also served the Jewish troops in Okinawa, Taiwan, Thailand, the Philippines and Vietnam. During my monthly visits to Korea, I worked with Rabbi Chaplain Louis Barish, a visually-impaired career military chaplain, who wrote an excellent book on the liturgy of the Jewish high holy days and was the first to write a history of the Jewish chaplains.

In 1968, when I was in Japan as the rabbi of the Jewish community, I met Rabbi Milton J. Rosen, who served in Korea during the Korean War. While there, Rosen became a correspondent for the Yiddish press in New York, and in 1950–1951 he wrote many exceptional articles for *Der Morgan Journal*, the popular Yiddish daily newspaper. He wrote under difficult circumstances in the thick of battle during the Korean War and under brutal winter weather conditions.

Years later, Rosen returned to Japan, where he served as an auxiliary Jewish chaplain at Camp Zama and married the librarian there. He studied at the prestigious University of Tokyo and became an expert on Buddhism and Sanskrit. He knew so much in this rather esoteric, intellectual field that I pleaded with him to write the definitive volume comparing and contrasting Judaism and Buddhism, but he died before ever writing a word, always saying that he was not sufficiently knowledgeable about that subject to write about it. I am haunted by Rabbi Rosen's decision, and since I am a man of a certain age, it was part of my motivation to write this book.

Rosen loved to tell the story of Corporal Abraham Geller, a soldier raised on New York's Lower East Side. Even on the frontlines of Korea, where sleep was at a premium, Geller always woke up thirty minutes before anyone else except Captain George O'Connor. Geller awoke early to recite his morning prayers, and O'Connor awoke early to survey the terrain and strategize on how to deploy his troops.

One day, after they had crossed the Han River on their way to Seoul, the Korean capital, it was Yom Kippur, the Jewish high holiday, the Day of Atonement. When O'Connor told Geller to get some food and coffee after he finished his early morning prayers, Geller replied that on Yom Kippur observant Jews fast all day and that he had enough calories packed away for twenty-four hours. In the course of that very tough battle day, Geller took three bullets intended for O'Connor and was operated on for the resulting wounds to his abdomen, injuries that usually would have been fatal. Rosen told the story as a religious miracle and credited Geller's survival to the fact that he had fasted on Yom Kippur and his stomach was empty.

I also traveled with Rabbi David Seligson, a most prominent rabbi of Central Synagogue in Manhattan, and escorted him on military planes and jeeps to meet with troops in Japan and Korea and boost their morale. During World War II, Seligson served as chaplain in the China/Burma/India theater, where the loss of lives was staggering. In this region, planes had to fly over the Himalayas to deliver vital supplies to China via the "back door" (China's Western front), since the "front door" (China's Eastern coastline) was in Japanese hands. The building of the Burma Road through thick jungle, with Japanese snipers and aircraft everywhere, was a major story during World War II and resulted in the creation of the "Flying Tigers." The "Flying Tigers" was an elite force of American airmen fighting for Chiang Kai-shek, the leader of the Chinese government who helped liberate China from Japan via the Western front.

Rabbi Chaplain Elihu Rickel was a career chaplain who served as the base chaplain for all the troops, which were overwhelmingly Christian, at Iwakuni Marine Corps air base near Hiroshima. It was my assignment to visit the Jews in the US Marines at this base, to conduct services and to provide for their spiritual needs. During these visits I learned so much from Chaplain Rickel, who told stories in a way that made the listener see and hear what it was like to be in battle under fire. He served as chaplain with the Marine Corps on Iwo Jima and later in Korea during the Korean War.

Chaim Potok, the noted author and novelist, also served as a chaplain in Korea, and Rabbi Herman Dicker, a refugee from Europe, served as a chaplain to servicemen in both Korea and Japan, where he also served as a rabbi at the Tokyo Jewish Community Center. Dicker wrote the first book about Jews in the Far East.

During a retreat for chaplains serving in the Far East, I met Rabbi Bertram W. Korn, noted American Jewish historian and rabbi of Congregation Keneseth Israel of Philadelphia. Rabbi Korn was the first rabbi to hold the rank of admiral in the navy and the first rabbi to achieve two-star rank in the American military chaplaincy. After World War ii, he served as the only rabbi in North China, and he traveled by plane, jeep and rickshaw to Beijing on Tuesdays and Wednesdays, to Tsingtao on Thursdays and Fridays, and to Tientsin (now Tianjin) on Saturdays, Sundays and Mondays.

Tsingtao then was home to about two hundred Jews, most of them refugees and professionals. In 1945, Rabbi Korn addressed them at their Hebrew Association and expressed concern that they had an association rather than a synagogue. The force of this young rabbi chiding them for not having a synagogue jarred them. Rabbi Korn encouraged them to create a synagogue library and stock it with books on Jewish history, poetry, fiction and contemporary issues for free circulation in the community. He also encouraged them to pursue Jewish music and provide a Jewish education to their children. The community was inspired to implement Rabbi Korn's suggestions.

Word spread that the refugees in Tsingtao wanted to build a synagogue against all odds. Soldiers, marines, sailors, airmen, Jews and non-Jews offered their help not only with money but also with the actual building of the synagogue. By the spring of 1946, the synagogue was ready to open. For the servicemen, the event was the sweetest fruit of the war's victory; for Rabbi Korn, it was the fulfillment of his calling.

I learned from Rabbi Korn that without help from President Abraham Lincoln, there might never have been any Jewish chaplains in the military. The concept of a military chaplain, however, precedes Lincoln. It goes all the way back to the Book of Deuteronomy where the Bible relates that in times of battle the priest would encourage and inspire the troops to victory. Rabbis, however, were not permitted to serve as chaplains in the American military until 1862. An earlier law passed by the US Congress stated that a military chaplain must be a "regularly ordained minister of some Christian denomination." Surprisingly, however, in July 1861, a congressman from Ohio lobbied for an amendment which would substitute the phrase "religious society" for the words "Christian denomination." He believed that the number of Jewish men in the United States was growing and that these Jews were just as good citizens and true patriots as any others in the nation. He was ignored by everyone except Rabbi Isaac Mayer Wise.* Wise understood that a law granting rights exclusively to Christians violated the constitutional rights of non-Christians.

In September 1861, a YMCA worker visited a military camp in Virginia where a Philadelphia regiment that included many Jews was stationed. He was horrified to discover that a Jew, Michael Allen of Philadelphia, was serving as the regimental chaplain; it seems others did not know of the law that forbade Jewish chaplains. The YMCA worker promptly began a campaign in the press that forced the government to publicly state that only a regularly ordained clergyman of a Christian denomination could serve as a chaplain in the military. Allen resigned his commission blaming ill health rather than suffer the humiliation and dishonor of being dismissed. Allen was unqualified for two reasons: he was not Christian and he was not ordained.

Colonel Max Friedman, the commanding officer of this regiment, decided to try again to secure a Jewish chaplain for his Jewish troops. He and the Jews in his regiment elected Rabbi Arnold Fischel, an ordained rabbi, who would apply directly to Secretary of War Simon Cameron for a commission. Cameron's rejection read in part, "We regret that we cannot appoint a member of your faith as a chaplain of the US Army. The laws of Congress strictly direct that all chaplains be of the Christian religion." Needless to say, the Jewish community and the press were outraged. Rabbi Fischel instead accepted a position to serve as civilian chaplain in the Washington, DC, area. On December 11, 1861, Fischel appeared at the White House, which was open to the public at

---

* Rabbi Isaac Mayer Wise (1819–1900) is the father of Reform Judaism in the United States. He was ordained as a rabbi in Europe and came to the US in 1846, accepting a rabbinic position in Albany, New York. His reforms, such as having men and women sit together during services, sing together in the choir and be counted together as part of a minyan, offended many congregants in Albany, and he relocated to Cincinnati, Ohio, where he remained as rabbi of the same synagogue for over forty years. He wrote many books and published a newspaper in which he conveyed his thoughts against slavery, in favor of Reform Judaism and in favor of rabbis serving as chaplains in the US military.

the time, and personally presented to President Lincoln his case for religious acceptance and constitutional rights for the Jewish community.

President Lincoln told Fischel that he was unaware that Jews were prohibited from serving as military chaplains and that he believed it was altogether unintentional on the part of Congress. He noted the justice in Fischel's presentation and agreed that action should be taken to correct the problem. On December 13, 1861, President Lincoln wrote to Fischel, "I find there are several particulars in which the present law in regard to chaplains is supposed to be deficient, all of which I design presenting to the appropriate committee of Congress. I shall try to have a new law broad enough to cover what is desired by you in behalf of the Israelites." On December 20, a resolution went to the House allowing ordained men of any religion to serve as military chaplains; on January 8, 1862, a bill to repeal the discriminatory law was introduced and subsequently passed by the House and then passed by the Senate in March 1862; and on July 17, 1862, the bill became effective, and rabbis with proper recommendations and qualifications were permitted to serve as chaplains in the US military, thanks to the perseverance and patience of Rabbi Arnold Fischel. Since rabbis are exempt from the draft, every Jewish chaplain is a volunteer.

The first chaplain assigned to the Marines was Rabbi Roland B. Gittelsohn, an exceptional man and successful rabbi who served in Rockville Centre, New York, before the war and at Temple Israel in Boston after the war. Born in 1910 in Cleveland, Ohio, where his father was a physician, Gittelsohn attended Western Reserve University and then Hebrew Union College in Cincinnati where he was ordained as a Reform rabbi. He was married with a family when he enlisted and was assigned to the Fifth Marine Division which served on Iwo Jima.

Gittelsohn was a pacifist, a civil rights activist and a supporter of liberal causes. Later, he was a member of President Truman's commission on civil rights. I am still friends with his assistant, Sammy Bernstein, who was with Rabbi Gittelsohn in the foxholes of Iwo Jima, a small volcanic island 650 miles south of Tokyo. The military mission was to seize a 554-foot mountain, Suribachi, that dominated the full length of the beach, and to wrest the island from its 22,000 defenders. The first surprise was the black volcanic sand that made it impossible to get any traction while walking. On February 19, 1945, although Iwo Jima was the most densely fortified piece of real estate in the world, 110,000 soldiers assaulted the island in a ferocious battle that lasted thirty-six days. More than one-third of the 19,000 Marines who were killed in World War II died on Iwo Jima. The dedication of the Fifth Marine Division Cemetery took place even before the end of the battle.

The senior chaplain, Reverend Warren Cuthriell, had originally planned a joint service. First there would be a secular dedication with the address given by the commanding general. Immediately thereafter, all three faiths were to unite in a combined religious service, after which any group that so wished would be free to hold its own denominational service. As an eloquent expression of his own devotion to the teachings of Christianity, as well as to the high truths of democracy, the chaplain invited Gittelsohn to serve as spokesman for the smallest religious minority in the division and to preach the memorial sermon. Immediately after Cuthriell's plans became public, two Protestant chaplains visited him to express their vigorous objection to the Jewish chaplain preaching over graves belonging mostly to Christians. Cuthriell explained that the right of the Jewish chaplain to preach such a sermon was precisely one of the rights for which they were fighting a war.

Then six Catholic chaplains on the island sent their senior representative to speak for all of them. They were opposed to any joint memorial service, and they were opposed especially to a sermon preached by a Jewish chaplain. If Cuthriell insisted on carrying out his original intention, they would refuse to participate or even attend. Ten days passed between Gittelsohn's receiving the invitation to preach at the cemetery and Cutheriell's telling Gittelsohn of his dilemma. He could withstand the two Protestant chaplains, but the objection of what felt like the entire Catholic church would have made a major incident out of the matter, so Gittelsohn decided to withdraw.

First minyan by a Jewish chaplain on Japanese soil during World War II, Iwo Jima, March 2, 1945. Chaplain Roland Gittelson, *far right*; courtesy of Samuel Bernstein, *fourth from left*.

After a brief secular dedication, each faith went to its own specified corner to hold its own memorial service. Gittelsohn gave the exact sermon to the twenty-five Jewish servicemen in his corner that he had prepared for the large group at the joint service. "You try to serve men of all faiths and no faith," he said, "without making denomination or affiliation a prerequisite for help. Protestants, Catholics and Jews have lived together, fought together, died together, and now lay buried together. But we the living could not unite to pray together." Gittlesohn's service for his twenty-five Jewish

This photo is of Chaplain Adler in the United States prior to his assignments in the Philippines and Japan; courtesy of Photo Archives of Congregation Shaarey Zedek, Southfield, Michigan.

servicemen was the first Jewish ceremony on captured Japanese soil during the war. A Protestant chaplain made copies of Gittelsohn's sermon, and it was widely disseminated by newspapers, magazines and radio stations. It was a most pioneering sermon in which Gittlesohn also included black servicemen; the sermon rightly earned a place in the *Congressional Record*.

Rabbi Morris Adler was born in Slutsk, Russia, where his father heard stories about Abraham Lincoln and a country where everyone was free – no persecution and no Siberia. The family migrated to the United States in 1912 and lived on New York's Lower East Side. His father, who became a prominent rabbi and educator in New York, would dress in a tuxedo and top hat to vote on election day and often thanked God for being alive and living in a free country. Adler attended the City College of New York and the rabbinical department of the future Yeshiva University. During this period he met Goldie Kadish, and the couple married in June 1929. Adler took a position at an Orthodox synagogue in St. Joseph, Missouri, before returning to New York to attend the Jewish Theological Seminary. Upon ordination, Adler received a rabbinic appointment at the oldest synagogue in Buffalo, New York.

In 1943 Adler enlisted in the military, serving with the Eleventh Airborne Division in the Philippines, and was the first Jewish chaplain to arrive in Japan after the country's surrender in 1945. During the six months Adler served as chaplain in Japan, he went anywhere and everywhere, searching every corner for Jews to care for them, advise them and help many of them migrate to the United States. He wrote letters in Yiddish to parents and grandparents of soldiers and translated letters in Yiddish that came to some of the Jewish soldiers. He was available for Jewish soldiers who wanted to talk to him, and he made the chapel a place to enjoy Jewish foods, listen to phonograph records, meet Jewish girls who were nurses or WACs (Women's Army Corps) and experience a little normalcy. On the Jewish New Year, Adler reserved a large room for thousands of Jewish soldiers to attend religious services, and he also arranged for transportation to take them there.

Adler's intelligence, vitality and personality were impressive. When he spoke to you, you felt you were the only person in the world who mattered, no matter who you were. Nothing that was human was beyond his concern. Having faced death close up and personal, he embraced life.

Back in the United States, Adler became the senior rabbi of Congregation Shaarey Zedek in Southfield, Michigan. In 1966, on Abraham Lincoln's birthday, a twenty-three-year-old, mentally ill congregant named Richard Wishnetsky read a brief statement condemning the congregation in front of seven hundred congregants including his parents, sister and grandmother. He then took out a .32 caliber colt revolver, fired it first into the ceiling and then into Rabbi Adler's arm and head at point blank range before finally shooting himself. Wishnetsky died three days later, and Adler died three weeks later.

In the 1970s, while I was serving as a rabbi in Tokyo, I suggested to the travel agencies handling visits to the Far East by Jewish groups, such as Hadassah, American Jewish Congress and B'nai B'rith, that they include synagogues and Jewish communities on their tours, and they agreed. One day a group came with the American Jewish Congress and, as they sat in the synagogue, I asked them their names and the names of their hometowns. One woman said she was Goldie Adler from Detroit. I asked her if she was Rabbi Morris Adler's widow; she was. I told her and the entire group that I was walking in Rabbi Adler's footsteps.

Rabbi Morris Gordon was born in 1914 in Baronovich, Poland, which was under Russian control at that time. His father went to the United States alone to earn money so he could send for his family. Gordon really did not know his father until the family was able to start a new life together in Albany, where his father worked as principal of the community Hebrew school. Gordon learned English and read the dictionary every day. There was a great deal of tension in the house except on the Sabbath. Then, he and his father played a relaxing game of chess and studied Torah, and the family enjoyed the Sabbath tranquility together as they read classic Hebrew literature. Gordon studied at the City College of New York, Columbia University and the Jewish Theological Seminary from where he graduated as a rabbi with distinction, winning awards for excellence in Jewish literature, public speaking and cantorial music. After serving as a rabbi at the Millinery Synagogue in Manhattan, Gordon accepted a rabbinic position in Youngstown, Ohio.

During World War ii, Gordon enlisted in the military and was sent to the China/Burma/India theater, landing in Burma in a camouflaged mail plane where he was dropped off without the pilot ever turning off the engine. A soldier wandering by directed him to his tent, which he had to share with a cow (a sacred animal in Burma), which had taken up residency there. He was the first Jewish chaplain in Burma and served as the chaplain for all faiths. Gordon joined the one thousand troops whose mission it was to build and protect the Burma Road. The flights over the Himalayas, referred to as "over the hump," were the most dangerous because of the treacherous cross winds, and during this time 460 planes crashed and 792 airmen lost their lives. Gordon was almost attacked by a python, a reptile valued by the Burmese for its skin and meat, but Gordon prevailed, a victory noted in many newspapers, including *The New York Times* on June 22, 1945.

General Claire Chennault, commander of the "Flying Tigers," requested a meeting with all the chaplains in the Burma theater for an important announcement with a reward attached to it. The mission to open the Burma Road was vital to preventing the Japanese from winning the war. Chennault was looking for a chaplain who would be willing to make the first trip on the Burma Road, conducting religious services in the camps along the way. Gordon's hand shot right up. He thought it would be a great honor to open the Burma Road, and he was surprised when he looked around and saw that he was the only volunteer.

Chennault congratulated Gordon for his wisdom and bravery and told him to select a sidekick and be ready to leave early the next morning. Gordon picked Eddie, a black, Catholic, piano-playing sergeant who agreed to accompany him. During World War ii, this pairing of a black and white soldier was unique. Blacks and whites lived in segregated tents and ate at segregated tables in the mess hall. As they packed up their heavily armored jeep, the Catholic chaplain gave Eddie rosary beads; Protestant chaplains gave them Bibles; and Gordon found room for his Torah and a kosher salami. With hundreds of soldiers waving goodbye and wishing them well, they started their eight-hundred-mile journey winding through the treacherous Himalayas, at the end of which General Joe Stillwell would welcome them in China with a marching band and a huge press contingent.

Traveling during daylight proved too dangerous, but driving at night with lights, which were needed to see the narrow road with steep drops on both sides, was equally dangerous, so they decided to travel at night without lights as they climbed from an altitude of eight thousand feet up to fourteen thousand feet. Along the way, they conducted services for men who were hungry for God, with Eddie playing the harmonica or flute. Soldiers showed up from everywhere in the jungle to connect with the United States and to a man who represented a higher power. There are no atheists, it seems, in foxholes. And there were also very few white soldiers along the way; black soldiers built the Burma Road. These soldiers, who endured malaria and yellow fever, rampant in the jungle, were never given credit for their back-breaking work. After the war, when Gordon attended ceremonies honoring those responsible for the opening of the Burma Road, shamefully there was not one black face in the crowd.

Gordon and Eddie never completed their mission to open the Burma Road. About six hundred miles into the trip, everything went wrong. They came to a washed-out bridge over a river which their jeep could not cross. They jerry-built a kind of ferry or raft to float them in their jeep across the river, but a Japanese plane strafed them, causing the jeep to explode, killing Eddie instantly and throwing Gordon into the river. He grabbed his Torah and tried to swim to shore, but his heavy gear dragged him under where he swallowed massive amounts of polluted water, and he felt too weak to pull himself out. It was a miracle that a Chinese officer heard the explosion and saw Gordon go underwater. He saved Gordon and the Torah and radioed for a plane which flew Gordon back to an army hospital, where for three weeks he suffered with bacterial dysentery that almost cost him his life. When he recuperated, he held a memorial service for Eddie and later officiated at a large Catholic service for him.

Gordon returned to his camp when he was healthy again and became known as "Flash Gordon." In Burma, he saved the life of a villager who had taken his army-issued dagger, an act punishable by death in the village, and that man went on to become indispensable to Gordon and everyone else in the camp. The Chinese officer who saved Gordon in the river made an ark from teak wood for the Torah and put Roman numerals on each side to represent the Ten Commandments. After the war, Gordon kept the ark, polished and oiled, positioned at the entrance to his home. Gordon was awarded a bronze star for his heroic deeds. When the war was over, Gordon, officially part of the "Flying Tigers," was chosen to speak in Shanghai to celebrate the victory and to be honored for making the first trip along the Burma Road. In the Shanghai ghetto, Gordon learned of the twenty thousand refugees there and soon conducted the first bar mitzvah in the ghetto. Gordon also arranged for school supplies to be delivered to the two Jewish schools in Shanghai and he filled a ship headed to Palestine with Jewish children.

Rabbi Chaim Nussbaum was born in 1909 in Auschwitz, Poland, was raised in Holland and served as a chaplain on the River Kwai in Thailand. Stranded in Lithuania at the beginning of the war, Rabbi Nussbaum, his wife and their two young children made their way across Russia into Japan and waited for their visas to Canada or South America, but they never came. The Dutch consul advised him that science teachers were needed in Java in the Dutch East Indies, where the Jewish population also had no rabbi. The consul suggested that Nussbaum consider Java as his new home, and he went there.

After Pearl Harbor, the Dutch empire fell quickly, and despite an opportunity to escape to Australia, Nussbaum remained as a volunteer chaplain to the Dutch and allied forces. Soon, however, Nussbaum and his comrades were overrun by the Japanese and held as prisoners of war (POWs). Despite his loss of freedom, separation from his family, cruelty, torture, death marches, disease (especially cholera) and starvation, Nussbaum did not want to be a victim. Instead, he wanted to be an "observer of human suffering and survival." Suffering did not diminish his faith. Throughout the war he recited his prayers, observed the Sabbath and served as chaplain wherever he was. Rabbi Nussbaum could communicate with any person of any race, any religion and any social status. Each prisoner was special, but all were part of the family of man.

Rabbi Nussbaum was a Renaissance man of extensive and varied learning who kept a journal during the war years about his experiences as a POW in Singapore, Indonesia, Burma and Thailand under the Japanese. During his years as a POW, 1942–1945, there were many Jews in the POW camps, and Nussbaum managed to build the only synagogue in a POW camp, organized religious services, wrote a prayer book, edited a literary magazine, produced a Jewish calendar, held study groups whenever and wherever possible and taught others to conduct services and even how to bury Jewish soldiers.

Nussbaum's courage and hope in such a hostile environment influenced other POWs. On Chanukah, a twenty-year-old POW carved a menorah and a Star of David out of scraps of wood. When the Japanese found it, they were furious, and that night the Dutch officers, fearing for the safety of Jewish prisoners, instructed the Jews to remove all Jewish symbols from sight. Chanukah, nevertheless, was observed properly with all the blessings and traditions.

The oldest son of an Orthodox rabbi of a synagogue in Washington, DC, Alexander David Goode was born in Brooklyn in 1911. He grew into an exceptional student and a superb runner and boxer. After receiving his rabbinic ordination from Hebrew Union College, Goode married his long-time sweetheart, served as the rabbi in York, Pennsylvania, and earned a PhD from Johns Hopkins University. At the start of the war, he volunteered for the military. While on his way to his assignment in Greenland, traveling on an old, rusty and slow freighter, the SS Dorchester, he and two Protestant chaplains and one Catholic chaplain learned that the signal officer had received a warning that a Nazi submarine was following them.

At one o'clock in the morning on February 3, 1943, an explosion erupted as a torpedo ripped through the ship and fires broke out. One thousand soldiers were told to abandon ship; seven hundred men died that night. All the chaplains gave their life preservers and gloves to enlisted men who did not have theirs, and it was widely reported that the four chaplains stood with their arms linked together in their conviction that they must give up their lives to save others as the frigid ocean became their grave. Rabbi Goode posthumously received the Purple Heart and Distinguished Service Cross.

A chapel at Temple University in Pennsylvania, known as the Chapel of the Four Chaplains, was dedicated to Rabbi Goode and his three chaplain colleagues on February 3, 1951, the eighth anniversary of the sinking of the SS Dorchester. President Harry Truman was the keynote speaker. At the front of the chapel there are three revolving arks – Protestant, Catholic and Jewish. Above the main entrance there is an eternal light and an inscription etched in stone that reads: "Chapel of four chaplains, an interfaith shrine, here is sanctuary for brotherhood, let it never be violated." I own the first day cover of the 1948 postage stamp dedicated to the four chaplains.

There was a small Jewish community in the Philippines whose members included refugees escaping from the Nazis. Their synagogue was Temple Emil and, in 1944, the Japanese occupied it and used it as an ammunition depot. Fortunately, the Jews had emptied the synagogue and had hidden the Torah scrolls among members of the community, because in February 1945, during the Battle of Manila, the Japanese naval troops set Temple Emil, filled with ammunition, on fire. Little remained of this synagogue where Jews had worshipped for decades.

In October 1945, under Captain/Dr. Adolf Nachman's leadership, several Jewish servicemen met to plan the rehabilitation of the Jewish community of Manila, a fitting memorial to the Jewish servicemen who died in the liberation of the Philippines. The plan included the rebuilding of Temple Emil on its former site, where the foundation and outer walls were still intact. In November 1945, American service men and women jammed the open space that was the synagogue's main sanctuary to commemorate the seventh anniversary of Kristallnacht and to commit to the rebuilding of Temple Emil. A fundraising event was held at which $15,000 was donated. In December 1945, during the celebration of the Jewish holiday of Chanukah, a formal presentation by Lieutenant General William D. Styer, commanding general of the US forces in the Western Pacific, was made on behalf of Jewish soldiers to the Jewish community. "Our forces came to the Philippines not as takers of freedom, but as givers of freedom," Lieutenant General Styer said. "Tonight's celebration is an expression of the true spirit of giving.... This synagogue [which] ... it is believed, was the only synagogue under the American flag to be destroyed by the enemy in this war, shall be rebuilt." And it was.

On October 24, 2011, at Arlington National Cemetery, a plaque with the names of fourteen Jewish chaplains who died in the service of the United States was dedicated. These were rabbis from all the Jewish movements who lost their lives on land and sea in North Africa, Europe and the Far East. It was a time when Reform, Conservative and Orthodox rabbis came together and served Jews and non-Jews in the military. It was a time when "matzah" could serve as "communion bread" when necessary. War is a sad time that ironically brings the kind of cooperation among people of different beliefs that puts smiles on their faces and offers hope that cooperation among people also can exist in times of peace.

Chapter Six
Jacob Schiff: How $196,250,000 Changed History in Japan in 1904

S oon after my arrival in Japan in 1968, the Israeli ambassador to Japan told me a story. When he was participating in the formal and elaborate ceremony of the presentation of his credentials and documents to Emperor Hirohito of Japan, he was surprised at how warm and welcoming everyone was. He was especially surprised when the emperor said, "We will never forget what one of your people, Jacob Schiff, did for us." The same gratitude was expressed by a member of the Imperial Household Agency, who told the Israeli ambassador that "we can never forget what Schiff did for us during those crucial years of our history." Since the ambassador did not know who Jacob Schiff was, he remained awkwardly silent in response to all the words of appreciation he was receiving.

When the ambassador returned to the embassy and asked his staff who Jacob Schiff was, they did not know either. Since I was the only rabbi in Japan, the ambassador called me, hoping that I could enlighten him. I agreed to meet with the ambassador to tell him the amazing story of Jacob Schiff and what he did for Japan. I told the ambassador that Jacob Schiff is the only Jew who is found in the standard history text of Japan. He is described as a Jew from the United States who helped Japan enter the industrial world to become a major world power and saved Japan from defeat and humiliation. The unusual role that Schiff played in the history of relations between the Jews and the Japanese resonates to this very day.

In 1973, wanting to learn more about Jacob Schiff, I asked Stephen Birmingham, author of *Our Crowd*, a book about German Jews in New York, about his research on the Schiff family and Jacob Schiff's connection to Japan. He kindly

replied that he was not particularly interested in the Japanese connection, and he
suggested that I write to John Schiff, Jacob
Schiff's grandson, and ask permission to
read Jacob's journal written during his visit
to Japan. From Japan, I sent my request to
John Schiff at Kuhn Loeb, a major investment banking firm in New York at the time,
and explained that the diary would be very
helpful to my research on the Jewish experience in Japan.

John Schiff responded that his grandfather's journal was his most precious possession, a treasured legacy for the entire
Schiff family that he could not let out of

Jacob Schiff, 1847–1920

his hands to send to me in Japan. Therese, Jacob Schiff's wife, had gathered
his diary entries into a book, *Our Journey to Japan*, had it printed on Japanese
paper and then presented it to him on his sixtieth birthday. I understood John's
reluctance and tried to assure him that I would treasure the book, too, treat
it with the utmost care and return it to him in the same condition in which I
received it, but he still respectfully declined. I was very eager to read the diary,
and Birmingham insisted that I read it, so I wrote again and restated the significance of the diary to research and scholarship, promising again to return
the book safely into his hands. As luck would have it, this time there was a
partner at Kuhn Loeb who was a former congregant of mine, and he assured
John Schiff that he could trust me. I was delighted when he wrote that indeed
he would send the book to me. When it arrived I was incredulous that I was
actually holding it in my hands, and I was ecstatic as I was about to read it.

My ecstasy soon turned to concern, however, when I was not able to read
the book. You see, although the book had been printed about seventy years
before I received it, it was still in excellent condition, but the groupings of
four pages were sealed together at the edges, so I could not turn them. With
great care, I used a single-edge razor blade to slit them open. Unbelievably,
this copy of the priceless family treasure, the precious diary, in fact, had never
been read by anyone!

Jacob Henry Schiff was born in Frankfurt, Germany, on January 10, 1847. He
was the second son in a family of four boys and one girl. He was a descendant

of a long line of rabbis, including the notable seventeeth-century rabbi Maharam Schiff who died at age thirty-six after writing a commentary on the Talmud* that is studied in every yeshiva (a Jewish religious school) to this very day.

Another of Schiff's ancestors served as the rabbi of the Great Synagogue of London in the eighteenth century. Schiff himself was raised in a traditional, Orthodox Jewish home where he received an excellent religious education. He was an observant and proud Jew who recited his Hebrew prayers daily and regularly attended Sabbath services in a synagogue. He attended Jewish schools in Frankfurt, Germany.

At the age of eighteen, Schiff, penniless, moved to the United States and found employment as a bank clerk. At the age of twenty-eight, he joined the investment banking firm of Kuhn Loeb and Company (named after Abraham Kuhn, the German spelling for Cohen, and Solomon Loeb, the German spelling for Levy), and later Schiff married Therese, Solomon Loeb's daughter. Within ten years, Schiff was head of the firm, which had the reputation of being a young, creative and aggressive investment banking house that assisted in the rapid development of America's industrialization. Financial expert B.C. Forbes said that Kuhn Loeb "issued more good investments and fewer bad ones than any other banking concern in America." The most brilliant bankers and financiers were impressed that Kuhn Loeb committed so few investment errors. It seems fair to say that Schiff, who singlehandedly directed the firm and understood both industry and politics, had a sixth sense or intuition about investment and banking and an amazing grasp of economics.

Under Schiff, Kuhn Loeb financed and guided AT&T, Westinghouse Electric, US Rubber, Western Union and Armour Meat Packing in their early days. In addition, Schiff financed and guided every major railroad line and encouraged the development of the underwater tunnel and the building of Penn Station (next to the Hudson River) so that trains could come right into the center of Manhattan in New York City. There were no bridges, so before this tunnel was built travelers to Manhattan had to disembark in New Jersey and take a ferry across the Hudson River to Manhattan.

Many charities also received funds and guidance from Schiff. He made

---

* The Talmud is the massive record of discussions held by rabbis and scholars in ancient Babylonia and Palestine about the Bible, laws, ethics, wisdom, etc. that serves as the foundation of every aspect of Jewish life.

charitable contributions to the Red Cross, the Salvation Army and to the YMCA. Schiff was president of the Montefiore Home, a Jewish home for the elderly and disabled in need of nursing care. Thanks to Schiff, it boasted a kosher kitchen and a beautiful synagogue on the premises. Schiff's special involvement was such that for thirty-five years he attended all board meetings, knew most of the residents by name and visited them almost every Sunday. All major Jewish charities of the era were recipients of Schiff's philanthropy.

He also gave money to, among others, Barnard College and Columbia University, and he donated funds to establish a Semitics museum at Harvard University. He created an endowment for the Technion, located in Haifa, Israel, which still remains a primary institute for Israeli researchers and scientists. He financed the publication of the *Jewish Encyclopedia*, the first major classic encyclopedia of Jewish civilization and culture in English. He also financed the translation of the Jewish classics into English as a compilation entitled *Schiff Classic Series*, which is studied to this day. The Judaica collection of two hundred thousand volumes at the Library of Congress started with Schiff's donation of ten thousand volumes. And as a patron of the Metropolitan Museum of Art in New York, Schiff sponsored an exhibition of Japanese art, decorations and medals, the first major exhibition of Japanese art in America.

In his attempts to fight anti-Semitism and provide opportunities for Jews, Schiff encouraged the appointment of qualified Jews to major national positions, including Oscar Straus (the first Jew appointed to serve as a member of a US president's cabinet), Louis Brandeis (the first Jew appointed to the Supreme Court), and Paul Warburg (the first Jew named to the Federal Reserve Board).

In 1903, there was a horrifying pogrom (an anti-Semitic attack on a Jewish community) in Russia, echoes of which were heard across the continent and even across the ocean, and this pogrom soon would serve as the impetus for Schiff's generous act on behalf of Japan. During the Easter holiday on April 6–7, 1903, which coincided with the Jewish holiday of Passover, Minister of the Interior Vyacheslav Plehve and other high government Russian officials provoked an attack on the Jews of Kishinev, a Russian commercial and industrial center in Moldavia in the area of the Ukraine.

The violence started with a poisonous anti-Jewish campaign instigated by the chief of police after the dead body of a Christian child was found, and a rumor spread that Jews committed the murder in order to use the dead child's blood for the baking of matzah (unleavened bread) for the Passover holiday.

During the brutality and cruelty that followed, forty-nine Jews were killed, five hundred Jews were injured, seven hundred Jewish homes were ransacked and destroyed, six hundred shops were looted and destroyed, and two thousand Jews became homeless. The local garrison of five hundred soldiers took absolutely no action to stop the violence. Not only is blood not used to bake matzah, which is made from only flour and water, but also it was later learned that relatives of the dead child were, in fact, the murderers.

There was a public outcry in England, France and the United States. Leonid Tolstoy expressed sympathy for the victims and condemned the czarist authorities. The poet laureate of the Jewish people, Hayyim N. Bialik, wrote a moving poem about the pogrom titled "In the City of Murder." Jacob Schiff asked the American government to denounce the actions of the Russians, and President Theodore Roosevelt sent a letter to the Russian czar, but he refused to accept it. Schiff appeared several times at public meetings, including one at Carnegie Hall, to show his personal support for the protests against the Russian czar. Schiff's efforts raised $1.5 million to provide aid to those who had suffered during this pogrom.

Schiff was so outraged by Russia's actions that he refused to participate in any loan, no matter how profitable, if the czar or Russia benefitted in any way. He also told a friend, one of the Rothschilds, that eventually Russia would turn to the European money market for assistance and would apply to Jewish bankers for financial aid and loans. When that happened, Schiff said, everyone should decline to cooperate with, or supply financial help or any loans to, the Russian government. Whenever Russia needed money, Schiff would remind his fellow Jewish financiers that Russia had promised to behave honorably toward its Jewish citizens but never kept its promises. At Schiff's suggestion, in 1906, three years after the Russian pogrom, the American Jewish Committee was established to handle this sort of crisis, and Schiff became a valuable member of the executive committee.

In February 1904, war broke out between Russia and Japan. The conflict grew essentially out of rivalry between Russia and Japan in Manchuria and Korea. Both the failure of Russia to withdraw from Manchuria and Russian penetration into North Korea threatened Japan's attempts to maintain spheres of influence in these areas. Diplomatic exchanges were unproductive, and relations were severed in February 1904. Two days later the Imperial Japanese Navy attacked and blockaded the Russian fleet at Port Arthur in southern Manchuria.

Few people followed this war, and most knowledgeable Europeans were skeptical about Japan's chances to be victorious. No Asian power had defeated a European nation since the Mongol conquests in the thirteenth century. Everyone thought that when the tall, powerful, healthy and muscular Russian sailors waved their *pilotkas* (Russian sailor hats) at the short, thin Japanese sailors, the Japanese sailors would immediately turn around and run for their lives. The Russian czar, who referred to the Japanese as "yellow monkeys," believed that not only did the Russians have a superior army and navy, but that they also had superior finances, could secure limitless loans and would fight to victory, quickly bringing the Japanese to their knees.

Baron Takahashi Korekiyo. In the early 1900s he was vice governor of the Bank of Japan; he later went on to serve seven terms as finance minister of Japan and then became the nation's prime minister.

At the start of the war, Japan had sufficient funds for only a few months of warfare, and its gold deposits were diminishing. The Bank of Japan reserves fell from 116,962,184 yen in December 1903 to 105,921,628 yen in January 1904 to 67,442,130 yen in May 1904. The Japanese government, after many meetings in Tokyo, decided to send the vice governor of the Bank of Japan, Baron Takahashi Korekiyo, to secure war bonds to be floated overseas. Accordingly, Takahashi, an illegitimate child and self-taught man, sailed for London, the principal international financial market at that time, to arrange for the war loans.

While in London, Takahashi was invited to dinner at the home of Arthur Hill, a London financier, and there he met many of England's bankers and financiers. He paid little attention to the man sitting right next to him, Jacob Schiff, who was returning to New York after visiting his family in Germany. Schiff was very interested in what Takahashi had to say, but Takahashi didn't know who Schiff was. The next day Arthur Hill informed Takahashi that the man who was sitting next to him at dinner was interested in supporting Japan's war efforts, but Takahashi had never heard of Schiff or of Kuhn Loeb and, though he was excited, he thought it was premature to mention this to any government official in Japan.

Takahashi sent a cable saying that his efforts in London were likely to fail. Not only were British banks and financial institutions willing to provide only a small percentage of the money, they also added more insult by insisting that, despite precedent, a British official would have to supervise the customs office in Japan to guarantee the return of their investment. Takahashi wrote, "We will receive in London only small amounts under humiliating and embarrassing conditions." In addition, there were racial comments suggesting that the Russian czar's family was related by blood to the British monarchy, leading the London office of the Yokohama Specie Bank, a quasi-official bank of Japan, to conclude that this was a "color war" between the white and the yellow races and that the British would probably side with the Russians. Having failed to secure in London the amount of money Japan needed, Takahashi would have returned home in shame but for the encouraging news he had received from Arthur Hill about Jacob Schiff.

The United States at the time was not accustomed to foreign investment, and there was little financial connection between the US and Japan. Bankers were sympathetic but not encouraging, except for Jacob Schiff who asked Takahashi to accept the money the British had offered, assuring him that he would provide the remainder of the loan. Takahashi joyfully reported to the Japanese government that he had secured the entire initial war loan of £10 million, and the first Japanese war bond was issued on May 2, 1904, at 10:00 a.m. at the Kuhn Loeb office in New York. By 11:00 a.m. the next morning the subscription was closed as it was already oversubscribed by 500 percent. Later, in referring to that lucky dinner at Arthur Hill's house, Takahashi wrote in his diary, "…little did I think that this was to prove the beginning of his [Schiff's] important relations with Japan and of a valuable friendship to me!" Schiff's action also led to the uniting of England and the United States in support of Japan against Russia, an outcome for which King Edward VII later thanked Schiff personally at a private luncheon.

Why, you may ask, would Schiff, a brilliant but atypical investment banker, gamble so much money on Japan when everyone else thought Japan was such a bad risk? He believed that gold is not essential for war, if the war is a national effort. His knowledge of Japan was minimal, but his intuition, the sixth sense mentioned earlier that had served him so well, led him to perceive how corrupt Russia was; its pogrom against the Jews in 1903 substantiated his suspicion. Schiff reasoned that while the government had used the diversion of the pogrom against the Russian Jews to get the masses to forget their own lack of food, poor housing and hopelessness, he did not believe that the czar could convince the downtrodden and impoverished masses to exhibit heroic devotion to their homeland during a war against the Japanese that was being fought in Manchuria, not in Russia. Schiff's impression of the Japanese, however, was that they were loyal and willing to sacrifice out of devotion for their country, and he considered himself "a true friend of Japan." Schiff also prided himself on being fair and just. Russia had stymied Japan's major efforts in the Far East and even had excluded Japan from the spoils of the Sino-Japanese war. Schiff wanted to teach Russia a lesson and thought that if Russia lost the war against Japan, perhaps Russia's leaders would mend their ways and improve the lives of their own citizens.

As a devout Jew, Schiff also believed in the Bible and in the concept of divine providence. Frequently the Bible states that God uses nations to do the work of history. During the Russo-Japanese war, he believed that perhaps Japan was the rod to punish the Russians for their cruelty to the Jews and, therefore, he would support Japan's efforts and hope they would pummel the Russians. Schiff's support stimulated the Japanese, increased their confidence and raised their morale, while discouraging Russia and promoting the United States as an important influence on, and financial source for, Japan.

The first loan was not enough to guarantee victory for Japan, so there was a second (£6 million in November 1904), third (£15 million in March 1905), fourth (£10 million in July 1905) and fifth loan (£3.25 million in November 1905). When the third loan was offered to the public at Kuhn Loeb's offices in the Wall Street area in New York, *The New York Times* (March 30, 1905) reported that "when the office force arrived for work, the lower corridor outside the doors of the banking house was jammed with people so that it was hardly possible to reach the elevators. Outside the portal, there was a double line of people extending across William Street and two or three doors up on Pine Street." One employee reported that "they nearly tore us to pieces" for a few hours. In all, about $500 million in subscriptions were received for the $75 million American share of this Japanese war loan. The five loans underwritten by Schiff in New York totaled $196,250,000, the amount almost equal to the entire cost of the war.

Takahashi always was assured by Schiff that if the loans could not be secured, he personally would come to the rescue. Schiff promised that not only could he secure loans in New York and London, but that also he would contact his relatives in Germany to secure loans from Jewish bankers there, an amazing coup since Germany was supporting Russia, not Japan. Japan grew financially stronger, and Russia lost all its credit as the war progressed. Ironically, after the Sino-Japanese war, Russia, Germany and France had been united against Japan, leaving Japan isolated from the major world powers. Now, thanks to Jacob Schiff, Germany, England, the United States and France were united for Japan, and Russia was isolated from the major world powers.

These loans boosted Schiff's reputation nationally and internationally. Kuhn Loeb eclipsed the major banking house of J.P. Morgan, and Kuhn Loeb became the primary manager of American accounts held by the Japanese government. Thanks to Jacob Schiff, these loans represented, according to *The Wall Street Journal*, July 3, 1905, "New York's first big step toward the position of an international market." And *The New York Times*, earlier on March 30, 1905, described the Japanese war bonds as the reason to consider that "New York bankers should be consulted when new international loans are made." Thanks to Schiff, New York's Wall Street, not London's Fleet Street, became the international financial center.

Japan won the war, and the peace treaty was signed in Portsmouth, New Hampshire, on September 5, 1905. In 1911, the Russian minister of finance declared, "Our government will never forgive or forget what that Jew, Schiff, did to us. He alone made it possible for Japan to secure a loan in America. He was one of the most dangerous men we had against us abroad."

Schiff's actions would play a significant and ironic role in the relationship between the Jews and the Japanese many years later during the Nazi period. During World War II the members of Japan's cabinet spoke openly about the opportunity to save the Jews of Europe: "Now," they said, "we can do for Schiff's people what he did for us" and thus, wipe the slate clean, because in Japan it is undesirable to owe someone a favor, and Japan owed Jacob Schiff a big favor.

Takahashi returned to Japan where he served seven terms as finance minister and later became prime minister of Japan. His friendship with Schiff continued throughout his lifetime. Schiff was invited to Japan as the personal guest of the Japanese government and the emperor of Japan. He and his wife Therese arrived in Yokohama on March 25, 1906, and traveled by private rail car to Tokyo, where a long line of people were waiting to see, welcome and hail this amazing American friend of Japan. Schiff kept a diary about his activities during their brief stay in Japan. Accompanied by thirty-five-year-old Kitashima-san, a Harvard graduate assigned to be the couple's guide, they took a rickshaw ride and visited a teahouse and a Buddhist temple as well as other places of interest to tourists. He also visited Samurai Shokai, the largest curio and souvenir store in Japan. In another shop, Schiff bought a bonsai tree. But, oh, the cherry blossoms! Schiff wrote, "The entire town was covered in cherry blossoms. There was a delicate pink everywhere you looked, under the deep blue sky above, and all nature seemed to be rejoicing in her spring dress."

Schiff visited the prime minister, the finance minister, leading US diplomats based in Japan, the foreign minister and even the emperor. On Wednesday, March 28, 1906, promptly at 11:30 a.m., Schiff was escorted to a private meeting with the Meiji Emperor, which was followed by a luncheon. Dressed in military uniform, the emperor extended his hand in friendship to Schiff and told Schiff how pleased he was to be able to thank him personally for the important assistance he had given to Japan during a crucial time. Schiff was given the Order of the Rising Sun, a medal the emperor also wore. Schiff wrote, "This was the very first time that the emperor had invited a foreign and private person to a repast at the palace." At the luncheon there were nine Japanese dignitaries, and no foods prohibited by Jewish dietary laws were served out of respect for Schiff, so the repast was, one might say, a kosher luncheon.*

The emperor was in splendid humor; he felt quite relaxed and ate well. Schiff told the VIP sitting next to him that he would like to make a toast to the emperor, an act that represented a complete break with Japanese tradition and protocol since the Japanese even avoided making direct eye contact with the emperor! The dignitary asked another dignitary until finally someone courageously told the emperor of Schiff's sincere and honest request. The emperor agreed and signaled Schiff to proceed. Schiff decided to repeat the words of the first US president, George Washington: "First in war, first in peace, first in the hearts of his countrymen." He then went on with a toast wishing the emperor a long life filled with happiness for himself and his family and for the world that so respected him. After everyone drank to that, they were surprised and shocked that the emperor reciprocated with a toast to Schiff's good health and success and a wish that Schiff enjoy his visit to Japan and remain such a good

---

* Schiff also observed Jewish dietary laws in the Imperial Hotel during Passover in April 1906 while he was in Japan. He wrote, "Mother has prepared a festive table like at home. Nothing is missing for the ceremonies, and we all read the Haggadah (the book that retells the story of the Jews' slavery and their hasty exodus from Egypt) and thus, in a homelike way, we celebrated the old festival in a distant land."

friend to Japan. After the almost three-hour luncheon, people noted that they had never known the emperor to be so gracious to a stranger.

The festivities continued later that day with a dinner at the foreign minister's residence, where Schiff was greeted as the "most distinguished guest we ever had from the USA" and where his actions in 1904 were recounted: how he went to London during such dark days for Japan and how after a single conversation he amazingly arranged for Japan to secure war loans. The foreign minister thanked Schiff profusely saying, "Words fail to express our gratitude to you, not only mine, not only our government, but the nation at large, and I have not language suitable to the national feeling of thankfulness."

Schiff considered his visit to Japan as the most interesting episode in his life. During fourteen weeks, ending in June 1906, he traveled twenty thousand miles. He described his perception of the Japanese people, noting that they cherished simplicity and frugality and that they were loyal to their emperor, their country and to each other. He admired their piety and respected the sensitivity the young displayed for the elderly and the way the elderly doted on the young. He also was impressed with the rigorous athletics taught in the schools and the compulsory education mandated by the Meiji Emperor during which "education was as free as the air." In addition, Schiff admired the control the Japanese had over their passions. They were modest about their incredible victory over the Russians and held no victory parades and expressed no desire for continued hostility. They were happy to return to living life modestly.

Schiff admired – and tried to bring to the United States – Japan's system of seeking advice from its elder statesmen, four or five men whose active careers had ended after they had served their country for many years. With their immense experience and knowledge they served as advisers and counselors to government officials and the emperor and were always consulted on major issues and during any crisis. In the United States, however, even ex-presidents who are of sound mind and body generally are not consulted by the sitting president.

With tongue in cheek, Schiff also wrote of the faults of Japan, specifically their souvenir shops where the curio dealers were willing to let shoppers keep at least enough of their money to return home. In 1910, though, Schiff's disappointment in Japan was more serious. They allied themselves with Russia, and Schiff realized that Japan had become more aggressive and was determined to establish firm control over Korea and Manchuria and to dominate China.

I visited the Takahashi family when I lived in Tokyo, and some of them remembered Jacob Schiff's visit to Japan. Frieda Schiff Warburg, Schiff's daughter, told me the story of one of her parents' most unusual experiences during their visit to Japan. Baron Takahashi introduced his teenage daughter Wakiko to Schiff. Schiff loved children and tried to make conversation with this Japanese girl who spoke no English and whose father tried to serve as interpreter. Schiff asked, "How would you like to go to the United States one day?"

The next day, Takahashi told Schiff that he and his wife had discussed his wonderful invitation to Wakiko, and while it was not customary for Japanese girls to leave home, this was such an unusual opportunity that they had decided Wakiko could live with them in the United States for two years. Mrs. Schiff refused to take responsibility for this young girl who spoke no English, had never slept in a western-style bed, and who had never worn anything but a kimono and sandals, unless they sent someone trustworthy with her. So the Takahashi family selected Miss Suo, a tiny, Japanese Christian woman who spoke some English and who had been head nurse in the naval hospital during the Russo-Japanese War, to accompany Wakiko to America. The Schiffs returned home with Wakiko dressed in a badly cut tan suit, tiny Miss Suo rubbing her hands on her knees saying repeatedly "Yes, Mrs. Skeef, certainly Mrs. Skeef," and two little Japanese spaniels, Fuji and Kittie – the oddest group you ever saw.

Wakiko, who soon called the Schiffs "Aunt" and "Uncle," was never homesick, it seems. She lived for almost three years with the Schiff family in New York, where she was raised tenderly as their own daughter with the complete confidence of her family in Japan. After Wakiko returned to Japan, the Schiffs found little loving notes Wakiko had written to them and hidden behind cushions and pillows all around their home. She married in Japan when she was about twenty-one years old, three years after she left New York.

In 1936 Baron Takahashi was assassinated in his home by rebelling military officers, but the Schiffs continued to correspond with Wakiko and her oldest daughter Yurika, one of Wakiko's five children. The Schiff family always remembered how Wakiko would prance around in a beautiful satin dress – with a long flowing train – that Mrs. Schiff had bought for her, admire herself in the mirror and, with a grand gesture, swing the flowing train around behind her.

In 1917–18, World War I was raging in Europe. At the same time, during the Bolshevik Revolution in Russia, Jewish immigrants were in Japan en route to the United States. When the Russian czar was overthrown by the

Bolsheviks, rubles (Russian currency) became worthless. US immigration officials thought all Russians were hated Communists, so the American government blocked their entry into the United States. Jacob Schiff intervened and asked the Japanese government to let the Jewish immigrants stay in Yokohama until the situation settled, and he convinced the US government that the Jewish immigrants were legitimate, enabling all of them to get to America. During the heavy immigration of Russian Jews to New York's Lower East Side, the area became very crowded, so Schiff arranged the logistics for letting ships continue to Galveston, Texas, where there was more space for the Jewish immigrants to settle.

Schiff remained active in banking and philanthropy until his death on September 25, 1920. In 1921, Schiff Parkway was built in Lower Manhattan in his memory. The Japanese consul in New York participated in the ceremony, and sometimes when Japanese government officials visit New York, they place flowers on Schiff's grave (in Cypress Hills on the border between Brooklyn and Queens) so that they might never forget Schiff's amazing efforts on their behalf during the war with Russia. To this day New Year greetings are sent from Japan's imperial family to the Schiff family, although some of the imperial family now may have no idea why.

In a tribute paid to Schiff by Gaspard Ferrer of Baring Brothers, an investment banking firm in London, Ferrer said, "No one on Wall Street stood on a higher plane than Schiff; in character, ability and humanity, he was in the very foremost rank, and that in a generation which grew the biggest kind of men – Morgan, Hill, Harriman and many others. Those were the days when the individual had full scope for his energies and abilities, and Mr. Schiff certainly made the most of his opportunities."

Chapter Seven
A Chinese Torah in Texas and Other Chinese Torahs Elsewhere

It is hard to believe that there has been a Chinese Torah at Southern Methodist University (SMU) in Dallas, Texas, since 1963, although SMU did not know it was a Chinese Torah. How did the Chinese Torah become part of the Harrison Bible collection that is housed in the Bridwell Library in the Perkins School of Theology at SMU? Who wrote it? When and where was it written? Are the texts of Chinese Torahs different in any way from the texts of other Torahs throughout the world? Where are other Chinese Torahs and what do these Torahs tell us about the people who wrote them?

A Chinese Torah is one written in Hebrew by a Chinese rabbi or Chinese Jewish scribe in China, and the appearance and style of the one at SMU looks different from the Torahs found in synagogues in the United States and Europe. Since Torah scrolls record no dates, no names of the scribe or scribes and no place of origin, they offer little definitive information. The desire to have correct information about Chinese Torahs was fueled by the 1972 publication of the seminal book by Australian sinologist Donald Daniel Leslie, *The Survival of the Chinese Jews*, a book that remains the most significant and reliable academic study of the Chinese Jews.

In 1972 an SMU librarian sought information from Michael Pollak, who owned a local print shop and filled most of SMU's printing needs. Michael had attended an Orthodox Jewish day school in Brooklyn, New York, before eventually settling in Dallas, Texas, and the librarian hoped Michael would be able to shed light on their unconventional Torah. Initially, Michael was flummoxed. In December 1972, however, he met Dr. Morton Rosenbaum, a dealer of antiquarian Hebrew manuscripts and books. Dr. Rosenbaum also had no clue about SMU's Torah, but he strongly suggested that Pollak consult Dr. Menahem Schmelzer, the librarian at the Jewish Theological Seminary (JTS) in New York. Pollak photocopied several columns of the Torah at SMU and sent them off to JTS. Within two weeks, he received a reply that the writing style of the Hebrew letters in the Torah was, indeed, that of Chinese Jews. This information was the key to unlocking doors as Pollak continued searching for more answers.

Pollak visited several libraries and universities in the United States and Europe and corresponded with those with an interest in, and knowledge of, the Chinese Jews. He learned that the first synagogue in China was built in Kaifeng, China's capital, in 1163, but later it was damaged or destroyed and then repaired and rebuilt several times. In 1642, for example, during a battle between the emperor in Kaifeng and his opponents, those enemies diverted the Yellow River as a military strategy, and the flooding that resulted caused casualties to more than one hundred thousand people, including members of the Jewish community, and also completely leveled the synagogue.

A stone stele, erected in Kaifeng twenty-one years later in 1663 (see chapter 21), describes how the synagogue's thirteen Torah scrolls floated away. It also tells how two young Chinese Jews retrieved ten of those scrolls and twenty-six synagogue books from the flood waters. The Torahs were waterlogged and badly damaged, but they were dried in the sun and delivered to the rabbi. From the least damaged parts of these Torahs, the rabbi and congregants put together one complete Torah, which they named the "Scroll of Moses." Two other Torahs were restored fairly well, but seven were unusable and were discarded.

Torah scroll, Kaifeng, China, seventeenth century; housed at the Bridwell Library in the Perkins School of Theology at Southern Methodist University, Dallas, Texas

Eventually ten new Torahs, copied from "The Scroll of Moses," were completed by the rabbi and members of the Jewish community. When the rebuilt synagogue in Kaifeng was dedicated in 1653, there was again a total of thirteen Torahs gracing the Ark. It is inspirational – and demonstrates great emotional dedication to Judaism – that after enduring floods and war, members of the Chinese Jewish community served as amateur scribes to help the rabbi rewrite ten massive Torah scrolls and rebuild the synagogue.

Chinese Torahs were written in black ink on sheepskin or goatskin, and only Chinese Torahs were sewn together with silk, rather than with thread made of animal tendons as is the case with conventional Torahs. The ink that was used has not been affected too badly by the passage of time, and the text still is quite legible. A numbering system from one to twelve was used to distinguish the individual Torah scrolls, with the original "Scroll of Moses" being left unnumbered. The Torah number was written in Hebrew in black ink on the lower portion of the reverse side of the last skin of the Torah.

When Chinese Jews read from the Torahs in the Kaifeng synagogue, they placed the scrolls on a table called the "Chair of Moses." Kaifeng was the only place where the Torah reader wore a veil, imitating Moses who, it is said, wore a veil when he read the Torah to the people of Israel in the desert. The Torah states that when Moses returned from forty days on Mount Sinai, which he ascended in order to bring the Ten Commandments down to the people of Israel in the desert, his face was "beaming," and the people were frightened of him. Since one cannot be a successful leader if one's followers are frightened, Moses wore a veil. By the way, it is also possible that the inaccurate accusation that "Jews have horns" came from the misunderstanding by Christian scholars of the meaning of the Hebrew word for "beaming," which they translated incorrectly as "horns."

By the middle of the nineteenth century, though, the Jewish congregation in China was isolated from the rest of the Jewish world; the rabbi's children no longer became rabbis; the Jewish school closed; no one knew Hebrew anymore or observed Jewish holidays; and Jews intermarried and assimilated completely into Chinese society. They were in dire financial straits, living in poverty on the premises of their own synagogue and selling tiles from the building and even topsoil to assuage their hunger.

The London Society for Promoting Christianity among Jews (referred to in this chapter as the London Society), founded in 1809, received a generous contribution to establish a mission to convert the Chinese Jews. In November 1850 two Chinese converts to Christianity left Shanghai in a mule cart and arrived in Kaifeng in December 1850. They observed that many members of the Jewish community were so poor that they were living in the synagogue compound and selling parts of the building. During their six days in Kaifeng, they purchased synagogue books from these poor Jews, until the police accused them of being spies and they fled back to Shanghai, arriving in January 1851.

Their tales about the Jews in Kaifeng and the books they bought from them created quite a stir in Europe and encouraged the Chinese converts to return to Kaifeng for more. In July 1851, their pockets filled with missionary money, these two men returned to Kaifeng, where this time they stayed for about two months. When they arrived in Shanghai after this trip, they had six Torah scrolls, around fifty manuscripts, twelve prayer books, two Passover Haggadahs (the text used at the Seder [meal] celebration during the Passover holiday), and the Kaifeng Jewish community's Memorial Book which contained their "history," all bought for a total of about £140. Between 1851 and 1866 the synagogue building was demolished and was never rebuilt.

It is disheartening that loyal Jews, albeit very poor Chinese Jews, would have permitted the holy scrolls and books to pass into the hands of these Chinese converts to Christianity, but probably it is true. Chinese Jews later complained that foreigners – they did not know whether they were Jewish or not – came, took the artifacts to study and promised to return them but never did, a claim without much credibility.

So what happened to the six Torahs that were taken by the Chinese missionaries? Well, one was given to the library of the Missionary College in Hong Kong and later found a home with the Bishop of Victoria in Hong Kong, but this Torah has disappeared. Some reported seeing it on display at the Hong Kong library; some remembered seeing it in the Hong Kong City Hall; and there were even accounts that it was housed in the Hong Kong synagogue. Most believe that this Torah was destined for the Hebrew University in Israel, but there is no record of it at the university or anywhere else in Israel.

I tried to obtain information in the library at St. Paul's College in Hong Kong about a Torah scroll that some visitors reported seeing in 1862–63 in the City Hall there. I discovered that in 1926, Arthur Sopher wrote that this Torah had then been transferred to the Museum of Hong Kong, where it remained until 1910, when the city authorities gave the Torah to Ohel Leah, the synagogue in Hong Kong, from where it was destined to go to the synagogue of the Hebrew University in Jerusalem.

According to Professor Irene Eber, professor of Chinese at Hebrew University, the Torah, in fact, did reach Hebrew University in Jerusalem. She asserts that the Torah was stored at the Mount Scopus campus in Jerusalem which was overrun by Arabs during the Israel War of Independence in 1947. When Jerusalem was reunited and the Mount Scopus campus became part of Israel again during the Six Day War in 1967, the Torah was no longer there. Sadly, as of now, no one has found the Torah in either Hong Kong or in Jerusalem, and no one

Close-up of handwritten Chinese Torah at Southern Methodist University

knows if it still exists. The mystery of this Torah remains unsolved.

The other five Torahs were sent to London. According to the September 22, 1852, minutes of the London Society, one complete Torah was presented to the British Museum, another was given to the Bodleian Library at Oxford and a third is at Cambridge University. The London Society kept two Torahs, one of which has since disappeared. The Torah in the British Museum is labeled #2; the Torah at Cambridge is labeled #4; and the Torah at Oxford is labeled #5.

Around 1868, a few young Chinese Jews appeared in Peking (now Beijing) with three Torah scrolls, from the seven that remained after the London Society acquired six of the original thirteen. One was purchased by W.A.P. Martin, a missionary; another was acquired by S. Wells Williams, also a missionary; and the third Torah scroll was obtained in 1870 in Beijing by Karl von Scherzer, an Austrian diplomat. The Torah purchased by Martin was then sold first to John Wylie Barrow (a wealthy accountant with a large, impressive rare book collection and a cousin of Charles Dickens), and then to Judge Mayer Sulzberger of Philadelphia, who wrote in 1900, "If I should live long enough to see the Chinese troubles settled, and a new synagogue dedicated at Kaifeng, it would give me great pleasure to contribute the scroll for the edification of the descendants and successors of the original owners."

In 1903–04, Sulzberger's Chinese Torah scroll, labeled #7, and other books and manuscripts in his superb Judaica collection, found their way to the library of the JTS. This Torah is 141 feet long and 24.5 inches wide, with 234 columns, some of which contain scribal errors. The Torah that was acquired by Williams, now at the American Bible Society in New York City, is incomplete and in poor condition; and the one that was bought by the Austrian diplomat, labeled #6, went directly to the Austrian National Library in Vienna, where it remains to this day.

Since the London Society always was evasive about the whereabouts of the two Chinese Torahs they had, no one knew for certain where those Torahs actually were or how many the London Society really owned. Consequently, many people tried to purchase them from the London Society. In March 1918, Sir David Sassoon (see chapter 8) offered to purchase all the Chinese Torahs and manuscripts held by the London Society, but his offer was not accepted. In 1929, the library of Hebrew Union College in Cincinnati, Ohio, also attempted to buy the Torah scrolls from them, but that offer also was rejected. The Torah kept at the London Society (reorganized eventually as the Church Ministry to the Jews) for more than seventy years after its purchase in 1851, seems to have disappeared, and the London Society claims that they do not know what happened to it.

We do know, fortunately, a great deal about the other Chinese Torah that the London Society owned. It is now at SMU and is labeled #12. In 1955, a bookseller in Pennsylvania informed Thomas J. Harrison (a Bible collector in Oklahoma) that a Torah scroll was on the market and that it had been identified in England as a seventeenth century Torah from the Middle East. The bookseller, who had never seen the Torah, thought it was probably written in Syria or Turkey and later, after seeing it, said that it was the finest Torah he had ever seen. Harrison agreed to buy it for about $450. Following Harrison's death in 1963, his biblical collection, including the Torah, went to the Bridwell Library at SMU.

For nine years, the staff at Bridwell, not satisfied with the bookseller's information about the Torah, unsuccessfully tried to establish its origins. In 1972, with Michael Pollak's help, their efforts were rewarded at last, and the scroll was identified with certainty as one of the six Chinese Torahs purchased from the Jews of Kaifeng in 1851. It is 96 feet long and 23 inches high, is made from 68 skins, has 239 columns and weighs 18.5 pounds. It is exquisite, priceless and worth seeing when in Dallas, Texas.

In April 1974, I became involved in the mystery of the whereabouts of some of the other Chinese Torah scrolls from Kaifeng. On Cat Street in Hong Kong, there are both genuine antiques and fake items; it is a thieves' market where items stolen during the day can be purchased at night. A Catholic priest was walking through Cat Street when he saw four Torah scrolls and some Hebrew books for sale on a table. The seller had no idea what these items were or what their value might be, but, of course, when anyone shows interest the price goes up. According to the seller, these abandoned items had been purchased from a warehouse in Shanghai.

The Catholic priest informed Lord Lawrence Kadoorie (see chapter 8), the titular head of the Jewish community in Hong Kong, about what he had seen on Cat Street, and Kadoorie sent Ezekiel Abraham, formerly of Shanghai, to rescue the Torahs at any price. Were these Chinese Torahs from Kaifeng? Michael Pollak, who was still conducting research on the Chinese Torahs at the time, asked me to visit Hong Kong to investigate these Torahs.

I learned that they were in a wooden chest marked "Shanghai," along with a prayer book printed in Germany in 1907 and two albums of family photographs. I examined the Torahs on July 17, 1974, and determined that they were the property of the German Jewish refugee whose name was on the 1907 leather prayer book, were not very old and had no characteristics of, or connection to, any Chinese Torahs.

Other incomplete Chinese Torah sections (not part of the thirteen from the Kaifeng synagogue), as well as other Jewish artifacts from the Jews in China, are housed in the Royal Ontario Museum in Toronto and at Hebrew Union College in Cincinnati, Ohio.

The mystery surrounding some of the thirteen Torah scrolls from the Kaifeng synagogue continues. One Torah scroll was reported to have been used to make trousers for some Chinese ladies. There are rumors that another Chinese Torah scroll from Kaifeng may be hidden in the mosque in Kaifeng. In October 1907, there was an article in *National Geographic* magazine on Chinese Jews, and there is a photograph in front of the mosque in Kaifeng of a Torah case from the synagogue in Kaifeng. According to the article, the location of the actual Torah is a secret but is widely suspected of being hidden in the mosque.

Knowing that SMU's questions about the Torah in their library finally were answered allows us to hope that remaining questions about all of the Chinese Torah scrolls from the synagogue in Kaifeng will have answers someday, too.

Chapter Eight
The Amazing Sephardim of Shanghai

W hen I served as rabbi in Japan, China was off-limits. We could not visit China or buy even a toothpick that was made there. Upon entering the United States from the Far East, we needed a Certified Certificate of Origin (CCOR) showing that no part of any purchase came from Communist China.

Often, however, I visited Hong Kong, a former British colony, where the air is not only filled with the aroma of sandalwood but also with energy. The language spoken there is English; it has a historic Jewish cemetery; and the main street connecting Kowloon, Hong Kong's major shopping center, to the mainland is named Nathan Road. Built by, and named for, Sir Matthew Nathan, the talented Jewish governor of Hong Kong, the road was called "Nathan's folly," but it was really Nathan's stroke of genius to connect Hong Kong to the mainland.

Hong Kong is also where more than one million Chinese refugees sought sanctuary between 1951 through 1964. In 1937, 100,000 refugees fled to Hong Kong. With the fall of Canton (now Guangzhou) to Japan in 1938, 500,000 more refugees escaped to Hong Kong. From 1948 to 1949, after China fell to the Communists, 750,000 refugees found safety in Hong Kong.

From the 1980s to the present, whenever I lead Jewish tours of Japan, China and Hong Kong, there is always a free day for shopping in Hong Kong, a duty-free port. In the past I would use that time to visit with Lord Lawrence Kadoorie and his brother Sir Horace, exceptionally successful Sephardic Jews, at their prestigious office in the St. George's building across the street from the Mandarin Hotel.

Lord Lawrence Kadoorie was born in 1899 in Hong Kong and spent several years as a student in London, where during the 1920s King Faisal 1 of Saudi

Arabia and Emperor Haile Selassie of Ethiopia stayed for months at the Kadoorie family home. Lord Lawrence studied law but never completed his legal education and did not become an attorney. Instead he became a businessman who owned cotton mills, a carpet company and a furniture company, and he was a principal shareholder of the prestigious Hong Kong and Shanghai Bank until he was forced off the board of directors by the Arabs in the 1970s. In 1930, Lord Lawrence joined the board of China Power and Light, and in 1935 at age thirty-six he was appointed chairman of the board, the youngest ever. He served as chairman of China Power and Light from 1939 to 1940 and again from 1946 until the 1980s.

Lord Lawrence Kadoorie, 1899–1993

Lord Lawrence was president of the Jewish community of Hong Kong and was the first resident of Hong Kong to be named to the House of Lords in London. Lord Lawrence and his brother Sir Horace were the majority stockholders of the Peak Tram, the Star Ferry (that ran between the two sides of Hong Kong) and the Peninsula Hotel. Interestingly, these two brothers always shared a checking account, and no questions were ever asked about any checks that were written. Together, they founded the New Territories Benevolent Society, which established small hospitals and clinics in rural areas of Hong Kong.

Sir Horace Kadoorie, who was born in London in 1902, created a school for Jewish refugee children who arrived in Shanghai during the Nazi period. The school became known as the Kadoorie School and included so many services it was a city unto itself. Managed as a student-run enterprise to foster the development of skills for the future, the students were chefs, plumbers, engineers, electricians, shoemakers, tailors and bankers, handling student money. In addition, Sir Horace created the Shanghai Jewish Youth Association (SJYA) and also built the first school where the Chinese studied martial arts. He endowed a chair in physics at Hong Kong University and later founded the Kadoorie Aid Association to ameliorate the needs of the millions of refugees in Hong Kong. Sir Horace also owned a magnificent ivory collection, catalogued in seven volumes.

In 1951, Sir Horace, who always wanted to be a farmer, created the Kadoorie Agriculture Aid Association to explore three areas of feasibility in the development of farms for poor refugee farmers in rural areas of the new territories in Hong Kong: what the role of the Hong Kong government would be and did it have the necessary knowledge; whether every person receiving assistance would join in the work to help others help themselves; and how the Kadoorie family would supply the necessary funding. To understand the magnitude of the amazing contributions the Kadoorie Agriculture Aid Association made in Hong Kong, consider these accomplishments. It helped 312,000 refugees from China to gain sanctuary in Hong Kong; created 1,218 villages with a minimum of fifty families in each village; provided 21,013 tons of cement; built 194 miles of road, 316 dams, 474 wells, 8,626 retaining walls, 23 reservoirs, 1,443 floodgates and 4,376 houses; cultivated 80 orchards with 89,279 fruit trees; managed 13,795 pigsties with 48,299 pigs and 921 chicken coops with 1,034,346 chickens and 89,675 ducks; raised 3,367 head of cattle; produced 112,234 bags of feed; cared for 17 fishponds; built 23 school ball fields and administered 189,834 inoculations.

Their father, Sir Elly Kadoorie, was born in Baghdad in 1865, left Baghdad in 1880 for India and China, married Laura Mocatta in 1897, created the firm Sir Elly Kadoorie and Sons and died in Shanghai in February 1944, during the war. An important philanthropist, he built Jewish schools and was the first to provide educational facilities for girls in many parts of the Middle East. He also established schools with open enrollment that both Jewish and non-Jewish children could attend, and much of the property where Hebrew University stands on Mount Scopus in Jerusalem was acquired through Elly Kadoorie's generosity. He also built hospitals in Iraq, Persia (now Iran), Israel, India, Syria, Turkey, France, Portugal, England and Shanghai. When the owner of China Power and Light died, his family did not have the money to pay the estate taxes, so in 1928 they sold shares of the company's stock, many of which were purchased by Elly Kadoorie. Kadoorie insisted on hiring qualified local workers, a practice unheard of at the time. In 1926 Elly Kadoorie received the honor of the Knight Commander of the British Empire (KBE). Elly's wife, the mother of Lord Lawrence and Sir Horace, was the first woman in Shanghai to drive a car.

The Kadoorie family was known for attention to details, which ensured efficient and correct work; praised for their breadth of vision with an eye to the future; and appreciated for their amazing generosity. Sir Elly's brother

Ellis was no exception. He built schools with open enrollment in China, Hong Kong and Palestine that both Jewish and non-Jewish students could attend, as well as two agricultural colleges in Israel, one for Jews and one for Arabs. He was vice president of the Anglo Jewish Association in London and president of an international Sephardic organization based in Paris. Among the Sephardic Jews, Lord Lawrence and Sir Horace's father and uncle were respected as prominent Zionists.

Lord Lawrence stood tall and always was dressed well in a 100 percent wool pinstripe suit, looking very regal and royal, and to me he was Jewish aristocracy or nobility. He was very cordial to me, perhaps because he appreciated that I was the only rabbi who never asked him for a donation but asked only for his time. And over time he shared with me documents relating to the history of Jews in Shanghai and Hong Kong and personal stories that I am telling now for the first time.

Shanghai, Lord Lawrence said, was a city of contrasts, and he loved to describe what Shanghai had been like before the war. It was a mixture of East and West, the Paris of the Orient, filled with both good and evil, he said, and it was a paradise for adventurers and citizens of the world. His eyes lit up when he waxed nostalgic about his home and his sukkah (the thatched roof outdoor space where Jews eat during the joyous autumn holiday in remembrance of the temporary desert shelter Jews used after their exodus from slavery) on his front lawn that could seat hundreds of friends and family. He said that no matter how much wealth he had and no matter how high his standard of living had reached in Hong Kong, nothing equaled the quality of his life in Shanghai before the war. When I asked him what he remembers besides his sukkah that made life so special then, he smiled and said, "French toast and ice cream."

He spoke lovingly about his parents and of Marble Hall, his famous, huge home whose 80-foot long and 50-foot wide living room boasted a 65-foot high ceiling. Built by an alcoholic architect in the 1920s, Marble Hall had a 225-foot-long veranda surrounding rooms on the second floor and was the first air-conditioned home in Shanghai. When China fell

Shanghai Children's Palace (formerly Marble Hall), built by Sir Elly Kadoorie as the family's residence

to the Communists, Marble Hall became the Children's Palace, where music, art and dance lessons still are provided after school to gifted children.

Lord Lawrence returned from London to Hong Kong in the 1930s, and in 1938 he married Muriel Gubbay. She gave birth in 1940 to their daughter Rita Laura and in 1941 to their son Michael David. After Pearl Harbor, since Lord Lawrence had British citizenship, he was interned at Stanley Camp in Hong Kong with his wife, eighteen-month-old daughter and six-month-old son. There they survived on nine hundred calories a day from a daily diet of one small tin of rice, boiled lettuce and soup. Later they were moved to Chapei Camp in Shanghai and assigned to one room shared with another family of four. After the war, many dignitaries from England stayed at Marble Hall, and British diplomats and military generals used it as their base of operations. Lord Lawrence, a wise entrepreneur, was eager to return to Hong Kong as soon as possible, but transportation was limited.

The first flight to arrive in Shanghai after the war brought Sir Alwyne Ogden to serve as the British consul, and he went straight to Marble Hall. That flight was continuing to Chongqing, and from there Lord Lawrence hoped to get a flight to Hong Kong. From the airport in Chongqing, he headed to a hotel in town, traveling in a military jeep which had a protruding nail that ripped his only pair of pants. Some GIs, seeing him looking distressed on the street, came to his rescue and dressed him in their GI garb. When they told him there were no passengers on the flight to Hong Kong, Lord Lawrence produced a letter of introduction from Sir Ogden and received approval to travel there as "freight," the only person to receive permission to do so. His plane, which was carrying British bank notes, arrived in Hong Kong in November 1945.

Upon his arrival, Lord Lawrence requested a room at the Peninsula Hotel, of which he was a major shareholder, but his request initially was refused before the staff realized who he was. In Hong Kong he met with American Jewish chaplains, explained that the Japanese had frozen Sephardic Jewish funds intended for Jewish refugees in Shanghai and obtained their help in getting those funds released to the refugees.

Lord Lawrence was successful in aiding the refugees, but he found his own company, China Power and Light, a shambles. Both J.P. Braga, the oldest and smartest employee, and I.N. Murray, the deputy manager, had died during the war. G.I. Angus, the assistant supervisor, had been taken prisoner and died as a POW in Japan, and H.P. Samuel, an efficient statistician, was killed in the battle of Hong Kong. Lord Lawrence essentially had to rebuild China Power and Light from the ground up.

No matter what business problems Lord Lawrence had, he always found time to help Jews in need. After the war ended in 1945, he assisted twenty-two Jewish refugees who had escaped the Holocaust by going to Shanghai to obtain transit visas to Hong Kong so they could depart by ship to Australia. The Joint Distribution Committee (JDC) guaranteed payment for the ship tickets, but the Kadoories always were ready to help out by lobbying to obtain transit visas to Hong Kong, providing pocket money and securing accommodations, as well as helping with other matters as they arose. In July 1946, for example, about 283 Jewish refugees in Shanghai were scheduled to travel to Australia on the *SS Duntroon*, an Australian ship. The ship then was rescheduled to depart for Australia from Hong Kong on August 5. When the refugees arrived in Hong Kong on July 30, the Kadoories assumed responsibility for the 141 men, 125 women, 15 children and 2 babies, just as they had promised the government they would do.

The Kadoories' five-star luxurious Peninsula Hotel was full, so they put the public area to use: the roof garden would be for the men, and the Rose Room would be for the women. Women with children would be housed on the mezzanine floor in the hotel. The Kadoories provided cots, mattresses on the floor, meals, bathing facilities and safe storage for their luggage. Lord Lawrence also dealt with health issues, listened to their heartbreaking stories and wrote letters to their families as needed.

Out of the blue, a telegram arrived from Australia announcing that the *SS Duntroon* was being taken out of service because it was needed by the military. Weeks turned into months, but the Kadoories, their staff and the local Jewish community never stopped providing for the refugees. The refugees were treated to picnics and played soccer, and Lord Lawrence even brought many refugees to his home. When the Jewish New Year approached in September, the Kadoories created a small synagogue in the hotel and served holiday meals to all the refugees. Lord Lawrence's wife Muriel served as president of the Jewish Sisterhood they created, coordinated activities for the stranded refugees and organized committees for the elderly, children and teenagers. The Kadoories even established a small school emphasizing the teaching of English. Finally, in October the elderly were able to leave for Australia, followed by the women and children. The last of the refugees left in December.

During the entire time when the Jewish refugees were in limbo in Hong Kong, the Kadoories never let them down.

The Kadoorie corporate office was on the twenty-fourth floor of the St. George's building in Hong Kong. Lord Lawrence told me that in the 1960s and 1970s, representatives of the People's Republic of China would come to Hong Kong each year to meet with him in his office, and he was always courteous. Over a cup of tea, they invited Lord Lawrence to visit China, and each time Lord Lawrence explained that he did not believe in communism; that Communists had confiscated his home in Shanghai; that they had frozen his assets; that they had taken the family's ivory, jade and porcelain collection without compensation; and that he had no desire to visit a communist country. Year after year, they paid Lord Lawrence a visit and invited him to China over a cup of tea, and every year Lord Lawrence declined the invitation.

Lord Lawrence recalled the year that the Chinese officials realized their method was failing and devised a new strategy. When they arrived for their annual visit, they decided to play on the respect that both Chinese and Jews had for parents and ancestors. Over their tea, they asked, "Sir, don't you want to visit your parents?" Lord Lawrence said that of course he wanted to visit his parents (their graves) who had died in Shanghai! The Chinese visitors told him, true or not, that the maid was still in their home and that she visited the cemetery weekly and washed the gravestones out of respect for his parents whom she remembered so well. Finally, Lord Lawrence said that he would go to China, but only if he cruised down the Yangtze River into Shanghai.

In May 1978, Lord Lawrence traveled to Shanghai, visiting his former home and the cemetery, and he was treated royally. There is no privately owned property in China; the government owns all of it and leases it to the people. Lord Lawrence explained that the government made an exception for him, however, and demarcated his parents' graves as the private land of the Kadoorie family, perhaps the only such private property in China. While visiting Shanghai Lord Lawrence learned the reason the Chinese had been begging him to return to China: energy. They needed help getting more power and electricity. There was a need to prepare for the future by introducing nuclear power to southern China, including Hong Kong.

The Kadoories already were studying nuclear power, and between 1973 and 1975 Lord Lawrence went regularly to England and France to observe their nuclear reactors. In 1977, he produced a nuclear power plant study, and when the Chinese came to Hong Kong for their next visit and cups of tea, he presented them with one hundred copies. They had never seen such a comprehensive study, asked for two hundred more copies, and that study set the standard in China for the large projects they had in development. The nuclear power plant was built in 1979 in the city of Shenzhen, thirty miles from Hong Kong, to benefit China and Hong Kong.

I personally experienced the Jewish sensitivity of Lord Lawrence. During one of my visits to Hong Kong, a Jewish man died unexpectedly, and I was contacted about the immediate burial in the Jewish cemetery (Jews bury their dead within twenty-four hours if possible). Since the deceased man had no family or friends in Hong Kong, I had difficulty organizing a minyan (quorum for prayer), so I called Lord Lawrence. As one might expect, he was in a meeting, but the secretary put me through to him and after I explained the situation, he left his meeting, came directly to the cemetery and assisted in the ritual washing, dressing and burying of this man, a stranger to him. To Lord Lawrence this was not an imposition. When I thanked him for coming and helping, to my surprise he thanked me for calling him.

On another occasion, in Hong Kong I had purchased a rosewood coffee table to be shipped to me in Tokyo. When it arrived, it became clear it was defective. When the wood expanded and contracted with changes in the weather, it would expose a hole in a knot in the wood. All of my letters, with photographs of the defective table included, went unanswered. On my next visit to Hong Kong, I went to the furniture store, told them the story and asked for a replacement or a refund. They told me I would have to wait for at least an hour to meet with the manager/owner. I informed them I could not wait because I had a meeting with Lord Lawrence Kadoorie. That was the magic name, and I received a replacement table without further discussion.

Another time, a close Chinese friend told me she was ill with cancer but there was a very long wait to see the doctor and to receive the needed surgery and treatment. The long wait understandably frightened and devastated her, so I called Lord Lawrence seeking his guidance and assistance. He made the necessary phone call that resulted in immediate and complete medical care for my friend, and he paid for all of it. She is alive and well to this day.

As philanthropically minded as Lord Lawrence was, he admired David Sassoon (1792–1864), the man who set the standard for philanthropy in Bombay (now Mumbai) and put the Baghdadis on the map. The Kadoorie family and the Sassoon families are related, and both families were bankers in Baghdad. Lord Lawrence used to say that his family drew inspiration from the Sassoon legacy and that the Rothschilds were the Sassoons of the West, not the other way around. To the Kadoories, the Sassoons were the giants who set the standard for community leadership, scholarship and philanthropy.

Sassoon tradition has it that their family is descended directly from King David. Indeed, in Baghdad the head of the Sassoon clan was titled *nasi* (prince) or *sheikh* (chief) in Arabic. The family had come from Toledo in Spain and left at the time of the explusion from Spain, with Baghdad as their final destination. Three centuries later, David Sassoon fled from Baghdad and settled permanently in India in 1832. He arrived penniless and worked as a peddler, but eventually he founded David Sassoon and Company, which traded and exported silk, spices, metals and opium,* a valuable commodity at that time. Treated as we now treat cigarettes and alcohol, opium was frowned upon everywhere but not prohibited in England until the twentieth century. England sold opium to China and made a fortune, but the Chinese always talked about the two evils from foreigners: missionaries and opium. The missionaries, however, spoke out against opium, while, sadly, there does not seem to be any evidence that the local rabbis did. David married twice and had thirteen children, including eight sons, all of whom he dispatched to open offices in Shanghai, Hong Kong, Yokohama, Saigon, Nagasaki, Rangoon and other strategic places.

David, who was an Orthodox Jew, never dressed in western clothes, wearing instead a turban and flowing robes that when combined with his long, white beard made him look very biblical. His office was closed on Saturday (the Jewish Sabbath) and on Jewish holidays. In addition, he took time for midday and evening prayers, built a *mikveh* (a ritual bath) in every location where he had offices and provided a Hebrew teacher and kosher food for his Jewish employees. David became the illustrious leader of the Jewish community of Bombay and served as the judge for all disputes in the Jewish community. Being a judge was the most respected and honored position, and his decisions were final.

---

* In the eighth century, the Arabs introduced opium to China as a medical treatment. At the end of the eighteenth century, the British East India Company had a monopoly and was the only company allowed to sell opium, selling most of it to China. After the opium wars in the early nineteenth century, the Chinese were forced to accept opium from India via the British, and by the 1830s, several countries competed to provide opium to China. Opium was the single most valuable commodity in the nineteenth century, but by the end of that century, Jewish opium traders were investing their profits in real estate and stocks and were no longer dealing in the opium trade.

David built the Sassoon Mechanics Institute in Bombay, the illuminated clock tower located in Victoria Gardens at the Bombay Zoo, and the only statue of Prince Albert, which is now in the Victoria and Albert Museum in India and which includes a Hebrew inscription. In addition to responding charitably to the needy of his community, David built the Jewish school in Bombay, the first public library in India and the first reformatory in the Far East for youthful offenders, as well as synagogues and hospitals. In the Sassoon home and the Sassoon Jewish school in India, "God Save the Queen" was sung in English (although David never learned English), Hebrew and Arabic. David Sassoon's estate, valued at £4 million, was amassed in thirty-two years.

Albert Sassoon (1818–1896), David's oldest son, financed the Gateway to India in Bombay, built the docks of Bombay (which are still called the Sassoon docks) to make Bombay a major port and employed fifteen thousand workers in the Sassoon cotton mills in India. In addition, Albert financed the construction of a college of science as well as the Knesseth Eliyahu (sometimes written Eliyahoo) Synagogue in Bombay. A shrewd businessman, he knew that during the American Civil War there would be a blockade of the southern ports which exported cotton, thereby creating a shortage in the world market that India could easily fill, and he made a fortune doing so. He also knew that when the war ended there would be an oversupply of cotton and prices would drop, so he never expanded wildly or was overstocked with cotton, mistakes made by others. Albert was awarded British knighthood, and one thousand people attended the celebration in his home.

Edward Albert Sassoon (1856–1912) was Albert's youngest son and the first Sassoon to choose politics as a profession, becoming in 1899 the first Sassoon elected to the House of Commons, part of the British Parliament, a seat he held for the remainder of his life. He married Aline Caroline de Rothschild, the daughter of Baron Gustave de Rothschild, and the chief rabbi of France officiated at their marriage.

Rachel Sassoon (1857–1927) was the daughter of Sassoon David Sassoon, who was one of David Sassoon's sons with his second wife. Sassoon David Sassoon established the Sassoon Bank; today it is the Bank of India and remains on the same site. In its time, it was the most respected bank in India, and Sassoon checks, written and signed in either Hebrew or Arabic, were the most trusted checks. Rachel edited both the *Sunday Observer* and the *Sunday Times*, both London newspapers, and married Frederick Beer, who was not Jewish, creating a huge scandal.

Sir Victor Sassoon, 1881–1961

Flora Sassoon (1859–1936) managed the Sassoon Company with great skill and was a founder of the London Jewish Hospital. She was both beautiful and brilliant and spoke English, French, German, Arabic, Hindi and Hebrew. At age eighteen, Flora married Solomon Sassoon, eighteen years older than she was, Albert's half-brother and her great uncle. A devout Jew, Flora was a Torah scholar who lectured on the Talmud at Jews College in London. It was expected that everyone eating at Flora's table would wear a yarmulke (skull cap). Flora's brother, Philip Albert Gustave David Sassoon, served as a member of the British Parliament for twenty-seven years, was the youngest member of the House of Commons, and later held many government positions in England.

Sir Victor Sassoon (1881–1961), a grandson of Elias David Sassoon (1820–1880), David Sassoon's second son and the most prominent and successful great-grandson of David Sassoon, was born in Naples, Italy. Educated at Cambridge in England, Sir Victor was a pioneer of civil aviation in India and in World War I was a captain in the Air Force. He had a suite at the Taj Mahal Hotel in Bombay, owned a small yacht and drove a yellow car with the license plate "EVE 1." Eve, as he was nicknamed, is a combination of his two given names, Ellice and Victor. A discreet, handsome, smart, witty, dashing and rich playboy who knew how to keep his public and private lives separate, Sir Victor loved the theater, fast horses (he owned horses in Shanghai and England and won the British Derby three times), fast cars, fast airplanes and fast women. He fell in love with a non-Jewish girl, but his family rejected her and he never got over it. Although he had a string of women, he did not marry until he was seventy-seven. While his mother was alive, Sir Victor never violated the Jewish Sabbath or Jewish holidays publicly, but after she died, he attended a theater performance on Yom Kippur, after his secretary mistakenly ordered the tickets for that night. He was quoted as saying, "There is only one race greater than the Jewish race, and that's a horse race."

Despite serious injury from a plane crash that resulted in his suffering from broken and crushed bones, a disparity in the length of his legs, and both emotional and physical pain, Sir Victor threw fabulous costume parties in Shanghai. These parties had different themes on different nights and were great fun, but they were not rowdy and did not include excessive drinking. Guests might be asked to come dressed one time as a circus performer or another time as something related to a toy, and prizes were given for the best costumes. In one case, during a party on Sir Victor's yacht, for which guests were instructed to arrive dressed as if ready to abandon ship, the winning couple, who were taking a shower together when an alarm bell rang, came as survivors of a shipwreck who had just been taken off a lifeboat, dressed with only a towel around them!

Sir Victor had the best business head in the Sassoon family and was the senior member of the fourth generation of Sassoons, impressing everyone with his intelligent questions, sharp mind and ability to grasp a balance sheet. When Lord Reading, a British Jew whose name was Rufus Isaacs, was appointed governor of India, Sir Victor gave him £37,500 to be distributed among needy Indians. When a Jew in Shanghai who did not work for Sir Victor asked him for financial help, Sir Victor threw his checkbook at him and told him to write a check for what he needed but never to come back. The man wrote a check for five figures, but when he returned for more money, he was denied entry. Another story concerns an employee who was stealing and was fired but, nevertheless, asked for a letter of recommendation. Sir Victor gave him a letter that stated, "There is no question of his business ability; he should not however be empowered to sign checks." Surprisingly, the man was hired immediately by another firm.

In Bombay, Sir Victor was a pioneer in providing health and welfare benefits for Sassoon employees, setting an example for others. He served on the Indian legislative council for five years, and in 1930 he was appointed chairman of the newly created E.D. Sassoon Banking Company. In the early 1930s, Sir Victor moved his corporate headquarters to the penthouse of the hotel he had built in Shanghai, the Cathay Hotel, which arguably remains the best-known building in the city today. The building, now known as the Peace Hotel, was prime real estate even then, and Sir Victor, the richest person in that city, was known as "Mr. Shanghai," and even as "Mr. China."

When the refugees arrived in Shanghai during the Nazi period, they had nothing and needed everything (see chapters 9 and 10), so the Kadoories met with Sir Victor Sassoon to discuss the pressing issue. They reminded him of his heritage as a benevolent Sassoon and essentially advised him to put aside his "party boy" activities and instead become the leader and philanthropist for which the Sassoon family was known. They told Sir Victor what was needed, and he rose to the occasion by providing transportation from the port, temporary housing, milk, food, furniture, cotton, silk, money, vocational training and hundreds of jobs for the talented refugees.

Luckily, Sir Victor was in Bombay on December 7, 1941, the day the Japanese bombed Pearl Harbor. When the Japanese wanted to show that they now were the dominant regional power and controlled Shanghai, they searched for an image that would convey that point clearly. An iconic image would be more effective than boring speeches. So the Japanese docked the warship *Izumo* across from the Cathay Hotel; Japanese Navy Captain Inuzuka Koreshige then strode across the street into the hotel, took the elevator up to Sir Victor's penthouse office suite, sat in Sir Victor's chair at his desk, and had his picture taken. The next day the picture appeared in the newspapers, unequivocally illustrating that a Japanese man was now "Mr. Shanghai," not Sir Victor; such was the power of Sassoon's chair.

Sir Victor is often quoted as having said, "I gave up India, and China gave me up." Unlike the Kadoorie family, whose investments were diversified not only within mainland China but also in Hong Kong, which was protected by the British, Sir Victor's assets were primarily in China, and he lost much of them when China fell to the Communists.

During the years following the end of World War II in 1945, Sir Victor searched for a place to relocate his office and a place to live, because colonial India, which was under British control, became the Republic of India, and the Republic of China became the People's Republic of China or Communist China. In 1954 Sir Victor relocated to the Bahamas. In 1959, already seventy-seven years old and quite ill, he met Evelyn Barnes, a thirty-year-old nurse, from Dallas, Texas, and they married in the Bahamas that year. Evelyn took care of him, but sadly, two years after they married, when Evelyn was about to give Sir Victor one of his shots, he said, "I'm not going to need that one, Barnsie." Sir Victor died in 1961.

The four generations of the Sassoon family accomplished so much, including the building of five synagogues: Ohel Leah in Hong Kong, Ohel Rachel in Shanghai, Magen David in Bombay, Ohel David in Pune (India), and Knesseth Eliyahu in Bombay. The Sassoon family – merchants, industrialists, statesmen, scholars and philanthropists – counted among their friends over the years the Shah of Iran, King Edward VII, Lawrence of Arabia, the Duke of Windsor,

Charlie Chaplin and Dr. H.H. Kung (finance minister of China). Collectors of antique Hebrew manuscripts, rare Jewish books and Judaica carefully monitor auctions of materials from the Sassoon collection. The two outstanding survivors of the Sassoon dynasty were, ironically, Solomon Sassoon (an Orthodox rabbi and Flora Sassoon's grandson) and Siegfried Sassoon (now deceased), a prominent British Catholic poet.

A successful beneficiary of the Sassoon family was Silas Hardoon (1851–1931). His birth date may have been around 1846, because when he died in 1931, both *Israel's Messenger* and the *North China Daily News*, newspapers in Shanghai, reported his age as eighty-four. Whether it was in 1846 or in 1851, Hardoon was born in Baghdad, and he came as a young child with his parents to Bombay, where his father worked for the Sassoons. Hardoon's father died when Silas was very young and, penniless, he moved to Hong Kong, where he worked for the Sassoon Company but eventually was dismissed. In 1874 Hardoon moved to Shanghai, where he would live for the rest of his life, and S.J. Solomon took pity on him and convinced the E.D. Sassoon Banking Company in Shanghai to hire him. Hardoon began working there as a minor clerk earning a meager salary and sometimes as a watchman or a rent collector, all of which were embarrassing jobs for a Sephardic Jew. Despite the low weekly salary of twelve shillings that Hardoon was paid, he managed to save one shilling every week.

While working for Sassoon, Hardoon created his own enterprise involving both real estate and opium. The press referred to Hardoon as a dealer in *tu*, which, depending on the pronunciation, means either opium or land. Realizing which parts of Shanghai were likely to develop, and using money from his opium trading, he slowly acquired vacant land that later became prime real estate. From 1892 to 1901, he served on the municipal council of the French Concession (an area of Shanghai), and from 1900 to 1903, he served on the municipal council of the International Settlement, which was British and American. He was the only foreigner to serve on both councils in the same year. In 1911, he severed his ties to Sassoon and soon became the largest individual land owner in Shanghai, running his business out of a spartanly furnished office with no shades, no carpets covering the unpainted floor, no heat – requiring that he work with his coat on in the winter – and a few, mostly broken, pieces of furniture.

By 1916 Hardoon was the major owner of the property on Nanking Road (now Nanjing Road), the "Fifth Avenue" shopping street then and even now, and the first two department stores, Wing On and Sincere, which introduced modern shopping to Shanghai, were built on his property. He owned about eighteen acres of the most valuable real estate in Shanghai, land which became primarily residential dwellings for the Chinese. Despite being the largest individual landowner and having become a multimillionaire, Hardoon personally would collect the rent from his tenants, even sitting in their apartments waiting for them to come home so he could collect the money. Lord Lawrence Kadoorie, while laughing about Hardoon's dilapidated office and the strange behavior of his fellow Baghdadi Jew, eventually became disappointed in him and angry at him, too.

Hardoon married a Eurasian woman named Luo (Liza) Jialing (1864–1941), the daughter of a French-Jewish policeman and a Chinese seamstress. Rumored to have been a prostitute before she married Hardoon, Liza lived on the Hardoon estate, forty acres known as Aili Gardens, which was located on Hardoon Road in Shanghai. It was believed that the Hardoons had a staff of nine hundred in their house, including a group of Buddhist monks, one of whom had designed the house, and several eunuchs from the Forbidden City (the Imperial Palace in Beijing where commoners were not allowed). Liza, a faithful Buddhist who used Chinese medicine and believed in ancestor worship, established close contact with important personalities in the Chinese cultural, political and religious worlds. The Hardoons had no biological children but adopted about twenty children, raising both Western orphans (mostly Russian Jewish children whom they raised as Jews) and Chinese orphans (whom they raised as Buddhists).

Since Hardoon had married a Eurasian woman, he was considered an outsider to the foreign community, so he also cultivated relationships with Chinese politicians, former generals and warlords. Even Chinese presidents paid their respects by visiting Hardoon's estate. The Hardoons also owned magnificent homes in Beijing and Hangzhou (on a lake), but their Shanghai home was the center of many activities.

Hardoon gave huge sums of money to Chinese charities but little money to Jewish causes, and that was one of the reasons for Lord Lawrence Kadoorie's anger at Hardoon. On their premises the Hardoons established the Buddhist University of China, where traditional Confucian studies constituted the basis of the curriculum. In 1902, they supported the improvement of textbooks for Chinese schools. In 1913, Hardoon spent $750,000 to reprint 8,416 volumes of the complete set of Buddhist scriptures to be distributed to university libraries throughout the world, and he also financed the publishing of the Koran in

Chinese. He supported many schools in China, was the primary support for victims of the floods in northern China, and on many Chinese New Years he gave a dollar to every beggar he saw. Known as the Western Buddha, a man of noble character and a compatriot, Hardoon received twelve decorations, and in 1924 he received the Zhao Wu Order, the highest Chinese award ever bestowed upon a foreigner. These honors were confirmation of his acceptance into Chinese society, an acknowledgment that was very important to him.

There were eight hundred Sephardic Jews in Shanghai at that time, and most of them aspired to become British gentlemen, but Hardoon strove to become a Confucian gentleman. Acceptance by the Jewish community mattered less to Hardoon, although in 1925 there was a reception for a Zionist envoy, and the meeting was held in Hardoon's home. Around the same time, Hardoon also had a dream that he reported to D.E.J. Abraham, a religious member of the Sephardic community. In his dream, his father, just as Lord Lawrence Kadoorie did later, questioned his choice of doing so much for the benefit of the Chinese people but so little for his own people.

Abraham advised him to build a synagogue and name it for his father. In 1927 Hardoon had the Beth Aharon Synagogue built on Museum Road near the Bund (the waterfront of Shanghai). Years later, in 1941, when the yeshiva students arrived in Shanghai from the city of Mir in Poland via Lithuania and Kobe, Japan, this synagogue became their location for studying and praying during the entire war. The Mir Yeshiva was the only yeshiva to survive the Holocaust intact. I remember the mezuzah (the ritual prayer scroll Jews affix to entranceways as a sign of faith) and the Star of David on the front of the building, and I also saw the synagogue razed in 1985. The *Shanghai Newspaper* eventually occupied the site, now the location of the Peninsula Hotel.

Beth Aharon Synagogue, Shanghai, China, built in 1927 by Silas A. Hardoon in memory of his father

When Hardoon died on June 19, 1931, at age eighty-four, his funeral created much emotional agitation among the two thousand mourners. Many decades later, Lord Lawrence still was so angry at Hardoon that I thought he would have a stroke when he described the incredible event to me. Hardoon was not buried in the traditional manner in a Jewish cemetery. The funeral procession was more Chinese in character than Jewish, with hundreds of burning incense sticks placed around the casket, and he was buried in his garden with both Jewish and Chinese officials leading the service. An elderly Jewish cantor praised his philanthropy, while his adopted Buddhist children got down on their knees to honor their dead father, and the adopted Jewish children recited kaddish (the mourner's prayer) at their father's grave. No rabbis officiated, and some thought that the two cantors who were there along with the president of the Jewish Burial Society should have walked out; the president of the Jewish Burial Society eventually did tender his resignation. The event divided the community, and the newspapers covered it all. Thirty days after the funeral, five thousand people attended a Chinese Buddhist memorial service to lead Hardoon's soul to paradise, with a wax statue of Hardoon overlooking the ceremony.

It is difficult to convey the indignation of the Baghdadi Jewish community when they discovered that Hardoon had left his entire fortune of $150 million to his wife. There were indications that the will Hardoon signed on June 10, 1931, just a week before he died, was signed under undue influence from his wife while he was critically ill, and from June 1932 to February 1933 people filed legal claims for some of that money. Not only were there questions about the validity of the will, there also was the question of who had jurisdiction over his estate. Should it be adjudicated under Chinese law, Jewish law, British law or Iraqi law? Was his wife Jewish as claimed, even though no one ever saw her conversion documents or ketubah (Jewish marriage document)? Every country wanted to claim Hardoon as a citizen because of the hefty estate taxes, and people like S.J. Solomon, who had helped Hardoon along the way, were upset that they also were not remembered in his will.

On February 19, 1933, Judge Penrhyn Grant Jones announced his decision, granting almost all of Hardoon's money to Liza, who, according to the judge, was Hardoon's wife "by reputation." England did receive £500,000. Shanghai was awarded $900,000 in estate taxes, and Hardoon's wife had to borrow money to pay those taxes because her inherited assets were mostly real estate, not money. The judge's decision kept the community divided, but ultimately no one benefitted from these vast holdings because after 1948 real estate was confiscated by Communist China.

Hardoon's wife died in 1941, after having been blind for four years, leaving an estate valued at $40 million. In 1943 there was a fire which destroyed almost all of Aili Gardens. In addition, after the establishment of the People's Republic of China, the Communist government demanded that the family remove Hardoon's remains from the mausoleum in Aili Gardens and take them outside the city. The mansion and remaining gardens were razed, and in 1958 the Soviets, who in 1949 had become China's closest ally, erected the Sino Soviet Friendship Building, now called the Shanghai Exhibition Center, on the site of the Hardoon estate.

Hardoon was one of the best known of the Sephardic Jews and foreigners (along with Sir Victor Sassoon) in China, becoming the subject of much fiction and even a soap opera. He was the only prominent Baghdadi who acculturated into the Chinese environment, and he spoke the Shanghai dialect of Chinese, the spoken language in that city (rather than Mandarin Chinese). He understood the regional real estate market and had foresight and good instincts about how much its value would appreciate. He was loved and hated, cursed and praised.

While no one denies that Hardoon's story is truly a rags to riches tale, the Jewish community believed, probably correctly, that Hardoon's wife had tampered with his will while he was ill. They also were disappointed, like Lord Lawrence, that Hardoon had not assumed a leadership role, had not sought to strengthen the structure of the Jewish community and had not served as a bridge between the Jewish and Chinese communities, and that neither he nor his wife showed much interest in helping Jews.

Chapter Nine

Laura Margolis: The Right Person for a Difficult Job in China

I met with Laura Margolis (1903–1997) in Teaneck, New Jersey, in the latter part of her life and found her to be cordial, friendly, humorous, honest, forthright and outspoken: what was on her mind was on her tongue. We talked about what I knew and what she knew of the experiences of the twenty thousand Jewish refugees in Shanghai, and I came away from that meeting feeling inspired, knowing that I had spoken face-to-face with the woman who had saved the lives of so many of those refugees in China during the Holocaust.

One day, years earlier during my tenure in Japan, Michael Kogan, one of my congregants, came to my office and opened a huge *furoshiki* (kerchief) – a cloth that could be folded and tied for use as a bag to carry goods – that was filled with about eight thousand pages of top-secret Japanese Foreign Ministry documents detailing the fate of Jews in the Far East in the 1930s and 1940s. He said that since I had a fervent interest in Jewish history in the Far East and was asking so many questions on this subject, I should read these secret government documents carefully.

Among the names that frequently were mentioned in these documents was that of Japanese Navy Captain Inuzuka Koreshige. He was high on my list as I looked for the Japanese who had been enemies or friends of the Jews, as well as those who had been "experts" at making policy regarding the Jews. Inuzuka was one of those "experts" on the Jews in Shanghai beginning in 1939 when the Japanese were the dominant power in that city. He died shortly before I arrived in Japan, but in Tokyo I did meet and visit often with Inuzuka Kyoko, who had been his mistress in Shanghai and later became his wife in Tokyo, and she told me many stories about Laura Margolis. And when I met with

Laura in Teaneck, New Jersey, Kyoko was our mutual friend about whom we shared fond remembrances.

Kyoko lived a life of intrigue and had a superb library of documents dealing with the Jews of Shanghai. I have many of her letters to me as well as those she exchanged with Laura. Kyoko described Laura as an exceptional and talented woman who was the right person for a very difficult job. At the time, Japanese women had no rights and were considered incompetent. Laura stunned the Japanese men in Captain Inuzuka's office because she was a talented and competent woman in charge of twenty thousand refugees, and her capa-

Laura Margolis, circa 1935; courtesy of American Jewish Joint Distribution Committee

bilities were beyond anything they could imagine for a woman. When she entered the office, they would point to her and whisper, "*Yudaya-jin*" (the Jew). How did Laura – a tall, stately, efficient-looking thirty-nine-year-old female – come to be assigned to tackle one of the largest and most complicated migrations of refugees the world has ever seen?

Laura was born in Constantinople (now Instanbul), Turkey, where her Austrian-Hungarian maternal grandfather, Dr. Solomon Schwartz, was the private physician to the Sultan Abdul Hamid of Turkey as well as president of the Ashkenazic (Jews from Europe, with the exception of the Sephardic Jews in Spain) Jewish community of Turkey. Laura's mother, Cecilia was a musician, and her father, Herman Margolis, who had left behind his Zionist family in Russia to travel to Palestine, was sent from Palestine to Constantinople to direct a school that would prepare Russian Jews to live as pioneering farmers in Palestine. He and Cecilia were married on May 25, 1902, in Constantinople, where they lived in primitive conditions. On October 18, 1903, for example, Herman took Cecilia by ox cart to her father for help with Laura's birth. When Laura was five, they moved to the United States, settling in Dayton, Ohio.

When Laura arrived in America, she was able to speak French, German, Greek, Turkish and Spanish, but not English. She learned quickly, though, graduating from Ohio State in 1926 with a BS degree. In 1927, Laura earned a degree in social work from the School of Applied Social Sciences at Western

Reserve University. In 1929, at the start of the Depression, Laura accepted a position with the Jewish Welfare Society in Cleveland, training volunteers to work at the Jewish Big Sisters Association for Jewish girls. It was a job Laura later described as a challenge: "It seems to me that I was always reacting to challenges!" she said during her 1990 interview with the United States Holocaust Memorial Museum (USHMM).

After leaving Cleveland for about a year, Laura returned to train volunteers for the National Council of Jewish Women. It was in Cleveland that Laura established her pattern of successfully completing an always challenging, often dangerous job and then moving on. As Eleanor Roosevelt wrote in one of her syndicated "My Day" columns, "I shall never cease to marvel at the courage of people like Miss Margolis who, after having escaped from one dangerous situation, seems anxious to return to another."

Her next job was in Buffalo, New York, where the Jewish leadership had a terrible reputation as a dictatorship of the wealthy with no structure or professional standards. Although everyone told Laura not to go, in 1934 she went there anyway, becoming director of the Jewish Welfare Society. Decades later, I began serving as the auxiliary rabbi for the High Holy Days of Rosh Hashana (the Jewish New Year) and Yom Kippur (the Day of Atonement) in Buffalo. It was there that I met Professor Selig Adler, author of *From Ararat to Suburbia: The History of the Jewish Community of Buffalo.*

Professor Adler shared with me many stories about Laura's time in Buffalo. He explained that a few wealthy German Jews who knew nothing about social work had the power to dictate the programs because they could write the checks. There was great tension and conflict between Laura and this group, because Laura wanted to establish health and social services, not just distribute money directly to poor people as charity. When Laura trained Betty Warner, the daughter of a major donor, however, she gained a spokeswoman who was able to promote Laura's objectives by explaining to the major contributors the purpose of social work as it related to their community. Despite overwhelming odds, Laura met her goal successfully and, ready for the next challenge, she left Buffalo in 1938.

At that time, there were about five thousand Jewish refugees residing in Cuba, and they already had successfully dealt with the bribery and corruption surrounding their efforts to enter or exit Cuba. But ships continued to dock weekly, each one carrying at least five hundred Jewish refugees who had escaped from the Nazis and hoped to reach the United States. In May 1939, the

German ship *St. Louis* (part of the Hamburg America Line) arrived in Havana, but only 29 of the 937 passengers were allowed to disembark. Is it any wonder that voyage was sometimes referred to as the "Voyage of the Damned"?

The Joint Distribution Committee (JDC) was now in the picture and, since Laura could speak Spanish, she went to work for the JDC in Cuba. She provided food, supplies and support for those Jews who had to remain on the ship while she searched for alternative ports for these refugees. The United States sadly and shamefully refused to accept them. Those who remained on board, rather than pursue an option to head for Shanghai, had no choice but to return to Europe since that is where the ship's captain was scheduled to go. The refugees were permitted entry into Western European countries, but many of them ultimately lost their lives in concentration camps when those countries were overrun by the Nazis.

Laura was able to assist the five thousand Jewish refugees already in Cuba by helping them to process their American visa applications. The United States government appreciated Laura's assistance and language skills so much that Avery Warren, in the visa office of the State Department in Washington, DC, asked the JDC to send her to the American consulate in Shanghai. No one on staff at the time spoke German, and a bottleneck had resulted as the crowd of German-speaking Jewish refugees applying for American visas grew larger. Warren thought that since Laura could speak German, she would be able to speed up the process.

Moses Leavitt, JDC head at the time, called Laura and asked her to go to Shanghai, to which she replied, tongue in cheek, "Where is that?" Laura started to learn Chinese during her trip, which lasted a full twelve days. It first took her five days (because of numerous stops on the way) to fly from San Francisco to Hong Kong; she then had to spend a week in Hong Kong waiting for the next Allied ship sailing to Shanghai. With so much time on her hands, she walked the streets of this fascinating British colony, where she passed a sign that looked familiar.

While working in Buffalo, NY, Laura had helped raise funds for the Chinese Defense League for the benefit of poor and disabled Chinese children, and it was a sign for this charity she now saw on the storefront. The organization's clerk asked her for her name and the name of the hotel where she was staying, which she gave gladly, explaining that she was only visiting Hong Kong en route to Shanghai. When Laura returned to the hotel, she was surprised to find a message from Mme Sun Yat-sen, also known as Soong Ching-ling (see chapter 1), inviting her to have dinner that night at her home, and the note informed Laura that General Two-Gun Cohen (yes, the same Two-Gun Cohen from chapter 1) would be her escort.

At the dinner, attended by many prominent people, Mme Sun Yat-sen pulled Laura aside and asked her to return to dinner the next night so they could talk alone. Two-Gun Cohen was assigned to guide and protect Laura during her week in Hong Kong, and he escorted her to the dinner the next night as well. The year was 1941, and Mme Sun Yat-sen wanted to know what Laura would be doing, what the issues were in Shanghai, and whether Laura needed any assistance. She gave Laura the names and addresses of both Chinese and foreigners in Shanghai who could be trusted and who would be helpful, and those people became resources for Laura. In fact, she later wrote in a letter to me that she found those names to be of "inestimable value" in Shanghai.

While Laura had been very helpful to Jewish refugees in Cuba, in Shanghai she found a much bigger and messier problem. Shanghai was a paradoxical place where luxury and misery existed side by side. Laura saw dead Chinese lying on the streets among the garbage, a stark contrast to what she saw at her dinners at Mme Sun Yat-sen's home. The Jewish refugees also were suffering enormously. The housing situation was intolerable. Many destitute refugees were crowded into five small buildings, and every forty people shared two toilets. These people not only lacked proper housing, but also lacked food, clothes, medicine and leadership. Laura was the right leader for this difficult job, capable of making order out of chaos.

By befriending the Japanese leadership, Laura was able to obtain authorization from the Red Cross to release five thousand sacks of cracked wheat for the refugees, an act that led Laura to describe those Japanese as doing more for the refugees at that moment than anyone else. Because Laura spoke German, she indeed was of great assistance to the American consulate, helping to organize files and process visa applications from Jewish refugees in Shanghai who wanted to immigrate to the US. She informed the JDC in New York that it was very important for her to be able to listen to, record and then inform them of proposed activities relating to the Jewish refugees in China, but her stay in China was cut short.

When Germany invaded the Soviet Union in 1941, there was fear of a war in the Far East. Laura received a cable ordering her to leave immediately for Manila in the Philippines. It was difficult to find passage, but eventually she was able to travel on a troop ship sailing to Manila via Hong Kong.

Laura sent a cable to Mme Sun Yat-sen informing her that she would be stopping in Hong Kong in June 1941 on her way to Manila. Passengers were not permitted to disembark in Hong Kong, but Laura heard her name announced over the loudspeaker, and there was Two-Gun Cohen waiting to escort her to visit with Mme Sun Yat-sen, after which he accompanied her around the city for the day. Laura and Mme Sun Yat-sen would have no further contact for almost forty years, until 1979.

In October 1941, Laura returned to Shanghai, where she was responsible for feeding the eight thousand refugees who were destitute, as well

Heime in Shanghai, China, the shelters where refugees lived in crowded conditions during World War II; photo by Arthur Rothstein

as running a hospital and a Jewish school. Funds to help the Jewish refugees now were sent directly to Laura, rather than to the hated committee of rich Jews, who often referred to the refugees as "coolies" (unskilled workers hired for low wages). Laura asked the JDC for help and, at her request, Manny Segal, a JDC employee with whom Laura had worked before, was sent to assist her, arriving on December 1, 1941. On December 13, 1941, Laura was "authorized to borrow [$30,000 from wealthy Jewish philanthropists], on the promise of us [JDC] to repay the amount of money which is required to take care of the needy," providing Laura with the amount needed to feed eight thousand Jewish refugees and to house twenty-five hundred. Laura was authorized to extend that loan for six months for a total of $180,000. One of the lenders became my congregant years later in Tokyo, and he told me that he was repaid in full.

When Pearl Harbor was attacked, and Shanghai immediately was overrun by the Japanese, Captain Inuzuka, who was in charge of the twenty thousand Jewish refugees, moved to Sir Victor Sassoon's penthouse in the Cathay Hotel, home of Sassoon's corporate headquarters (see chapter 8), where Laura was also staying. She called him, and he invited her to tea prepared by his future wife Kyoko. Laura told him that since Japan and the United States were now at war, American money could not be transferred to Japan. She explained that she could help him by keeping the Jewish refugees from rioting but would need to borrow money to feed them and to fix other inefficiencies in the system. Michel Speelman, Ellis Hayim and David Ezekiel Joshua (known as DEJ) Abraham had asked the same from Captain Inuzuka earlier, but he considered them anti-Japanese and summarily dismissed them.

Captain Inuzuka knew Laura from their previous meetings, however, and he liked and trusted her. She was American and patriotic, but she was a wiser and more diplomatic negotiator than the above-mentioned three men. Captain Inuzuka immediately agreed to let her borrow money as long as she gave him the names of the lenders, who had to be from neutral countries (meaning no Americans, British or Dutch), conditions which she had no choice but to accept. Soon afterward, in a kind gesture, Captain Inuzuka also secured the release of JDC funds that had been frozen in the Chase Bank of Shanghai.

The JDC fed eight thousand destitute Jewish refugees daily, but the kitchens were inefficient, and charcoal, the fuel used for cooking, cost fifty cents per meal. Each meal cost a total of sixty cents, which meant that only ten cents went to pay for the food itself. Laura learned from one of the Jewish refugees, Polish engineer A. Levenspiel, that there were two brand-new boilers belonging to the Sassoons sitting outside in a lot, and they would make meal preparation more efficient and cost-effective by using steam rather than charcoal. She asked someone in Sassoon's office for the boilers, but her request was denied because as a British company, they, like Americans, were considered "enemy aliens" and so were prohibited from granting her request. Captain Inuzuka, however, gave Laura permission to take the two boilers. Laura gave someone in the Sassoon office an IOU, and at midnight under cover of darkness, while the streets were teeming with distracted people, several Jewish refugees moved the boilers. Levenspiel then created a new kitchen for about $500. There, the staff of ten to fifteen people was able to feed the refugees for just ten cents per meal, with only two cents going to fuel, a tremendous saving.

Not only did the staff create a simple, efficient, steam kitchen, but Laura also organized the community as an "experiment in democracy under the Axis." Under her leadership the refugees organized a laundry, tailor shop and vegetable gardens, as well as a skating rink and a dance pavilion, both of which would be rented out to provide income. The refugees thus became active on their own behalf.

Laura also organized a committee comprised of non-enemy aliens (all Jews

from Russia, Germany and Poland) to continue what she already had started –
taking care of the refugees – because she assumed it was just a matter of time
before she would be arrested and interned as an enemy national. They would
need money, though, and that was a problem. In 1942, M.L. Hoffman, on staff
in the Office of Foreign Funds Control at the US Treasury Department, said
that all communications and transfer of funds were prohibited as a matter of
policy and if asked, he must say no. "Of course," Hoffman added, "if you [the
JDC] wanted to send a cable, you are at liberty to do so, but the Treasury
[Department] could not authorize the sending of such a cable." The JDC and
other major Jewish organizations, behaving as super patriotic Americans, did
not accept Hoffman's hint for them to proceed with business as usual without
authorization, and in May 1942 they cut off all communication and funding, a
tragic and catastrophic decision for the twenty thousand Jewish refugees from
Europe. The amazing Laura soon came to their rescue.

In February 1943, long after the attack on Pearl Harbor, Laura was among
the last to be interned in the Chapei camp. She was kept in an old schoolhouse
and roomed with forty other women – missionaries, widows, diplomats and
prostitutes – all of whom were understandably miserable. After a while, when
Laura could take it no more, she hatched a plan. Faking illness, Laura was sent
to a hospital, where an Italian doctor who was her friend secured a semi-pri-
vate room for her. Her roommate was the Russian mistress of the director of
the German bank in Shanghai. She was very helpful and asked Laura if she
wished to have visitors.

Of course Laura wanted visitors, her committee members! They were
allowed into her room by saying that they were there to visit the Russian
patient. During the two months Laura managed to stay in the hospital, she was
able to continue her activities on behalf of the Jewish refugees. Laura created a
plan for coded messages to be sent to the committee members wherever they
were. She told one of her visitors, committee member Joseph Bitker, that when
he got a message wishing his daughter "Happy Birthday," it would mean that
money from JDC in the United States was on the way again. These funds were
vital in preventing refugees from starving and in stopping Jewish mothers from
giving away their babies because they lacked enough money for food and milk.

When Italy surrendered and became America's ally, Laura's friend, the Italian doctor, was considered an enemy of Japan, and Laura was returned to the
Chapei Camp. In preparation, Laura wrote on toilet paper the vital information

concerning the funds she had borrowed, the names of her committee members, those who could be trusted and other important, secret facts and figures. Then she rolled up the toilet paper and hid it inside the elastic of her underwear.

In September 1943, Laura was repatriated to the United States via the *Gripsholm*, an exchange ship. Unlike Mr. Hoffman's official negative response (with the ignored clue) earlier, US Secretary of the Treasury Henry Morgenthau said "yes" to Laura when she asked him for authorization to transfer money to Shanghai. By circumventing the JDC and seeking permission from Morgenthau directly, Laura finally was able to send the "Happy Birthday" cable to Bitker in 1944.

In 1945 World War II ended, and in 1948 the state of Israel was created. Laura eventually moved there and obtained Israeli citizenship. One day in 1978, while Laura was visiting New York, she saw in a Chinese bookstore an article written by Mme Sun Yat-sen in the magazine *China Reconstructs* (Mme Sun Yat-sen also was the editor). The article included a photograph as well, and Laura learned that not only was Mme Sun Yat-sen still alive, but also she was the vice-premier of the People's Republic of China. Now, since China was a Communist country, the United States no longer had diplomatic relations with China, but there was a Chinese Mission at the United Nations, so Laura wrote a letter to Mme Sun Yat-sen and delivered it to the Chinese Mission, hoping they would send it on.

In February 1979, Laura received an answer in which she was invited to visit China to spend time with her old friend, an invitation she accepted. In December 1979, Laura arrived in China, sent a cable to Mme Sun Yat-sen announcing her arrival and received a reply, "Welcome." A car picked Laura up, and the two women sat alone for two hours over tea, waxing nostalgic over the past, including their memories of Two-Gun Cohen. Laura left with a gift of Peking dates to bring home to share with her family and later described that reunion as one of the most exciting evenings of her life.

Laura considered Mme Sun Yat-sen, who died in May 1981, to be a nationalist who cared deeply for her own people and for people throughout the world, feelings the Chinese leader had in common with Laura. China was one of the first nations to support the Balfour Declaration,* and Mme Sun Yat-sen's

---

* The Balfour Declaration was the November 2, 1917, letter from the United Kingdom's foreign secretary Arthur J. Balfour in support of establishing a national home in Palestine for the Jewish people.

late husband had written a letter supporting the efforts of the Jewish people to establish a Jewish homeland. In 1985, the Chinese People Association of Friendship with Foreign Countries invited Laura to China, and while there Laura visited Mme Sun Yat-sen's grave, a very emotional experience.

Laura's career spanned three continents: she served in Cuba in the Americas; in Shanghai in Asia; and after her repatriation, rather than disembarking in South America, Laura insisted on going to Europe even before the end of the war. She was in Amsterdam twenty-four hours after the Nazis left and then went on to Paris. The JDC asked her to head European operations, charged her with helping the survivors, especially children, with food and medical supplies and, eventually, with arranging for their transfer to Israel. Laura was the first female overseas representative of the JDC and the first JDC female director of a European country after the end of World War II. "If I had been a man, I would have joined the navy and seen the world," Laura once said, "but since I am a woman, I joined the JDC."

When asked what made her do all these things, Laura said, "Well, I went around the world looking for my husband, and I found him." Marc Jarblum worked for JDC headquarters in Paris. He was a very active person and worked for the Jewish community there as a layman, while Laura worked there as a professional social worker. It was in June 1946, after the war, that Laura decided it was time to get married, and when she met Marc, an active Zionist, she knew he was the right person.

After they married in 1950, Laura said she was very tired and suggested to Marc that they move to Israel. Three years later they did, and Laura became director of Malben, JDC's care facility for the nation's elderly and disabled. Laura did an excellent job there, just as she always did everywhere she went. Marc died in 1972, but Laura stayed in Israel from 1953 to 1983, when her family urged her to return to the United States, which she did with some ambivalence. "To this day," Laura said in her interview for the USHMM in 1990, "I don't know whether I did the right thing.... For the first time [in Israel] I felt that I belonged, that I had roots.... I felt real good and at peace."

Laura, who told me that she "lived in a laboratory of saving lives," died in Brookline, Massachusetts, on September 9, 1997, at the age of ninety-three. On July 17, 2007, JDC president Judge Ellen M. Heller wrote that "one of the most remarkable chapters in JDC history is the assistance given to the World War II Jewish refugees in Shanghai, directed by the only woman professional of the Joint [JDC] at that time, Laura Margolis."

In 1993, at a reunion in Chicago of Shanghai refugees, Laura had received a scroll signed by the attendees and presented to her by Ernest G. Heppner, the first refugee from Shanghai to write a memoir, *Shanghai Refuge*. In a testimonial after Laura died, Heppner said, "If there is one deserving hero in the whole Shanghai episode, it is certainly Laura Margolis."

Chapter Ten

From Poverty to Culture: The Refugee Jewish Community in Shanghai

My congregation in Tokyo, Japan, consisted primarily of former residents of Shanghai, China. They were either born in Shanghai or had migrated there from Harbin and Tientsin (now Tianjin), Manchuria. All of them, however, shared deep nostalgia for their time living in the French Concession area of Shanghai, and by the end of my stay in Tokyo, I knew the streets and landmarks of Shanghai almost as well as they did. In fact, in the early 1980s, when I finally visited Shanghai for the first time – I went to lead a tour of China after Americans were permitted to travel there – I surprised the local guide, who did not know anything about the Jewish presence there, when I was able to tell stories and give directions to the bus driver although I had never been to Shanghai before. I knew the history of the Jews in Shanghai, recognized buildings, landmarks and theaters, and even knew the original names of many of the streets. Later, on another one of my tours, there were three generations of one family: the grandmother who had been a refugee in Shanghai, her daughter who was born in Shanghai, and her grandson who was born in the United States.

From 1938 to 1943, there were more than twenty-five thousand Jews living in Shanghai, twenty thousand of whom were Jewish refugees, with ten thousand Jews arriving within a six-month period at the height of Jews escaping from Europe. More than five thousand others were Russian Jews, Baghdadi Jews and German/Austrian/Polish Jews who had been residents of Shanghai before the war and, therefore, were not considered refugees.

I was invited to a reunion of many of these refugees at a hotel in New York's

Catskill Mountains in the late 1980s. We reminisced about their experiences in Shanghai, and I brought them up to date on the status of former synagogues, Jewish schools, community buildings, familiar streets and homes, and the heroes who helped them in Shanghai, like Laura Margolis whom the reader met earlier (see chapter 9).

The Sino-Japanese War (China's war with Japan) began in 1937. Hitler had already come to power in 1933, and Jews were fleeing from Germany and Austria. Some Jews had gone to Shanghai earlier, and on a 1932 list of the ninety-nine members of the Shanghai Stock Exchange, thirty-eight of them were Jewish, mostly Sephardic. In February 1939, there were 248,000 German Jews waiting for American visas, which they never received, and immigration to Palestine was drastically reduced by the British. Shanghai, however, then with a population of about four million out of which six hundred thousand were unemployed, did not require a visa. In 1939, Dr. Julius Seligson, a leader of the German Jewish community, wrote a report detailing how undesirable Shanghai was, but, sadly, there was no other place for Jews to go.

In order to leave Germany and Austria, the Jews had to relinquish all their property and valued possessions and were allowed to take with them only ten German marks (then equal to four dollars). The typical travel route to Shanghai was by ship from Genoa, Italy, via the Suez Canal in Egypt, to Aden, Bombay, Ceylon (now Sri Lanka), Singapore, Dutch East Indies (now Indonesia), Manila and Hong Kong. Not every ship stopped at every port, but the trip generally took a month or longer. Often, it was the women who had to make all the arrangements because their husbands already were in concentration camps, even though it was in the late 1930s. Still at that time, if a Jew had a ticket to leave the country, he could be released from the concentration camp. Family dynamics changed because the wife had to take care of all the details, including getting the ticket, finding out to which concentration camp her husband had been sent, getting him released, completing all the paperwork and deciding what was important enough to take with them.

Shanghai was the cultural and economic center of China, but its reputation in Europe was terrible. It was known for unbearable heat and humidity in the summer, flooding in autumn from the typhoons, and cold, wet winters. In addition, the crowded, unsanitary conditions were exacerbated by mosquitoes, worms, bedbugs, flying cockroaches and crushed bugs on the walls, much of which in turn led to rampant dysentery, cholera, malaria, typhoid, typhus and spinal meningitis. The first impression Shanghai made on the refugees was that

Refugees selling their belongings on the streets in Shanghai, China, during World War II

it was a crowded, foul-smelling, dirty and noisy place, and that the Chinese language sounded like people yelling.

While the refugees saw attractive foreign influences on some of the impressive buildings, they also saw corpses in the street, which included dead babies wrapped in rags or newspapers who were picked up every morning and cremated. The refugees were advised to study English, to be aware of pickpockets, and not to drink the polluted water without boiling it first. Vegetables and fruits had to be boiled, or boiling water had to be poured over them. Making matters worse, vendors often injected watermelons with polluted water to make them heavier so they could sell them for a higher price. Bread, when it was available, had to be sliced very thin and held up to the light so any parasitic worms could be picked out by hand.

On a more positive note, placards welcoming the refugees to Shanghai read, "Now you are no longer Germans, Austrians, Czechs or Romanians. Now you are Jews, only Jews. The Jews of the whole world have prepared a home for you." Each refugee received a blanket, a spoon, a cup and a dish; Jewish doctors performed their work admirably despite the lack of medications and medical instruments; and there was a refugee hospital, albeit poorly equipped. In addition, the Japanese authorities controlling Shanghai had a positive attitude

Bunk beds for refugees in Shanghai, China, during World War II

toward the Jewish refugees because they remembered Jacob Schiff, the Jewish banker who financed their war against Russia (see chapter 6). When the Nazis pressured their Japanese allies to hand over their Jewish refugees, they refused.

Sir Victor Sassoon (see chapter 8) owned some buildings and purchased more to be used immediately to house refugees. Upon disembarking the ship, those refugees with no prearranged housing boarded animal-transport trucks to get to their shelter. The first refugees (about eight thousand) who arrived in Shanghai either had someone waiting for them or had money or valuables to sell, and they wisely chose to live in the pleasant French Concession area of the city where neither the Chinese police nor the military could enter. They also were able to open businesses or find jobs. The second group to arrive fell into poverty soon after arriving in Shanghai and each family squeezed into one rented room, sometimes shared with another family, and survived by selling everything they had and eating only the one free meal a day that was provided to the refugees. The third group of refugees arrived penniless and had nothing to sell. The second and third group numbered about twelve thousand in total, all of whom were taken immediately to live in Hongkew.

Hongkew, a slum in Shanghai where one hundred thousand poor Chinese and twelve thousand poor Jews lived (before an additional eight thousand Jewish refugees were forced to relocate there from the French Concession in 1943), had endured terrible housing conditions that worsened after the dilapidated neighborhood was bombed heavily in 1937 at the start of the Sino-Japanese War. People lived in what was known as a *heime* (Yiddish and German word for "home," but meaning "barracks" here), in which between thirty and forty moldy and bug-infested bunk beds were so close together that there was no room for chairs or tables. There were only two flush toilets for every forty people, so usually the toilet was a foul-smelling honey bucket used by everyone, with the contents later used as fertilizer after it was emptied daily by an unskilled, low-paid laborer known as a coolie. Cooking took place outside in the alley between buildings on a kind of hibachi that could not be used inside because of the smoke and fumes it emitted. Just to cook a pot of plain rice was a time-consuming task.

Tempers flared and fistfights erupted. With only a sheet providing any privacy, the well-educated, successful Jews from Europe found the situation difficult, to say the least. Many were musicians, dentists, doctors, merchants, actors, opera singers, comedians and professors, but finding employment was almost impossible. Those who did find menial jobs earned between twenty-five and fifty cents per day. The refugees sold whatever they had for food; a few even sold their babies. Sometimes they had to make clothes for themselves out of flour and potato sacks. When suits became worn out on one side, they were turned inside out; sometimes women had enough yarn, thread and cloth to knit sweaters or make clothes they could sell. Some refugee Jewish girls worked as nannies to the children in the foreign community; some women became prostitutes just to survive. And some men and women simply gave up and committed suicide. We know, however, that the Jews who did not escape from Europe to Shanghai faced a much more devastating fate, one over which they had no control.

In February 1943 all Jewish refugees were ordered to move by May 18, 1943, to the already crowded designated area in Hongkew. This directive included all eight thousand Jews residing either in the French Concession or elsewhere in Shanghai, as well as even those Hongkew residents living just a few feet outside the designated area. The sudden announcement in 1943 was a demoralizing, shocking and frightening event for the Jewish refugees living outside Hongkew. They were forced to close their businesses or relinquish their jobs, and they panicked at the prospect of being forced into a "Jewish ghetto." The Japanese never used the word ghetto or referred to the refugees as "Jews." Rather, they were referred to as "stateless refugees who arrived in Shanghai after 1937." By the May 18 deadline, eleven hundred refugees, including several doctors, had not moved to Hongkew, and several of them were arrested and sent to Bridge House Prison, where typhus was rampant and they paid for their resistance with their lives.

Beginning on August 10, 1943, Hongkew residents with a pass could leave in the morning to go to school or work, but getting that pass was easier said than done. *Pao Chia*, the title of the border patrol, was in charge of enforcing the pass system. To secure a pass, a refugee had to appear before Ghoya Kanoh (whom I met years later, in the 1960s), a Japanese police officer who worked for the Bureau for Stateless Refugee Affairs. Married and a father of two, fluent in English and a violin player, Ghoya seemed conventional enough. He was short, however, which gave him an inferiority complex, and if a tall refugee asked for a pass, chances are he would stand on a desk or chair and beat the tall refugee before throwing him out of his office. One refugee waited in line for a pass wearing a top hat. Ghoya asked if he were making fun of him, to which the refugee replied, "No, Sir. Whenever I meet an important person I wear a top hat." From then on that refugee always received a pass. Ghoya was so strange that he abused and intimidated the refugees on the one hand and, on the other hand, he attended their concerts and soccer matches and called himself the "King of the Jews."

When I met Ghoya, he tried to elude me after I surprised him by calling out his name, but I finally cornered him. I asked him if he were still "King of the Jews," and he gave me a dirty look. He told me he was aware of a secret transmitter in the Ohel Moshe Synagogue in Hongkew, but I think he heard the rumor about a possible transmitter in the synagogue only after the war. He said he personally never sent anyone to the Bridge House Prison, which meant certain death from typhus, but that his colleagues did. He argued that his violent behavior was his way of masking his attempts to save Jews, but this also is unlikely. The Jewish refugees hated him with a passion; after the war he was beaten by Jewish youth group members who probably left him for dead in the street.

The Mir Yeshiva, which traveled from Poland to Lithuania and Kobe, Japan, and was the only European yeshiva to survive the Holocaust intact, was already in Shanghai in 1943, and their presence in the city engendered tension on several fronts. One major source of conflict was the fact that the yeshiva had an independent source of money in addition to the money the institution was receiving from the Joint Distribution Committee (JDC). They argued that they needed more money than the German and Austrian Jewish refugees because of their kosher dietary laws and other restrictions, and they prevailed. In addition, they refused to relocate to Hongkew in 1943, arguing that unlike the German and Austrian Jews who indeed had lost their citizenship status, the yeshiva students were not "stateless citizens" but Polish citizens since there was a Polish government in exile in London. All of this eventually created a riot in Hongkew when students from the Mir Yeshiva broke into the offices of the Shanghai Ashkenazic Collaborating Relief Association (SACRA), smashed furniture and then threw some of it out the window. Some of the rioters were arrested and sent to prison. Eventually the Mir Yeshiva did move, although by that time conditions in Hongkew were somewhat better, and in 1945, after the war, the Mir Yeshiva relocated to Brooklyn, New York, and Jerusalem.

To paint a complete picture of the refugees in Shanghai, one must mention another source of tension among the refugees, the tension between the Polish Orthodox refugees – some called them religious fanatics – and the German-Austrian refugees, most of whom were not observant Orthodox Jews but rather liberal and progressive individuals who ignored the most basic Jewish traditions. Many German Jews felt they were intellectually superior to the Polish Jews, while many of the observant Polish refugees looked down upon the German refugees, and some even considered them as the cause of the Holocaust. The destitute German and Austrian Jews, who had been poor and unemployed for so long, would walk around in their clothes made out of flour or potato sacks and would see Mir Yeshiva students purchasing luxuries like new suits for the Passover holiday in the spring and the Rosh Hashanah holiday in the fall, and they would see the wives of Mir Yeshiva rabbis and faculty purchasing expensive delicacies like butter and kosher chicken. There were rumors that the leaders of the Mir Yeshiva were arrested for black marketing, demanding twice the food allowance of the other refugees because of their religious needs and then selling what they did not use. Families often sent their children to the school at the Mir Yeshiva because there were better meals there than they could provide at home.

On July 17, 1945, due to poor visibility, American bombers missed their intended target and directly hit Hongkew instead. Houses that had been rebuilt after the bombing by the Japanese in 1937 were demolished again, and fires burned everywhere. Human limbs littered the streets, and thirty-one Jewish refugees, including Felix Kardegg, the president of the German Jewish refugee community, were killed. In addition, more than two hundred Jewish refugees were wounded, seven hundred became homeless and thousands of Chinese also were wounded or killed. Jewish doctors treated and cared for the wounded Jewish and Chinese victims equally, and the next day the Chinese brought small food gifts to the Jewish refugees as tokens of their appreciation. As often occurs during a terrible crisis, everyone came together to help in every way possible, and this was one of the finest hours of the Jewish refugee community in Shanghai.

Despite the horrible living conditions and internal tensions, the Jewish refugees created an amazing community. Playing mah-jongg, creative Monopoly and other games offered an initial distraction; the refugees also created a café life on the streets filled with opportunities for intellectual stimulation from the arts, theater, music, the sciences, lectures and discussions on every subject. The Hongkew area began flourishing and was affectionately named "Little Vienna" as restaurants, shops and cafés were rebuilt with financial help from Jewish organizations. The Jewish refugees produced plays, and Jewish refugee musicians formed an orchestra and gave concerts. Light opera, operettas, the Yiddish theater and comedies offered relief from the intolerable living conditions and, of course, were very popular. Scripts for plays and operas were written from memory. Art exhibits were mounted on the streets. The Jewish refugees even operated a radio station that delivered news and journalists' reports, as well as medical reports from doctors, legal advice from attorneys, and popular synagogue liturgy sung by cantors. There were also performances by the talented refugees.

The Jewish refugees managed bookstores such as Book Mark, The Lion, Paragon and also managed the Western Art Gallery. In addition, they published newspapers in German, Polish, Yiddish and English, and the yeshiva produced a journal in Hebrew. At a time when even large Jewish communities produced only one newspaper, it is extraordinary that the Jewish refugee community in Shanghai managed to publish three German dailies, two in the morning and one in the evening. The *Shanghai Jewish Chronicle*, one of the morning dailies, was published in German from 1939 to 1945, and after the war it continued under the name the *Shanghai Echo* until 1949.

The other daily German morning paper was *Die Gelbe Post* (the Yellow Post). It started in May 1939 as a monthly paper published by Adolf Joseph Storfer (1888–1944), five months after he arrived in Shanghai. Storfer was a psychologist who became a loyal pupil of Sigmund Freud after meeting him in 1910; he also was an author, linguist and intellectual who studied law, philosophy, psychology and linguistics in Romania and then at the University of Zurich. From 1921 until 1932 he served as director of the International Psychoanalytic Publishing House, where he published journals with Freud. During the 1930s he published two books about the etymology of words. Storfer left Vienna at age fifty, and, after failing to gain admission to either the United States or Switzerland, traveled to Shanghai, reaching Hongkew in December 1938.

The German evening paper in Shanghai was *8-Urh Abendblatt* (Eight

O'Clock Evening Newspaper), published by Wolfgang Fischer. The German weekly *Shanghai Woche* (Shanghai Week) was also very popular, and the Russian newspaper *Nasha Zhin* (Our Life), published in Shanghai from 1941 to 1946, eventually added a page in Yiddish and a page in English. There were three medical journals, and more than one hundred religious books were published. In 1941, the Polish refugees published original, scholarly Talmudic commentaries in Hebrew, and on October 10, 1941, there was a fabulous celebration when the entire text of the Talmud – a twenty-volume work known as the Shanghai Talmud – was printed in Shanghai. Clearly there was an active press in Shanghai with publications in six languages, thanks to the Jewish refugees.

There were nine lending libraries in Shanghai, and we know that the Kadoorie family (see chapter 8) established a school and youth association that improved the quality of life for the Jewish children. Horace Kadoorie said that for his family "education is our hobby," and in their schools and summer camp the children were taught not only all the basic subjects, but also civics and etiquette, and they participated in calisthenics and afterschool activities such as preparation for bar mitzvahs, chess, dancing and sports.

After the war, Americans landed with chewing gum, candy and cigarettes for everyone and nylon stockings for the women, and they provided high paying jobs for fifteen hundred refugees who worked as drivers, office workers and service people in the PX, the store for military personnel. There were rumors in Shanghai that extermination camps there were ready for Jews, but there is no evidence supporting that rumor. Finally, starting in 1947, it was time for the Jews to leave. World War II was over; the Civil War in China had intensified; Palestine became Israel, the Jewish homeland; and the United States began accepting displaced persons. Some Jews went to the US, some went to Israel, some went to Australia, and a few even returned to Europe. Again, there was tension as complaints surfaced that the religious Polish refugees monopolized the American consulate and, in fact, they were the first refugees to arrive in the United States.

The Jewish refugees survived the Shanghai experience with courage, honor and dignity, but they did not do so alone. Besides the Sassoon and Kadoorie families (chapter 8) and Laura Margolis (chapter 9), there were the Jewish musicians (see chapter 14) and other Jewish artists, like Willie Tonn, who accomplished some of their best work as refugees in Shanghai and helped to raise the intellectual quality of life for their fellow Jewish refugees. Born in 1902 to a wealthy, German Jewish family, Tonn studied Chinese in Berlin and, after losing everything, lived from 1939 to 1948 in Shanghai, where he attempted to bridge the cultural gap between Jews and Chinese. He created People's University, also called Asia Seminar, an adult education effort that met regularly at the Kadoorie Jewish School. The program involved thirty lecturers teaching Japanese, Sanskrit, Hebrew, Chinese, Chinese language for doctors and lawyers, and Chinese history and culture. Tonn himself taught not only the Chinese language but also Chinese customs, Chinese culture, Chinese civilization, Chinese classics, sciences and liberal arts. After the war, he also offered an American school for those going to the United States and an Israel school for those heading to Israel, and his many articles about China were published in Chinese newspapers. In 1949, he went to Israel, where he was not successful. He died in 1957, and his archives are at the Center for Jewish History in New York as part of the collection at the Leo Baeck Institute.

Friedrich Schiff (1908–1968) was an Austrian Jewish artist who made superb drawings of the Chinese such as his "Rickshaw Boy," "Wheelbarrow Boy," "Chinese Barber," and artistic renditions of beggars. He taught at the Shanghai Art Club and was universally praised by all the newspaper art critics in China. His drawings frequently were used as covers for magazines, on postcards and in Christmas collections. His artwork helped chronicle Chinese life in Shanghai. After the war, Schiff moved to Argentina.

David Ludwig Bloch (1905–2002) was a German Jewish artist who was orphaned when he was only one year old. After Kristallnacht in 1938, Bloch was imprisoned in the Dachau concentration camp but he survived and arrived in Shanghai in 1940. A member of ARTA, an association of Jewish artists and lovers of fine arts, he made hundreds of woodcuts depicting every aspect of life in China, and in 1942 he published a portfolio titled "Rickshaw," containing sixty of his woodcuts. After the war he immigrated to the United States. When Lyndon B. Johnson became president, Bloch was invited to dinner at the White House. I met him in New York, and he gave me a book of his woodblock prints of life in China.

Austrian film director Jacob Fleck (1881–1953) directed hundreds of films in Austria and Germany, where he had the best-equipped and most modern studio during the silent movie era. Paul Muni, a famous actor, was one of his students. Fleck was imprisoned in both Dachau and Buchenwald but eventually fled to Shanghai. There, along with the famous Chinese film director, Fei Mu (1906–1956), he made one of the best films of the period, *The Children of the World*, starring Ying Yin, one of the most popular Chinese film stars of that time. *The Children of the World* was the only feature film ever directed by a foreigner in the history of Chinese cinema. Fleck planned to create the Chinese Academy of Movie Arts for training filmmakers, but the attack on Pearl Harbor ended that dream. Fleck survived the war in Shanghai.

Arthur Gottlein (1895–1977) revived the puppet shows that had disappeared from the Shanghai stage after the start of the Sino-Japanese War in 1937. He accomplished this by having *The Puppet's Paradise*, a three-act play, translated from German into both classic Mandarin and Shanghai dialect languages. He then arranged for the show to be performed in Shanghai, and his success revived the genre of puppet shows there by encouraging Chinese puppeteers to keep the art of puppetry alive.

R.O. Shoemyen (1892–1982) was born to religious Jewish parents in Vienna. When the family moved from Vienna to Hungary, they changed his original name, Rudolph Schlesinger, into a Hungarian name. Shoemyen played the violin, attended art school, and studied building design before finally becoming a construction engineer. He served as a lieutenant in the Austro-Hungarian Army during World War I, was awarded the Iron Cross, and learned the Russian language when he was taken as a prisoner of war by Russia. After the war, Shoemyen moved to China where he worked as an architect and designed the Jewish school in Harbin. Highly successful in Shanghai, where he owned a horse, a motorcycle and a car, Shoemyen was among the architects who designed the East Asia Bank, the Shanghai Jewish School (which is still standing), several theaters, the Sun-Sun Department Store and many mansions for rich Chinese families. Shoemyen also made charcoal drawings of Chinese and Mongolians.

Hans Adolf Georg Hamburger (1899–1982) escaped the anti-Semitism in Germany by going to China in 1935. In China, he taught engineering and German at several universities in Shanghai, worked for Shanghai public works, translated seven engineering books from German into Chinese and also translated books from German into English, all of which were published by leading publishers in China. Hamburger mastered not only German, English and Chinese, but also French, Latin and Greek. Every morning he practiced Chinese shadowboxing and always dressed in the ordinary coat the Chinese wore. He was among the last Jews to leave China. During the Cultural Revolution (1966–1976), when his friends were afraid to associate with him, he finally decided it was time to leave. When he visited China in 1972, he was surprised to be invited to review the National Day (October 1st) celebration in Tiananmen Square.

A less known name is Charles Bliss (1897–1985). Born Karl Blitz in Vienna, Blitz studied music, mathematics and chemistry and worked for a large electronics company before his arrest in the 1930s. He spent thirteen months in concentration camps after which he escaped to China and changed his name to Charles Bliss. He is known as the author/inventor of "Blisssymbolics," a simple, clear script similar to Chinese script which he first demonstrated at the Shanghai Jewish Club in 1943. Bliss thought that "Blisssymbolics" could unite the world. He settled in Australia after the war, and when his work was rediscovered in the 1970s, it was found to be very useful as a method of communication for learning-disabled children, particularly for those immobilized by cerebral palsy and those with mental disabilities. Bliss dedicated his book to his thirty-four relatives who perished in the Nazi gas chambers and the millions who died with them.

About four hundred children were born to the refugee Jewish community in Shanghai. Former president Jimmy Carter's secretary of the treasury, W. Michael Blumenthal, known as the "Shanghai kid," was raised in Shanghai and has returned there many times. Jewish artist Peter Max also was raised in Shanghai, and it was there that he received his first paintbrush.

There were extraordinary Jews like Laura Margolis and the Kadoorie and Sassoon families who did so much to help the Jewish refugees in Shanghai, but the refugees themselves, who did not tell their stories publicly for decades, were heroes, too. They invented ways to cope with a terrible situation and built a community out of nothing, demonstrating their vitality, determination and defiance in overcoming numerous obstacles to create familiar institutions in an unfamiliar environment. It is fair to say that the Jewish refugees in Shanghai did more than just survive dehumanizing conditions against all odds. Amazingly, they triumphed and left Shanghai a better place than they found it.

Chapter Eleven
A Comedy of Errors Reveals a Long-Lost Community of Chinese Jews

I magine seeing a synagogue that looks like a pagoda and a rabbi who looks like a Mandarin. Imagine Jews who are not known as Jews, Hebrews, Israelites, Juifs, Yahuds, or Yehudi, but rather as "blue hats" or as "the sect that extracts the sinew," based on a verse in Genesis 32:33, "therefore the children of Israel eat not the sinew." Imagine Jews who do not live in the cities associated with Jews such as Jerusalem, Tel Aviv, Paris, New York, Miami, London, Buenos Aires and Toronto, but, rather, live in Kaifeng or Xian. Imagine Jews who do not have names like Cohen, Levy or Goldberg, but who have Chinese names like Li, Shi and Zhao. And imagine Jews with yellow skin and dark, almond-shaped eyes rather than blue-eyed blonde or dark-eyed brunette Jews. The Jewish community in China, which numbered between two and five thousand people, was there for six hundred years before anyone knew it existed, but that all changed in the seventeenth century.

On a hot, humid day in June 1605 in Peking (now Beijing), there was a knock on the door of Father Matteo Ricci, a Catholic Jesuit missionary who had arrived in 1583 to convert the "heathen" Chinese to Christianity. When Father Ricci – standing over six feet tall with a curly beard, blue eyes and a voice like a bell – opened the door, he was greeted by Ai Tien, a sixty-year-old ethnic Chinese man who looked slightly different from the typical Chinese person. Ai, who thought he was standing at the door of a synagogue and who did not know who Father Ricci was, asked him if he had come from so far away to teach the Chinese about his belief in the one God of the universe. Much to Ai's pleasure, Father Ricci said that, indeed, he had come to teach the Chinese about the one God. Ai continued and asked Father Ricci, who

Stamp in honor of Father Matteo Ricci

had mastered the Chinese language and customs, if he taught the traditions of the holy, moral and ethical way of life. Again, Father Ricci answered affirmatively. Ai said that it was difficult to maintain that way of life so far away, but far away from where he did not say. Ai was one of the Chinese Jews who, like other Chinese Jews for centuries before him, lived isolated from the global Jewish community.

Intrigued by Ai's questions, Father Ricci invited him into his home, which contained a chapel, to share tea and become better acquainted. Ai was disoriented as he looked around the small interior. The furniture, carpet, curtains and artwork were not oriental but European. Ai had read in a book titled *Things I have Heard Tell* that a learned foreigner, not Muslim and with no connection to Islam, had arrived in China, lived in Peking and claimed to believe in the one God of the universe. Since there were no Christians in China at this time, a monotheist would be Jewish. The comedy of errors began when Ai assumed that Father Ricci was the learned foreigner he had read about and that he was a rabbi who could offer so much help to the Jewish community of Kaifeng which was struggling to survive. As they continued talking to each other, Father Ricci remembered that in prior centuries there were Christians in China who had disappeared, but no one knew where they were or even if they still existed. So, since Ai believed that there was one God of the universe and was knowledgeable about the holy way of life, Father Ricci assumed Ai was Christian or a descendant of a Christian, and Ai assumed Father Ricci was a rabbi! Neither one, however, said aloud what he was thinking.

There are two versions of what happened next during the meeting between Ai and Father Ricci. One comes from books about Father Ricci, and the other comes from my Chinese Jewish friend, Lieutenant Colonel Shih Hung-mo, who escaped with Chiang Kai-shek to Taiwan. I met Shih in 1974 when I lived in Tokyo. He had been in the Chinese Air Force but was living as a recluse when I found him, and in the ensuing years, I visited him several times and corresponded with him for many years.

It is hard to be certain which story is the most accurate, so here are two versions of one story. In version one: A painting on the wall caught Ai's attention, so he got up from his chair to move closer to take a good look and then bowed down flat on the floor. Father Ricci, surprised, asked Ai if he was familiar with the painting, and Ai explained that in his home there was great reverence for that painting. The painting was of the four evangelists, so when Ai inquired if the four men were part of the twelve, Father Ricci answered affirmatively. He was thinking of the twelve apostles. In version two: According to Shih Hung-mo, when Father Ricci asked Ai why his family revered the painting, Ai answered that it was a painting of Jacob in the center with his twelve sons, the founders of the twelve tribes of Israel, and Father Ricci said the painting was of a table with a holy man sitting in the center with six men to his right and six men to his left, the familiar scene of the Last Supper.

Here are two versions of another story about their meeting: On the other side of the room from the painting there was a scene in the adjacent chapel with figurines of a woman, a baby and a man, which to Father Ricci, of course, were the Virgin Mary, John the Baptist and baby Jesus. Coincidentally, it was June 24, 1605, and St. John the Baptist Day, a Catholic holiday. When Father Ricci asked Ai to kneel in front of the statues, however, Ai realized that Father Ricci was not a rabbi and explained that in his tradition one does not kneel before figurines but that he would do so out of respect for his ancestors.* Version one: according to the book I read about Father Ricci, the "ancestors" to whom Ai was referring were Rebecca and her two sons, Jacob and Esau. Version two: Shih told me that his relatives told him the figurines were of Abraham, Sarah and the baby Isaac, and that version makes more sense because the scene was of two adults and one baby. Regardless of which are the correct scenarios, the important facts are that the two men met, that a comedy of errors followed, and that history changed.

Ai did not know the word *Jew*. He called his people "Israel," but because Chinese have difficulty pronouncing the *r* sound, he pronounced it as "Yisuloyeh." Father Ricci had a Bible written in Hebrew, and Ai recognized the letters. He told Father Ricci that his brothers preferred Hebrew studies to

---

* Jews abandoned kneeling at the start of Christianity, but some Orthodox Jews prostrate themselves on the floor on Yom Kippur.

Chinese, were active members of the synagogue and could read Hebrew. When Father Ricci was searching for Christians in China, he had to invent the word for "cross" as there was no Chinese word to convey the concept. The Chinese number ten, however, is written as +, which resembles a cross, and Ai remembered that there was a small sect in his neighborhood known as "Muslims of the Ten", and they made a cross over their food and drink.

Many factors led to the confusion and the comedy of errors, but in 1605, with so few differences in their respective theological positions, Ai asked Father Ricci to succeed the chief rabbi of the Jewish community of Kaifeng, on condition that he no longer eat pork and no longer preach that the Messiah already had come – as the Kaifeng rabbi said the Messiah would not come for another ten thousand years – but Father Ricci declined. He wrote to the Jesuits in Europe telling them that he found a Chinese Jew, however, so Europeans at the beginning of the seventeenth century suddenly became aware of the existence of Jews in China. When Ai was in Peking to accept his official appointment as a school supervisor, Father Ricci wrote, "His face was quite different from that of Chinese in respect to his nose, his eyes and all his features." From 1605 to 1723, the Jesuit missionaries provided an abundance of information about the Jewish community through their writings and sketches of the interior of the synagogue and the synagogue grounds.

Photo found inside a tomb in Xian, China: a Jewish traveler with a long nose, wearing a floppy hat

The discovery that there were Chinese Jews is one of the most fascinating finds relating to the Diaspora. For the first time, Europeans learned that a Jewish community was established more than one thousand years earlier, when Jews traveled from Persia along the Silk Road to Kaifeng, about five hundred miles southwest of Peking. Kaifeng, with three sets of city walls and a forbidden city in the center, at the time was China's capital and the largest city in the world, with a population of more than one million people.

The Chinese Jewish merchants from Persia met the emperor of China at the Imperial Palace in Kaifeng and gave him a gift of dyed cotton cloth, a fabric then unknown in China, and these Jews were experts in the dyeing process. The emperor greeted them warmly. Carved on the stone stele in 1489 are the words the emperor said to their ancestors centuries earlier: "You have come to our China; revere and preserve the customs of your ancestors and hand them down in Kaifeng." (Later generations of Chinese Jews also wrote about their heritage on stone steles in 1512, 1663 and 1669. We have the rubbings of all four steles, but only two steles remain.) As descendants of the Persian tradesmen, today's Chinese Jews still know some ancient words of Farsi, their prayer book and Passover Haggadah (liturgy which describes the exodus from slavery in Egypt commemorated by the Passover holiday) contained Persian Farsi words, and they count the number of letters in the Hebrew alphabet and the sections of the Torah in the same unique way as was done in Persia.

The Jews in Kaifeng built a synagogue, called the Temple of Purity and Truth, and the synagogue compound was dedicated in 1163. Like all Chinese temples, inside there was a long table on which there were five ceremonial objects: two candlesticks, two flower vases and an incense bowl. As required by the emperor for all Chinese temples, an inscription declaring loyalty to him was engraved on one wall. Above that inscription was the familiar Hebrew phrase: "Shema Yisrael…" (Hear O Israel…).

There is a model of the synagogue of Kaifeng on permanent display in the Diaspora Museum in Tel Aviv, and in 1988 Israel issued a beautiful Rosh Hashanah (the Jewish New Year) postage stamp with a picture of the Kaifeng synagogue. The synagogue was built on about two acres, with the structure measuring 60 by 40 feet and the compound about 400 by 150 feet. The synagogue, entered from the east, faced west (the same as their Jewish cemetery) toward Jerusalem (Chinese temples face south) and had a series of courtyards, a *mikveh* (a ritual bath), a room for preparing kosher meat, a

Photo of the model of the synagogue in Kaifeng; the model is on permanent display at the Diaspora Museum in Tel Aviv, Israel

communal kitchen, a study hall and a hall of ancestors. Chinese Jews would burn incense in front of the inscriptions of their ancestors' names, but there were no statues or images in the hall.

The ark contained thirteen Torah scrolls (see chapter 7) numbered one to twelve, with the thirteenth being the "Torah of Moses," the original one from which the others were copied. Each Torah was in a gold lacquered case, and a magnificent elevated chair with embroidered cushions was used for the reading of the Torah. The Chinese Jews said that their Torah had fifty-three sections and their sacred Hebrew script had twenty-seven letters. Europeans and Americans divide the Torah into fifty-four sections and their alphabet has twenty-two letters. The Chinese Jews recited exactly what was recited by the Persian Jewish community, thus confirming their origin. The seventeenth-century missionaries reported that people removed their shoes before entering the synagogue; that the Torah reader wore a veil on his face (the source of which is Exodus 34:33; see chapter 7); and that they observed the Sabbath, circumcision and all the Jewish holidays. The rabbi's name in the seventeenth century was *Lieh-wei*, which translates to Levi.

The first synagogue was destroyed by a terrible flood in 1461 and was rebuilt but destroyed by fire in 1600. We now know that there were Jewish communities in Hangkow, Canton, Nanjing, Ningbo, Xian, Peking and a few other cities in addition to Kaifeng, but as of now, no one has found records or artifacts relating to the communities in these other places. The search by Chinese scholars for such records has already started, however, and we do know that the Jewish community in Ningbo donated a Torah scroll to the Jews of Kaifeng after the flood in 1461.

The third synagogue was swept away in the flood of 1642 during which one hundred thousand people, including many Jews, lost their lives. The last synagogue was dedicated in 1663. Twelve new Torah scrolls then were written to replace those lost in the flood, but the amateur scribes made hundreds of spelling errors. After the death of the last rabbi around 1810, there was no one to take his place, and the reading of the Torah was beyond the ability of any community member. Even earlier rabbis could not remember much of their ancestral language and faith. Around 1825 there was even a Torah on display in the Kaifeng marketplace with a sign offering a reward to anyone who could read the text. No one could claim the reward.

Chinese Jews, like other residents, were weakened by the repeated military, economic and natural disasters that Kaifeng experienced over the centuries.

Fires, floods and revolutions created havoc, and eventually Kaifeng was no longer the national capital or even an important city. Some of the city's Jews moved elsewhere, but their new surroundings were not as conducive to maintaining and transmitting their Jewish heritage to succeeding generations. For those who remained, poverty and ignorance were rampant, and the Jews in Kaifeng debated back and forth for decades concerning "saving face," an important concept in the Far East, about their declining fortunes and numbers. They had arrived in China as proud, loyal and observant Jews and created a vibrant Jewish community, but over time they had intermarried, had become assimilated and were uneducated. How could they face their ancestors without guilt and shame? If they went public with the humiliating truth and a cry for help, would a teacher or rabbi and others come to their aid out of respect for their ancestors?

Such a cry for help finally was sent to the outside world on August 20, 1850, in a letter written by Zhao Nien-tsu. He wrote, "Morning and night, with tears in our eyes and with offerings of incense, do we implore that our religion yet again flourish. If we can rebuild our synagogue, it will give great joy to our community...our synagogue has no rabbi. Our *mikveh* and Ark are in ruins. The sight of our synagogue brings grief to our hearts and....If we could again have a rabbi and teacher and rebuild our synagogue, our future will be secure....We have everywhere sought about but could not find anyone who could understand our scriptures."

The letter reached London and New York, and the rabbis in those places asked congregants to help their brethren in China. Jacob Touro, a prominent and philanthropic American Jew, left a fortune for any teacher, rabbi or layman who would go to China for as long as was necessary to teach basic Judaism to the Jews of China. Tragically, no one rose to the occasion, and the Chinese Jews felt humiliated by the lack of response. Rabbi Isaac Leeser in the United States endorsed the letter, and in 1853, Rabbi Nathan Marcus Adler, chief rabbi of the British Empire, wrote to the Sassoons in Shanghai (see chapter 8) asking for their help to send a rabbi to Kaifeng to open a Jewish school and help the Chinese Jews in that city. The response was slow and discouraging, but in 1864, eleven years after Rabbi Adler's letter but in response to it, two Jews from Kaifeng arrived in Shanghai to live with a Jewish family and learn basic Judaism.

The synagogue in Kaifeng was demolished around 1860 when poverty and ignorance was so widespread that some of the remaining Jews sold two stone lions from the Kaifeng synagogue to a Buddhist temple, and the tiles from the synagogue were sold to the local mosque for use on its roof. Today, that mosque also has a Torah case and a lotus stone bowl from the Kaifeng synagogue,* and a *National Geographic* article about Chinese Jews (October 1907) reported that one of the Torah scrolls from the synagogue is hidden in the mosque as well. Other artifacts from the Kaifeng synagogue, including Torah scrolls, valuable books, genealogy reports, and a memorial book with inscriptions dating from the fifteenth century to 1670, are currently in libraries and museums in England, Canada, the United States and Austria.

In the Washington, DC, Anglican Cathedral one can see another lotus stone bowl, and there is a major exhibition of artifacts from the synagogue of Kaifeng on display in the Royal Ontario Museum of Toronto. While visiting the museum, I had the thrill of sounding an amazing black marble chime that once was rung three times a day at the synagogue as a call to prayer. The Jewish Theological Seminary in New York has a Torah scroll and a few books, but the largest collection of prayer books, genealogy and other Kaifeng Judaica – except for Torah scrolls – is at the Hebrew Union College in Cincinnati, Ohio.

In the seventeenth century both Catholics and Protestants, many of whom considered Jews as the devil or anti-Christ, were eager to obtain one of the original Chinese Torah scrolls, because if, as they hoped, the Jews had arrived in Kaifeng before the start of Christianity, then their Torah scrolls would contain text prophesying the birth of Jesus. Christian theologians believed that ancient rabbinical authorities had excised from the Torah all references to Jesus as the Messiah, but if the Jews saw Jesus mentioned in one of the original Chinese Torahs, then they would know they had been deceived by their rabbis, see the error of their ways and embrace Christianity. To the great disappointment of the Christian clergy and theologians, the Torah scrolls were exactly like every other Torah and did not contain any Christological passages.

The Canadian Anglican missionaries, under Bishop William Charles White, who in 1942 wrote three volumes titled *Chinese Jews*, purchased the land where the synagogue stood. Later the government built a hospital which, amazingly, contains the vestiges of the original *mikveh* (ritual bath) of the synagogue down some narrow steps in the boiler room. These steps are constructed of bricks from the Ming Dynasty, which places the *mikveh*'s origin in the 1300s.

---

* The lotus is a Buddhist design symbolizing that out of dirt sometimes comes beauty. It has no religious significance in Judaism, but Chinese Jews appreciate the meaning behind the lotus symbol.

The street was, and still is, named Teaching Torah Lane South. One Chinese Jewish family still lives at number 21, where they maintain a mini museum (well worth seeing) in their tiny, one room home. In the multi-story Kaifeng Museum, which was completely looted, one item remains because it is was too heavy for thieves to carry. On the top floor of the empty museum building one can see the original stele the Chinese Jews etched in 1489.

True stories, nonsense and jokes about Chinese Jews have proliferated over the centuries. True stories from long ago that refer to Jews in China include the following: In the ninth century, Ibn Khordadbeh, a geographer and reliable scholar, noted travels of Jews on the Silk Road from Europe and the Middle East to China. During the same era, a Muslim historian wrote of a massacre in Canton (now Guangzhou) in which many Jews died. Marco Polo visited China and reported in 1286 that he heard Hebrew spoken and saw Jews in Peking. Kublai Khan (1215–1294) mentioned Jewish festivals in his writings, so Jews must have lived in the empire or been part of his inner circle. In 1326 Andrew of Perugia wrote that Jews in Peking refused his pleas to accept baptism. An Arab visitor to Hangkow wrote in 1346 that he entered the city through the Jewish gate and that many Jews lived there. And during the Ming Dynasty, the emperor, who could not pronounce the Jewish names of the recently arrived foreigners, gave his new subjects many Chinese family names, only seven of which remain today, in appreciation for a Jew exposing treason that was planned by a member of the royal family. About 1653, Ying Sheng (1619–1657/1658), whose Hebrew name was Moses Ben Abram, wrote a history of the Chinese Jews, as well as the basic tenets of Judaism. What a great discovery it would be if a copy of that book were found!

A nonsensical story started during the Opium War of 1839–1842, when it was said that an unnamed British commander sailed in an unnamed naval ship along an unnamed river into China and discovered an unnamed city inhabited by one million Chinese Jews. Some of the other nonsense relating to Chinese Jews stems from the fact that the Hebrew word *sin*, which is found in the Bible, was incorrectly thought to mean China, since sinology is indeed the study of China. "Sin" in the Bible, however, is the geographical name for southern Egypt and has nothing to do with China.

Among interesting stories from more recent times that refer to Chinese Jews are the following: In the 1940s, the Jews of Harbin in Manchuria reported that a Chinese Jew attended their synagogue on Yom Kippur. In the mid-nineteenth century, there was a report in a San Francisco newspaper that among the brigades of Chinese laborers who arrived on the West Coast was one man who claimed he did not work on the Sabbath. In 1942 Japanese intelligence sent a delegation to Kaifeng to determine whether the Chinese Jews were part of the alleged international Jewish conspiracy to control the world. And in 1948, Nobel Laureate Pearl Buck (1892–1973), daughter of Presbyterian missionaries who brought her with them to China, wrote *Peony* about the heroic attempt of the Chinese Jews to survive and not be swallowed by China.

Robert Lury, who was born in Nagasaki, followed in his father Meyer's footsteps to become president of the Jewish community of Japan. When I arrived in Tokyo in 1968, Robert was a member of my congregation, and he told me a fascinating story. His family came from Nikolaevsk on the Amur River in far northeastern Siberia, where they operated a fishing fleet manned by a mostly Chinese crew. For one trip out to sea, one could earn a year's salary, and if one gambled that salary and won, he could come home with two years' salary. If one lost, however, he would arrive home with empty pockets. On the return trip, therefore, gambling and odds increased as losers tried to make up for their losses, and violence, including murders, escalated as the losers became more desperate to come back with money in their pockets. Consequently, a rule forbidding gambling on the return trip to port was put into place.

One night, when the Lury family searched the ship to be sure there was no gambling, they came upon a circle of Chinese crewmen, stripped to their underwear because of the heat, engaged in the forbidden activity of gambling by candlelight in a dark, steamy area near the boiler. They had chosen that space thinking it was a good place to hide because people stayed away to avoid the darkness and stifling heat. As the Lurys looked around the circle of gamblers, their eyes focused on one man whom they detained after letting all the others go. The Lurys wanted to know why he was wearing what looked like an undershirt with fringes. The crewman said he did not know what it was or why he was wearing it; he knew only that all the men in his family wore it. The Lury family believes that this man was wearing a Jewish prayer shawl, a ritual item of clothing which also has fringes (called *tzitzit*). It is possible, however, that the fringe just might have been the result of the poor man wearing cheap clothes made from the end of a bolt of cloth that had strings hanging down.

Before the Chinese Jewish community declined into poverty and ignorance of their identity, they had grown to an estimated population of between two and five thousand individuals. Members of the Jewish community dressed like other Chinese, wore pigtails, bound their daughters' feet, spoke the local dialect and engaged in the same professions. Some Chinese Jews shaved their head to disguise their curly and/or red hair. They did not eat pork, however, and they would make their own ersatz matzah for the Passover festival, which falls at the same time as the spring full moon. They also had a unique tradition of placing a drop of rooster blood on their doorposts during this springtime holiday. This custom relates to the biblical story of the exodus of Jews from slavery in ancient Egypt when God passed over the homes of the Israelites who made their presence known by placing a drop of blood on their doorposts.

Drawing of prominent Chinese Jew in Kaifeng, China

The Chinese Jews lived in an open and tolerant society. In proportion to their numbers, Chinese Jews seem to have been quite successful. Many obtained Mandarin rank, held responsible government posts, and not once did any Chinese emperor or ruler deny them access to any form of employment or single them out for the persecution that Jews experienced in the Christian and Muslim worlds. Sometimes at school, however, children were laughed at when they were asked where they were from and answered "Israel," a place no one in China knew.

Appointments to China's most prestigious and highly paid posts in the education field, civil service and armed forces required candidates to pass three specialized examinations designed to evaluate the extent of the candidate's mastery of the classic texts of Confucianism. Preparation for these exams, open to all Chinese citizens, took years, and for the Jews that meant forgoing their Judaic studies for a time. A Chinese proverb says that one has to spend at least ten years studying to take the qualifying exam to be a scholar and a Mandarin. Education and studying scriptures are Jewish values, and soon Jews were passing the exam and becoming Mandarins. From the 1400s through the 1700s, the Golden Age, Jews were judges, school supervisors, newspaper editors, members of the imperial household, military officers and physicians. If a Jew scored high enough on the exam and received an appointment, however, it often meant that he and his family would be sent far away from Kaifeng to an area with no Jews, and they could be lost to their people.

In 1900, the Society for the Rescue of Chinese Jews was organized in Shanghai, but without financial help and encouragement from American and European Jews, it was forced to close in 1904. In 1932 David A. Brown, an American Jew, visited the Ai family in Kaifeng, and they told him, "We need a school for our children that they may learn who they are ... we are eager for them to walk in the footsteps of our ancestors." Bishop White was at that meeting and asked Brown, "Are you Jews really interested in saving these people?" Brown said he would make some inquiries when he returned to the United States and let White know. Tragically, as in 1850, it seems the answer again was "no."

In 1952, soon after the establishment of the People's Republic of China, government officials discussed who, exactly, the ethnic minorities were in China. They estimated that the Han Chinese comprised over 90 percent of the population, and identified about fifty-five registered minorities in China. The Chinese Jewish minority was asked to meet in Beijing with Mao Zedong, Zhou Enlai, and Deng Xiaoping, the leaders of China. Ai, a descendant of Ai Tien (the man who met with Father Ricci centuries earlier) met with the three leaders of China. When they asked him if his community spoke the language and observed the rituals of their ancestral religion, he responded "no." The government, therefore, decided that since they were completely assimilated within the greater Chinese population, there was no basis for Chinese Jews to be recognized as a distinct minority.

Ancestry is very important in Asia, including in China, and everyone carries an ID card with name and nationality. There are thousands of Chinese today with an ID card that lists *Youtai* (Jewish) as their nationality without really knowing why. Preserving one's lineage and loyalty to ancestry is significant, and carrying the ID card that says *Youtai* may be the only remaining way for Chinese Jews to do that. With the introduction of computers, however, even this link to the past may be lost. Since *Youtai* is not considered an official minority, sadly it cannot be entered as one's nationality in the computerized population database.

In 1981, there was an article in the journal *Shehui Kexue Zhan Xian* titled "Wo Xi Zhonguo Youtai Ren" (I Am a Jew), written by Jin Xiaojing, a prominent young sociology professor. In the article, she wrote that sometimes, when she gave her name at professional conferences, someone would tell her that there was another professor with that name, and that he was Jewish. She discovered that he was her uncle, and she found out about a second "academic uncle" while also attending a conference. Her relatives confirmed that she was a descendant of the Chinese Jews. Her daughter, Qu Yinan, who was a writer for a prominent newspaper, took this news very seriously. She came to the United States in 1984 and lived with Rabbi Joshua Stamfer in Portland, Oregon, where she studied Judaism and Hebrew. She also studied at the University of Judaism in Los Angeles, where she excelled in her English, Hebrew and Jewish studies. Qu Yinan eventually married a Jewish man and remains in the US.

Several years later, during one of the tours I led to China, a member of my tour group, Jamshid Zar, a Persian Jew from the city of Mashad in northeastern Iran, always sat next to me during meals. One Friday night, as we were just about to start our Sabbath dinner in the dining room of our hotel, I said to him, "I think your cousin just entered the room. He's over by the door, and you should talk to him and welcome him." Jamshid gave me a strange look and then gave me an even stranger look when he looked over to the door and saw a tall Chinese man. He asked me if the visitor spoke English, to which I replied, "Not a word." When Jamshid asked then in what language he should speak, I said Farsi. Jamshid returned from his conversation pale as a ghost, incredulous that an ethnic Chinese person would be familiar with ancient Farsi, a dialect that Jamshid himself spoke but which most Iranians today would not understand.

Once, during the late 1990s, I heard a knock on my hotel door in Beijing. As soon as I began opening the door, I heard "*Ani Yehudi Sini*" (I am a Chinese Jew) and immediately opened the door wider. It was Professor Zhao Xiangru, a friend to this day. Born and raised in Kaifeng, his family name is one of the popular Chinese Jewish family names, and he is widely published on the history of Chinese Jews and other minorities dispersed among China's large and diverse population.

Another time I was in Beijing with a group visiting the Forbidden City, formerly the Imperial Palace. Several members of our group were wearing black yarmulkes (skull caps). One of the Chinese guards looked at the black skull caps and, although he spoke no English, conveyed to us his surprise. I responded, "*Youtai*" (We are Jewish). He said that could not be, because some elders in his family also wear skull caps, but they are blue. He was correct that the Jews of Kaifeng wore blue hats, to distinguish themselves from the Muslims, who wore white skull caps. I tried to locate his family – the elders who wear blue hats – but the guard did not understand and did not respond to my phone calls or letters, so I never found them.

On a visit to Kaifeng, my tour group and I met Shi Lei, a young college graduate who had majored in English and spoke it perfectly. He asked me many questions about Jewish history, Jewish religion, Jewish culture, Israel and the Jews of the world. We stayed in touch, and during the Palestinian intifada (violent uprising) against Israel in 2001, I asked him if he would be willing to go to Israel for one year to experience the Jewish calendar of holidays and study basic Judaism in English at a university. He said "yes" immediately, as did his parents, so I facilitated his acceptance into Bar-Ilan University in Israel, and my tour group participants provided the funding. The student ended the year with an amazing B+ average and told me that there was so much more he wanted to learn that he wanted to attend a yeshiva in Israel. With the assistance of the organization Shavei Israel, we arranged for him to study in a yeshiva in Jerusalem for two years. He returned to China, settled in Kaifeng and created a school where he teaches English and basic Judaism. He also passed the examination that qualifies him to serve as a national and local guide for visitors to China and was the pioneer for future Chinese Jews to study in Israel.

Several Jewish Chinese girls from Kaifeng went to Israel to study and have remained there. Recently, seven young Jewish men from Kaifeng went to study in a yeshiva in Israel, and one was planning to become a rabbi. At the rabbinic conversion exam, which they all passed with flying colors, the last question was added for comic relief. Many Jews recite blessings before eating, with specific blessings for the different food groups, and the surprise question was, "What blessing is recited for a Chinese egg roll?" Silence swept across the room as tension grew. Finally, the Kaifeng rabbinic candidate asked, "What is an egg roll?" Contrary to common belief, egg rolls are not eaten in many Chinese communities – including those in Kaifeng. Once the ingredients of an egg roll were provided, they all answered the last question correctly.

In a small way, I also attempt to assist the community of Chinese Jews by assisting with their medical needs, by providing scholarships for students to attend universities and by helping the poor. In addition, I am honored to be on the board of directors of the Sino Judaic Institute, created in 1985 to exchange information on the historic Jewish communities of China, to promote the growth of Jewish and Israel studies in China and to assist Kaifeng Jewish descendants in reconnecting with their Jewish heritage. The Institute issues an excellent periodical that disseminates scholarly research on these subjects.

There is a small renaissance taking place in Kaifeng. In 2012, Beit Hatikvah (House of Hope), a Jewish school, opened. It was founded by an American

Jewish university student who was studying in Kaifeng. On a visit to the school, I heard everyone sing *Hatikvah*, the Jewish national anthem, in both Hebrew and Chinese. Sadly, however, in Kaifeng there is also a messianic Jew, a member of Jews for Jesus, who is attempting to convert the surviving Chinese Jews to Christianity. He is supported with substantial funds from a church in Hong Kong. The city of Kaifeng, on the other hand, built Riverside Park to attract tourists with a recreation of what life was like in Kaifeng one thousand years ago, and in this park, there are two magnificent pavilions dedicated to the Chinese Jews.

Pearl Buck's novel *Peony* ends with the demise of the Chinese Jews who become completely assimilated into Chinese society. I visit Kaifeng every year, however, and the Jewish community still dreams of rebuilding their synagogue. Loyalty to ancestors is a powerful concept in China, and with young Chinese Jews studying Judaism and Jewish history in Israel, and with the recent introduction of Jewish studies in China's leading universities, one has reason to feel optimistic that surviving Chinese Jews will return to Judaism.

Chapter Twelve
Emily Hahn: The Eccentric Writer with an Unusual Companion

Emily Hahn (1905–1997), known to many as "Mickey" throughout most of her life, was an amazing character, and character is the operative word here. Amidst her eccentricities, however, she was a genuine intellectual who wrote fifty-four books and more than two hundred articles under four different editors at the *New Yorker* magazine. Emily lived in Shanghai from 1935 to 1940 and in Hong Kong from 1940 through 1943, when she was repatriated to the United States. Much of her writing introduced China to foreigners, mostly readers in the United States. She was a character I wish I had known.

From the late 1960s through the 1970s, my congregation in Tokyo consisted primarily of Russian Jews, mostly from Siberia, who fled south of the border to Manchuria in northern China either before or after the Soviet Revolution. They had lived first in Harbin, Manchuria, which had a Jewish community of about twenty-three thousand, and then migrated to Shanghai, China, before finally settling in Tokyo, Japan, after World War II. Their remembrances, however, were mostly about their time in Shanghai. It was from my congregants that I frequently heard Emily Hahn's name, not only because they saw her out and about, but also because of her exceptional articles and books about China, especially Shanghai and Hong Kong. Americans, and even some Israelis, in my congregation were curious about life in China, especially Jewish life in Shanghai, but since we were not permitted to enter China at that time, we asked the Russian congregants to lead a discussion about Shanghai, and they happily did.

The president of the Jewish community of Tokyo, Walter Citrin, and his wife Judy, led the discussions to a standing room only audience in the library of the Jewish Community Center in Tokyo. Walter's father was the last leader of the Jewish community in Shanghai, and Walter had stayed behind in Shanghai, already under Communist rule, until the last disabled Jew was on a ship to Malben, a residential center for the disabled in Israel. Judy, who was born in Vladivostok, Russia, but later migrated to Shanghai, served in Tokyo as the female leader of the city's Jewish community and as president of the Japan-Israel Women's Welfare Organization (JIWWO), a philanthropic organization to assist disabled children in Japan and Israel.

Emily Hahn with her pet gibbon

The Citrins and my other congregants suggested that we use Emily Hahn's writings as our textbook. In truth, though, we seldom actually discussed Emily's books. Instead, inevitably the discussion turned to memories of China, Harbin, Shanghai and Emily, whom they all saw, met or knew before the war. And they read her articles, too, as she was a correspondent for the *North China Daily News*, the local newspaper. The Jews lived in the "French Concession," an area populated primarily by foreigners and somewhat isolated from mainstream Chinese culture. So it was through Emily's newspaper articles, a kind of bible to them, that the Jewish residents learned what was happening in China.

My congregants were familiar with all the gossip about Emily and knew about all her eccentricities. They knew that Emily had been the intimate girlfriend of Sir Victor Sassoon (see chapter 8), and the anticipated wedding of these two accomplished Jews was to be the wedding to end all weddings. Everyone talked about the beautiful Chevrolet he gave to Emily and knew that she posed nude for Sir Victor's photo album. The Jewish refugees used to see Emily, with or without Sir Victor, at the bar of the Cathay Hotel with her pet gibbon named Mr. Mills, a short ape, eighteen inches tall, with a round head, very long arms and no tail, who usually was dressed in a diaper and dinner jacket. They saw her at cocktail parties, in the chocolate shop and even on the street smoking cigars. Emily took Mr. Mills everywhere, no matter how exclusive the occasion, and if her pet was not invited to a dinner party or other

Cigar-smoking Emily Hahn, 1964

event, she refused the invitation. In Shanghai, and later in Hong Kong, Emily, who drank too much, was rescued frequently at drinking parties by Two-Gun Cohen (see chapter 1), who prevented her from gambling when she was intoxicated. Emily certainly had an eye for the curious and offbeat; wherever she was, there was "a happening."

Emily did not have a really strong Jewish identity and did not observe Jewish holidays. Although she was aware of and wrote about the travails of the thousands of Jewish refugees who flooded Shanghai, she did not play an active role in any relief effort. In 1959, however, she wrote *Aboab: First Rabbi of the Americas*, about the first rabbi of the Americas (in Brazil), a book that was compulsory reading at the Hebrew school of the Jewish Center in Tokyo.

Emily was born in St. Louis on January 14, 1905, to Jewish parents. Her father Isaac Newton Hahn was a dry goods salesman, and her mother was an independent thinker, just as Emily was. The fifth of six children, Emily as a child dreamed of being a famous lion tamer or an expert on ghosts, and she ran away from home briefly when she was ten. She and her family moved to Chicago when she was fifteen. When Emily was older, she was an early feminist and wanted to be a mining engineer, but because she was a woman she was denied registration for a chemistry class at the University of Wisconsin in Madison. Typically for Emily, she simply dug her heels in deeper after she was denied registration in the chemistry class and changed her major from English to engineering. While Emily's college adviser told her that women were incapable of grasping math and science and discouraged her from becoming a mining engineer, her lab partner told her that despite being a woman, "You ain't so dumb!" Thanks to her intelligence and perseverance, in 1926 Emily became the first woman to receive a degree in mining engineering.

Emily also studied mineralogy at Columbia and anthropology at Oxford, and she taught geology at Hunter College. Emily worked briefly for a mining company in Illinois before she and a girlfriend, dressed as men, drove across the continental United States in a Model T Ford. Her brother-in-law was so impressed with the letters she wrote from the road that he sent them to the *New Yorker*, and the magazine bought some of them in 1924. During the late 1920s Emily worked as a screenwriter in Hollywood, where she had a serious affair with Eddie Mayer, a married playwright and screenwriter, and she was devastated when they broke up. She also worked as a tour guide in New Mexico, and in 1930 she began working for the Red Cross in the Belgian Congo, where she lived with a pigmy tribe for a couple of years before walking alone across Central Africa. Headstrong, self-confidant and, yes, eccentric, Emily felt at home anywhere in the world.

Emily's first book was *Seductio ad Absurdum: The Principles and Practices of Seduction – A Beginner's Handbook* (1930), a light-hearted look at how men court women. In 1935 the *New Yorker* hired her as its China correspondent. She moved to Shanghai, where she lived among prostitutes while supporting herself by writing her articles, and her apartment became a salon of sorts for artists, poets and intellectuals who stopped by anytime for warm welcomes and friendly conversation, whether Emily was there or not. Among her friends were Mao Zedong and Zhou Enlai, two rising leaders of Communist China.

One night Emily accepted a ride home from a Chinese poet/publisher, Sinmay Zau. He was an aristocratic intellectual, sophisticated and witty, who lived in both the Chinese and Western cultural spheres. He drove a sports car and had studied at Cambridge in England, but he also wore his hair in a pigtail and dressed in a Chinese gown rather than in Western clothes. Although he was married and had five children, Emily became romantically involved with him, eventually becoming his concubine. In China, this form of relationship represented a legal arrangement accompanied by appropriate documents, but it still was shocking to foreigners, who thought that with this action Emily had crossed the line. Emily's attitude about China's legal polygamy was that at least there were no illegitimate children. Her relationship to Sinmay Zau allowed her to be considered Eurasian, the label given to white people married to Chinese people. Sir Victor finally told her she was "getting too damn Chinese."

On the one hand, Sinmay Zau gave Emily the credibility for the introduction she needed to write a biography of the three Soong sisters. Each of these three women married important members of Chinese society: one married Dr. Sun Yat-sen, the first president of the Republic of China; another married Generalissimo Chiang Kai-shek, the leader of the Kuomintang (Nationalist Party); and the third married H.H. Kung, a prime minister of China who also became famous as the nation's highly successful finance minister. Emily's friend, John Gunther, had suggested that she write about the Soong sisters, recommending that she focus her writing on personalities in China rather than on politics.

On the other hand, Sinmay Zau introduced Emily to the practice of smoking opium at a time when opium was illegal in China, and the penalty for being caught with opium was death. Emily wanted to become addicted but actually had to work hard for over a year to do so. She then realized that if she were to travel to Chongqing to interview the three Soong sisters for her biography of them, she would have to be drug free. She found a refugee Jewish doctor from Germany who hypnotized her and succeeded in ending her addiction very quickly. In the summer of 1940, Emily completed the first draft of the biography and gave it to Sir Victor who told her that he fell asleep while reading it. She then rewrote it, and *The Soong Sisters* (1941) became a best seller in America.

Mr. Pan (1942), another book Emily wrote, showed Americans what life in China, primarily in Shanghai, was really like for the Chinese. Since Mr. Pan was really her lover, Sinmay Zau, Americans could read her insider's look at Chinese intellectuals: what was in their journals, what they ate, what their family life was like, what their opinions of foreigners were and what they aspired to and dreamed. Sinmay Zau did not like the book because he thought he was portrayed as an idiot. More recently, in 2005 author Wang Pu wrote his book *Xiang Meili* (the name Sinmay Zau gave Emily). It tells the story of the loves and life Emily had in Shanghai.

In the early 1940s, while Emily was living in Hong Kong, she began having an affair with Major Charles R. Boxer, the British chief of military intelligence of Hong Kong, who was a heavy drinker and an unhappily married man. He also had served for two years with a Japanese army unit, a major coup for a chief of military intelligence, because he learned Japanese and could study the strategy behind Japanese military plans. He was fluent as well in Chinese, Dutch and Portuguese. A military man rather than an academic, he nevertheless later became the ranking expert on the Dutch and Portuguese in the Far East, and even taught at Yale despite his lack of university degrees. Emily told Boxer that she was not getting any younger, was not married but wanted to have a child, so he offered to help with the latter.

With Boxer, Emily became pregnant, a condition she did not hide. She gave birth to a daughter, Carola Militia Boxer, on October 17, 1941, several weeks prior to the attack on Pearl Harbor. It was rumored that Ernest Hemingway offered to accept responsibility for fathering the child, but Emily declined.

Sir Victor told her not to tell Carola (who now lives in New York City) that she was born out of wedlock, advice Emily ignored. While she did not marry Sir Victor as everyone expected, they remained good friends until he died. Is it any wonder that everyone talked about Emily's scandalous life or that she was the subject of so much gossip and storytelling among my congregants!

When the Japanese asked Emily why she had a child with Boxer, she reportedly answered, "Because I am a bad girl!" She also reportedly slapped the Japanese chief of intelligence across the face, and he returned to see her the day before she was repatriated on the *Gripsolm* in 1943 and slapped her back. Boxer, who had promised to make Emily a respectable woman and their daughter legitimate, became a prisoner of war and was reported to have been decapitated. That turned out not to be true and, after his divorce was finalized, he and Emily married on November 28, 1945. They settled in Dorset, England, had a second child, Amanda Boxer, who now lives in England, and Emily and Charles remained married for more than fifty years.

In 1950, Emily rented an apartment in New York City, where she continued writing for the *New Yorker*; she visited her husband and family in England periodically. I corresponded with Boxer for many years about the Dutch Jews and Portuguese Marranos in the Far East, and he was very helpful to me in my research. I never knew, however, that he was Emily Hahn's husband and I was both surprised when I finally learned this and very sad at the missed opportunity. Had I known, I certainly would have asked him about Emily, as well as about his days as a POW of the Japanese.

Emily Hahn's writing – saturated with anecdotes, vignettes and conversations – provides the readers with such colorful close-ups of people and places that they feel like they are there. She studied the Chinese language and the fears and thoughts of the Chinese people, and she was comfortable placing herself in the story, giving the reader a glimpse of her unconventional private life. Her writing is known for its charm, tolerance, compassion, determination, depictions of the unconventional and humor. In *China and Me* (1944), for example, Emily asked, "Why have the Chinese never learned how to make good chairs to sit in? They can boast all they like about their centuries of civilization, and [they] can tell me as much as they wish of Chinese paintings and bronzes, and I myself grow lyrical over their food, but how, how, how can they have gone all these thousands of years sitting on stiff, slippery, shallow, spindly chairs?" In *China: A to Z* (1946), Emily wrote charming poems for children about Chinese objects, such as a bowl of rice for the letter "b," a panda for the letter "p," and the Yangtze River for the letter "y." While there is no alphabet in the Chinese written language, Emily's poems are illustrated beautifully with Chinese scenes and the Chinese symbols that depict each object. When Westerners want to understand China, they read Pearl Buck and Emily Hahn. She was a rare talent and a funny, charming, independent and intelligent woman.

While some may be disappointed in Emily's lack of effort on behalf of the Jewish refugees in Shanghai, there is much to be said for her underground relief work in Hong Kong at the start of the war. Since she was considered Eurasian because she had been Sinmay Zau's concubine, she could walk the streets with impunity, while Caucasians were arrested and interned. Emily's clandestine activities certainly were helpful to the prisoners and the foreign community, and she gained access to the world of espionage by providing English lessons to Japanese individuals who sometimes gave her useful information.

On January 23, 1940, the Jewish historian/author Theodore White wrote a letter from Chongqing, China, to his mother in New York in which he said, "Mickey Hahn is here, too – a superb mad woman. Brilliant, beautiful, Jewish, extremely clever – smokes cigars, talks Chinese, writes like a saint, has every man in love with her, lives with a Chinese poet."

Roger Angell of the *New Yorker*, for which Emily wrote for sixty-eight years, said that Hahn "was, in truth, something rare; a woman deeply, almost domestically, at home in the world. Driven by curiosity and energy, she went there and did that, and then wrote about it without fuss." On February 18, 1997, at the age of ninety-two, after living a most colorful life, Emily died following complications from surgery after a fall. Upon hearing of her death, the *New Yorker* wrote that Emily Hahn is "considered a forgotten American literary treasure."

Emily's granddaughter and Carola's daughter, Alfia Vecchio Wallace, said it best in her eulogy: "Chances are your grandmother didn't smoke cigars and let you hold wild role-playing parties in her apartment. Chances are that she didn't teach you Swahili obscenities. Chances are that when she took you to the zoo she didn't start whooping passionately at the top of her lungs as you passed the gibbon cage. Sadly for you, your grandmother wasn't Emily Hahn."

Lucky for all of us that Emily was such a prolific writer and made the East so familiar to the West.

Chapter Thirteen

Sex Therapist, Poker Buddy, Doctors and other Jews in Mao's Circle

The margin of error in the Chinese census is larger than the entire world Jewish population. China now has a population of 1.3 billion people, and the total world Jewish population is very small in comparison. Jews, nevertheless, played a prominent role and made enormous contributions to modern China. What was China's attraction? Why did Jews align themselves with China when at times China was considered an enemy of the West?

For thousands of years Jews had suffered from the results of anti-Semitism, and the dream of the Russian Revolution in 1917 was to produce a society of intellectuals, change the world for the better, end the cruelty of the czar and prevent fascism. Communism was embraced by many as a great cause because it had the potential to emancipate humanity. It offered a messianic vision of making human life worth living, especially during the worldwide economic depression in the late 1920s when millions of people were struggling to survive. Communism presented a dream of what the future could be, and it attracted Jewish intellectuals and liberals who read Marx, Trotsky and Lenin. Marx and Trotsky were Jews, but Joseph Stalin, who became the leader of the Soviet Union (USSR), was among history's cruelest haters of Jews.

In the latter part of Stalin's life, during one of his infamous anti-Semitic tirades, he arrested the leading Jewish doctors in the USSR who, he claimed, were planning to poison government leaders; this became known as the "Doctors' Plot." Lavrentiy Beria, the feared and hated chief of security of the USSR's secret police (NKVD), requested that Colonel Nicolay Novik send an officer to China to arrest the Jewish doctor who was treating Mao Zedong.* No one knows for certain who this doctor was, but we do know that in 1949 Mao was in a hospital in Moscow, a fact that gave Stalin's accusation against Jewish doctors some credibility. Soon thereafter, Stalin died suddenly, and Soviet officials dropped the investigation of the alleged plot by Jewish doctors as there was no basis for it whatsoever.

Jewish doctors, in fact, played important roles in Mao's health care. When Mao turned sixty in 1953, for example, he feared that the end of his sexual activity was imminent, a thought that troubled him enormously, and there was no Viagra at that time. Mao was fond of young women and actually had a harem of concubines. He believed that his sexual desire and potency were indicators of the status of his health, and he believed in the centuries-old imperial view that one could become immortal by making love to one thousand young virgins. The more sex one had, he thought, the longer one's life would be. He had frequent injections of an extract of ground deer antlers, an aphrodisiac according to traditional Chinese medicine, but his impotence persisted. Since he was determined to live as a healthy and sexually active man until he was eighty, he expected his doctors, some of whom were Jewish, to help him with his sexual problem.

Mao heard that there was a woman whose name was Dr. Leshinskaya, a Jewish doctor in Romania who was a "sex therapist" of sorts, and Mao sought her help. There is a dearth of information about Dr. Leshinskaya, but it is said that she claimed to have a treatment which, when taken daily in small doses, lengthened life, renewed strength and endurance, and enhanced sexual potency. Her secret "H3 injection" was actually the anesthetic drug novocain. Mao agreed to the treatment on condition that his personal doctor, who was only thirty-five years old and had no sexual issues, would take the injection first. He took the injection without any adverse effect, so Mao agreed to take these injections – unfortunately without success – for three months, when, although he still feared becoming a eunuch, he decided to abandon the treatment.

Dr. Magdalena Robitscher-Hahn (1899–1977) was a female Jewish dentist who was born in Karlsbad, Bohemia in Austria-Hungary, to Jewish parents. Her father was an attorney and her grandfather was a farmer. She had a strong

---

* Chairman Mao Zedong (1893–1976) was a Communist revolutionary who founded the People's Republic of China in 1949 and served as chairman of the Central Committee of the Communist Party of China.

sense of social consciousness and empathy for the poor and downtrodden, as well as for soldiers. After completing the dental studies program in Munich, Germany, and qualifying as a dentist, she pursued advanced studies in dentistry in Leipzig and Freiberg. She finished her studies in 1922 and returned to Prague. With the frequent shifting of government authorities as borders changed, however, her dental license was not always recognized, so she was allowed to work only as a dental assistant. She married and had a son, but sadly lost her husband to tuberculosis and was forced to become sole provider for herself and her child. After earning a doctorate in dentistry at Charles University in Prague, she opened her own dental clinic, and all was going well until, soon thereafter, the Nazis arrived.

Knowing that this was a harbinger of serious trouble to come, she escaped through Holland, France, England and Cuba to Bolivia in South America. There were many Nazis within the government of Bolivia, however, and after one Nazi informer denounced her for being Jewish, she was limited to treating ethnic Indians on a private basis. Her son went to America to study medicine, and luckily, this impoverished, now fifty-year-old female Jewish dentist obtained a temporary position at the United Nations Relief and Rehabilitation Administration (UNRRA, 1943–1946).

UNRRA suggested that Dr. Robitscher-Hahn go to China to open a dental clinic, and she arrived in Shanghai in the spring of 1946. Initially, she worked as a dentist in several cities in China under Chiang Kai-shek's jurisdiction, where she witnessed horrendous conditions in the hospitals and corruption everywhere. Former Nazi and Japanese doctors who committed war crimes were there working in disguise. Finally, she arrived in Yan'an (located in north central China and the wartime stronghold of the Chinese Communists from the 1930s to 1949), and the contrast between Mao and Chiang Kai-shek was obvious; under Mao Dr. Robitscher-Hahn saw dedication to a cause, not corruption. Although life was very difficult and Dr. Robitscher-Hahn was living in a cave under very primitive conditions, she saw civilized behavior and human dignity that she had not seen in China before.

Suddenly Dr. Robitscher-Hahn was called upon to examine Mao's teeth. She was very concerned that the problem might be an impacted wisdom tooth that would require special instruments that she did not have, but she responded to the summons and, together with her translator, traveled a great distance to the farm that served as Mao's living quarters. They were greeted by Mao's wife and six-year-old daughter.

Mao asked about her dental facilities and hygienic standards, and he wondered if her students could carry on her treatment with him after she left. She assured Mao that they could. Mao adhered to the peasants' custom of cleaning teeth by rinsing their mouths with tea rather than using a toothbrush. After all, Mao reasoned, tigers do not brush their teeth, yet their teeth are sharp and clean. To Dr. Robitscher-Hahn's relief, Mao's problem was minor compared to wisdom teeth. He had receding and inflamed gums, as well as some cavities. In her memoir, Dr. Robitscher-Hahn describes treating Mao on ten occasions, filling his cavities and treating his gum disease. She also revealed that Mao always was very polite and interested in how China compared to Europe and what she thought about dental amalgams. Despite Mao's consistent courtesy, Dr. Robitscher-Hahn always felt that there was a barrier between them, so she preferred talking to another patient of hers, Zhou Enlai.*

Sadly, Dr. Robitscher-Hahn's son died suddenly and unexpectedly in 1975, and she died in 1977 in Germany, in an old age home run by the Jewish community in Frankfurt – alone, lonely, alienated and disillusioned.

Among the Jewish doctors in the People's Liberation Army (the PLA, founded in 1927, was the military arm of China's Communist Party until 1949 when it became China's national army) who fought against the Japanese were Dr. Hans Miller, Dr. Wilhelm Mainzer and Dr. Ianto Davidov Kaneti. Dr. Miller (1914–1994) was born in Germany and in 1939 he traveled to China, where he attained a high rank in the PLA. In 1949, he became vice president of the Beijing Medical School. Dr. Mainzer (1909–1984), migrated to Israel in 1949. Dr. Kaneti (1910–2004), a Bulgarian native, was among the few Bulgarian volunteers who helped the Republicans during Spain's Civil War in the 1930s. In the summer of 1938 he was wounded near the Ebro River during one of the battles that marked the beginning of the Fascists' victory under General Francisco Franco. After the Republicans' defeat, some of the wounded and most of the foreign volunteers returned home. Dr. Kaneti and a few friends crossed the mountains into France, where he was placed in an internment camp under horrible conditions. In 1939 Dr. Kaneti was freed by the Red Cross and granted asylum in China, where he met his future wife, Zhang Sunfen, a graduate of the prestigious Yenching University, and together they joined the PLA in the war against the Japanese.

---

* Zhou Enlai (1898–1976) was the first premier and foreign minister of the People's Republic of China and worked under Chairman Mao Zedong.

After the war, Dr. Kaneti and his wife returned to Sofia, Bulgaria, where his wife worked as a translator at the Chinese embassy and opened a Chinese school for the city's Chinese immigrant children. The Kanetis became well known in Sofia, and their home in Sofia on Oborishte Street was recognizable by almost everyone in the city. Dr. Kaneti, considered "the last Western volunteer who fought with Mao," died at the age of ninety-four.

Friedrich Albert Jerusalem, another physician in Mao's circle, was born in Prague in December 1903. The prosperous and liberal family soon moved to Vienna, where as a teenager Friederich witnessed the fall of the Austro-Hungarian monarchy, economic distress and political tensions after World War I. Friedrich's politics shifted to the left when, during his medical studies, he witnessed the right-wing terror in Austria. At some point he changed his name to Fritz Jensen. He joined the Austrian Communist Party in 1929, and in 1934 he was arrested by the Nazis in Austria and spent one horrible year in a concentration camp which, understandably, left a deep emotional scar. He served as a doctor in Spain where he joined the Republicans, and after their defeat by Generalissimo Franco in 1939, he moved to China, where he worked for the Red Cross of China as part of a medical team attempting to rid China of cholera. Since Dr. Jensen was close to the Soviets at the time, he also was the personal physician to Chiang Ching-kuo, the oldest son of Chiang Kai-shek, who was educated in the Soviet Union. Chiang Kai-shek (1887–1975), the leader of the Kuomintang (Nationalist Party)*, was a close ally of Sun Yat-sen, and he fought against the Communists. Dr. Jensen's dream was to change the world for the better, and in China he was disillusioned by the enormous corruption of the Kuomintang Party of Chiang Kai-shek, and he gravitated to Mao and the Communists.

In 1949, Dr. Jensen wrote a book about China in German called *China siegt* (China Triumphs), and during the 1950s he wrote many articles for European journals describing events in China and the Chinese people. In 1955 he was assigned to report on the Bandung Conference, the Asian-African conference in Indonesia. He was on a scheduled flight to Indonesia with Zhou Enlai, whom he had met years earlier, but at the last moment Zhou changed planes. The plane Dr. Jensen boarded was sabotaged with a bomb and went down at

---

* The Kuomintang Party, the Chinese Nationalist Party, was founded by Sun Yat-sen in 1911 and was dominant in China under Chiang Kai-shek from 1928 to 1949 when the Communists took power.

sea, leaving no survivors. Press reports stated that the bomb was placed by the Kuomintang to assassinate Zhou Enlai. A posthumous volume of Dr. Jensen's writings in German was published under the title *Opfer und Sieger* (Victims and Victors), and a tombstone in the Cemetery for Heroes of China in Beijing carries his name.

Another important Jew in Mao's circle, but not a physician, was Hans Shippe (1896–1941). He was born Mojze Gryzb but also used the names Heinz Moller, Heinz Gryzyb, Asiaticus and others. Born in Krakow, he later moved to Germany, where he studied philosophy, economics and journalism and changed his name to Hans Shippe. Beginning as early as the 1920s, Shippe was already involved with the revolution in China. To Shippe, socialism was modern wisdom. Aristocracy, the foundation of the old world, was a relic of the past, and socialism seemed to Shippe to be the answer to the world's problems. He organized political circles whose members studied Marx, Lenin and Engels.

In 1925, Shippe arrived in China to serve as a reporter for the *People's Tribune*, the voice of China's Kuomintang Party. In 1926, he wrote the book *From Canton to Shanghai* in German under the name Asiaticus. After he was expelled from the Communist Party of Germany for being too democratic, he continued writing articles on many subjects, including the economic problems of China, Dr. Sun Yat-sen, and the developments in China at the time. His articles appeared in the *New Yorker, China Today, Pacific Affairs, Voice of China, China Weekly Review, Amerasia, Izvestia* and other publications. He met and interviewed both Mao Zedong and Zhou Enlai and wrote an eighty-thousand-word manuscript that, sadly, never was found.

The first writer to report first-hand on the aggression and atrocities the Japanese committed against the Chinese, Shippe was critical of Japanese expansionist ambitions and of the international community for appeasing Japan and ignoring China. He wrote of the discipline, careful planning, spirit and dedication of the Chinese Communists and their intense campaigns against the heavily equipped Japanese invaders.

From 1934 to 1937, Shippe was active in the peace movement and spoke out passionately against war and fascism. He gave many lectures, trying to create a united front against fascism and the Nazis. During the Nazi era, the German ambassador to China fumed against Shippe's anti-fascist, anti-Japanese articles. Upon realizing the corruption and treason of the Kuomintang, Shippe joined Mao, serving as editor of international publicity and translating many of Mao's speeches and articles into German and English.

In China, Shippe lived the spartan, simple life of the Chinese. Wearing the typical thin cotton uniform and straw sandals even during the very cold winters, he slept on the ground, coped with terrible and insufficient food and marched with the PLA for thirty-six miles a day without food. He noticed that the soldiers would work in the peasants' fields as a gesture of goodwill and also paid for everything they took.

Shippe raised funds to provide medical supplies for China and its military, and in 1941 he acquired a medical ID card, and his wife Trude Rosenberg acquired a nurse ID card. With these pieces of identification, they planned to cross the Japanese military lines to reach the PLA. When the Chinese warned Shippe and begged him not to attempt to cross enemy lines, he insisted that he must be there in order to correct the information the world was receiving. He explained that it was important to publish in influential world magazines and newspapers what was really happening in remote areas of China. Indeed Shippe never went anywhere without his typewriter, and any available surface – whether a rock, grass or a log – served as his desk.

When Shippe reached his destination, he found himself in the middle of an intense battle between the ill-equipped PLA and five thousand well-armed Japanese troops. Shippe's bodyguards and interpreter were killed instantly, and then, while using their guns to continue their battle, Shippe was hit with six enemy bullets. He died facing fascism, becoming the first reporter and first foreign volunteer to fall in battle on Chinese soil. After his death, his wife returned to Shanghai. In 1942 a monument was erected by the PLA. It reads, "To the eternal memory of Comrade Hans Shippe, advocating international humanitarianism between Europe and Asia, sacrificing his life in Yinang, with a war of resistance against Japan."

A strong, tall, Jewish man with brown hair and blue eyes, Shippe greeted every Chinese person he met with "*Nihao* (hello), my name is Hans Shippe." He was dearly loved by the Chinese, who were impressed with his dedication and heroism, and Chinese journals described him as active, sharp, diligent, perceptive, inquisitive and totally committed to getting the truth. In this case, his seeking of the truth cost him his life. On October 1, 1979, the thirtieth anniversary of the victory of the Chinese Communists, Mme Sun Yat-sen stated, "Many foreign friends have fought shoulder to shoulder with us on our own soil, some laying down their lives. We shall never forget them." Hans Shippe was one of those people.

Sidney Shapiro (1915–) is another Jew in Mao's circle. Born in Brooklyn,

New York, Shapiro's roots were in Lithuania and the Ukraine. His grandparents, who had suffered through the czar's pogroms in the late nineteenth century, came to America, worked hard and put their son through college and law school, and he became a successful corporate attorney. Sidney Shapiro graduated from St. John's University Law School, which he attended at night, and worked briefly during the Depression in his father's law firm. His specialty was entertainment law, primarily helping young performers obtain royalties they had not received and the money they were owed by the hotels and clubs where they had performed.

During World War II Shapiro volunteered for the army, starting as an anti-aircraft gunner protecting New York from attack, and then volunteering for a coed language training program offered by the army at Cornell University. He preferred to study French, but there were too many students in that class, so he was assigned to the Chinese class. He had never thought of, or had any interest in, China, but he became fascinated by the language and chose to spend two years in Hawaii with the army studying Chinese before they transferred him to the Japanese language section to read the coded messages from Japan. He volunteered to continue his study of Chinese at the University of Hawaii, and after the war, under the GI Bill,* Shapiro moved forward with his Chinese studies at Columbia University and then at Yale, where he was given a Chinese name, Sha Boli (the *Sha* from Shapiro, the *Bo* meaning knowledge or extensive learning and the *li* meaning reasonable or intellect). While at Yale he also gave English lessons to a Chinese woman in exchange for an opportunity to practice his Chinese conversation with her.

At age thirty-one, Shapiro decided he no longer wanted to be an entertainment law attorney. Since there was no need for anyone with knowledge of Chinese in Brooklyn, and since he had no girlfriend or wife to object, in 1947 he headed off to China with $200 in his pocket, speaking broken Chinese. He planned to use his knowledge of both law and Chinese in China where there were few US or foreign attorneys. His Chinese friend at Yale recommended he make contact with a woman in Shanghai who also would exchange conversational Chinese practice for English lessons, and he eventually married his Chinese "tutor," a beautiful actress, correspondent, writer and editor, who was a kind, wise and hospitable woman. Her English name was Phoenix; her

---

* The Servicemen's Readjustment Act of 1944, known as the GI Bill, was a law that provided a range of benefits to World War II veterans, including tuition for education.

Chinese name was Fengzi. In 1947 Shapiro was an attorney working at one of only four US law firms in China.

"China is an easy place for Jews," Shapiro said. "The Chinese are similar to Jews with their family life, respect for elders, love of learning, decent behavior and devotion to parents." When Shapiro was going to marry Phoenix, he requested his mother's blessings. She answered, "If she is a nice girl, marry her." Shapiro's mother did spend six weeks with them in China, cooking all the Jewish delicacies he missed.

Phoenix, however, had been heavily involved in the Communist underground in the 1940s when she and Shapiro met, but he did not know that. During the Cultural Revolution (1966–1976), furthermore, she opposed Mao's wife (the leader of the powerful group known as "the gang of four"), who persecuted Phoenix and ordered that she be sent to a labor camp for five years. Shapiro does not know why he also was not arrested as a spy, although his movement was restricted. Phoenix could not return home, and their teenage daughter was sent to work in a paper mill, so Shapiro rarely, if ever, saw either of them during the Cultural Revolution. He, nevertheless, stayed in China throughout the Cultural Revolution, except for a brief visit to the United States.

In 1971, after President Nixon reestablished diplomatic relations with China, Shapiro became the first Chinese tourist to visit the United States. He thought, "If a Chinese scholar in the United States can visit China to see his mother, why can't an American in China visit his mother in New York?" He had become a Chinese citizen in 1963 and had a Chinese passport, but since the country had no diplomatic relations with America, he had to travel first to Montreal, Canada. If worse came to worst, he reasoned, his family could visit with him there.

In Ottawa, Shapiro went to the American embassy and requested a visa to the United States. His Chinese passport puzzled them, as he was the first Chinese citizen to apply for an American visa, but ultimately, after considerable bureaucratic red tape, he received the visa and returned to the United States for the first time in twenty-four years. There he noted the open prostitution, the drug scene, the miniskirts and the homeless people sleeping in the park, but he also felt nostalgic for the slapstick comedy of the Marx Brothers trio and for US science and technology. Of course, everyone wanted to meet and interview him, to which he responded that he was just a "particle in a centrifuge that created momentous change in Chinese history."

Shapiro's interest in the Chinese Jews of Kaifeng (see chapter 11) came about by accident and grew out of embarrassment. Everyone knew he was Jewish, but when he was asked about the Chinese Jews of Kaifeng, he knew absolutely nothing about them. In 1982 he started to study the subject and he found excellent research by Chinese scholars, research which remained unknown to Western scholars and others who could not read Chinese. So Shapiro translated this research into English and published it in an excellent volume, *Jews in Old China* (1984), which he revised later after visiting many of the cities where Jews had been residents one thousand years earlier.

Shapiro became a leading translator of Chinese literature into English, and he improved English translations of Chinese literature, both classical and modern, including Ming Dynasty masterpieces like the fourteenth-century classic *Water Margin*. He translated more than twenty volumes into English and also had an excellent reputation with the foreign language press as a translator of Chinese poetry. He wrote about some of the dramatic changes that took place in China over the fifty years prior to, and during, his residency there. His translation of *Outlaws of the Marsh* is one of the classics of Chinese literature. In his translation of *Deng Xiaoping and the Cultural Revolution*, Shapiro helps the reader to understand some of the reforms Deng sought as a reformist leader of the Communist Party during the post-Mao era.

Considered the preeminent translator of Chinese literature, Shapiro believes that the revolution in China provided the Chinese with a better life and a chance for peace and prosperity, but he longs for the good old days of the China of 1949, the days of liberation and egalitarianism, not those of corruption and graft. Shapiro, who still lives in China, wrote two autobiographies, *I Chose China* and *An American in China*. In 1983 he was appointed to the Chinese People's Political Consultative Conference, which evaluates the government on behalf of the people, but he was never admitted into the Chinese Communist Party.

In 1989, the same year as the Tiananmen Square protests (to which Shapiro thinks the government's reaction was excessive), he went to Israel. This was even before there were diplomatic relations between China and Israel, but Shapiro was able to travel as a special tourist, with the blessings of the Chinese government, to search for his roots as a Jew, as well as to speak about his book on Chinese Jews (*Jews in Old China*) and to arrange for its translation into Hebrew. Shapiro is fond of saying that he is an ethnic Jew, not a religious Jew, and he has difficulty intellectually with biblical epics. He has a strong emotional attachment to Jews and Judaism, nevertheless, which he expresses culturally, ethnically and ethically, and his Brooklyn accent and other Jewish mannerisms convey his Jewish roots.

I saw Shapiro in New York in the late 1980s, but I had met him and Phoenix at their home in Beijing in the early 1980s. He was friendly, witty, charming and refreshing, and Phoenix told me she was honored to have a rabbi in her home as their guest. Phoenix also said Shapiro was a good husband and was good to her people and to China.

Sidney Rittenberg (1921–) lived in China for thirty-five years, sixteen of which he spent in solitary confinement as a political prisoner, an idealistic young Marxist who suffered greatly through the Cultural Revolution. The only child of a prominent, prosperous southern Jewish attorney, Rittenberg was raised in Charleston, South Carolina, and had a gift for learning languages. In high school he was the best student in French and Latin, and at the University of North Carolina, he excelled in German.

His political beliefs were probably influenced by his maternal grandfather, a Russian Jewish revolutionary. While attending the University of North Carolina, where he also studied philosophy, Rittenberg joined the radical student movement, and at age eighteen, he joined the American Communist Party. He helped organize steelworkers and coal miners, lent his support to cotton mill workers and was arrested in Birmingham, Alabama, fighting for civil rights. He dropped out of college at nineteen, was drafted into the US Army in 1942, quit the Communist Party and was sent by the military to Stanford University to study Chinese. He arrived in China in September 1945, when World War II was over, and the Chinese Civil War had just started.

One of the turning points in his life came shortly after he arrived. An American soldier driving a truck while drunk accidentally killed a Chinese girl, an only child. Rittenberg made a plea to the US military on behalf of the poor, devastated family for adequate compensation, which was determined to be twenty-six dollars, six dollars of which the family gave to him. Rittenberg also was assigned to serve as an interpreter for the American military attorneys in Kunming, a city in southwest China on the Burma Road. He was so shocked by the poverty he saw that his belief in Marxism was reinforced. One of the people he met around this time was Mme Sun Yat-sen, who found a position for him at UNRRA after his discharge from the military.

In 1946–47, UNRRA was supplying food to millions of Chinese, and Rittenberg was dispatched as a relief observer. It was then that he met Zhou Enlai, who invited him to Yan'an to meet Mao Zedong. Rittenberg leaped

Mao Zedong (*left*) and Sidney Rittenberg

at the invitation, traveling for six weeks by foot, horse and mule to get there. Within minutes of arriving, he found himself in a crowded dance hall, where a band was playing a foxtrot, and Mao was gliding across the floor with his wife. When the dance ended, Rittenberg – then just twenty-five years old and exhausted from his five-hundred-mile trek – was introduced to Mao and began chatting with him as an equal. He was meeting the Mao he read about daily in the newspaper, the Mao whose words he had studied at Chinese language school at Stanford, and the Mao whose philosophical brilliance he already respected and admired. Rittenberg later wrote, "I could scarcely believe my good fortune," and he wrote also that Mao's attention was intense and flattering. Later that evening he danced with Mao's young wife, Jiang Qing, a frail, shy woman who seemed nothing like the virago she later became, when her foul-mouthed tirades as leader of the "gang of four" angered the Chinese during the Cultural Revolution.

The next day Mao took a jeep and drove Rittenberg to a labyrinth of caves where the Communist Party broadcast its version of the news to the world. Because he was the only bilingual person there at the time and also was sympathetic to their politics, Rittenberg immediately was asked to handle the English language portion of the broadcast. He soon was welcomed into Mao's inner circle, becoming the first American to join the Chinese Communist Party. He frequently played poker and gin rummy with Mao Zedong and Zhou Enlai, gave Mao's children piggyback rides and was given the name *Li Dunbai* (a famous Chinese poet's name that means "upright").

In early 1949, before the Communists had seized power in China, Rittenberg was arrested on false espionage charges. As a prisoner of the Chinese government, he was locked in solitary confinement and routinely interrogated, beaten, drugged and starved. He kept boredom, despair and madness at bay by studying the teachings of Mao and singing biblical hymns he had learned in Hebrew school at his synagogue in Charleston. On April 4, 1955, he was led out of his cell into a brightly lit room and permitted to sit on a chair. A party member informed him that he had been wrongly charged and imprisoned and that his second wife (Chinese) had divorced him and remarried. It was Stalin, Rittenberg learned, who had falsely accused him of being an American spy and ordered his arrest. After Stalin's death, the falsity of the charge was acknowledged and he was released. Surprisingly, Rittenberg bore no hatred toward his captors. In fact, his imprisonment strengthened his loyalty to the Communist Party. He refused to return to the United States, fearing that doing so would be considered an admission of guilt and that he would never be allowed to return to China, to the country and people he loved.

In 1955 Rittenberg began working at the broadcast administration, a top-level agency that manages China's national and international radio stations. Using the pseudonym "Lord Haw-Haw," he often broadcast Mao's propaganda in English on the Communist station Radio Peking. His language skills were in constant demand, and his high-level party membership afforded him access to vital information. Mao and other top party leaders regularly would seek him out as a source of inside information. For two years Rittenberg also worked with an elite team of scholars to translate Mao's writings into English.

At the broadcast administration, of which Rittenberg was named chief in 1967, Rittenberg met his current wife, Wang Yulin. Before their marriage he revealed his Jewish roots to his wife-to-be. He told her that while he was not a religiously observant Jew, he felt a strong affinity to what he had learned in Hebrew school about the Jewish people – their ancient culture and the many similarities they seemed to share with the Chinese in terms of family values, traditions, respect for parents and elders, education and delicious food. Rittenberg and his wife had four children.

When the Cultural Revolution started in China, Rittenberg was one of its most passionate supporters. He wanted to recapture the zeal of the early Chinese Communists and spoke everywhere about the importance of change. He was a well-known orator, and people sought his autograph. Ritttenberg was enthusiastic about the prospect of building a world without classes, without war and without poverty and believed those were the goals of the Cultural Revolution, but the Revolution turned out to be a disaster for China. It was also a time when many people informed on their family, friends, classmates and coworkers, and Rittenberg used his authority over the radio stations to inform on some of his fellow foreigners, putting them into serious trouble.

Indeed, when I once mentioned Rittenberg to Sidney Shapiro, he became very angry and could not find one nice word to say about him.

In 1967 Rittenberg became the victim of Mao's wife and her "gang of four" and was arrested. During this imprisonment he was kept in solitary confinement for nine years, eight months and one day. He later would learn that his wife also had been imprisoned for three years, during which time she was beaten, ridiculed and forced to wear a sign that read, "This is the unrepentant wife of a dog, an imperialist spy." His children, who most likely lived with relatives during this period, also were beaten, pummeled with rocks and humiliated by their classmates. Despite all the persecution, Rittenberg's wife and children waited for him with great love.

Upon his release from prison, he decided to return to the United States, which he did in 1980. A legend in his lifetime in China, a man who rose to a higher level in China's Communist Party than any other foreigner, Rittenberg today comes across as honest, funny and a great storyteller who can educate and entertain at the same time. There is a documentary about him called "The Revolutionary," and his book, *The Man Who Stayed Behind*, was published in 1993.

He is now a capitalist, living in Arizona with his wife, teaching at a university and heading Rittenberg Associates, his firm that promotes trade with China. Rittenberg's complete lack of anger or bitterness about the sixteen years he spent in prison gives him a measure of trust and easy entrée to Chinese leaders who have known him for decades. This status enables him to forge important business relationships for the benefit of the major US corporations who are his clients.

Under Mao, an estimated thirty-six million Chinese died during a famine between 1958 and 1962, and millions of others were casualties of the Cultural Revolution, but Rittenberg, who was the consummate propagandist, public relations man, translator and liaison with foreign journalists on Mao's behalf, still considers Mao a brilliant historic leader, albeit one who sometimes behaved in monstrous, criminal ways. As he grows older, however, he does concede having some regrets about participating in the victimization of innocent people and acknowledges having done so because life under Mao was very good for him. While admitting to acting out of self-interest, Rittenberg still finds rationalizations for all he did, insisting that his intentions were to be part of creating a better world. Rittenberg, it seems, has very little remorse about his life or activities during the thirty-five years he lived in China.

Yakob Rosenfeld has a very different story. In 1992, China established diplomatic relations with Israel, a move that was long overdue and most welcome.
When the new ambassador Lin Zhen arrived in Israel, protocol expected him
to present his documents to the Foreign Ministry to establish cultural, economic and diplomatic relations between the two countries. This is standard
operating procedure and is usually a simple, brief and friendly ceremony, but
the Chinese ambassador, upon presenting his papers to the East Asia desk of
the Israeli Foreign Ministry, said unexpectedly, "I have orders from our government to show my respect to Yakob Rosenfeld, and I would appreciate your
assistance." The ministry promised to help him locate Rosenfeld, and the meeting came to a close, ending with a toast to future cooperation between both
countries. After the ambassador left, everyone at the Israeli Foreign Ministry
asked who this Yakob Rosenfeld was and why he was of interest to the Chinese government.

There must be fifty thousand Yakob Rosenfelds living in Israel! It is, after
all, a common Jewish name. There is an organization in Tel Aviv, however, the
Society of Former Residents of China (Igud Yotsei Sin), which consists of
Russian and Sephardic Jews who lived in Harbin, Shanghai and other cities in
China, that could help find the right Yakob Rosenfeld. The organization was
founded by Teddy Kaufman, who was born in Harbin and served as its first
and only president until his death in July 2012. Someone from the Foreign
Ministry called Kaufman, who said Yakob Rosenfeld was not familiar to him,
but he offered to check with me.

At first, I did not take Kaufman's call seriously, but when he told me the
circumstances that led to the call, I told him that China actually had issued a
postage stamp for Yakob Rosenfeld, that there is a statue of him in China, that
there is a hospital named for him there, that he was a general in the PLA, and
that he was chief of medicine and also personal physician to Zhou Enlai. In
addition, Yakob Rosenfeld's picture appears on the cover of a book published
about foreigners who were helpful to China. In short, I said, Yakob Rosenfeld
is considered one of the great heroes of China. I went on to explain that he died
in Israel in 1952 and is buried in the Kiryat Shaul Cemetery in Tel Aviv. The
new Chinese ambassador was seeking to pay his respects to General/Doctor
Rosenfeld at the cemetery and wanted to know where it was located. To this
very day, when members of the Chinese government and visitors with any
connection to the Chinese government visit Israel, they bring flowers to the

cemetery and pay their respects to one of the heroes of the People's Republic of China, Yakob Rosenfeld.

Yakob Rosenfeld (1903–1952) was born in Lemberg/Lvov, Austria. His father Michael served as a military officer until the monarchy collapsed after World War I, and in 1918 the family moved to Vienna where his father owned a hat factory. Rosenfeld adored his mother, whom he admired for her generosity to the poor and her exceptional kindness. She later died in a Nazi concentration camp, and Rosenfeld always felt guilty that he could not save her. Rosenfeld excelled at school in all subjects and studied to become a doctor, graduating from medical school in Vienna in 1928. The faculty praised him for his humane qualities, surgical skills and organizational talents. Having received awards for excellence in the practice of urology and gynecology, he went on to hold a prestigious position in the urology department of a hospital in Vienna before entering private practice with his sister Sabine* who was both a general physician and a dentist.

Keenly aware of the growing Nazi threat, Rosenfeld was arrested for being a liberal intellectual and outspoken anti-fascist when German troops marched into Austria in 1938. He was sent to Dachau and Buchenwald where he was beaten mercilessly and brutally. He covertly treated patients, nevertheless, and his commitment was such that when a building collapsed in the Buchenwald concentration camp and people were trapped underneath, he screamed for everyone to take off their shirts for use as bandages and sought to rescue the victims – despite the Nazis' orders to continue working. When he finally was released in 1939, he was given fourteen days to leave the country. The only option Rosenfeld had was to travel to Shanghai, via ship, and it is believed that he received a visa from Dr. Ho Feng Shan, the Chinese consul in Vienna. Once in Shanghai, where he was appalled by the poverty and lack of acceptable health care, he practiced medicine, specializing in diseases of the liver, bladder and prostate. He spent his free time with friends and fellow Jewish refugees in the local chocolate shop discussing politics and events of the day. It was there that Rosenfeld met Hans Shippe and joined his group, eager to

* Sabine studied medicine under two handicaps: she was a woman and was Jewish. Although she was brilliant, professors deliberately gave her failing grades until Rosenfeld intervened on her behalf and she finally received her MD degree. Soon it became clear that Austrians would not seek care from a Jewish, female doctor, so Sabine studied dentistry, but since Austrians would not seek treatment from a female, Jewish dentist, either, she joined Rosenfelds practice and specialized in obstetrics and gynecology.

fight fascism and to study Marxism and the future benefits it would bring to the world. Rosenfeld became a zealous advocate of communism, losing all confidence in Chiang Kai-shek, whom he considered a terrible tyrant who should be removed from power.

Rosenfeld also met with and was interviewed by Dr. Shen Qizhen. Dr. Shen was an active member of the Communist underground, a doctor serving in Mao's army who, by masquerading as a successful businessman, was able to buy medications for the PLA. Rosenfeld's vow to take revenge on fascism for his suffering in the Buchenwald and Dachau concentration camps inspired him to join Mao's army, which was fighting Japanese aggression and also defending itself from the attacks of Chiang Kai-shek's nationalist army. Dr. Shen, who later would become the high-ranking Chinese minister of health, warned Rosenfeld of the hard life he would face if he enlisted, but Rosenfeld assured him that if he could survive life in the concentration camps he could survive life in Mao's army. So in November 1941, Rosenfeld, traveling incognito as a missionary – with a German cross on the inside of his jacket in case he was stopped by the Japanese – journeyed with Dr. Shen through the Japanese lines and reached Mao's army headquarters.

As a member of the army's medical staff, Rosenfeld established health clinics, instructed medical personnel on the fundamentals of proper hygiene and sanitation and treated soldiers and civilians who had malaria, typhus, dysentery, scabies, trachoma, malnutrition, anemia and recurring fevers. He even made his own surgical tools out of silver (they are now lost), because there was no stainless steel. Rosenfeld, one of about ten thousand doctors (mostly Chinese) serving a population of five hundred million, was impressed by the enthusiasm with which the peasants embraced his medical advice. To train more doctors, Rosenfeld helped build many medical schools and also recommended shortening their curriculum of study. He rose to become chief of medicine for the PLA, and with the rank of general in the military, was known to both the military and civilians for his dedicated service in all fields of medicine.

Rosenfeld was on the reviewing stand in Tiananmen Square in October 1949, when Mao proclaimed in front of hundreds of thousands of people the creation of the People's Republic of China. Shortly thereafter, Rosenfeld returned to Vienna to obtain medical treatment for a cardiac health issue, a long-term condition that had been exacerbated by his time in the concentration camps and his chain-smoking habit. Troubled by receiving treatment in a hospital where many of the doctors were former Nazis, he traveled to Switzerland but could not obtain appropriate care. He went to Israel, where his brother lived, settled there and practiced medicine in Assuta Hospital. In 1952, while working in the hospital, Rosenfeld suffered a massive heart attack and died.

Rosenfeld also wrote poetry; kept a diary – found decades after his death – which he dedicated to Mao, "the genius of the new China"; wrote a play that was never published or performed; gained membership into the Communist Party; and compared Mao's long march to Moses leading the Israelites across the desert.

Referred to as "*Herr* Dr. from Vienna," or Luo Shente, Yakob Rosenfeld was loved, honored, revered and respected for his work as both a physician and an educator. The Chinese also called him "the tiger balm doctor," a reference to the herbal ointment that many believed could heal every ailment. He worked hard and effectively and was an outstanding human being. An excellent doctor in every field of medicine, Rosenfeld genuinely cared about the Chinese, and they knew he loved them. Every individual he met and treated would have voted for him for any office, so complete was their trust in him.

A hospital in Graz, Austria, is named for Rosenfeld, and in 1992, in honor of what would have been his ninetieth birthday, the Rosenfeld Hospital was built in Shandong, China, with a large statue of him placed at the hospital's entrance. Rosenfeld Memorial Hall, also in Shandong, houses many of the photos, maps and records that document his enormous achievements in China. A photo exhibition about Rosenfeld was held at the Diaspora Museum in Tel Aviv, where it was viewed by 250,000 people. In 2003, another major photo exhibition about Rosenfeld was held in Beijing. To this day, one wall of the Military Museum in Beijing features a photo of Yakob Rosenfeld, the Jewish doctor who was a general (he was called General Luo Da Bizi, Chinese for "Big Nose") in the PLA for eight years.

My introduction to Israel Epstein (1915–2005) occurred in the mid-1960s. China and the United States had no diplomatic relations, and US citizens could not travel there. During a visit to Hong Kong, however, I read the news bulletins from Communist China posted in English on the pillars of the Bank of China building and saw they had been written by one "Israel Epstein." In the early 1980s, when diplomatic relations between America and China had resumed, I wrote to Israel Epstein and told him I was coming to China with my oldest son, Amiel, then thirteen years old, and would like to meet him. Eppy, as he was known to everyone, invited us to visit with him in his apartment at the Friendship Hotel. His entire living room wall was adorned with a larger-than-life painting of Mao Zedong.

Eppy became my dearest friend in China from our first meeting in 1983 until his death in 2005. I learned a great deal from him and looked forward to seeing him on my trips to China; in fact I spent more time with him than with anyone else in China. We usually spent the Sabbath together in Beijing, during which time I would speak to him in Yiddish, the language of his childhood, but he would respond in English. He often asked me to bring him American cigarettes when I came to Beijing; sometimes requested kosher corned beef, pastrami or salami; and always asked for cinnamon or chocolate *rugelach* (small pastries).

Eppy was born in Warsaw, Poland, in 1915. In 1919 his mother took him to Harbin, Manchuria, where they joined his father who arrived from Kobe, Japan, where he had been working for an insurance company. In 1920, they left for Tientsin, now Tianjin, the port of Beijing, where they lived until 1937. Eppy attended an English-language school (for foreigners) where he learned nothing about China and for the first time experienced anti-Semitism, which came from the heavily white Russian community and some Germans. As a teenager he wrote his first article; it was published in the *Jewish Daily Forward*, the Yiddish newspaper in New York. At sixteen, he became a reporter for the *Peking and Tientsin Times*, where he honed his journalism skills and even wrote editorials. In 1934, at age nineteen, he married his Jewish childhood sweetheart, and although the marriage ultimately failed, they remained very good friends. It seems she wanted to raise a family, and he wanted to see China, a problem of irreconcilable differences.

In 1937, Eppy's parents went to the United States, but he stayed in China, becoming a correspondent for United Press. He went on to work with Mme Sun Yat-sen on literary and social projects, the beginning of a forty-year professional relationship. In 1939, Eppy wrote his first book, *The People's War*, about the Sino-Japanese War. Eppy also was a writer for the *South China Morning Post*, the leading newspaper in Hong Kong. In 1940, Eppy was in Chongqing, the capital of China at the time, and there he married his second wife, Elisee Fairfax Cholmeley, a marriage that lasted until Elisee's death in 1984. Eppy was in Hong Kong on December 7, 1941 (or December 8, 1941, because of the International Dateline), and knew that he was on Japan's "wanted list." At the time he was in the hospital for some type of infection , and he avoided detection by growing a beard, using a false name and making sure that it was reported that he had died. He, nevertheless, was captured by the Japanese in 1942 and imprisoned in Stanley Prison, along with Two-Gun Cohen (see chapter 1), Emily Hahn's husband Charles Boxer (see chapter 12), and other foreigners.

In 1942, Eppy escaped from prison. He then wrote an article about it, hoping his story would inspire others to do the same, although he did not divulge the actual details of his escape so as not to alert the Japanese to one of the lapses in their prison security. In any case, his method of escape would not have helped some of the other prisoners. Eppy was short and thin so he was able to use the lightweight wood he found on the Stanley Prison beach (where prisoners were allowed) as a raft to simply float away. This wood, however, would never have supported the tall and husky Two-Gun Cohen.

In 1944, Eppy was in Yan'an. There he became a writer for *The New York Times*; met Mao Zedong, Zhou Enlai and US General Joe Stillwell, who was known as "Vinegar Joe"; joined the Communist movement; and became a follower of Mao. That year Eppy also traveled first to England and then to the United States, where he remained for several years. In 1951, during the nation's McCarthy era, when there was a witch hunt against American Communist sympathizers, Eppy returned to China.

After his arrival in China, Eppy edited the English-language magazine *China Reconstructs* for Mme Sun Yat-sen. He remained editor of the magazine until retiring at age seventy, becoming editor emeritus. Eppy also wrote *The Unfinished Revolution* (1947); *From Opium War to Liberation* (1980); and *Women in World History: The Life and Times of Soong Ching Ling*, about Mme Sun Yat-sen (1994), among others. He made four visits to Tibet, where he reported what he saw as anti-Tibet and pro-China activities, and he wrote about Tibet's slavery in his book *Tibet Transformed* (1983). Eppy became a citizen of China in 1957 and became a member of the Chinese Communist Party in 1964. He participated in the translation of four volumes of the writings of Mao and Deng Xiaoping (chairman of the Central Advisory Committee of the Communist Party from 1982 to 1987 and a powerful leader of the People's Republic of China from 1978 to 1992).

Eppy was imprisoned in 1968 during the Cultural Revolution. There was no trial, no conviction and no admission of guilt, but Eppy, nevertheless, was placed in solitary confinement until 1973. He later would receive an apology from Premier Zhou Enlai. In 1983, Eppy was elected to the Chinese People's Political Consultative Conference which, as noted earlier, reviews the opinions, attitudes and laws of the government on behalf of the people.

When asked about the activities of Communist China and about China's progress, Eppy, who called everyone *Tongzhi* (comrade), always conceded there were mistakes and bad judgment, but he insisted that while China's history was not a straight line, it was one which eventually straightened out and took China in a positive direction. He saw China as having been invaded and humiliated by foreign imperialists. Surprisingly, however, Eppy was silent about the 1989 Tiananmen Square uprising, and he was a loyal and faithful Communist to the end.

At a 1992 conference at Harvard on Jewish history in China, Eppy spoke about his life experience as a Jew in China. It was at that conference that he shared with me the secret detail of his escape from Stanley Prison! In 2004, Eppy attended a reunion of the former Russian Jewish community in China and government-assigned, prominent Chinese scholars of the Jewish community. The reunion took place in Harbin, and the Russian Jews, who all knew him as a good Communist, were impressed to see the sharp salute he received from the police as his government car brought him to the conference.

Over the years, Eppy always considered biblical epics as fairy tales, but as he and I discussed Judaism, studied the Torah and read books about the Jews, he came to realize that Jews were leading actors on the stage of history, producing a moral code that has sustained and ennobled civilization for more than four thousand years. He regretted not having had a Jewish religious education, and he became more appreciative of his Jewish roots and the Jewish people. The result was that he was not hostile, anti-Israel or anti-Zionist, as had been expected by the former Jewish residents of Harbin at that reunion.

Often when I led tour groups of Americans, Europeans and Israelis to China, we would spend the Sabbath in Beijing, and Eppy would be our Saturday afternoon speaker. One year he was in the hospital but insisted that I bring my group of tourists there to hear him speak. Eppy was so erudite, polite, fair, honest and likeable that although none of the tourists were Communists, there were no confrontations. Eppy did not proselytize. He just wanted us to understand China's struggles, achievements and future. He was candid about the errors in judgment he felt had been made along the way, both the Communists' mistakes – including an unnecessary famine that starved millions – and his own mistake, for which he felt guilty, of believing everything the Chinese government said. At each gathering, he signed and distributed his books at no charge and won the hearts of everyone.

Eppy's eightieth birthday in April 1995 was celebrated in the Great Hall of the People (which can accommodate ten thousand guests for dinner) with all

Israel Epstein (*left*) with Hu Jintao, president of China, April 17, 2005, on the occasion of Epstein's ninetieth birthday

leading government officials in attendance, including President Jiang Zemin and Premier Li Peng. The event was broadcast for two hours on national television. Just before his ninetieth birthday, China's President Hu Jintao personally visited him and saluted him for his many years of writing about the dramatic changes that took place in China, calling him an "outstanding intellectual soldier."

The last time I visited with Eppy, his mind was strong but his body was frail. He was in a wheelchair, and as his third wife, who was Chinese, wheeled him toward the elevator at the hotel where I was staying, he looked at me and said, "Moishe, next year when you visit, I will not be here." I told him to take good care of himself and to work on his memoirs. After all, he had spent most of his life in China, was the chronicler of modern Chinese history, personally had witnessed the Sino-Japanese War, had lived in China, where he became a citizen and a member of the Communist Party, had served as a member of the Chinese government and had edited the prestigious magazine *China Reconstructs* (now known as *China Today*). He said he was using all his energy and resources every day to work on his memoirs.

From inside the elevator, he asked me what the title of his memoirs should be. I was standing outside the elevator, but before the door closed, I said, "Reb Israel (my term of endearment for him in Yiddish), if you choose to align yourself with China, I do not know if China will remember you in one hundred or five hundred years, but if you align yourself with the Jewish people, you will

1948 1999

1930 1995

1909 1971

1904 1961

1900 1955

Evolution of the famous Shell Oil logo (Shell trademarks reproduced by permission of Shell Brands International AG)

Photo found inside a tomb in Xian, China: a Jewish traveler with a long nose, wearing a floppy hat

Photo of the model of the synagogue in Kaifeng; the model is on permanent display at the Diaspora Museum in Tel Aviv, Israel

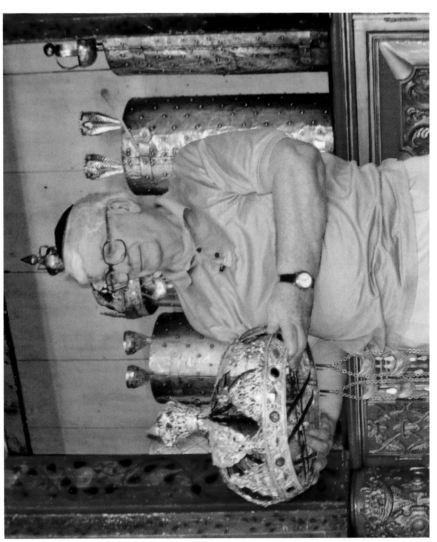

Rabbi Marvin Tokayer holding jewel-encrusted gold Torah crown, a gift from the local maharajah to the synagogue in Cochin, India

Musmeah Yeshua Synagogue in Rangoon, Burma

Silver Torah cases in Musmeah Yeshua Synagogue in Rangoon, Burma

Buddhist images found in Cave 45 at "The Caves of the Thousand Buddhas" (known also as the "Magao Grottoes") in Dunhuang, China; courtesy of Dunhuang Academy

Knesseth Eliyahu Synagogue, built in Bombay, India, by Alfred and Jacob Elias Sassoon, 1885

be permanently and forever part of Jewish history, because Jews never forget."
He smiled, waved goodbye and said he would consider what I had said.

Several months later I received a call from China informing me that Israel
Epstein had died. I asked if he had completed and published his memoirs and
learned that he indeed had finished the manuscript before his death but had
not lived to see it printed, and that it would be published later that week. The
title is *My China Eye: Memoirs of a Jew and a Journalist* (2005), but I will never
know for certain whether the title is a reflection of the conversation we had
and the advice I offered.

Eppy died at age ninety in Beijing Union Hospital on May 26, 2005. His
state funeral on June 3, 2005, was attended by more than one thousand people,
including China's president Hu Jintao and premier Wen Jiabao. His casket was
covered with white lilies and the flag of the People's Republic of China. He
was eulogized as a treasured comrade and friend and a virtuous person whose
death was a great loss to China, a country he loved, inhabited by people he
admired. The *name* "Epstein" may have been of no significance in China,* but
the *man*, Israel Epstein, was honored and respected by all.

---

* In fact, because the Chinese thought "Epstein" was a typical American name, the writers
of a popular Chinese film gave the name "Epstein" to the generic character of a downed
WWII American pilot.

Chapter Fourteen
Jewish Contributions to Classical Music in the Far East

The Japanese have been great admirers of classical music dating back to the Meiji Era (1868–1912), and Japan was the largest market for classical records in the 1930s. Many might say that the greatest Jewish impact on prewar and wartime Japan was in the field of music. In the 1920s, most of the classical musicians who visited Japan were Jewish, and in the 1920s, 1930s and early 1940s, many prominent Jewish musicians settled in Japan and taught at the prestigious music schools and in the colleges and universities. In fact, the first concert of the Tokyo Symphony Orchestra in 1923 was conducted by a Russian Jew named Jacques Gershowitz, and most of today's major musicians in Japan were students of Jewish musicians and Jewish professors who were refugees in Japan because of the Nazis and anti-Semitism.

Hans Alexander Straus (1901–1977) was among the German Jews who lived in Japan before the Nazi era. I met him in 1969, corresponded with him for many years after he retired to Locarno, Switzerland, and recently corresponded with his family. Straus was an employee of Columbia Records when it was purchased by the Japanese in 1935. One of the first letters received at the Japanese headquarters of Columbia Records after Hitler came to power was from Germany advising them that recordings of Jewish artists would "no longer be available." Straus told me and wrote in his memoir that Mr. Suginami, head of the foreign artists' department at Columbia Records, approached him and said, "Mr. Straus, as you know our government is very friendly with the new German government, and I imagine that measures similar to those taken in Germany may be taken by the Japanese government as well." Then, handing him the Columbia Records catalog, he continued, "Please mark in this catalog all the artists of Jewish ancestry, and if you are not sure who is Jewish, the German embassy will assist you."

Straus opened the artists section of the catalog and started with the violinists: Elman, Goldberg, Heifetz, Huberman, Kreisler, Menuhin, Szigheti, Zimbalist, and he marked them all. Suginami looked over his shoulders and answered with deep understanding, "Oh, I see. So-called Aryans – I think that's the word the Germans are now using – are not allowed to play the violin." The Japanese heard that so many violinists were Jews and assumed that Aryans were not permitted to play the violin, so every violinist on the list, Jewish name or not, was listed as being a Jew. Columbia Records continued representing Jewish musicians.

An unusual person was Manfred Gurlitt (1890–1972), who became very prominent in promoting and popularizing opera in Japan. He first denied being Jewish and joined the Nazi party in his native Germany, but, fearing arrest, he fled from Germany to Japan in 1939. There is now evidence of his Jewish ancestry. Hans Pringsheim, music and art critic for the *Japan Times* and the son of the famous conductor Klaus Pringsheim, who knew the Gurlitt family, told me in the 1970s what everyone, including the Nazis, knew: Manfred Gurlitt was Jewish.

As of this writing, Manfred Gurlitt's family has been in the news frequently. In the spring of 2012, but made public in late 2013, Bavarian authorities seized about fourteen hundred paintings, lithographs and drawings that had been hidden away in the Munich apartment of Cornelius Gurlitt, the partly Jewish, reclusive eighty-year-old son of Nazi art dealer Hildebrand Gurlitt. While Manfred Gurlitt consistently denied his Jewish ancestry, the news articles do mention the family's Jewish roots. As of early 2014, it had been determined that several hundred of the items legally belong to Cornelius Gurlitt, many items are not that valuable, and a few hundred of the artworks were created after 1945 and, therefore, were not looted by the Nazis. In addition, because of Germany's thirty year Statute of Limitations, Gurlitt can claim ownership of all of the works, but he has agreed to return art pieces to anyone who can produce proof of ownership. On May 6, 2014, Cornelius Gurlitt died in his Munich apartment of heart disease at the age of eighty one. He left no known heirs, and in his will he left all his art to the Kunstmuseum Bern in Switzerland.

As for Jewish musician in Japan, I received a phone call from Hans Pringsheim, with whom I maintained a cordial friendship. He directed me to a book produced by the NHK (Japan's government television and radio network),

Joseph Rosenstock, conductor/composer, 1895–1985; photo by G.D. Hackett

and I purchased it. It contains a history of NHK music concerts with the program name, date, soloist and conductor of every concert. In the book appears the names of the conductor Klaus Pringsheim (whose twin sister was married to Thomas Mann), Maxim Shapiro (accomplished pianist, soloist and teacher), his cousin Constantin Shapiro (a cellist and composer), pianist Leo Sirota (father of Beate Sirota Gordon; see chapter 4), soprano Margarette Netzke-Loewe, Willy Frey (a violinist), the best-known piano instructor Leonid Kreutzer (who was chief piano instructor at the Berlin Music University until the Nazis dismissed him in 1933), Joseph Rosenstock and so many other Jewish musicians.

Perhaps the most famous Jewish musician in prewar and wartime Japan was Joseph Rosenstock (1895–1985). Born in Krakow, Poland, he graduated with honors from the Academy of Music in Vienna, where at age twenty-one he accepted the position of conductor of the Vienna Philharmonic Choir. In 1933, the Nazis forced him to give up his position as director of the Mannheim Opera House. When all the Jewish musicians were dismissed by the Nazis, Rosenstock founded a Jewish cultural association in Berlin that gave employment to two hundred Jewish musicians and stagehands who put on operas, concerts and theatrical productions exclusively for Jewish audiences. At first, the Nazis had no objections since it was for Jews only and could not "pollute" the minds of Aryans, but eventually they shut it down.

In 1936 Rosenstock was appointed conductor of the Japan Symphony, later renamed the Nippon Philharmonic Orchestra, where he remained throughout World War II. Soon after Rosenstock arrived in Japan, however, he complained to the press that the cultural policies of the Nazis were lowering the level of German music. Rosenstock's statement caused the protests from the German embassy to escalate with a demand that Jews not be allowed to conduct, perform or teach music in Japan. The German embassy tried from the beginning to stop Rosenstock from conducting, offering the Japanese a "pure German conductor." Rosenstock told me and writes in his never-published memoir (I have a copy) that Japan's Foreign Ministry replied, "It is well known that the Japanese public attitude toward Jews is totally different from the German official position, and that there are groups in Japan who would sympathize with the Jewish refugees. Our government cannot do anything that might be interpreted as supporting racial discrimination or taking a position against the Jews." Jewish musicians performed and taught in Japan even when Japan was an ally of Nazi Germany, despite protests from the German embassy in Tokyo, which the Japanese – who loved their music – generally ignored. The orchestra, being independent, also steadfastly refused to replace Rosenstock with a German Aryan conductor.

In 1938, Hitler annexed Austria, and Rosenstock lost his citizenship and became stateless. When war broke out in Europe in 1939, the Germans increased their anti-Semitic propaganda in Japan and displayed terrible pictures and statistics about Jewish "ruthless" and "dangerous" activities around the world, using the image of a snake wrapped around a globe in their propaganda material which was posted everywhere.

When the Japanese attacked Pearl Harbor in December 1941, Rosenstock was rehearsing with the orchestra in Tokyo. American Ambassador Joseph Grew and his wife were scheduled to attend the concert, but the tickets had been sold by mistake to another party. Rosenstock telephoned the American embassy several times to make other arrangements for the ambassador and his wife to attend the concert. The Japanese, who monitored phone calls to the American embassy, assumed the conversations about concert tickets were code words for wartime information, and the story continued that Rosenstock was arrested for espionage during the rehearsal. There is truth to this story except for the ending: neither Rosenstock nor the ambassador was arrested.

Germany sent Gestapo Chief Colonel Joseph Meisinger, alias "The Butcher of Warsaw," to Tokyo with two lists containing the names of spies, nationals and foreigners, a total of two hundred people who should be arrested. Rosenstock was on one of those lists. The Japanese, however, were resentful of a foreign nation interfering with their internal policies, and, content with their own investigation – which turned up no evidence of illegal actions by those on the two lists – arrested no one.

During the course of the investigation, Rosenstock's students were questioned and reported back to Rosenstock, and Rosenstock told me when we met that, with the exception of one person, the Japanese musicians behaved very decently. A regulation was issued, nevertheless, forbidding all foreign artists from participating in any public activities, and police advised them to leave Tokyo.

February 1944 was the last time that Rosenstock would conduct the orchestra until after the war. He relocated to the town of Karuizawa, where the parents of one of his students offered him shelter, albeit in a shack with no heat, next to their country house. Life was very difficult with temperatures inside the shack falling below freezing and hunger always a threat. When the people who had fled to Karuizawa complained to the police about how cold their shacks were, the police advised them to cut down trees in the nearby hills and use them for firewood, but they had no tools to do so and no way to transport the trees even if they could cut them down. Fortunately, Rosenstock had his library, his piano and the camaraderie of other foreign embassy personnel, all of whom would exchange articles of clothing, or anything else they had, for rice or potatoes.

Nobody knew how long their clothes, the food or the war would last. In fact, it was less than one year later, on September 2, 1945, that the Japanese surrendered to the Allies, and the war was over. Even then, however, foreigners were warned to stay inside, behind locked doors, in case the Japanese went on a rampage against them, but very soon a jeep appeared with both a Protestant and a Jewish chaplain (Rabbi Morris Adler from Detroit; see chapter 5) and a member of the Red Cross, all wearing US Army uniforms. They brought soap, chocolates and razor blades, and they collected the addresses of family members who were abroad so that they could inform them of the survival of their relatives in Japan.

After Japan's surrender in 1945, Rosenstock was invited back to Tokyo to conduct the orchestra, but he refused to return until every "pro-Nazi Japanese scoundrel" in the music field was gone. One week later Rosenstock received a message that they all had been dispersed, so he returned to Tokyo. Following a meeting at General MacArthur's Occupation headquarters, Rosenstock decided to stay in Japan, resume his position and reorganize musical life in Tokyo. The first postwar concert, attended by Japanese residents of Tokyo as well as members of the Occupation, took place on October 24, 1945. For this inaugural performance, Rosenstock chose for his program "The New World Symphony," which had been forbidden during the war. Every Sunday he also conducted special concerts for Occupation members only. Yehudi Menuhin was the first foreign artist to perform in Japan after the war.

In 1946 Rosenstock submitted his resignation, which the Japanese refused to accept. He explained that after ten years of isolation, statelessness and separation from his family, he wanted to go to the United States. The Japanese understood but convinced him to sign an agreement that he would return to Japan after taking as long a leave of absence as he needed. During his residence in New York, Rosenstock conducted the Metropolitan Opera and served as manager of the New York City Opera. After five years, Rosenstock indeed did return to Japan, where he learned that the orchestra had been paying the rent on his apartment so that it would be there for him upon his return, and he was very moved by their generosity. Rosenstock continued to work in both New York and Japan until his death in New York in October 1985, at age ninety.

In 1956, on the occasion of the thirtieth anniversary of the NHK Symphony Orchestra of Japan, the program read: "Rosenstock may not be the literal father of this musical ensemble, but he has certainly become its closest mentor in his long association with the orchestra. Other conductors have come and gone mostly as 'visiting professors' and have added invigorating touches of diverse techniques and stimulating personalities. Yet Rosenstock alone has guided this orchestra from tenuous beginnings through wartime upheavals, and on to a level where it has become the standard-setting symphonic organization in Japan." Rosenstock received the Japanese Imperial Award, the Order of the Sacred Treasure, and to this day, he is considered the father of the best symphony orchestra in Japan.

When I met Rosenstock in Tokyo in the 1970s, he was exceptionally kind, forthcoming and cooperative. He told me that he was not an observant Jew, although in Europe he had a bar mitzvah, and he did not observe Jewish dietary laws, but as a courtesy to me he never ordered pork or other forbidden foods in my presence. Rather, he always had fish when we met for dinner at the Imperial Hotel in Tokyo. Rosenstock never offended my religiosity and always was proud of his Jewish roots.

Rosenstock knew I was collecting information about amazing Jews in the Far East, and he wanted me to write about what I learned and shared with me what he knew. He said that in time it would be shown that the greatest contribution of Jews in the Far East had been in the field of music. Since there were no books on this subject, he believed that the only "historians" would be the people with remembrances, and their knowledge eventually would be lost when they died.

Rosenstock was the first one to tell me about Aaron Avshalomov, the composer of the opera *The Great Wall*; about Herbert Zipper, the exceptional conductor (and survivor of Dachau) of the orchestra in Manila during the war; and about Klaus Pringsheim, the German Jewish adviser on music in Bangkok, Thailand, who had been expelled from Japan under intense Nazi pressure. Rosenstock, however, never would mention Manfred Gurlitt, who denied his Jewish ancestry.

I always have felt guilty about not writing in English about the Jewish musicians in the Far East (I had written about them in Japanese) and hope that my doing so now would not only please Joseph Rosenstock were he alive but also will ensure that these musicians will be remembered forever.

China also received its fair share of refugees. People in every profession, including fifteen orchestra conductors and other musicians, fled to Shanghai between 1933 and 1939. Some of the musicians would work at menial jobs during the day and in the evening they would play at dance halls and coffee shops that were owned by Jewish refugees. Other musicians were invited to teach at the Shanghai Conservatory or at universities, and among the musicians were ten who immediately became members of the Shanghai Municipal Orchestra, which later became the Shanghai Symphony Orchestra.

The most famous of these musicians were the violinist Alfred Wittenberg and the composer Wolfgang Fraenkel. Alfred Wittenberg (1880–1952) was born in Breslau, Germany, and educated in Berlin. At age twenty, he became first violinist at the local opera house, where he was noted for his beautiful tone. He was not only a brilliant violin teacher but he also was an accomplished pianist. He could play pieces from memory on the piano and the violin and could demonstrate the musical styles of different musicians on both instruments. In 1939 Wittenberg fled to Shanghai, where he taught violin and piano at the Conservatory of Music and at the university, while also giving private lessons. He was dearly loved by his students, and their families frequently offered him free room and board.

The warm relationship Wittenberg, a tall man, felt with his students was in sharp contrast to the fear and humiliation he felt when he was asked to play piano accompaniment for Ghoya Kanoh, a sadistic Japanese official who handled Jewish affairs in the Shanghai ghetto (see chapter 10). A short man, Ghoya called himself "King of the Jews," and he frequently stood on a chair yelling at, and sometimes slapping, the refugees who requested the permit they required to leave the ghetto to go to their jobs. Ghoya had a violin and mistakenly thought of himself as an accomplished musician, and he directed most of his hostility toward the taller refugees. Once, when he had a clash of musical opinion with Wittenberg while Wittenberg was accompanying him on the piano, he threatened, "You play as I direct or I kill you."

After the war, although Wittenberg was invited to teach in the United States, he preferred to remain in Shanghai to teach violin. He died in Shanghai, with a violin in his hand and a Bach solo sonata on his music stand. Later his violin was sent to Israel.

Wolfgang Fraenkel (1897–1983) was born in Berlin, Germany. By profession an attorney, his avocation was music. Some of the pieces he composed in Germany were not published because he was Jewish, but they later were expanded, revised and published in China. He was serving as a judge in Germany when he was arrested and interned in a concentration camp. Upon his release in 1939 he fled to Shanghai, where he joined the Shanghai Municipal Symphony and also taught composition, harmony and counterpoint at the National Conservatory of Music. Fraenkel could play not only the piano but also all of the string instruments. He played in the string section of the Shanghai Municipal Symphony, where he could switch from the violin to the viola or any other string instrument depending on where he was needed.

Fraenkel was a versatile musician known for both innovative composing and brilliant performing, and he also possessed a photographic memory. Once, when a violinist with the Shanghai Municipal Symphony wanted to play Mozart's Violin Concerto #3 in G Major but had only the piano score, he turned to Fraenkel for help. From memory, Fraenkel wrote the entire score for the whole orchestra, and that score was later confirmed to be note perfect. Fraenkel also was the first person to introduce Arnold Schonberg's treatise on harmony and the bar-less music system to China. Many of Fraenkel's students went on to become preeminent composers in China.

In 1970, Fraenkel settled in Los Angeles, and in 1990, his student Sang Tong, a prominent composer and director of the Shanghai Conservatory of Music, wrote an article in *The Journal of the Shanghai Conservatory of Music* titled "Remembering My Teacher Wolfgang Fraenkel," in which he described Fraenkel's superlative teaching.

The orchestra conductor at the Shanghai Municipal Symphony from 1932 to 1952 was Arrigo Foa (1900–1981), a Jew from Vercelli, Italy, who taught me the correct way to eat spaghetti when I met him in Hong Kong in 1969. He studied in Milan, graduated in 1918 and became concert master at the Shanghai Municipal Symphony in 1921. He had a sense of absolute pitch, rhythm and balance as well as excellent baton technique, and he was promoted first to vice conductor and then to conductor of the Symphony. In 1938, under Foa's direction the Chinese musicians first became regular members of the orchestra, and the Shanghai Municipal Symphony improved greatly during Foa's many years there.

In addition, Foa was one of the first professors at the National Conservatory of Music, one of the first schools of its kind in China. He was in charge of the violin section and was a very conscientious and demanding instructor for twenty years. It is no surprise that among his former students is one who became a violin teacher at the Juilliard School of Music in New York.

In 1952, Foa was dismissed from the Shanghai Municipal Symphony primarily because he was a foreigner. His dream that the Shanghai Municipal Symphony would be comprised entirely of Chinese musicians came true shortly thereafter. Foa left for Hong Kong, where he served as conductor of the Hong Kong Philharmonic Orchestra from 1952 to 1969. In 1952, Foa received the prestigious Star of Solidarity Award from the People's Republic of China, and in 1969, the Italian government honored him as a *cavalier merito della republica.* Foa is buried in the Jewish cemetery at Happy Valley in Hong Kong.

Otto Joachim (1910–2010), a composer, teacher and cellist, was born in Dusseldorf, Germany, to a Jewish family that included an opera singer. Initially, Joachim studied violin and viola in Cologne, Germany, and went to China in 1934. There he taught and performed with the Shanghai Municipal Symphony. He also organized a very popular and successful orchestra, comprised exclusively of Jewish musicians, that was dedicated to performing religious and secular Jewish music, and he also opened a music store where musicians could purchase the instruments and scores they needed. A ninety-year-old Chinese violinist recently recalled with gratitude that his complete sets of music by Mozart, Brahms and Schubert were made possible with Joachim's help. After the war, when China became a Communist country, Joachim immigrated to Canada, where he joined the Montreal Symphony as principal violinist, and taught at McGill University, where his major contribution was in composing.

Otto Joachim's brother, Walter (1912–2001), a cellist and teacher, also studied in Cologne, performed across Europe and Asia, and in 1940 arrived penniless in Shanghai. During the day, he worked at menial jobs, and in the evenings he played the cello in cafés and dance halls. One day Foa heard him play and, recognizing his talent, invited him to join the Shanghai Municipal Symphony and teach at the Conservatory of Music. Among Walter's students was Situ Zhiwen, the chairwoman of the China Cellist Association. Like Otto, Walter left for Canada when China fell to the Communists and in 1953 became first cellist of the Montreal Symphony Orchestra, where he remained until 1979. In 1987, he returned to Shanghai to attend the sixtieth anniversary of the Shanghai Conservatory.

Music flourished in China, and many guest artists traveled there to perform. In April 1935, Arthur Rubinstein arrived in Beijing to give a concert. He was faced with a piano that was not only out of tune but irreparably broken. Since there were many diplomats and other important people scheduled to attend the concert, canceling it would have created chaos. An American living in the Range Hotel heard the commotion and suggested contacting Elizabeth Lyon (known as Elsie), the daughter of Joseph Grew, the US ambassador to Japan. Elsie was living in China with her husband Cecil B. Lyon, the American consul in Beijing. The couple had a new Steinway grand piano, and she agreed to loan it. Elsie Lyon is the same woman whom Moe Berg (see chapter 3) claimed to be visiting when, instead, he gained access to the roof of St. Luke's Hospital in Japan, where she had recently given birth. Rubinstein waited anxiously, worried about the care needed to move a piano. Soon twenty men singing in rhythm entered the concert hall carrying the piano, with legs and pedals well attached, on ten huge bamboo poles. Their singing provided the rhythm they needed to walk in step without colliding, since they were unable to see each other. The piano was fine, Rubinstein was most appreciative, and the concert was very successful.

With the establishment of the People's Republic of China in October 1949, music continued to thrive. New conservatories, orchestras and choirs emerged, and these were headed by many of the musicians who had been trained so well in Shanghai by their Jewish instructors. Two world-famous Jewish violinists later helped introduce Chinese musicians to the world. In 1979, Isaac Stern visited the Shanghai Conservatory of Music, then known as the National Conservatory of Music, and was astonished at the number of prodigies. Stern's Oscar-winning documentary, *From Mozart to Mao*, caused a sensation in the Western world and highlighted the excellent quality of Chinese musicians.

Also in 1979, Yehudi Menuhin was invited to lecture and perform in China. During his visit, he invited a gifted youngster from the Shanghai Conservatory's

Aaron Avshalomov, composer/
conductor, 1894–1965; courtesy of
his grandsons David and Daniel
Avshalomov

primary school to study at no cost at his boarding school for musically talented children near London. The support, guidance and encouragement of these two prominent Jewish musicians, Isaac Stern and Yehudi Menuhin, played a vital role in fostering the careers of many young Chinese musicians.

Jewish musicians served as teachers and composed, conducted and played beautiful music, but Fritz Alex Kuttner and Aaron Avshalomov were directly involved with saving and adapting Chinese music. Fritz Alex Kuttner (1903–1991) felt more German than Jewish, but Hitler put an end to his career and he sailed for Shanghai in 1939. During his ten years there, Kuttner, who held a doctorate in economics, owned a music store called Philharmonica. He also served as music critic for the *Shanghai China Press* and was considered to be a critic who withheld praise.

I met Kuttner in New York during the 1980s. He impressed me as brilliant and profound and, admittedly, I later had difficulty understanding his complex work on what is known as the "Pythagorean Tone System." Kuttner's treatise on the subject, *The Archaeology of Music in Ancient China: 2000 Years of Acoustical Experimentation,* was published in 1990 when he was eighty-six years old.

There is a Chinese legend that in the year 2700 BCE, the emperor sent a trusted friend to the far western borders of China where he was to invent music and singing. This emissary cut a piece of bamboo and made a flute with it, and he also developed a way of singing, imitating the phoenix birds. Thousands of years later, Kuttner spent forty years studying the origin of Chinese music, Chinese instruments and Chinese tones. His search for the ancient instruments he saw depicted in ancient Chinese art ultimately led him to discover a bronze seven-stringed instrument with flat jade discs and a hole in the center, bronze bells, jade bells, tuning devices, bronze drums and cymbals. In his book, Kuttner explored ancient Chinese instruments and the different tones that are produced by materials like bronze and jade.

Aaron Avshalomov (1894–1965) was born in Nikolayevsk-on-Amur, Siberia, to a Jewish family. He developed a close relationship with the elderly Chinese man who was his childhood caregiver and grew up singing Beijing Opera arias and Chinese folk songs. Avshalomov enjoyed the Beijing Opera performances he attended with his caregiver. He was fascinated by the unique blending of acting, posture, facial expressions, singing, dancing and orchestral accompaniment into the organic whole he heard and saw. Avshalomov spent his early years in Siberia, Manchuria and Japan before his father sent him to Zurich to study medicine, but instead, he enrolled in the Conservatory of Music.

Avshalomov went to China in 1916 to collect folk music, and in 1925 he produced his first opera, a composition about the Chinese Buddhist Goddess of Mercy, which was inspired by Chinese folk songs. He resolved to devote his life to the advancement of Chinese national music and to the Peking Opera and, in fact, he personally rescued a vast musical treasure embedded in Chinese folklore that had been neglected by the Chinese themselves when they became more interested in Western music than in their own. In Avshalomov's symphony, *The Hutungs of Peking*, for example, which was first performed in Shanghai in 1933 and conducted in the United States under the baton of Leopold Stokowski in 1935, the listener can detect all the street sounds heard for centuries in the *hutungs* (alleys) of Peking (now Beijing). Avshalomov also wrote the orchestration for China's national anthem.

Avshalomov's masterpiece, however, was the opera *The Great Wall*, based on a tragic love story that took place about twenty-four hundred years ago. This work represents a synthesis of Chinese music and themes with the addition of Western composition techniques and presentation styles. The opera, which he composed in 1942, premiered in November 1945 with great success and went on to be performed more than thirty times. The premiere was attended by Mme Sun Yat-sen, Mme Chiang Kai-shek, generals and other dignitaries, and *The Great Wall* was universally applauded by the critics. "*The Great Wall* is a worthy experiment…and a definite step in the right direction for the future of Chinese music drama," one critic wrote. Another wrote, "[*The Great Wall*] is richly inspired, full of distinction…a milestone of modern Chinese music and civilization."

Yet, despite all his talent and success, Avshalomov never held a steady job or learned how to make a living. He never had any money, was always looking for funds and failed at three marriages. On July 24, 1954, he wrote to one of his sons, "There are only seven dollars in my pocket and the rent is unpaid. There is no one here I can turn to. Within two weeks I may get a job in the liquor shop at Port Jefferson, Long Island [in New York]. In the meantime I must have something to stay alive."

In August 1982, sixty Chinese artists, including two musicians who played leading roles in Avshalomov's major work, *The Great Wall*, and Avshalomov's son Jacob (who was also a conductor and a composer) were seated at tables at the French Club in Shanghai, linked by their memories of the man they called "Aufu" because "Avshalomov" was too difficult to pronounce. One by one, each of the sixty guests shared his memories, and each one demonstrated his immense respect for Avshalomov. They spoke of his devotion to Chinese music, his perseverance during rehearsals, his patience when teaching them, his ideals and his modesty. Some remembered seeing him wearing a Chinese gown at home, and one couple spoke of his borrowing money in order to buy them a beautiful wedding present. Avshalomov lived in China for nearly thirty years and in the United States for a total of twenty-four years over three visits. He died at Mount Sinai Hospital in New York, and *The New York Times* chronicled his life with a long and respectful obituary.

Strong bonds were forged between Chinese and Jewish musicians during the war. Despite having instruments of inferior quality and personal hardships, they gave concerts at the Lyceum Theatre (now the Shanghai Arts Theatre) and also at the Russian Jewish Club (now the Shanghai Conservatory of Music). When I visited that building in Shanghai, there was still a mezuzah (the ritual prayer scrolls attached to entranceways in Jewish homes, synagogues etc.) fastened to the doorpost, and the photographs of the Jewish board members were still hanging on the wall.

Another eastern location that was graced by Jewish refugees was the Philippines. Herbert Zipper (1904–1997) was born in Vienna to an upper-middle-class family living in a large home near St. Stephen's Cathedral. His family life was filled with good conversation, humor and cultural outings. Zipper demonstrated unusual musical talent at a very young age, and his parents secured a piano teacher for him when he was only five. He practiced happily for two hours each day from the age of ten and was educated by the likes of Richard Strauss and Maurice Ravel. While music became the center of his life, he was also a mountain climber and became a political activist.

Zipper felt he was "struck by lightning" when he saw Trudl Dubsky for the first time. She was was only four feet ten inches tall, blonde, independent, a professional dancer and fourteen years old, although she told Zipper, who was six feet one inch tall, that she was seventeen. She taught him how to dance; he sent her roses; and Dubsky, the daughter of a Jewish father and Catholic mother, became Zipper's lover soon thereafter. Zipper took a job as conductor of Hakoah, the Jewish Sports Association Orchestra, and also conducted for union musicians, academy musicians and orchestras of local workers in Vienna. When Dubsky was seventeen, she accepted a job teaching dance at the Bedford College for Women in London, and their marriage plans were put on hold. When Hitler became chancellor, Zipper,

Herbert Zipper, conductor/composer, 1904–1997

familiar with the ideas Hitler expressed in his speeches, returned to Vienna at the end of June 1933 and composed anti-fascist music filled with political implications for the underground.

Zipper's family remained optimistic and proud Viennese Jews until the German annexation of Austria (the Anschluss) in March 1938, when they were blindsided by the deep-rooted anti-Semitism in their city that emerged after Hitler marched into Austria. Viennese Jews were reviled, humiliated and arrested. Zipper had tried to convince his family to get out earlier, but he was voted down. Jews had contributed so much to Vienna, his family argued, how could Viennese Jews expect anything other than decent treatment? In 1421, Vienna decimated its Jewish community by carrying out a pogrom during which Jews were forcibly converted, expelled and executed. That was the first, but not the last, time Vienna destroyed its Jewish community, despite the fact that in 1849, Emperor Franz Josef granted full constitutional rights to the Jews.

Zipper frequently did not sleep at home and would telephone before returning to be sure it was safe. In May 1938, a plainclothesman came to the Zipper home and ordered Herbert and his brothers, Otto and Walter, to bring a typewriter and go with him. So many people were being arrested that the Nazis needed more typewriters to process all the extra paperwork. Otto was physically weak, and Herbert managed to convince the Nazi authorities to get

Otto to a hospital, an act which saved Otto's life since he could not have survived in any concentration camp. Herbert and Walter were taken to the train station where they were brutalized before being dispatched first to the Dachau Concentration Camp and then to Buchenwald. At both camps Herbert and Walter were tortured even more brutally, and Herbert felt the immense sadness of having precious moments of his life taken away forever.

Zipper realized the immense power of the arts when he and another prisoner began reciting poetry and a crowd of prisoners gathered around them. The arts, Zipper learned, were essential to the existence of life, and without art, the human soul withers and dies. Eventually Zipper created a secret orchestra which he conducted and for which he composed the music, and they gave clandestine concerts in an unused latrine. Two of Archduke Franz Ferdinand's sons were in Dachau at the time, and one told Zipper, "If I owe my sanity to anyone it is to you for this contribution to our lives." Zipper composed the music (lyrics by fellow prisoner Jura Soyfer) for a song titled "Dachau Lied," a song that found its way into other concentration camps, where it became known as the "Dachau Song." Zipper was transferred from Dachau to Buchenwald and felt that the absence of birds there was a harbinger of even worse conditions. The brutal torture Zipper endured is too painful to recount here, but, nevertheless, he again exhibited amazing altruistic behavior.

After Zipper was released from the concentration camps with a death threat hanging over his head – if he were caught in the area he would be killed – he was, understandably, a changed person, more committed to the power of music to help humans survive inhumane conditions. He went to Paris where he met an actor friend from Vienna who asked him if he could write an opera in six weeks. After what Zipper had survived in the camps – and the speed with which he clandestinely had composed music there – of course he could do that! Then, in May 1939, Zipper received a telegram from the Philippines. The Viennese conductor Alexander Lippay, founder of the Manila Symphony and director of the Academy of Music of Manila, had died, and Zipper was asked to become his replacement.

It was a welcome offer on many levels. Zipper could continue working as a musician and teaching music; he could travel to a new part of the world and make new memories; and, most important, he could be reunited with his beloved Trudl, who had traveled to Manila in 1937 to serve as director of a dance studio and to found the dance department at the University of the Philippines. In fact, she was one of the reasons Zipper had received the offer. Not only had she choreographed and danced to many of his musical compositions, so faculty and administration officials were familiar with his work, but also she did a little "lobbying" on his behalf.

Zipper left for the Philippines on May 27, 1939, taught himself English while in transit, and reached the Philippines on June 23. Upon arrival, he initially was overwhelmed by the heat, but he immediately was cheered on by a huge and warm welcoming committee that included Trudl. Since she had not divulged that she and Herbert were romantically involved, she hung back for a while, and when introduced, he simply kissed her hand. It was only after Herbert had placed a wreath on his predecessor's grave and had attended his official installation and the reception in his honor that the two lovers finally could be alone.

It wasn't long before Zipper learned that the orchestra he would be conducting was comprised of both experienced and inexperienced musicians, and much of his time was spent on teaching them, instruction he gave with patience, kindness, intelligence and humility. His musicians developed a love and loyalty for him which would pay amazing dividends down the line. Zipper also organized a chorus that grew to one hundred voices, and when President Manuel Quezon heard them sing "The Requiem," he said, "That's what I want played at my funeral."

On October 1, 1939, Trudl and Herbert were married after having remained in love during the twelve years they had been separated by war and work. The orchestra season ended in March 1940, but Zipper decided to extend the season by taking the orchestra, despite their fear and trepidation, to the northern mountain city of Baguio. When I served in the military, I visited this area frequently and understand why the orchestra members were frightened. It is the home of the Igorot tribe, a brown-skinned, medium-height ethnic group in the Philippines known for war-making and head-hunting. They bothered outsiders, however, only when they felt threatened and even punished their own tribesmen if they engaged in violence without provocation. Once, while the orchestra was playing, Zipper looked behind him and saw several hundred of these potentially dangerous mountain headhunters sitting there without their spears and shields. They just were sitting quietly and enjoying the music of a symphony orchestra for the first time. From then on, they came every day to hear the orchestra play, and when Zipper asked them why they came, they replied simply, "Because the music is beautiful." It is fair to say that for Herbert and Trudl, as horrible as 1938–1939 was, that's how wonderful 1940–1941 was. This dreamlike interlude was brought to an abrupt end, however, on

December 7, 1941, with the Japanese attack on Pearl Harbor, which was followed by the Japanese attack on Manila soon thereafter.

Once Pearl Harbor was attacked, Zipper knew that the Japanese invasion of Manila was imminent, so he closed the academy, disbanded the orchestra and hid the instruments in a distillery which had been emptied to prevent the Japanese from using the alcohol as fuel. Initially, Zipper would go to the distillery periodically to clean and care for the instruments, but after the Japanese invasion he was imprisoned for five months because the Japanese knew he was opposed to the Axis Powers, had met with MacArthur and sided with the Allies. When Zipper was asked for the location of the instruments, he gave his interrogators a false location, where he had planted empty crates marked "Property of the Manila Symphony." When he was informed that the crates were empty, he blamed Japanese soldiers for taking the instruments. Zipper was released because there was no evidence to keep him incarcerated, and the military authorities believed they had intimidated him enough.

In July 1942, a young man visited Zipper and asked if he would help organize an underground intelligence unit. He agreed and became part of a group of thirty-two mostly Chinese men who would meet in an old walled-in cemetery with huge trees and large gravestones. They had almost daily contact with MacArthur's headquarters in Australia. When MacArthur needed information about the Japanese warships in Manila Bay, Zipper started watching them from the top floor of an eight-story building, despite having been warned that there was an armed Japanese sentry on the roof day and night.

Zipper obtained a good pair of binoculars and a 1941 edition of "Jane's Fighting Ships." One morning in 1944 while in his lookout position, he heard footsteps approaching and turned to see a Japanese soldier approaching with a gun in his holster. The soldier stopped, gestured as if lighting a cigarette, and asked Zipper for matches, which he gave to him. Fortunately, that was all the soldier wanted, and Zipper's heartbeat returned to normal. On September 23, 1944, American planes started dropping bombs on Manila's harbor, destroying almost every ship that was anchored there. When Zipper saw that a cruiser was being loaded with ammunition and was ready to open fire on the city, he radioed the information to MacArthur's headquarters, and the next morning American planes sank that cruiser.

In addition to his espionage work, Zipper continued giving private music lessons in order to pay the rent and buy food, which was scarce in Manila, where starvation was prevalent during the war. Indeed, while before the war forty thousand inhabitants lived in just one area within the walls of Manila, after the war only 224 remained, because most had died of starvation. Through it all, Herbert managed to compose music; he even composed a full-length ballet called "Veritas" for his wife. Sadly, the score was destroyed during the bombing to liberate Manila, and the ballet never was performed.

The liberation of Manila began on February 3, 1945, but during the month-long battle, Manila was virtually leveled, and one hundred thousand of the seven hundred thousand residents died. The synagogue (Temple Emil) on Manila's Taft Avenue became a Japanese ammunition dump which was blown up, and only bare walls remained until GIs rebuilt it (see chapter 5). The devastation of Manila and its residents was enormous and unbelievable. One morning Zipper learned that a friend from Vienna was dying of tetanus in the hospital. Herbert obtained some anti-tetanus vaccine from a Spanish pharmacist and borrowed a stethoscope, while Trudl sewed a red cross on his white shirt. Zipper walked up the street past Japanese soldiers and went into the hospital, where he administered the vaccine to his friend who survived. A short time later, Zipper saw a young Chinese boy lying in the street with one bullet hole in his chest just below his heart and another hole where the bullet had exited through his back. Zipper and others rolled him in a small rug and kept him alive until they found a military ambulance and turned the boy over to the Red Cross.

In March 1945, just before the Japanese surrendered, Zipper wrote to General MacArthur asking for assistance in organizing the Manila Symphony Orchestra quickly to help boost morale. MacArthur sent a brigadier general to find out what Zipper needed, and Zipper brought the list to MacArthur's office the next morning. General MacArthur stuck his head out the door and said to Zipper, "Hi. I'm glad you're alive," and signed Herbert's list. Six days later all the musical supplies Zipper had requested arrived from San Francisco. After deciding that the concert would be held in the bombed-out cathedral, his next problem was to find as many members of the orchestra as still were alive in Manila and able to perform. By word of mouth, and then by bicycle and jeep, Zipper scurried around trying to put together his orchestra.

In a suburb of Manila, an old lady approached Zipper and asked if he was Herbert Zipper and, if so, was he looking for musicians. When he said "yes" to both questions, she pointed to an old tree and told him that there was a cellist in the tree. In a hollowed-out hole in the base of the tree Zipper saw a small figure reading. The tree-dweller looked up, recognized his maestro and reached down and pulled up his cello, his only other possession besides his book. He was thrilled with the idea of playing again but said he had no pants and, thus, could not perform in public. Zipper arranged for a US Army truck to deliver khaki pants and shirts to his musicians at several drop-off locations.

Many orchestra members, however, did not survive. The violin concert-master was one of many citizens who had been herded into a church and incin-erated by the Japanese. Others who had survived were not strong enough to play. The French horn player, who had almost starved to death, was too weak to blow his horn. Zipper immediately arranged for rice and canned food to be delivered to him and several others. As part of helping the orchestra, the US Army was not only happy to provide food, but also to conscript some American soldiers into the orchestra, along with an Australian lieutenant and some Filipino professional musicians. Rehearsals began on April 2, 1945, and when tickets went on sale, the line was ten blocks long, and twenty-four hun-dred tickets were sold. While they had stolen lumber, which they referred to as their "midnight requisitions," to build a platform for the orchestra, nobody could find chairs for the audience. The Chinese residents of the Chinatown area of Manila, however, provided two thousand chairs from their schools, all of which were closed.

The concert on May 9, 1945, became legendary. In front of military per-sonnel and Mrs. MacArthur, sitting in a destroyed city with no roof over their heads in what remained of a church lit by army searchlights, the orchestra played Beethoven's Eroica Symphony #3 and Dvorak's New World Symphony. Despite the sounds of war and death in the distance punctuating the beautiful music, this life-affirming concert became a harbinger of a new reality: instead of war, death and destruction there would be peace, life and creation. The day before, the war had ended in Europe.

American military personnel repeatedly requested more performances, and they rented an old, large movie theater in Chinatown where, for the next for-ty-five weeks, Zipper conducted rehearsals and often the orchestra performed seven times a week to full and appreciative audiences of soldiers and civilians.

After the war, Trudl and Herbert traveled to the United States where he was reunited with Otto, Walter and the rest of his family, none of whom he had seen since 1939. In the US, Herbert conducted the Brooklyn Symphony, to which he added eight women and four black musicians, and Trudl taught such students as Walter Matthau, Paul Newman and Tony Curtis in her drama workshop. Herbert also taught a course on the history of opera at the New School for Social Research in New York.

Unknown to many, Zipper's archives may be found in Santa Monica, California, in a private, progressive elementary and high school library. The blanket in which the young Chinese boy was wrapped is included. In 1951, when Zipper returned to the Philippines from the United States, that young boy, then a grown man, greeted him at the airport with a bouquet of flowers.

Zipper went on to found more than twelve community art schools, first in New York and then in Chicago, where Trudl and Herbert moved in 1953. He fought to provide the arts in schools attended by minorities, girls and underprivileged children. He played before forty thousand children in more than eighty-five schools every year. He also returned to the Philippines to conduct special concerts and accept awards, including the Philippines Presidential Medal, which he received on July 4, 1959. Zipper played in Taiwan, Korea, Hong Kong and Thailand and, beginning in 1981, went eight times to China, where he taught conductors, composers and musicians about Western music.

One legendary conversation between John D. Rockefeller III and Zipper took place at one of Zipper's concerts. When Zipper asserted that his success was the result of his fine teachers, Rockefeller retorted, "Don't forget, Zipper, this whole civilization of man has been built by very few people, and I'm talking to one of them."

Chapter Fifteen
The Only Place on Earth Where No One Knew When the Sabbath Was

When World War II began on September 1, 1939, first Nazi Germany and then the Soviet Union invaded and divided Poland, a country which thereafter ceased to exist for a time. Millions of Jews in Poland were trapped. Eighteen thousand, including many noteworthy Jews like Menachem Begin, legally and illegally crossed the border into Lithuania, which briefly gained its independence before being taken over by the Soviet Union. This short window provided the avenue of escape for thousands of Polish Jews in Lithuania, but only for the Jewish refugees; Jews who were citizens of Lithuania were considered citizens of the Soviet bloc, so they were not permitted to leave. Consequently, almost all of them were massacred by either the gentile Lithuanians or the Nazis. Even the Nazis were surprised by the sadistic cruelty the Lithuanians exhibited toward their own people. Fortunately, however, there were a few heroes who helped the Jewish refugees in Lithuania escape to the Far East during that brief window of opportunity.

One hero was Nathan Gutwirth (1916–1999), born in Antwerp, who lived with his family near The Hague in Holland. In 1936, he went to study in the Telshe Yeshiva in Telshe, Lithuania, a three-hour train ride from the Lithuanian city of Kovno. Once, while walking the streets of Kovno, he noticed on a storefront the name of the famous Dutch company Norelco Philips. Curious, he went inside and met the young manager, Jan Zwartendijk (1896–1976), a warm and friendly man who later became the Dutch consul in Kovno. At the time, there were only four Dutch citizens in all of Lithuania: a Dutch priest, Nathan Gutwirth, Jan Zwartendijk and Chaim Nussbaum (see chapter 5 for Nussbaum).

When war broke out in 1939, Gutwirth looked for a way to escape from Europe. He studied Zwartendijk's Dutch newspapers, and the two men discussed the situation in Holland. Germany conquered Holland in 1940, making it impossible for Gutwirth to return home. About the same time, Germany also conquered Denmark and Norway, blocking the escape route to the north via the Baltic Sea and Scandinavia.

Gutwirth had two options. As a Dutch citizen, the Dutch East Indies (now Indonesia) was available to him, as was the island of Curaçao, a Dutch possession in the southern Caribbean Sea off the coast of Venezuela. The Germans did not yet have control of either place. In Riga, Latvia, there was a Dutch embassy with responsibility for the region that included Lithuania. Gutwirth wrote a letter to the Dutch ambassador in Riga, L.P.J. De Decker, informing him that

Nathan Gutwirth, Dutch citizen who saved thousands of Jews during his stay in Lithuania at the beginning of World War II

he wanted to travel with his fiancée to Curaçao, since it was relatively close to the United States, where his fiancée had a sister. Gutwirth found out that to travel to Curaçao he would have to cross through the Soviet Union and Japan. There were no diplomatic relations between Holland and the Soviet Union but, upon asking Soviet authorities, Gutwirth learned that he would be permitted to travel through Russia to get to Curaçao, information that would prove to be valuable to the Jewish refugees.

Another hero was Zorach Warhaftig, an attorney from Poland and leader of the religious Zionist movement there, who would later sign the Israeli Declaration of Independence and serve as a longtime cabinet officer as the minister of religious affairs in Israel. He, his wife Naomi and their infant son Emanuel fled to Lithuania, where Zionists were considered criminals by the Soviets. A man of great fortitude and foresight, Warhaftig realized that all of the Jews in Lithuania were trapped. He explored Palestine as a safe destination, but that was blocked by the British. He tried to secure visas from thirty embassies and consulates in Lithuania, all without success. Not willing to give up, Warhaftig continued to seek a solution until, finally, he saw a ray of light for helping Jews to escape from Europe.

Since Gutwirth was a Dutch citizen, Warhaftig urged him to ask De Decker, the Dutch ambassador, for visas to Curaçao not only for himself and his fiancée, but also for his classmates, friends and other Jewish refugees. The ambassador responded that no visa was required for anyone, since entry into Curaçao was dependent solely on possession of a letter from the governor of Curaçao granting permission to enter. At Warhaftig's urging, Gutwirth requested official written confirmation that no visa was required, because without it they would not be permitted to pass through Russia and Japan on the way. De Decker wrote a letter to Gutwirth assuring him that he already had informed Jan Zwartendijk (whom Gutwirth had met earlier in the Norelco Philips store but who was now the Dutch consul in Kovno) that "entry of strangers into Surinam, Curaçao, and other Dutch possessions [in the Western Hemisphere] does not require a visa for entry," and that he deliberately had omitted the requirement of a letter from Curaçao's governor. De Decker's omission ended up saving thousands of lives.

One Saturday the NKVD (the Russian secret police) in Lithuania went to Warhaftig's home to arrest him. He was at synagogue, but they interrogated his wife Naomi before finally moving on. Fearing they would return, Naomi asked their gentile landlady, who also was questioned repeatedly about Warhaftig, to watch for her husband and to signal him to keep on walking and not enter the apartment. Warhaftig understood the signal and kept on walking. He then sent a message to Naomi telling her that he would take the train that night from Kovno to Vilna and that she and their infant son Emanuel should do the same; he would meet them on that train. A friend in Vilna hid them in his home overnight, and the following morning the three of them left on the train to Moscow, the next step in their long journey to Japan. During the trip through Lithuania, Moscow and Siberia, Warhaftig kept a low profile, correctly assuming that he and his family could make it safely to Japan before the NKVD

The Curacao visa with the Sugihara transit visa, August 1940 caught up with them. Like many Jews in Lithuania whom Warhaftig helped to escape before he left, he, Naomi and Emanuel also eventually arrived safely in Japan.

Gutwirth, who also made it safely to Japan, later praised Warhaftig for being the first person to realize the significance of the incomplete, phantom Curaçao visas. Warhaftig, who obtained visas for his family from Zwartendijk in Kovno, said he could not help but remember the Talmud's statement that "those engaged in pious deeds will meet no evil" (Babylonian Talmud, *Pesachim* 8a). Interestingly, years later Warhaftig met the former governor of Curaçao and asked him what would have happened if, indeed, the refugees had arrived in Curaçao, and he responded that he would not have permitted even one of them to leave the ship.

In Japan, Warhaftig tried to work with Nippon Yusen Kaisha (NYK), Japan's steamship company, to help more Jews escape to Japan. Warhaftig's goal was for every Jew to secure Japanese transit visas no matter where their final destination would be. He visited the NYK steamship company's offices in Yokohama to explore the viability of his new plan: since business was terrible for the steamship company in 1941, he proposed that he knew thousands of people who wanted to travel to the United States, Argentina, Palestine, Mexico and other countries, and he would arrange for them to travel exclusively on NYK's ships and pay in US dollars.

Unfortunately, Warhaftig's complicated strategy to get Jews out of Europe and into Japan where they could take ships elsewhere, with the payment being kept safely in an escrow account, was not taken seriously by Jewish organizations in America. Tragically, those organizations failed to deposit money into the escrow account, so Warhaftig's plan was realized only partially. From July 1940 through May 1941, Warhaftig helped more than three thousand Jewish refugees reach Japan rather than the tens of thousands more he could have saved if he had succeeded in obtaining the necessary finances.

To Warhaftig's great sadness, he could not help everyone who sent him telegrams pleading with him to save their lives; most of them perished later in the Holocaust. While Warhaftig's strategy did not materialize the way it should have, he succeeded in persuading Rabbi Eliezer Yehuda Finkel and his three hundred students of the Mir Yeshiva in Poland, the "Ivy League" of yeshivas comprised of students from almost every nation, to leave. As a result, the Mir was the only yeshiva to survive the Holocaust intact. In addition to the more than three thousand Jewish refugees whom Warhaftig helped escape to

Japan, he helped three thousand more Jews flee through Odessa-Istanbul and through Riga-Stockholm-Marseilles.

I knew Nathan Gutwirth, exchanged correspondence with him during the many years he lived and worked in the diamond business in Antwerp and later met with him on his visits to New York. I also met his family, including his son Pinchas, whom I met in Japan and introduced to all the people and places associated with the story of the escape of Jews from Nazi-controlled Europe. Gutwirth wondered his whole life why De Decker agreed to omit that requirement about the letter from Curaçao's governor and concluded that he was simply a "good man." He was an unsung hero of this great escape. De Decker died in 1948, leaving behind no family and no comment on why he had saved so many Jews by providing the successful text for their spurious visas. Gutwirth and I planted trees in Israel in his memory.

As for Jan Zwartendijk (who was known as "Mr. Philips Radio" and the "Angel of Curaçao"), in 1976 I sent him a letter from Tokyo with a list of the ages, genders and professions of the Jews who reached Japan from Lithuania; my letter arrived on the day he was buried. In 1996, the school named for Zwartendijk in Boys Town-Jerusalem organized a tribute to him in both Jerusalem and New York, and the school established an "institute for humanitarian ethics and values" in his memory. In October 1997, Yad Vashem bestowed the title "Righteous among the Nations" upon Zwartendijk, and in 2012 the Republic of Lithuania awarded him the life-saving cross. Records indicate that he issued 2,345 ersatz Curaçao visas in less than one month, helping to save the lives of thousands of Jews.

From Lithuania to Curaçao, one had to travel to Moscow, take the Trans-Siberian Railroad to Vladivostok, board a small, uncomfortable cargo ship to Japan, and then cross the Pacific Ocean and pass through the Panama Canal to Curaçao. The trip from Moscow to Vladivostok on the Trans-Siberian Railroad was more than fifty-seven hundred miles and took up to ten days. As noted, one also needed a visa from the Soviet authorities to enter and exit Russia and a transit visa from Japan to travel through that country. The knowledge of Stalin's terrible treatment of the Jews caused many Jews, including major religious leaders, to fear that if the Soviets granted an exit visa, their motive must be sinister and the Jews would be trapped and exiled to the death camps in Siberia.

There were two options: the Jews could sit and do nothing or they could stand up, be proactive and leave for Curaçao. Some decided not to leave. Some religious Jews turned to Providence for guidance, employing a system used only in times of great tension and danger to obtain divine answers to serious, life-and-death questions. These Jews prayed silently and fervently, and then a saintly person conducted a "lottery" by opening a Hebrew Bible to any page. The text on that page became evidence of a divine response. When some Jews were deciding whether to risk taking exit visas from the Soviets, the Bible opened to a page in the Book of Exodus 19:4, which said, "I have borne you on the wings of eagles and brought you to me." That divine answer was interpreted to mean that it was time to request the exit visas from the Soviets, despite the risks, and leave.

Still another hero was Rabbi Shimon Shalom Kalish from Amshinov, Poland. This pious man, known as the Amshinover Rebbe, arrived in Vilna, Lithuania, with thousands of other refugees. His father, Menachem, had been the Hasidic rebbe (pious Jewish spiritual leader) of Amshinov, and when he died in 1918, his son, then thirty-three years old, assumed his father's responsibilities and became the new Amshinover Rebbe. Whenever he and the other refugees came to a crossroads during their escape to Lithuania and were uncertain which way to proceed, the Amshinover Rebbe would get out of the wagon, stand in blind devotion and then point in a particular direction. His sense of direction, fortunately, was excellent. The others revered him, trusted him and believed that his choice of direction was Providence. Upon their arrival in Vilna, he became an influential leader who served as a father to the many orphans there and also helped every Jew he met as often and in as many ways as he could.

When the question of visas to Curaçao was raised, the Amshinover Rebbe declared simply and unequivocally that everyone should acquire a visa and travel that route. He urged everyone to prepare the necessary documents, passports and visas for Curaçao and Japan and to obtain exit papers from the Soviet Union. With great trepidation, thousands of refugees approached the Soviet officials, who added to their fear by taking their pictures as they arrived, interrogating them, making them fill out many forms and forcing them to return several times, standing in long lines each time. The Amshinover Rebbe promised that everyone who did as he recommended would be fine, and the many Jews who left with these life-saving documents did so thanks to the Amshinover Rebbe's adamancy on the matter. The Amshinover Rebbe was among the very last to leave and, like Moses in the desert, he was responsible for saving the lives of thousands of Jews.

Unexpectedly, in 1940 the Japanese opened a consulate in the Lithuanian city of Kovno, and Chiune (Senpo) Sugihara, perhaps the best-known hero to help Jews escape from Europe to Japan, became the Japanese consul in Kovno. I met Sugihara around 1975 in Tokyo, and I wish now that I had been older and wiser when we met; I would have asked more and wiser questions. I asked Sugihara if there were any Japanese in Lithuania in 1940, and he said "no." I asked him if there was any trade between Japan and Lithuania, and he said "no," and I asked him if there were any cultural relations with Lithuania and he said "no" again.

I asked him why he was assigned to Lithuania, and he told me that he was a spy. He explained that while Japan was a close ally of Nazi Germany, Japanese embassy officials in Berlin were not permitted full access to travel, but the Japanese government wanted to know the Germans' military intentions and troop movements. Since Sugihara and the other consuls could travel around their host countries with impunity and could take note of military activity and troop movements, the Japanese opened many consulates throughout Eastern Europe and made it clear to the consuls that they were to report to the authorities in Tokyo what they observed. Sugihara frequently went to border areas to monitor activities, camouflaging his visits as family picnics.

Sugihara also had the opportunity to meet the Jewish refugees in Lithuania and learned of the horrors taking place in Poland. On the morning of August 1, 1940, he heard unusual noises outside his home. Looking out his window, he saw a crowd of refugees standing outside his fence, crying as they begged for transit visas so they could reach other continents via Japan. For ten days he sent telegrams to Tokyo asking for guidance about issuing transit visas for the refugees, but he did not receive an answer. Finally, on August 11, Sugihara decided to distribute legitimate, ten-day transit visas to the waiting refugees, whether they had all the necessary documents or not. He continued doing so even after the Ministry of Foreign Affairs in Tokyo ordered him to stop because of the great turmoil that resulted when large numbers of refugees arrived both in the Siberian city of Vladivostok (the last stop on the Trans-Siberian train before boarding a boat to cross the Japan Sea) and in Tsuruga (the Japanese arrival port). After Warhaftig convinced Rabbi Finkel of the Mir Yeshiva in Poland to leave, it was Sugihara who provided everyone in the Mir Yeshiva with transit visas to Japan. Sugihara was expelled by the Soviets but requested a brief extension claiming illness and fatigue, and he continued writing transit visas and throwing them out the window to refugees even as his train departed from Lithuania on August 31, 1940.

When I asked Sugihara why he had written those visas when so few people lifted a finger to help the innocent trapped Jews who were trying to escape, he replied, "Everyone in life has an opportunity to do a good deed. Do it and leave it alone. Don't write about it or publicize it; don't make money from it. Just do what's right because it's right."

Sugihara told me that he had never heard from any of the refugees to whom he had issued visas, nor had he realized that his actions provided the teachers and rabbis for an entire generation of Jews in the United States. The Japanese visas provided by Chiune (Senpo) Sugihara were responsible for saving the lives of thousands of Jews, but Sugihara did not know that, and Sugihara's son Hiroki told me that when his father learned from me how successful his efforts had been, he stated, "This is the happiest day of my life." Today there are almost one hundred thousand Jews who are descendants of those who were saved by the Sugihara visas.

Yad Vashem (the Holocaust Martyrs' and Heroes' Remembrance Authority) reviewed a petition for Sugihara to be honored as a righteous gentile but denied the request because Sugihara's life was not at risk, one of the requirements for receiving the honor. Upset by this rejection, I played a minor role in having Yad Vashem's original decision amended, and in 1985 Sugihara received full recognition as a "Righteous among the Nations." Sugihara also was honored on a postage stamp in Israel, on a postage stamp in Japan and in a high school textbook in Japan that recounts his story, and I personally named him an honorary member of the Jewish community of Japan.

Surprisingly, during that brief window for Jews to escape from Europe, the Soviets for the first time also issued thousands of exit visas, but why they granted these visas is uncertain. Some academics hypothesize that the Soviets suspected they could not make good Communists out of these Jewish refugees and feared the refugees would be only a headache for them. Some speculate that the Soviets wanted foreign currency, especially the US dollar. Others think that the Soviets wanted to take credit for acting in a humanitarian manner. Some believe that the Soviets wished to recruit a few refugees as intelligence agents and also hoped to slip several of their own agents in with the thousands of refugees leaving the country. These are all theories; there are no definitive answers.

The payment for the railroad trip to Vladivostok to board a ship to Japan was originally $20, but the price suddenly rose to $170, to be paid in only US dollars. Rabbi Kalmanovitz, president of the Mir Yeshiva in Poland, was in New York

Refugees arriving in Kobe, Japan

raising money for the Mir Yeshiva when he received a cable urgently requesting help in raising funds for these train tickets for the hundreds of Mir Yeshiva faculty and students. On a Friday in the spring of 1941, he and a driver canvassed the garment district, the jewelry district, Wall Street (in vain) and the Crown Heights area of Brooklyn (a borough of New York City) to raise money, and he did not stop even when the Sabbath began at sundown.

Once the refugees made it onto the ship to Japan, they were still frightened because there were Soviet officials on board. When a ship left the port, local Soviet pilots who knew the location of mines and other dangers escorted the ship through local waters, but once the ship was in international waters, the Soviets disembarked, and the refugees sang and danced for joy. They were out of Europe, free from the Nazis and the Soviets and on their way to freedom. The trip from the Siberian waters in Vladivostok to Tsuruga, the Japanese port on the Japan Sea, took three days and two nights under normal weather conditions. About 90 percent of the Jews who traveled from Vladivostok to Tsuruga sailed on the *Amakusa Maru*, a ship built by the Germans in 1902 for the Russians who renamed it *Amur* and used it as a cruise ship. It was seized by the Japanese around 1904 during Japan's war with Russia, and in 1944, the ship was sunk by an American submarine. How ironic it was, though, that between 1940 and 1941 thousands of Jews sailed to safety on a ship built by the Germans for the Russians, both of whom wanted anything but to save Jews.

Once the refugees arrived in Japan, whether they had legitimate, incomplete or forged documents,* they gained entry. In one instance when seventy-two refugees were refused entry because they did not have Curaçao visas and were deported back to Siberia, Nathan Gutwirth interceded with the Dutch

---

* The forgeries the refugees used were quite good. Joseph Shimkin, a Jewish congregant of mine in Tokyo, was the chief forger. He would take a wet sliced potato, place it on an authentic visa, and then with fresh ink stamp it onto another document.

ambassador in Japan to issue the Curaçao visas, and even those refugees were returned safely to Japan.

Kobe, Japan, appeared as a Garden of Eden to the refugees. The weather was nice, the flowers and cherry blossoms were beautiful, the place was safe, the bureaucracy was efficient, and people were clean, neat and polite. The welcome the refugees received from the small Jewish community of Kobe, which numbered only about thirty, was warm, and their work on behalf of the refugees was indispensable. Mila Ionis and Alex Triguboff were members of the welcoming committee at that time, and years later they were congregants of mine. The refugees were also welcomed by the Japanese members of the Holiness Church, and doctors provided free medical care to refugees, particularly children, many of whom were ill after the long trip.

Upon his arrival in Kobe, the Amshinover Rebbe sent a telegram in Hebrew to Lithuania stating, "Six can get married under one *tallis* (prayer shawl)," and he signed it "Kalish." All telegrams were censored and could not be sent in an unfamiliar language. The Jewish community was contacted by Japanese authorities, and Triguboff responded. He was questioned about the meaning of the telegram, which he did not understand, but he recognized the word *tallis* and said that the Rebbe was asking that future refugees bring more prayer shawls with them. The telegram was approved, but when Triguboff saw the Amshinover Rebbe later, he asked what the telegram meant. The Rebbe smiled and said, "It is so difficult to obtain or forge one visa to Japan for just one person, but the Japanese require only one visa per family, so six people could travel as a family under one visa." That meant that with multiples of six traveling as a "family" under one visa, many more Jews could enter Japan.

Despite the friendly welcome the refugees received in Japan, they still had to adjust to the many differences between East and West. First, so accustomed to the unpunctuality of trains in Poland, the Jews almost missed the train on Friday afternoon from the Japanese port of Tsuruga to Kobe. Thinking they would not be in Kobe by sundown, the start of the Sabbath, they were tempted to wait on the platform for a train after the Sabbath ended twenty-four hours later. Only when the train to Kobe pulled into the station exactly on time and they were reassured that it also would arrive in Kobe exactly on time and before sundown did they hop on the train just as it was pulling out of the station.

One of the refugees who found it difficult to adjust to the differences was Irving Rosen, a young man who upon his arrival in Kobe broke down and simply sat on a curb, crying. He had left his parents, his family and his home and was now in Kobe after a difficult, dangerous escape. Sam Evans, president of the Jewish community, saw him and took him to his home, where he reassured and comforted the new arrival over a cup of hot tea. Evans, who became a Japanese citizen, prospered in Japan. He even owned the first car in Kobe, a red Buick, but since the emperor's car was red, Evans was asked to repaint his car, which he did; he painted it black. Irving Rosen also thrived during his time in Japan, moved to Shanghai and eventually relocated to the United States after the war. In the US, Rosen became a pearl dealer and returned to Japan often to purchase pearls.

The refugees had to adjust to a diet of mostly rice, vegetables, fish and eggs. Eating these foods with chopsticks was a challenge at first, and they missed the bread that had been their staple in Europe. On the other hand, citrus fruit was much more plentiful than it had been in Europe, and seeing bananas for the first time, many refugees ate them, peel and all. Since food was rationed in Japan, some Japanese complained that the refugees should not stand in line and take food but that this food should go first to the local residents. So the government authorities asked the refugees to forgo the food line, but every night freshly baked bread was loaded onto a truck and delivered along with other food to the Jewish community.

In addition, sleeping on tatami mats on the floor certainly felt odd, and to make their quilts, which were filled with straw, the refugees first had to dispose of the worms and rodents that were nestled there. Then there was the need to sit on the floor because there were few chairs, and the awkwardness of the Jap-

Local Japanese welcoming Jewish refugees with apples, 1940

anese bath houses, which were used by both sexes simultaneously. The Japanese, realizing that the refugees were shocked by seeing naked Japanese men and women bathing together, provided them with four single-sex bath houses.

When Passover was approaching, the refugees received a type of matzah (unleavened bread, like a big cracker) that was unfamiliar to them. These machine-made, oven-baked matzahs had been invented by the Man-ischewitz Company in the United States. There was the problem, fur-thermore, of getting the matzah and Passover wine through customs, but once the customs offi-

Professor Kotsuji Setsuzo wearing prayer shawl and tefillin

cials understood the Passover holiday, they were supportive. Officials also had to be persuaded to extend the ten-day visas the refugees held, which they did without any problems.

The Japanese had to learn about some of the other differences between them and the refugees. When the police confronted the Orthodox Jews for being disrespectful because they failed to remove their hats during a proces-sion of cars carrying the remains of dead war heroes from China, for example, they learned that Jews keep their heads covered as a sign of respect, whereas the Japanese take their hats off to show respect. In addition, the Japanese thought Jews were spies when they saw some of the observant yeshiva boys and men wearing tefillin, also called phylacteries. Tefillin are two small leather boxes that contain verses from the Bible. One tefillin box is worn on the arm, and the other is worn on the forehead, held together by long, protruding leather straps that the Japanese mistook for antennae that were transmitting and receiving secret messages.

The person responsible for convincing Japanese officials to extend the ten-day visas and to explain Jewish customs was Professor Kotsuji Setsuzo. Born in Kyoto in February 1899, the youngest son of a respected family of Shinto priests, Kotsuji also had been destined to become a priest. When he was about thirteen, however, he found a Japanese translation of the Bible, a book with which he was unfamiliar, in a used bookstore in Kyoto. He learned the con-cept of one God, or monotheism, so instead of following the path to become a Shinto priest, he studied Christianity in a seminary in Japan and then con-tinued his studies in the United States, where he earned a PhD. His doctoral dissertation was on the history of the Semitic alphabets. During his years in California, he showed a keen interest in Judaism, studying Hebrew intensely and paying frequent visits to a local synagogue. I came to know him well during my years in Japan and later exchanged about fifty letters with him.

Kotsuji was a guardian angel and a real hero to the Jewish refugees in Japan. He was the only professor of Hebrew in Japan, and throughout the Nazi period he wrote books favorably depicting the Jewish people and their culture. He also wrote the first Hebrew grammar manual in Japanese. In December 1939, at a conference on the Jewish communities of the Far East, Kotsuji gave his address in perfect classical Hebrew, and the Jewish audience was in awe.

In May 1941, a Japanese military agent came to the Jewish Center building in Kobe and asked for the highest-ranked refugees there. Japan is a vertical society, if you will, with everyone having a place on the social ladder, the emperor being at the top. Judaism, on the other hand, is horizontal, with everyone being equal in status. The agent insisted on getting the names of the highest-ranked refugees in Japan, so the Jewish representative told him about Rabbi Moses Shatzkes, whom he described as having been a child prodigy and a genius who, at age eighteen, had astounded the scholars and rabbis of Poland with his unique and brilliant mind. Prior to his escape to Japan, Shatzkes had served as the rabbi of the Polish city of Lomza. Years later, he would be responsible for ordaining Orthodox rabbis at Yeshiva University in New York.

The agent wanted to know who else there was in the Jewish refugee community of high status. The representative replied that there was Rabbi Kalish, the Amshinover Rebbe, who was next to God. They described his kind face, soft facial expression and twinkling eyes that had caused people to follow him in the streets in Europe. They also named another brilliant rabbi, Shlomo Shapiro.

The Japanese official said firmly, "Tomorrow morning...military officers' headquarters...Tokyo...interrogation. You will take the overnight train to Tokyo where we will meet you tomorrow at Tokyo Marunouchi Central Station. Be there. Goodbye." Despite their efforts to find the reason for this meeting in Tokyo, no information was forthcoming. Military interrogation sounded ominous, much worse than simply "questioning," and the refugees were frightened. After all, what do rabbis have to do with the military and with interrogation? Leo Hanin, a member of the Jewish community who spoke several languages, and Professor Kotsuji, who could serve as a translator, accompanied them. On the train ride they encountered Nazi soldiers who cursed at them, spit on them and pulled their beards, warning them that they were not safe anywhere. The rabbis ignored their assailants.

Upon their arrival the next morning, the Jewish delegation was welcomed at the VIP room at the Tokyo central train station before being trans-ported in a military lim-ousine, sirens blaring to clear the way for these VIPs on their way to mil-

Interrogation of Jewish refugees at Military Officers' Headquarters, May 1941; *left to right:* Rabbi Shlomo Shapiro, Professor Kotsuji Setsuzo, the Amshinover Rebbe, Rabbi Moses Shatzkes, Navy Captain Fukamachi and Leo Hanin

itary headquarters, the equivalent of the US Pentagon building. They were welcomed by a Japanese official to whom Rabbi Shatzkes responded politely. Throughout the discussions, Professor Kotsuji translated to and from Japanese to English, and Leo Hanin translated to and from English to Yiddish.

The first question the military officials asked the rabbis was what was so terrible, horrible, filthy, dirty and abominable about Jews that made Japan's German friends hate them so much. The courtesy of the first reply went to Rabbi Shatzkes, who turned pale and froze, fearing that what had happened to his family and other Jews in Europe was about to happen in Japan. He failed to respond. The Amshinover Rebbe quickly stepped in and answered, "The Germans hate the Jews because they know that we Jews are Asians," to which the Japanese responded, "We are Asians." The Amshinover Rebbe then told them that they, too, were on "the list" as non-Aryans. "What list are you talking about?" the Japanese asked angrily. The rabbi asked, "Don't you know what they say in Europe? Haven't you heard? In Europe they speak of the Jews, the Gypsies, the Slavs, the Blacks and the Yellows." The Amshinover Rebbe continued, "Since the Japanese, like the Jews, are not of the pure Aryan race made up of tall, blue-eyed, blonde-haired Caucasians whom the Nazis deem worthy to rule the world, you, like the Jews, are on the same list and will be next for extermination."

This response infuriated the Japanese officials, who demanded proof that what the Amshinover Rebbe was saying was true. The Amshinover Rebbe responded calmly and politely that it had been in the news that when a Japanese diplomat in the embassy in Berlin fell in love with a German girl and applied for a marriage license, he was denied the license on the basis that it was forbidden for an Aryan to marry an inferior person. After the Japanese authorities took a long recess to discuss this information, the doors swung open, the mood changed and a celebration with the rabbis began. At the end of this unexpected celebration, an official told the rabbis to return home and reassure their community that every effort would be made to protect their safety.

That meeting, which began at ten in the morning and lasted until three o'clock that afternoon, took place around the same table that was used a few months later to plan the attack on Pearl Harbor. I own a piece of this table, a very valuable souvenir to me. Meanwhile, the rabbis, now relieved, returned to Kobe, where the Jewish community remained cooperative and helpful to each other, while they and their Japanese neighbors lived together harmoniously as well.

In September 1959, at the age of sixty, Professor Kotsuji converted to Judaism at a ceremony in Jerusalem, in the presence of many of the refugees he had assisted. Years later, when I met with him for the last time, he was wearing a kimono and a yarmulke (skull cap). He had a Hebrew prayer book beside him, and we drank green tea together. He died in Japan in 1973, during Israel's Yom Kippur War. The civilian airport in Israel was closed for added security, but with the advice and consent of Zorach Warhaftig, I was able to arrange for Kotsuji's funeral and burial in Israel. His tombstone reads: "Here lies Professor Avraham Kotsuji, righteous convert, born 5660, died 5734." These are the Hebrew calendar dates for the years 1899–1973.

Between July 1940 and May 1941, about forty-six hundred refugees passed through Kobe, including the refugees from Poland, writers, journalists, businessmen, intellectuals, rabbis and yeshiva students and faculty. A farmer asked to meet all the refugee children, greeting each of them with an apple and an orange to welcome them to Japan, and teachers instructed the new immigrant children in the language and culture of Japan. Others welcoming the refugees upon their arrival also gave a small gift to anyone who answered affirmatively when asked, "Are you Jewish?" In Europe and elsewhere at this time, admitting to being Jewish was a death sentence, but not in Japan.

For the observant Jews who had overcome all the difficulties they encountered to escape from Europe to Japan from 1940 through 1941, one question still needed an answer. On which day was the Sabbath in Japan? Because the earth is round and the international dateline is in the middle of the Pacific Ocean, time and day are not the same everywhere. The line is not straight, Siberia almost touches Alaska, there are islands along the way, and it is completely arbitrary. Thus the question arises for religious Jews: if Japan is one hundred degrees east of Jerusalem, does the Sabbath start in Japan more than six hours before it starts in Jerusalem or more than eighteen hours after it starts in Jerusalem? So, is the Sabbath on Saturday or Sunday? Keep in mind that the Sabbath begins and ends at nightfall.

This is indeed a difficult and complicated question, posed during the war years by Orthodox refugees to the chief rabbi in Jerusalem and to leading rabbinic scholars around the world, but there was no unanimous decision. The majority of those consulted advised following the custom of the local community, making the Sabbath on Saturday. Other erudite and learned decision makers ruled that Sunday was the Sabbath, and advised that since the upcoming Yom Kippur (Jewish Day of Atonement on which Jews fast) would occur in most of the world from sundown on Tuesday until sundown on Wednesday, the Jews in Japan should fast on Thursday and eat on Wednesday before sundown. Still other rabbinic authorities favored a two-day Sabbath and a two-day Yom Kippur. These multiple views clearly demonstrate the conundrum that was created by crossing the International Dateline. In the Mir Yeshiva in Kobe, after a response came from a major Jewish scholar that the Sabbath should be held Sunday and not Saturday, Rabbi Ezekiel Levenstein approached the pulpit on Friday night, banged on the lectern and began prayers for an ordinary weeknight rather than for the Sabbath.

In 1941, Japan was the only place in the world where the Orthodox community did not know whether the Sabbath was on Saturday or Sunday. By the summer of 1941, months before the December attack on Pearl Harbor, the question was moot. Since the refugees had entered Japan with ten-day visas, and Curaçao was a false destination that no one actually reached, they were ordered to leave Japan for Shanghai, where the issues created by the international dateline were no longer relevant.

While the dateline controversy turned out to be little more than a heated debate of Jewish law, the Jewish refugees in Japan ended up having great significance for world Jewry, especially for Jews in the United States. In 1945, because of the Holocaust, few rabbis, Jewish scholars or Torah teachers had survived in Europe to come to North America. Then, however, the entire Mir Yeshiva from Poland arrived in the United States from Shanghai, and they became the educators of postwar Jewry until the US and Israel could produce a new generation of rabbinic scholars and Jewish leaders.

Chapter Sixteen
Garcia d'Orta: Militant Marrano of India in the 1500s

Garcia d'Orta (1501 or 1502–1568), a pioneer in Jewish history, changed my life, because his story illustrated to me how little I knew of the Jewish experience in the Far East; his story inspired me to uncover, document and write about the little-known history of the Jews from India to Japan. I had never heard of Garcia d'Orta, whose Hebrew name was Avraham, and he was not on my radar when a congregant of mine in Japan introduced me to several Japanese professors of Spanish and Portuguese history who asked me about him.

I later corresponded for several years with Professor Charles R. Boxer, Emily Hahn's husband and a former chief of British intelligence in Hong Kong prior to Pearl Harbor (see chapter 12). He studied the history of the Dutch in the Far East, but he also became a highly-esteemed expert on the Portuguese in the Far East, mainly in Macau (in China) and Goa (in India). He delivered a magnificent lecture on d'Orta on the exact date of the four hundredth anniversary of the publication of d'Orta's famous volume on botany and pharmacology, *Coloquios dos Simples e Drogas e Consas Medicinais da India* (usually referred to as *Coloquios*), which was published in Goa in April 1563. Boxer told me that the same excitement that surrounded the discovery of penicillin in the 1930s had surrounded the publication of d'Orta's book in 1563.

Of all the places where Jews lived, survived and thrived, there was only one country in the Diaspora where Jews experienced a "Golden Age" and established their finest community, and that country was Spain from 1000 to 1492 CE. In Spain there were Jewish prime ministers, military generals, rabbis, scholars, professors, poets, mathematicians, physicians, artists and philosophers. The Jews in Spain were superbly educated and also very literate in Judaism; few people know that much of the liturgy of the Jewish High Holy Days was composed in Spain. The Jews in Spain mastered Greek and Arabic literature and philosophy, and they lived in Spain with respect and tolerance from others.

Sadly, however, in 1492 under the Inquisition, the Jews were forced to convert and/or were expelled, tortured and murdered. Even many of the Jews who managed to escape on ships did not survive, as pirates were waiting for them in the Mediterranean. Others succeeded in escaping across the border to Portugal, but when King Emanuel I, who was Portugal's king from 1495 to 1521, wanted to marry Princess Isabella, daughter of Spain's King Ferdinand and Queen Isabella, King Ferdinand insisted that for the marriage to take place, Portugal had to be purified of the accursed Jews. The marriage contract was signed on November 30, 1496, and the expulsion of the Jews was ordered on December 4, 1496.

Jews in Portugal were forced under enormous pressure to become New Christians or "Marranos," a derogatory term that meant swine, pig or secret Jew. Some of the New Christians fled to Goa, but the numerical strength of the New Christians there became a major issue, and in 1527, in a letter from Goa to the king of Portugal, strong opposition was voiced about the concentration of local trade and commerce in the hands of the Marranos that created a major disadvantage to the Christian Portuguese population. In relating all of this to me, Professor Boxer reiterated that the Inquisition was not interested merely in establishing the preeminence of the Catholic Church; it also was an anti-Semitic entity that wanted to offer economic protection to the Christian community by persecuting Jews and even converted Jews. In 1540, in a report to the Portuguese king, a local clergyman listed three factors that he said would end Portuguese rule in India: the delay of payment to soldiers, the low moral practices of the Portuguese men who married local women although they had wives back in Europe, and the presence of so many New Christians and Marranos.

The Portuguese came to India not only as conquerors and merchants in search of spices, but also as bearers of the cross, aiming to convert the local Hindu and Muslim populations, as well as the Jews residing there. The Church reported that New Christians secretly were adhering to some Jewish beliefs, contaminating India and weakening the Christian faith. As a result, in 1545 Francisco Xavier, the foremost apostle of Jesuit activities in Asia, wrote to the Portuguese king that the Inquisition must come to India because there were many Jews living there without any fear of God or shame. In 1549, the vicar general of Goa, a fanatical enemy of the Jews, echoed this concern, writing that with so many New Christians living according to the rules of Judaism without fear or shame, the Inquisition must correct the situation. In 1560 the Inquisition did come to Goa and remained there for almost 250 years, until 1812.

Professor Walter Fischel at the University of California in Berkeley was a learned observant Jew and superb scholar who fully researched the epic story of Garcia d'Orta, whom Fischel referred to as one of the militant Marranos of sixteenth-century India. In 1492, d'Orta's parents fled from Spain and took refuge in Portugal. In 1497, King Manuel I ordered the mass conversion of all Jews, and d'Orta, his three sisters and his parents became New Christians. D'Orta matriculated at the University of Spain where he studied philosophy, the arts and medicine, and he practiced medicine in his hometown for eight years before relocating to Lisbon to teach philosophy at the local university.

Martim Affonso de Sousa, d'Orta's well-connected friend and captain major of the ship *Indian Ocean*, invited d'Orta to accompany him as his personal physician. They left for India on March 12, 1534, arriving in Goa in September 1534. For the next four years d'Orta traveled with de Sousa to Ceylon (now Sri Lanka), Cochin in India, and elsewhere before de Sousa returned to Portugal in 1538. D'Orta, however, remained in Goa, where in 1542 he married a cousin, Jewish by birth, from a wealthy merchant family. They had two daughters, and in 1548 d'Orta brought his mother, two of his sisters and their husbands to India from Portugal, where they already had been imprisoned by the Lisbon Inquisition.

In his study of diseases and drugs of India, d'Orta was a pioneer of the new spirit of scientific inquiry that developed during the Renaissance. He practiced medicine, worked in the Royal Hospital and devoted his free time to research and scholarship. He was friendly with everyone and had access to the highest circles of both secular and church society. A physician to the viceroys, his assistance also was requested by leading Christian dignitaries and notables. His fame as a successful physician spread, and Muslim rulers, too, invited d'Orta to their court. In the city of Ahmadnagar in India, he often visited his friend and patron, the Muslim sultan. D'Orta served as personal physician to the sultan and his family and also taught them the Portuguese language. This enabled them to communicate with the numerous scholars and scientists, including many "secret" Jews, who gathered at the palace to exchange ideas in an atmosphere of complete religious tolerance. Meeting with Muslim, Indian, and European physicians and philosophers gave d'Orta a welcome respite from the bigotry, tension and suspicion he and his family were subjected to in Goa.

The well-known and dignified d'Orta was respected as the best of the best in India intellectually, theologically, socially and medically. The Portuguese were so proud of their famous expatriate citizen that they gave him a gift: Bombay! It was not the same city in size and importance as it is today, but d'Orta proudly referred to it as "my island." In Bombay, d'Orta built a beautiful house which included a library, a museum filled with works of art and a spectacular botanical garden* that he used for his research and from which he sent plants and seeds to Portugal. This home, which is still standing, was the first western-style building in Bombay; it served as the residence of the governor of Bombay for 120 years.

It was here that d'Orta began his great work on medicinal herbs, and he became the first European writer on tropical medicine and a pioneer in pharmacology. *Nux Vomica* (strychnine), a poisonous but valuable medical agent made from a tree native to India, was unknown in Europe until d'Orta. It is generally believed that the China orange also was introduced to Europe from d'Orta's garden. His research on tropical medicine and medications made from plants, roots, leaves and bark remained the authoritative text for three hundred years and was translated into many languages, and he is credited with being the most important figure in pharmacology from the first century to his own time.

Coloquios, which d'Orta dedicated to the Portuguese viceroy, has fifty-nine chapters about tropical diseases and the medical plants and drugs in India used to treat them. Each chapter, written in dialogue style,** is devoted to a different remedy, including the medicinal uses of opium, cardamom, cloves, ginger, cinnamon and fruits such as mangoes, melons and coconuts. The volume also contains d'Orta's description of dysentery, malaria, typhoid, tuberculosis and several other infections. In addition, d'Orta observed and reported on the methods of Indian-Hindu doctors and the medicines they used, such as the use of lodestone for massage therapy. Lodestone is magnetic and has powerful negative polarity that can attract and repel, energize and sedate. It also has anti-inflammatory properties, so d'Orta often used it to treat bruised

---

* D'Orta's home and garden, a heritage site, is currently the headquarters of the Western Naval Command and is not open to the public.

** The dialogue question and answer style d'Orta used is similar to the Talmudic style in the *Kuzari*, written by Judah Halevi in Spain in the early twelfth century.

muscles and bone fractures. In addition, d'Orta was the first European to study snakebites (his research on the toxic venom of the cobra snake in India was extremely important), and he wrote the first modern description of the difference between European cholera and Asian cholera.

The symptoms of Asian cholera as described by d'Orta are weak pulse, very cold skin, cold sweat, burning throat, fever, inability to sleep, sunken eyes, severe diarrhea and leg cramps. Untreated, survival time then averaged ten hours to four days. When the Bishop of Malacca came down with Asian cholera in 1559, d'Orta treated him with external heat, hot irons to the soles of his feet, warm oils rubbed into his skin and, most important, opium, and the bishop was cured.

The third book ever printed in Asia and the first book printed in Asia on a non-religious subject, *Coloquios* was approved by the great inquisitor of Goa and enhanced by a dedication poem in the great inquisitor's honor, composed by the most famous poet of the day, Luis de Cameos. Unique for his time, d'Orta's amazing book contains no Christological elements and no references to the Trinity. D'Orta does refer to God and mentions his close contact with many of the Christian leaders of Goa. He also compliments Francisco Xavier, flattery which seems so out of place and unnecessary in a treatise on medicine and medical plants that it obviously was inserted because he needed church approval and wrote what he thought would help secure it. In some of his other papers, however, d'Orta makes many references to the Bible, Judea and Jewish law, even going so far as to point out that the Jews were the first ones to write about divine subjects. At that time, the Church had a monopoly on truth, and that meant truth according to Catholic beliefs, but d'Orta searched for truth based on observation, critical analysis and common sense.

Early biographies portray d'Orta as a happy man and a faithful Catholic who attended Mass regularly; lived a quiet, uneventful life; and died a bachelor at the age of eighty. All of this is incorrect and without any historical merit. When the records of the Inquisition became public in 1934, the truth was revealed. Far from living a charmed life, d'Orta lived a life full of affliction, tribulation, fear and terror for his own safety and that of his family.

D'Orta lived with tension and in fear for the simple reason that he secretly adhered to Judaism (it is said that if you look at d'Orta's signature, perhaps with a mirror, it spells "Abraham" in Hebrew) and lived life as a militant Marrano. D'Orta taught that the Torah of Moses was true, that one should honor the Sabbath by wearing clean clothes and that one should observe Jewish festivals and

Portuguese India stamp in honor of Garcia d'Orta

holidays on appointed days, especially Yom Kippur (the holiest day of the Jewish year). D'Orta went on to teach that the founder of Christianity was not the son of God, that the biblical prophesies were not yet fulfilled, that Jews did not kill Jesus, and that Jesus was the son of Mary and Joseph. Inquisition records and confessions by one of d'Orta's sisters also revealed that d'Orta's mother practiced Judaism, including preparing kosher meat in the proscribed fashion, serving unleavened bread (matzah) during the Passover holiday, and teaching her children the ways of Jewish life.

Under torture by the Inquisition, d'Orta's sister Catarina incriminated d'Orta and other members of her family who continued to live secretly as Jews. The Inquisition labeled her an impenitent Jewess and sentenced her to be burned at the stake on October 25, 1569, as punishment. Between 1561 and 1590, eighty-four Marranos were executed in Goa, and the records of those trials and executions are in the Torre do Tombo Library in Lisbon, Portugal. New Christians and Marranos made up 69 percent of those executed by the Inquisition, but not only Jews and former Jews were persecuted. In March 1546, the king of Portugal ordered the viceroy to forbid Hinduism, labeling it "gentile idolatry." Hindu temples were destroyed, all Hindu celebrations were prohibited, and all Brahmins were expelled.

D'Orta lived in Goa for almost thirty years until his death at about age sixty-seven. His funeral was held in accordance with Jewish tradition, and his wife clandestinely and courageously searched for special cloth so she could dress him in the traditional burial shroud. He was buried in Goa near the cathedral. On December 4, 1580, twelve years after d'Orta died, the Inquisition ordered that his remains be exhumed; they then counted his bones to be certain they had all of his remains, which they burned before throwing his ashes into the Arabian Sea. This was posthumous punishment for a militant Marrano they had initially chosen to leave alone, probably because of the prestigious standing and excellent reputation he enjoyed in Portuguese circles during his lifetime. Thus, the dark shadow of the Inquisition that motivated d'Orta to leave Lisbon and then hung over his head all through his days in India ultimately did not spare him even in death.

Garcia d'Orta's image on Portuguese currency

On the positive side, this great Jew was recognized when Portugal and Goa each issued postage stamps with d'Orta's face; Portugal also issued a banknote portraying d'Orta and minted a coin in his honor. In addition, in both Goa and Lisbon, there are gardens, hospitals and schools named for Garcia d'Orta. The name Garcia d'Orta stands head and shoulders above non-clergy in Portuguese India because of his contributions to science, medicine and statesmanship. Frederick August Fluckiger of Switzerland, frequently cited as the father of modern pharmacology, wrote, "No one has described the drug plants of India with so much care, with such accuracy...the *Coloquios* will always hold a place of highest honor in the history of pharmacology."

I have lectured in hundreds of synagogues, in many universities, and in Jewish community centers worldwide, on the unknown, fascinating Jewish experience and history in the Far East. When I told the story of Garcia d'Orta at Knesseth Eliyahu Synagogue in Mumbai, the congregants, like me years earlier, had never heard of d'Orta, although his home and garden stand on the naval base near this very synagogue. When I finished the story, they were so moved that they stood up with tears in their eyes and applauded.

The only time I ever cried when delivering a lecture was when the lecture was about Garcia d'Orta. I cried because the expulsion of Jews from Spain and the destruction of the amazing Jewish community in Spain five hundred years ago destroyed the magnificent Sephardic Jewish community which has not recovered to this very day. I cried because of that cruel destruction of the Jewish "Golden Age"; because of the hardship and courage of the Jews living their dual, secret lives; and because of the Inquisition's unconscionable burning of Garcia d'Orta's remains twelve years after his burial.

Chapter Seventeen
The Tragic Betrayal of Wolf Ladejinsky, Asia's Agriculture Guru

Several Jews played amazingly important roles in the Occupation of Japan after World War II. One of those Jews was Wolf Ladejinsky (1899–1975) who was born to a flour miller in Ekaterinopol in the Russian Ukraine. In Russia he had been surrounded by the poverty, starvation, alienation, indignity and persecution that the Jews – who were excluded from both farming and most urban occupations – had to endure. He saw, however, that genuine honor and reverence were accorded to learning and the educated, and this led Ladejinsky to scholarship. Because he was such an excellent student, he was one of the very few Jewish students who was permitted to complete high school, and he also was allowed to attend a Jewish school for his religious education. He continued his studies until 1920, when he fled across a frozen river into Romania to escape from the Bolshevik Communists.

In Romania, Ladejinsky worked briefly in a flour mill as a baker's apprentice before securing a job with the Hebrew Immigrant Aid Society (HIAS), serving as a counselor, accompanying Jewish orphans going to the United States and helping Jews to get out of Eastern Europe and make their way to the US and elsewhere. In 1922, Ladejinsky himself reached the United States, penniless and unable to speak English; Yiddish (the conversational language of most Jews in Eastern Europe before World War II) was his mother tongue. While learning English, Wolf washed windows and sold newspapers, and he eventually received his BA and MA degrees in agricultural economics from Columbia University.

His first published paper, "Collectivization of Agriculture in the Soviet Union," was intended to be his doctoral dissertation, but when one of his professors was called to Washington, DC, by the newly elected President Franklin D. Roosevelt, Ladejinsky left Columbia University at his professor's request to accept a position with the US Department of Agriculture (USDA) in the Department of Foreign Agriculture Relations. This position launched Ladejinsky's career that spanned four decades.

From 1935 to 1945, Ladejinsky's work was primarily academic. He published more than twenty research papers, mostly about agriculture in Asia.* He examined such issues as the expansion of agriculture in Manchuria, Thailand's agricultural economy, the Japanese cotton/textile

Wolf Ladejinsky, 1899–1975

industry, and Japan's food self-sufficiency. In 1937, he published "Farm Tenancy and Japanese Agriculture," and in 1939, he published "Agrarian Unrest in Japan." His work, which was influenced by several Japanese experts who had written about land reform, established him as the world's expert on Japanese agriculture.

General MacArthur was the supreme commander of the allied forces of the Occupation, and in 1945 Ladejinsky was sent to Japan to join General MacArthur's team. From then on, Ladejinsky lived modestly in Asia, where he spent thirty years of his life studying, explaining, reforming and advising on the agricultural and land tenure systems until his death in 1975. While Ladejinsky was familiar with published reports, statistics and views of high government officials, most of his research took place in the field. He wrote his reports based on what he observed; conversations with peasants, landlords, merchants and local officials; intuition; and long experience. His goal was to answer the questions: (1) how can we increase yield; and (2) how can we get farmers out of poverty. His reports were detailed and compelling and became the definitive guide for all the agriculture experts in East Asia.

During these three decades, Ladejinsky was devoted to implementing

---

* Fortunately, in 1977 a few of these reports were carefully collected, edited and published by Oxford University under the title *Agrarian Reform as Unfinished Business*.

agrarian reform for millions of submarginal farmers, tenants, sharecroppers and landless laborers in Japan about whom he cared deeply. He had a passionate dedication not only to Asia and learning, but also to democracy, a dedication that was intensified after Hitler inflicted the Holocaust on the Jews of Europe, and he wanted to ensure democracy for the independent countries of Asia.

To accomplish this goal, Ladejinsky believed that poor Asian farmers needed a piece of land to call their own, or at least reasonable rent for land they cultivated for absentee landlords. Ladejinsky was aware of how Lenin's promise of "land to the tiller" had influenced Russian peasants to revolt and how their revolt soon thereafter led to collective and state farms. This led Ladejinsky to a profound sense of the political role land played in society. He recognized the significance of ownership and tenants' rights in fostering the survival of democracy, which he deemed the more desirable alternative to the rural masses being seduced by the promise of communism.

Robert A. Feary, who was in Japan working as private secretary to the US ambassador to Japan, Joseph Grew, wrote a memo with Ladejinsky to the USDA about the importance of land reform to the future of democracy in Japan. The memo caught the attention of General MacArthur. MacArthur's prewar experience in the Philippines had convinced him of the merits of giving land to farmers, and his own father had advocated for land reform as far back as the early 1900s. MacArthur also had studied the land reform efforts of the Roman Empire. He and Ladejinksy soon were enjoying discussions about agrarian issues while they savored smoking their corn cob pipes, and MacArthur agreed with Ladejinsky that land reform was the best way to prevent a resurgence of militarism and to keep radical socialism and communism at bay.

In 1945 postwar Japan, almost 50 percent of the nation's residents lived on farms, but almost half of all land owned or cultivated was being worked by non-owners, and 70 percent of the country's cultivators were involved in some degree of tenancy. By the time land reform in Japan had been completed between 1947 and 1949, a dramatic transformation had taken place nationwide, and about 80 percent of tenant land holdings had been reallocated. The first stage of reforms saw the amount of property rented rather than owned fall from 46 percent to 10 percent, with 57 percent of rural families becoming farm owners and 35 percent becoming part owners/tenants. By the second stage of reforms, 90 percent of all farm land was being cultivated by independent growers, and the number of tenant farmers without land ownership had declined to only 7 percent. In just two years, Japan's agriculture had moved from a feudal, medieval system to a more progressive democratic one. The day the land reform bill became law, MacArthur issued a statement declaring the event as "one of the most important milestones yet reached by Japan in the creation of an economically stable and politically democratic society." He likened Japanese land reform to the efforts of the Gracchi brothers in the Roman era.*

On January 15, 1947, General MacArthur wrote the following to US Secretary of Agriculture Ezra Taft Benson: "Mr. Ladejinsky performed outstanding service in connection with the initiation of a comprehensive land reform program by the Japanese government, thereby aiding the attainment of important objectives of the Occupation. I wish to express my appreciation to you and the department for having made his services available."

As the principal architect of the successful land reform program in Japan after World War II, Ladejinsky had become well known, and he subsequently received requests for advice and assistance from many other nations. When Chiang Kai-shek fled from mainland China to Taiwan in 1948, many of his followers also went to Taiwan, overpopulating that country and creating a food shortage. Chiang Kai-shek turned to Ladejinsky for help, and Ladejinsky's solution became known as the "Taiwan Miracle." From the 1940s through the 1960s, Ladejinsky served as an adviser on land reform and irrigation issues in Korea, Nepal, Taiwan, Malaysia, Indonesia, India, South Vietnam, Iran and Mexico. He became known as "Mr. Land Reform," and his tireless work on land reform was fueled by his wish for all people to live with dignity.

Ironically, familiarity with Ladejinsky's name and work became greater after the notoriety he received in 1954, when the State Department returned responsibility for the work agricultural attachés were doing abroad to the USDA. Agricultural Secretary Benson, an active leader in the Mormon Church, refused to rehire Ladejinsky, declaring him a "national security risk." Benson said that his reasons for this designation were that Ladejinsky was a Soviet-born Jew who still had family living in the Soviet Union; he had received a visa in the 1930s to visit his family in the Soviet Union; he had worked in 1930 as an interpreter for a Soviet trade agency; and, some claimed, he once had been a member of two communist front organizations. Benson wrote that

---

* The two Gracchi brothers lived in the late second century BCE in Rome and attempted to pass land reform legislation that would redistribute large land ownership from the very rich to the peasants.

Ladejinsky was not only a Soviet-born Jew but also that Jews who turned into "Reds" (communist sympathizers) were the worst kind of traitors. In addition, he testified before the Senate Post Office and Civil Service Subcommittee that his real reason for suspending Ladejinsky was that this Soviet-born expert was "not equipped to represent American agriculture abroad."

Benson had engaged in a blatant anti-Semitic smear, and President Dwight D. Eisenhower and his administration fumbled badly, creating a bipartisan, international uproar. James Haggerty, Eisenhower's press secretary, wrote in his diary on January 4, 1955, "Benson and his people really have messed this one up like nothing has been messed up since I have been in Washington. Benson is very stubborn and refuses to flatly admit that he made a mistake."

Ladejinsky explained that he had taken the job with the Soviet trade agency because it paid more than he earned selling newspapers and that he had played no political role while working there. He said that when he visited his family in the Soviet Union he made periodic reports to the US embassy and had had little contact with his family in the Soviet Union after that visit. He denied ever having been a member of any communist organization and expressed his strong anti-communist beliefs, pointing to his published articles that touted land reform as a way to thwart "the communist menace" and prevent farmers from being attracted to communism.

When I met with Ladejinsky in Tokyo in the early 1970s, only the fact that I spoke to him in Yiddish gave him the comfort he needed to talk freely to me about this terrible period in his life. Before Benson's attack, Ladejinsky had been living the American dream. Then, suddenly, the Diaspora experience in Jewish history that Ladejinsky had experienced personally in the Soviet Union – bias, prejudice, hatred, anti-Semitism, pogroms – came out of nowhere in one flash for him. "I felt hurt and slandered by Benson's statements," he told me. Ladejinsky said that he was particularly devastated by Benson's suggestion that he lacked qualifications and the implication that he was incompetent at doing his job.

Ladejinsky's pain is palpable in a letter he wrote to Benson on October 24, 1955, in which he questions Benson's basis for making such allegations. "I must tell you in all humility," he wrote, "that your own objective examination of my performance record, or an examination by any group concerned with the promotion of American agricultural projects abroad, will conclude that I performed my salesmanship and representation duties with credit to the USDA and profit to American agriculture." After presenting a list of all he had accomplished, Ladejinsky then asked Benson again for an explanation. "Reflecting upon this record which is well known to the USDA, to the American embassy, Tokyo, as well as all those in American agriculture who are familiar with my professional work, I cannot help but wonder, Mr. Secretary, why you have elected to brand me unqualified or incompetent. My long years of association with the USDA, and my work in the fields in many parts of Asia, are hardly to be dismissed merely because I wasn't born on an American farm...."

While Ladejinsky suffered from Benson's action and words, he was also touched and encouraged by the response of others who came to his defense. There was a massive outpouring of support for Ladejinsky from the press; from professional associates; from prominent Americans such as Frank Carlson, Daniel Patrick Moynihan and James Michener; from Japanese government officials and from farm organizations. The brouhaha eventually led to Benson's issuing a retraction and an apology regarding his accusation that Ladejinsky was a national security risk, as well as to the government's revision of US national security procedures. In his 1955 letter to Benson, however, Ladejinsky writes, "You have had the courage of your convictions to disavow the security charge, and I hope you will have the courage to disavow the lack of qualifications when, having examined the record, you will find the charge wanting." It seems that, tragically, Benson never apologized for his accusation that Ladejinsky was incompetent. Ladejinsky went on to work for the Ford Foundation from 1961 until 1964; in 1964 he moved on to the World Bank, where he held a position until his death.

While Ladejinsky's life was devoted to his work on land reform, he also had a consuming interest in art, and during his decades in Asia he acquired an impressive collection. In 1962, in Asia, he began selling and donating a few of his art pieces. As a loyal Jew, when plans were being made for the construction of the Israel Museum in Jerusalem, Ladejinsky decided to give the bulk of his collection – more than seven hundred pieces – to that museum. Thus, his beloved art would remain in Asia, a continent he loved, but in the Middle East in Israel, the Jewish homeland, rather than in the Far East in Japan. He knew that in Israel his collection would be cherished, cared for and properly displayed.

A letter from Japan's minister of agriculture, Hirokawa Kozen, dated April 26, 1952, and inscribed on an impressive silver plaque, captures the importance of Ladejinsky's land reform efforts. Hirokawa wrote the following on behalf of the Japanese government: "Our country owes you a heavy debt for your share in

Charles Kades, 1906–1996

the successful accomplishment of the land reform program. The world knows that this is the most successful reform which Japan accomplished under the Occupation, and I know that the reform was carried out with the closest cooperation and the most friendly atmosphere between yourself and personnel of our ministry, and I am convinced that the effect of the land reform will remain forever and so will your name in Japanese culture."

In addition to Ladejinsky, other prominent Jewish men worked in the Occupation. One was Charles L. Kades (1906–1996), and he ranked third in importance in the Occupation, an unusual position for a Jew. Kades was deputy chief of the Government Section and was the "go to guy" to get things done during the entire time he was there.

Kades was born in Newburgh, New York. A graduate of Cornell University and Harvard Law School, Kades worked as an attorney in New York City. In September 1933, Kades went to Washington, DC, to serve as counsel to Harold Ickes, secretary of the interior, and in May 1940, Kades became assistant counsel to Henry Morgenthau, secretary of the treasury. He joined the army in 1942 at age thirty-five, graduated from the Command and General Staff School, a school for men with promise to be leaders in the military, and left the service with the rank of colonel.

Kades was offered the position of deputy secretary of state for occupied Germany, an interesting position to offer a Jew, but Kades refused the offer, believing he could make a far better contribution in Japan. In February 1946, Major General Courtney Whitney, second in command after General MacArthur, put Kades in charge of a sixteen-member task force assigned to write a draft constitution that would put Japan on the road to democracy. There were no official guidelines or blueprint for everything that the Occupation was doing. Kades's first act as task force director was to collect the few directives the Occupation had at the beginning, organize them and put them in a binder that he kept safe at all times. His binder, the guide to what needed to be done in Japan during the Occupation, became known as the "Kades bible."

His objectives were to remove feudal and aristocratic aspects from Japanese society and replace them with democratic ideas. He wanted to eliminate the influence of militarists and ultranationalists from Japan, and he made sure that the wishes of MacArthur, Whitney and Beate Sirota Gordon (see chapter 4) that there be no increase in armed forces in Japan would appear in the new constitution as a "no war" clause. Purging military leaders with the rank of major and above was a preventive measure, Kades believed, not punitive. Under pressure, he also added captains and lieutenants to this list. When Kades was offered the position of assistant secretary of state in 1947, MacArthur convinced him that it was more important for him to stay in Japan.

Besides fostering the development of democracy in Japan, Kades wanted to remedy two evils of postwar Japan. One was the political corruption that resulted from illegal disposition of Japanese military stockpiles, and the other was the widespread gangster activity reaching into the precincts of law enforcement, labor, business and politics. The first evil became known as the "great hoarded goods scandal," and the second was known as the "*oyabunkobun* menace." The second cause did not have MacArthur's support, but he did not interfere with the investigation Kades undertook. Kades used these two issues – hoarding and racketeering – to instruct the Japanese government members in the ways of democracy under the new constitution.

Kades also was involved directly with the disposition of the Akasaka Detached Palace, home of the imperial family, which was built between 1899 and 1909. Modeled after the Versailles Palace in France, it had more than three hundred rooms. Members of the imperial family became commoners after the new constitution was passed, and there was much speculation and debate as to who or what would occupy the palace. In February 1948, Kades held a meeting of the interested parties, and the next day the cabinet decided that the palace would be shared by the cabinet, the Diet (Japan's legislative branch) and the attorney general's office. Kades returned to the United States later that year.

Every step taken toward democracy during the Occupation was met with predictions that the consequences would be chaos, anarchy and communism, Kades wrote, and many believe that without him the constitution could not have been drafted as well as it was or in as timely a fashion. He had a winning smile; knew how to say "no" without offending; and was very popular with government and state officials, scholars, journalists and secretaries. He was smart, accessible, open to new ideas and enjoyed debates; and when he lost, he did so with grace and without blaming others. His name is mentioned forty-six times in the official minutes of the constitutional debates and discussions, more than anyone else's name. After MacArthur and his deputy Courtney Whitney retired, each retained Kades as his personal legal counsel. Kades later would say that the new Japanese Constitution and land reform were the two most important achievements of the Occupation.

Not surprisingly, possessing all the attributes just described, Kades also was quite the "ladies' man" and was married three times. His first wife was an Australian beauty who came to Japan to entertain the troops. They married and had a daughter Caroline who, after her parents divorced, returned to Australia with her mother. I still correspond with Caroline, who likes to joke that she inherited the best genes from each of her parents, both of whom she respected.

Kades died at the age of ninety. He had a Jewish funeral at which Rabbi Marvin Bash officiated, and both the funeral and the burial took place in Arlington National Cemetery with full military honors and representatives from the Japanese embassy in attendance.

Alfred C. Oppler (1893–1982) was division chief of the courts and law division of the Government Section during the Occupation, reporting to Charles Kades. Born in Germany to a Jewish family, Oppler's grandfather served in the Royal Prussian Army as a medical doctor during three wars and was a decorated hero who was buried with full military honors. Oppler's father was a judge and president of the courts of Berlin.

Oppler served for four years in the Imperial German Army during World War I, rising to the rank of lieutenant. He studied law at the universities of Munich, Freiberg, Berlin and Strasbourg, and at age thirty-nine he became associate justice of the Supreme Administrative Court and vice president of the Supreme Disciplinary Court, both in Berlin. Even though Oppler had been baptized, however, the rise of Hitler to power in 1933 disrupted his career. The Nazis believed that since Oppler had been born of Jewish ancestry (according to Nazi Aryan laws one was considered Jewish even with only one Jewish grandparent) he could not serve as a judge, and eventually he lost his job and his citizenship, becoming a "dehumanized outcast."

In March 1939, although he could not speak English, Oppler escaped to the United States, where he was assisted by Dr. Alfred Cohn, a friend of his family from Berlin. Oppler taught himself English, worked as a gardener, found a job as a librarian and taught German at the Berlitz School in Boston. From 1940 to 1944, he secured minor positions at Harvard University before entering government service as an adviser on German affairs.

In February 1946, Oppler was assigned to Tokyo, Japan, to assist General MacArthur on legal reforms. MacArthur, like many Americans, believed that democratizing Japan would result in its becoming a peaceful Japan, and that, in turn, would be in the best interest of the rest of the world. The Occupation used law as a tool to effect social change. Oppler was responsible for fostering the independence of Japan's judiciary, protecting and promoting civil liberties and bringing existing law into agreement with the Occupation's goals.

Although Oppler was born in Germany, spoke with a German accent and was a new American, both Kades and MacArthur believed he was the right person for the job. Knowledgeable about European legal systems, Oppler could better understand the Japanese system, which was modeled on the legal systems of Germany and France. In addition, having experienced discrimination personally, Oppler wanted to build a legal system in Japan that would prevent violations of human rights, and he became the principal architect of the legal and judicial reforms in Japan during the Occupation. His approach was not to "Americanize" Japan's legal system. Rather, Oppler worked to create a blend of American, Japanese and European legal systems, always looking for the combination that was the best fit for Japan. He did not allow his superiors to dictate his plans but followed the dictates of his conscience.

Oppler was known for his modesty, humility, wisdom and generosity. Among Oppler's contributions were the establishment of family courts, the Supreme Court and the Civil Liberties Bureau in Japan's Justice Ministry. And if Japanese lawyers and judges were to be asked to whom they owe their successful, democratic legal system, chances are Alfred Oppler would be the name they would give.

Theodore Cohen (1918–1983) became chief of the Occupation Labor Division in May 1946, and at age twenty-eight he was the Occupation administration's youngest division chief. Cohen read and spoke Japanese fluently, even though he was born in the Bronx section of New York City, to Russian Jewish parents. After graduating from public high school in the Bronx, Cohen majored in Japanese studies at the City College of New York (CCNY) and at Columbia University. His 1939 master's essay examined in two hundred pages the Japanese labor movement from 1918 to 1938.

Cohen's interest in Japan was actually accidental. He was going to write his master's essay on German anti-Semitism, but when the professor queried the members of the class for their topics, he asked them in alphabetical order, and a classmate whose last name was Chekanow took that topic just before it was Cohen's turn, so Cohen had to choose a new one. He decided on Japanese nationalism, which led to his immersing himself in every aspect of Japan, even learning the Japanese language.

At the start of the war, Cohen tried to enlist in the military, but at just under five feet tall, he did not meet the height requirements. After teaching briefly at CCNY, Cohen went to work for the foreign economic Japanese labor policy section in Washington, DC, where he drafted civil affairs guides on labor. Eventually he was recruited by the Occupation administration.

Cohen belonged to a generation of Jewish university graduates who were attracted to socialism and the labor movement. Applying his ideals to postwar Japan during the Occupation, Cohen was determined "to liberate Japanese labor from the savage repression of prewar Japanese authoritarianism, but at the same time prevent it from falling under the control of the communists." To this end, Cohen was responsible for the drafting of the labor relations adjustment law and the labor standards law, and for the establishment of procedures for resolving labor/management conflicts through conciliation, mediation and arbitration. He felt passionately about the creation of free, non-communist unions in Japan and led the American effort to support them. He also played a major role in preventing a general strike in 1947.

The philosophy and policies held by the New Dealers in Washington, DC, at the time, and not those of the Communists, drove the attitudes of those working in the Occupation. The New Deal believed in widely distributing income and the ownership of the means of production and trade, strengthening family farm ownership, breaking up monopolies, encouraging labor unions, and banning trade cartels, all by democratic government action. Cohen reported that the final order of the extreme East Asia League instructed followers to obey fully every directive of the Occupation promptly so that the Americans would see that force was not necessary and the US Army would withdraw. That same final order also advised the Japanese people to align themselves with Jews all over the world, because Jews had proven their invincibility when they triumphed over Hitler.

Cohen believed that the Japanese labor movement was not born after the war; rather, it was reborn and grew. Japanese labor unions, after all, had begun in 1883, and in 1936, there were about 420,000 non-agricultural workers in unions. By the end of 1946, four to five million Japanese workers were union members. Cohen enjoyed telling the story of the day a delegation of geisha girls arrived to tell him and MacArthur about their new labor union. Arriving in six-inch high heel shoes and colorful, elaborate kimonos, with towering hairdos and painted faces, these women put the entire staff of the Occupation out of action. Everything stopped while workers gawked at the spectacle.

Soon an American reporter accused Cohen of having leftist sympathies, so MacArthur removed Cohen from his position to avoid controversy and damage to his own presidential ambitions, even though he knew the reporter's accusation was untrue. As a child, in fact, Cohen, like many Americans, had known members of the Socialist and/or Communist Parties, including some of his relatives, but he had been a passionate anti-communist from the time he was eighteen years old and harbored an enormous fear of being labeled a Communist. His last name, nevertheless, was Jewish; he had a Japanese girl-friend and the Japanese were considered enemies; and he believed that since the Communists in jail had committed no crimes, they should be released. Cohen was very candid: what was on his mind was on his tongue, and some-times that got him into trouble. After MacArthur removed Cohen from his position as chief of the Occupation's Labor Division, he became economic adviser to the Occupation (1947–1950), where he continued to be very effec-tive in accomplishing his goals for Japan. After concluding his government service, he stayed in Japan, the country for which he had helped to achieve so much, married a Japanese woman and built a successful career with a Cana-dian import company.

Cohen considered the longest lasting influences of Occupation policy on the Japanese to be democratization and a unionized labor force. Improvement for workers was delayed until the end of 1947, but then real wages doubled over the following twelve months and then doubled again. In 1935, the dollar/yen rate of exchange was 34; in 1945, it was 31; in 1946, it was 71; in 1947, it was 200; in 1948, it was 324; and in 1949, the official rate became 360 yen to the dollar, and this was credited to Ted Cohen. The freeing of farmers from their debts and rents, and the unionization and collective bargaining of millions of white-and blue-collar workers, created a domestic mass market for consumer goods for the first time in Japanese history. Japan was elevated from a prewar exporter of poor quality items to an exporter of the finest quality goods on the world market. Many people, including Cohen, believed that increasing real wages saved the Japanese economy.

Cohen always wondered: since his parents emigrated from Russia to the United States in 1903, and since he had never been out of New York City until 1938, how could he have reached such a high level in the government? Under the circumstances, his accomplishments amazed him.

I knew Ted Cohen very well. We met in New York prior to my wife and I leaving for my rabbinic post in Tokyo. He briefed me on the Jewish community in Tokyo and on what life would be like there. I remember his telling me that no street names exist in Japan, but since the Occupation administration could not function that way, they had given names to major streets from A to Z in one direction, and from one to one hundred in the other direction. He expressed outrage that among the very first post-Occupation actions the Japanese government took was to take down the street names and numbering system the Americans had installed, the only time, he said, that anyone could find any place in Japan!

For seven years he and I jointly taught an advanced class in Jewish history at the Jewish center in Tokyo. For some time, Cohen was president of the Jewish community of Japan. I officiated at his son's bar mitzvah at the Tokyo synagogue and officiated at his daughter's wedding in Mexico, where Cohen ultimately retired.

Cohen's dog's name was L'Chaim (*L'Chaim* is a Yiddish expression, often used as a toast, meaning "To life!"). I told Cohen that he didn't need the "L," and the dog's name could just be Chaim, but everyone, especially the dog, had gotten used to "L'Chaim," and that's the name that remained.

Chapter Eighteen
Where and Why Did Prime Minister Indira Gandhi Say "Mazel Tov"?

In 1968, while serving as the rabbi of the Jewish community in Japan, I read a brief article in a magazine for stamp collectors saying that in December of that year the government of India would be issuing a postage stamp engraved with the image of the one remaining synagogue located in Jew Town, the ancient Jewish neighborhood in the southern Indian city of Cochin. The article identified the synagogue (Paradesi Synagogue) as the oldest in the British Commonwealth, as was the Jewish community there, and mentioned that Indira Gandhi,* the prime minister of India, would be speaking at a commemoration in Jew Town. Prominent, distinguished scholars and local residents also would be attending a conference in Cochin to study the history of the Jews there and to celebrate the four hundredth anniversary of this old synagogue.

I thought, "The oldest synagogue would not be in India! The oldest Jewish community would not be in India! Where is Jew Town, anyway? And why would the prime minister of India attend such a conference?"

I remembered that before I left for Japan in 1968, Rabbi Dr. Louis I. Rabinowitz, deputy editor in chief of the *Encyclopedia Judaica*, to which I was contributing articles, had told me that the most significant surprise I would find in the Far East would be Cochin, a small community off everyone's radar. News of the commemorative event in honor of the Paradesi Synagogue in Cochin

---

* Indira Gandhi, the only child of Jawaharlal Nehru, was the third prime minister of India and served from 1966 to 1977 and again from 1980 to 1984. In March 1942, she married Feroze Khan. There are many versions of why and how the name Khan became Gandhi. Some speculate that Mahatma Gandhi adopted him and, for political reasons, changed his name to Gandhi. Others think that Feroze's surname was a variation of Ghandy, a popular Parsi name.

confirmed his words. Two years later, when the Federation of Jewish Communities of Southeast Asia and the Far East was organized, I became responsible for the religious, educational and cultural activities of all the Jewish communities from India to Japan, including the one in Cochin. I realized how little I knew of this small city so far away, a city that continues to amaze me, just as Rabbi Rabinowitz predicted, no matter how many times I visit it. Every building in Jew Town has a Jewish story, each step is saturated with Jewish history and the synagogue is a magnificent treasure.

Jewish history started in India thousands of years earlier. The fleets of King Solomon most likely reached India, where they purchased items for the construction of the Temple of Jerusalem. The Romans recorded that there were already Jewish communities along both coasts of India in the first century. There are words in ancient Hebrew – like monkey, peacock, rice, sapphire, emerald, topaz and cinnamon – whose roots are Indian Sanskrit. And Maimonides* had a younger brother who tried but failed to reach India when, tragically, his ship went down in Indian waters, resulting in Maimonides falling into a deep depression.

The Jewish community proudly reiterates that in the year 379 CE there was a Jewish king of a Jewish state in Cranganore, a town in southern India about twenty-five miles north of Cochin, and the original copper plates establishing that principality or kingdom still are kept in the synagogue in Jew Town. The copper plates are etched in Tamil (a local language in southern India), and the Jewish king was Joseph Rabban, whose privileges of royalty existed for seventy-two generations until 1344, when Joseph Azar reigned as the last Jewish king. The Jewish community was very attached to the original settlement in Cranganore, which they called "Shingly." Rabbi Reuven Nissim, a poet who lived in Spain in the fourteenth century, wrote a poem, still chanted in the synagogue in Cochin, describing the Spanish Jews who saved their coins so they could travel to India to see with their own eyes the Jewish king of a Jewish state:

> I traveled from Spain.
> I had heard of the city of Shingly.
> I longed to see an Israeli king.
> Him, I saw with my own eyes.

---

* Maimonides, who lived in the Middle Ages, is regarded as the greatest Jewish philosopher. He wrote a code of laws to guide Jews on how to behave in myriad situations using the Torah and his code.

As an elementary school student, I wrote a book report about one of my heroes, Vasco da Gama, the late fifteenth-century Portuguese explorer who reached India by sea in 1498, built St. Francis Church in Cochin (the first Catholic church in India) in 1503, died in Cochin in December 1524 and was buried there (later his body was moved to Portugal). What I did not discover in elementary school is that in 1503 a man named Albuquerque followed Vasco da Gama's route to India and wrote to Portuguese officials asking for permission to "exterminate the Jews one by one as I find them."

The Jews were involved heavily in the spice trade, which flourished in India, and their successful business activities were a source of friction with both the Muslim and Portuguese merchants, who wanted to replace the Jews in the lucrative pepper trade. There was no pepper in Europe, and pepper was worth more than gold. Just a tiny amount of pepper provides so much flavor that everyone wanted it, and by 1524, the Portuguese made no secret of their resentment and anger that Jews were monopolizing the pepper trade. The International Pepper Exchange still is located on Synagogue Lane, the main street in Jew Town.

During the 160 years the Portuguese ruled in India, they brought terrible bloodshed and destruction to the innocent Jewish community, and when the Portuguese brought the Inquisition to their Eastern colony in 1560, it was the culmination of a very dark time for the Jews. The Portuguese were as cruel to the Jews in India as they were to the Jews in Portugal. Ultimately they destroyed Cranganore, including its two synagogues, a decimation so devastating to the Jews that they reacted as if it were the destruction of Jerusalem. After all, Cranganore was their Jewish state where they had lived for more than one thousand years in complete harmony with the people of India. Survivors fled to Cochin and established the tradition that a handful of soil from Jerusalem and a handful of soil from Cranganore were placed in the coffin when someone died, and when someone from Cochin had to be in the Cranganore area for any reason, he would leave by nightfall because it was considered to be cursed.

In 1568, under the protection of the local maharajah in Cochin and adjacent to his palace, the Jews built a synagogue that still stands in Jew Town. In the courtyard of the synagogue, the leading tourist attraction in Cochin, one still can see a clock tower in the shape of a cube. Hebrew numbers were seen from the synagogue; Malayalam (the language of Cochin) numbers were seen from the port; and Roman numerals were seen from the adjacent maharajah's palace. The queen of England visited this historic synagogue in Jew Town, which was

Rabbi Marvin Tokayer holding jewel-encrusted gold Torah crown, a gift from the local maharajah to the synagogue in Cochin, India

the extent of her 1997 trip to Cochin.

In the Holy Ark of the synagogue in Jew Town, the queen and other tourists also can see the Torah crown made of twenty-two-carat gold and embellished with rubies, emeralds and sapphires that was a gift from the maharajah in 1803. The carpet in front of the ark was a gift from Haile Selassie of Ethiopia, and the floor, dated 1760–1762, is made of Chinese tiles in a willow pattern with no two tiles alike. There are twelve windows in the synagogue corresponding to the twelve tribes of Israel. At the entrance to the synagogue there are two brass pillars in remembrance of the two pillars that were at the entrance to the Temple of Jerusalem, and the eternal light is a lamp filled with coconut oil.

The original synagogue music and liturgy are unique, historical, melodic and inspiring. The liturgy of Cochin has the longest Kaddish prayer (a prayer that magnifies and sanctifies God's name, recited by the leader of the prayer service and by worshippers mourning the death of a close relative) of any synagogue in the world. The synagogue had a minyan for 419 years from 1568 until 1987 when, because most of the Jews migrated to Israel, there were no longer enough congregants to have a minyan. In Israel, there is a solid gold Torah case from a synagogue in Cochin, perhaps the only one in existence; and in the Israel Museum in Jerusalem, one can find the interior of the synagogue from Synagogue Lane, Jew Town, Cochin.*

* The synagogue was erected of beautiful, carved teak wood between 1539 and 1544 and named Kadavumbagam synagogue, which means "Riverside." It was on a riverside in Cranganore, but after the Portuguese destroyed it, the Jews rebuilt it in Cochin, which is not on a riverside, but they kept the original name. The interior was purchased in 1991 and transferred to the Israel Museum. The exterior walls now enclose a warehouse in Cochin.

In 1949, the last maharajah of Cochin, H.H. Rama Varma, gave this touching farewell speech to the Jews who were leaving for Israel:

I thank you most sincerely for the hearty welcome that you have very cordially and warmly extended to me today. I am deeply touched by the spontaneous expressions of love and loyalty to my family and and myself and also by the very noble sentiments that prompted you to make kind references to my illustrious predecessors.

Cochin and its people owe much to you. The memory of your early association with this country has always been pleasant. It is recorded by historians that your people began to visit this coast as early as the days of King Solomon and they formed one of the earliest links binding the East and the West, fast with each other. It is told later on, in the early centuries of the Christian Era, some of them left their hearths and homes for good and finally settled themselves in Cochin. Without diving deep into the reasons that made you seek pastures new, the people of Cochin received you with open arms; the Ruling Family protected you from plunder and persecution. The tie of friendship between your community and the Royal Family became only stronger and closer in course of time. It may interest you to know that my grandmother used to tell us of the very pleasant hours she and the other princesses of her age spent in the company of your women-folk who usually gathered at the Palace in the afternoon.

The famous temple of historic importance that you have built here is not only a place of worship, but also a standing monument of the religious toleration and hospitality that prevailed in this part of the country from time immemorial. It is a thing of beauty and an architectural achievement in itself; a clear and visible evidence of the material prosperity and progress, attained by your community under the kind patronage of the Royal Family ever since you came here as the honoured guests of the people.

But I am glad to say that no other people deserved such treatment better. You have, on occasions more than one, shown your unflinching loyalty to the King and country that adopted you and gave you shelter. Of course, your community is small, but its historic importance is really greater. I assure you that all the legitimate interests of the minorities will always be scrupulously safeguarded, and will never be sacrificed for the selfish ends of the majority. The prosperity of the State and welfare of the people, irrespective of caste, community or colour, shall always be upper-most in my mind and I shall endeavour to promote them to the best of my abilities. It is very gratifying for me to learn that your co-religionists are now celebrating their national freedom in Palestine, the original home of your forefathers, and I heartily congratulate you on this very happy occasion.

Before I close let me thank you again for all your good wishes which I shall ever cherish in the innermost recesses of my heart with feeling of most sincere gratitude.

India is a huge country. A few foreign countries ruled in different parts of India over the centuries. The Portuguese, as noted, dominated this area from 1498 until 1663, a time of terror for not only Jews but also for Hindus, Muslims and even for Syrian Christians because they were not Roman Catholics. Sadly, not only did the Portuguese destroy the Jewish community in Cranganore, but in 1662 the Portuguese also plundered Jew Town, tragically burning all the historical records.

The Dutch period which followed from 1663 to 1795 is remembered as the Golden Age. On November 21, 1686, Moses Pareya de Paiva, a Jew, arrived from Amsterdam. He was fascinated by the Jews of Cochin and later wrote their history, and his account was translated into English for the 1968 commemoration of the Cochin synagogue. The community also assigned a special significance to the Jewish holiday known as Tu b'Av (the fifteenth of the Hebrew month of Av which coincides with July or August). For the Jews of Cochin, this day commemorates the arrival from Amsterdam of religious and holy books in Hebrew to replace the volumes destroyed by the Portuguese.

The British ruled in India from 1757 to 1947. (The Dutch were in a different part of India during the brief overlap with the British from 1792 to 1795.) Centuries earlier, however, the Cochin Jewish community played a decisive role in the history of the Jewish settlement in England. The Jews had been expelled from England in 1290, so when Shakespeare wrote *The Merchant of Venice*, he had actually never seen a Jew. Manasseh Ben Israel, a prominent Jew from Amsterdam, met with Oliver Cromwell between 1652 and 1655 to request that the Jews be permitted to reside in England again, but Cromwell was hesitant, as were his advisers. When Cromwell asked Manasseh Ben Israel if there was one place anywhere in the world where Jews were treated with honor, dignity and respect, he instantly responded by suggesting that Cromwell study the Jews of Cochin in India. Cromwell subsequently permitted Jews to live in England.

No matter which European power was in control, the maharajah, called the "King of the Jews" (the "Jewish King" in Cranganore was in a different time and place), was the protector of the Jews in Cochin who also were prominent in the maharajah's army. In 1550, when the maharajah was to go into battle, he informed his enemy that the Jews in his army did not fight on the Sabbath (Friday night to Saturday night), and amazingly, the battle was postponed for a day.

Cochin Synagogue commemorative stamp on the four hundredth anniversary of the synagogue's founding

Ezekiel Rahabi was the merchant/diplomat of the Jewish community in Cochin in the seventeenth century and set the standard for all his successors. He migrated from Aleppo, Syria, to Cochin around 1647 and became an important member of that community. He beautified the synagogue, corresponded with the world in Hebrew, produced the prayer book for the community and was, quite simply, "Mr. Cochin." When he died, his talented son David came from Syria to India.

It always was an honor to live in the area of Cochin called Jew Town, a gift from the maharajah, where the post office stamped all mail with the six-point Star of David. Jew Town is not now, and never was, a derogatory term, and Jew Town is not a ghetto. It is a unique, admired and exemplary place. It also was the most Hebrew literate and knowledgeable Jewish community, and that knowledge was passed on lovingly by parents to children, as there were no Hebrew schools, although over time there were eight synagogues in the Cochin area. And to this day, despite the fact that there are no longer any school-age Jewish children in Cochin, amazingly no tests are given in any school on Jewish holidays out of respect for this most honorable Jewish community.

On December 15, 1968, during the celebration of the four hundredth anniversary of the synagogue in Cochin, Prime Minister Indira Gandhi expressed the mutual respect that existed between the Jews and the people of India. Here are excerpts from that speech:

I am glad to have the opportunity to be with you at this historic celebration. This is not my first visit to this ancient synagogue. Each visit is a reminder of the long history of our country with which the Jews of India and certainly, the Jews of Cochin are associated and also of the tradition of religious and cultural tolerance, which is our very great heritage.

You have traced the history of the tiny but honoured Jewish community in India from the time of the Diaspora, and have paid eloquent tribute to the rulers of Cochin and to others.... We welcomed the Jews of India....

The Jewish community of India has rendered and continues to render notable service in many fields. It has contributed men of distinction to business and industry, to the civil services and the armed forces, and to the world of scholarship....

A stamp is only a bit of paper, but everyone recognizes and honours it, and it tells about our country to other countries. I am sure this stamp will enable our children to know more about the Jewish faith and the Jews of India. It is a matter of pride for us in India that all the great religions of the world are respected in our country. I offer my good wishes and say "*mazel tov*" (congratulations) to all our Jewish citizens on the occasion of this [four hundredth anniversary] celebration of the Cochin synagogue.

Indira Gandhi said she learned the word *mazel tov* from the musical *Fiddler on the Roof*.

In 1971, under the administration of Prime Minister Indira Gandhi, all property of the maharajahs was nationalized, and the princely estates were abolished. There would be one Republic of India. After the Indian government and the maharajahs spent many years unsuccessfully trying to negotiate an agreement about payment for the confiscated property, both sides decided to present their case to the Jewish community in the synagogue of Jew Town. Whatever the Jews decided would be accepted by both sides and, amazingly, it was.

A very short ferry ride from Cochin is the village of Ernakulam, which has a synagogue that dates back to 1200 and functioned until 1972. The building, shaped like an octagon, is still there intact at the edge of the food market and Jew Street. Early on in my visits to Ernakulam, I met and befriended Shabbetai Sattu Koder, an erudite, eloquent, respected and admired leader of the community. In the souvenir volume produced for the 1968 commemoration of the four hundredth anniversary of the Cochin synagogue, Koder is quoted as saying that "India is the only country where a Jewish community has lived without persecution [by the people of India] for two thousand years." His son-in-law, Samuel Hallegua, ably followed in his path and was a very articulate, learned and renowned leader of the Jewish community of Cochin.

Rabbi Marvin Tokayer holding the copper plates, Cochin, India

We must not forget that the Christian (Catholic) community also enjoyed a long history in Cochin and lived in peace with the Jews. As mentioned earlier, in 1503 Vasco da Gama built St. Francis Church in Cochin (the first Catholic Church in India). Catholics believe that Saint Thomas Apostle was sent from Jerusalem much earlier in the year 55 CE to bring the message of Christianity to the Jewish community. In fact there is an apocryphal book of the New Testament, "The Acts of Judas Thomas," which was found in Egypt and relates to this event. A popular Christian wedding song in Cochin also tells this story and refers to a Jewish flute girl who welcomed Saint Thomas.

Aramaic was the spoken language of the Jews two thousand years ago, and even the Talmud is written in Aramaic. I was most surprised to learn, however, that in the Saint Thomas Apostle Church in Cochin the prayers also were recited in Aramaic; hymns were sung in Aramaic; and the bishop's sermons were in Aramaic. In 1980, I was asked to preach to the congregation, and that was the first and last time I delivered a sermon in Aramaic. In the 1990s the community began using their local language, Malayalam, in their religious services.

In the year 849 CE, four Jewish witnesses also signed their names in Hebrew on another set of copper plates (the date of the first set, establishing the Jewish state of Cranganore, was 379 CE) acknowledging responsibility to protect the Christian community and their church in Cochin. Interestingly, when the Christian community had difficulty choosing a bishop many years later in 1747, representatives visited the synagogue in Jew Town. The Jewish community was considered to be so honest, respectful, intelligent and unbiased that they wanted the Jews to choose their bishop, which, in fact, the Jews did. (As mentioned earlier, in 1971 the Jews also successfully negotiated what had been an elusive agreement about the payment for the confiscated property that resulted from India's nationalization.) And local Muslims, Hindus and Christians visit the tomb of Nehemiah Mota, the poet, saint and mystic, who was buried in Cochin in 1615 in the old Jewish cemetery of Jew Town, and visitors always find candles, incense and people of all religions praying at his tomb.

Notwithstanding all the amazing contributions the Jews made in Cochin, and despite the respectful and tolerant relations the Jews had with local Christians, Muslims and Hindus in India, the story of the Jews of Cochin would not be complete without mentioning the tension that existed among the white, black and brown Jews who lived there. This tension was influenced, in no small part, by the caste system in India. Slavery, common in India, was abolished in 1855, prior to which time both white and black Jews had owned slaves. Black Jews, known as Malabar Jews, claimed ancestry from the original Jewish settlers two thousand years ago, and had their own synagogues. Brown Jews are freed slaves and also the offspring of white Jews and their black mistresses.

Abraham Barak Salem, known as A.B. Salem (1882–1967), was a descendant of a freed slave. Like each member of this group, Salem had two family documents in Hebrew, one declaring his freedom from slavery, and another affirming his conversion to Judaism. Sadly, however, in the primarily white congregation, he and his fellow brown Jews were not permitted to sit in a chair. Rather, they had to sit in the back anteroom on the floor. Brown Jews also were not called to the Torah and were not counted for the minyan. Years ago, when I entered the synagogue on the Sabbath, despite the fact that slavery had been abolished in 1855 and segregation among Jews ended in 1942, all the white congregants watched to see with whom and where I would sit. I sat with A.B. Salem's son Raymond.

A.B. Salem, with both a college degree and law degree, was the man in the community most knowledgeable about Judaism at the time, so he served as the unofficial rabbi of the community. Like Mahatma Gandhi, he went on hunger strikes, staged sit-ins and exhibited passive resistance to break the segregation in Cochin among Jews of different colors, all without much success. Finally, in 1942, white Jewish youngsters in the community joined Salem's protest. Every year on Simchat Torah, a much-loved holiday when the Jewish teenagers carried all the heavy Torahs with their gold crowns in a procession down the entire length of Synagogue Lane, thousands of Hindus, Christians and

Muslims would line the street eagerly awaiting the celebration. In 1942, however, the crowd waited much longer than usual. The teenagers, fed up with the discrimination against A.B. Salem and with the segregation among the white, brown and black Jews, protested by refusing to carry the Torahs in the procession.

Left to right: Indira Gandhi, S.S. Koder, Elias Roby, Isaac Hallegua, Samuel Koder; courtesy of Nathan Katz

Since the adults were not up to the task of carrying the heavy Torahs, the teenagers' strike finally ended the discrimination, and the celebration began.

When the Jews planned to migrate to Israel and worried about being accepted, it was A.B. Salem who was chosen to go to Israel to inform the officials in the Ministry of the Interior of the glorious history of this tiny Jewish community in Cochin. Salem impressed everyone in Israel, and the migration of the Jews went very smoothly. The street on which the Jewish cemetery is located in Cochin was renamed A.B. Salem Street.

Dan, my youngest son, was a teenager when I brought him to Cochin. He was so impressed with the story of A.B. Salem that he told A.B.'s son Gamliel how proud he was of his father and asked Gamliel for any souvenir or remembrance of his father. Gamliel gave my son A.B. Salem's door mezuzah (a parchment inscribed with Hebrew texts, placed in a decorative case and attached to doorposts in Jewish homes as a sign of faith) which to this day remains on my son's bedroom doorpost.

Despite the end of slavery and the end of segregation among Jews, problems continued. The first marriage of a brown Jew to a white Jew in 1950 was historic and confrontational when Balfour Salem, A.B. Salem's oldest son, married a member of the prestigious Koder family. In 1957 A.B. Salem's son Gamliel, whom I saw as recently as February 2012, married Reema Roby, also the daughter of a prestigious, white Jewish family. The discomfort with these marriages, expressed by many, existed despite the fact that the white Jews inquired about the matter to Rabbi David Ben Zimra in Cairo as far back as the early sixteenth century. He responded that white Jews are Jews, black Jews are Jews, and if brown Jews underwent a token immersion they are Jews, too, and all Jews are to be treated equally, with absolutely no discrimination whatsoever.

In the seventeenth century, another inquiry about the same issue was sent to Rabbi Jacob de Castro of Alexandria, Egypt, and he also replied that there is absolutely no racial discrimination in Judaism. A Jew is a Jew is a Jew. And in 1882 the same response came from Rabbi Raphael Meir Panigel (1804–1903), chief rabbi of Jerusalem and rabbi of the Ottoman Empire, and again from a rabbi in Baghdad who was furious at the discrimination by the white Jews of Cochin against Jews of different skin colors.

Irrational prejudices, however, seem to overtake law, logic and ethics. Prejudice dies slowly, as people's biases are slow to change. Despite the official stand that discrimination by Jew against Jew is never acceptable, descendants of freed slaves still are not buried in the center of the cemetery in Cochin but, rather, they are buried near the wall at the end of the cemetery.

In the meantime, several years ago I was leading a group on a visit to India, and as we entered an organic vegan restaurant in the city of Agra, the proprietor showered all of us with rose petals, explaining that we should "never forget that once you were kings here in India, and you should be welcomed as royalty." And we also should not forget that the larger history and experience of the Jews in Cochin is one that justly earned Jews great respect from Christians, Muslims and Hindus.

Chapter Nineteen

Beauty Queens, Military Heroes and More: India's Bene Israel

When Hellenistic Greece dominated the world more than twenty-two hundred years ago, the response of Jews in ancient Israel was to become "Jewish Greeks." They wanted to maintain their ancestral Jewish traditions but incorporate Greek wisdom, insight and engineering to enhance them. The Greek authorities based in Syria rejected this idea and went so far as to mandate the death sentence for anyone observing the Sabbath, following kosher dietary rules, circumcising boys or any other religious practices of the Jews. Greeks would enter a village, arrest the local sage, place a pig on the altar (kosher dietary rules forbid the eating of pork, among other things) and, upon penalty of death, force the sage to eat it. The Jewish people were not under attack; now it was their traditions and religion that were under attack. When Jews no longer could observe their way of life in their homeland of ancient Israel, some sought freedom in the forest, some hid in caves and some fled to India by boat. Tragically, the boats hit dangerous rocks and went down at sea south of Bombay (now Mumbai), but fourteen Jews survived out of possibly three boats that left ancient Israel, and they became the founders of the Bene Israel community in India over two millenia ago.

India always had a reputation for religious tolerance. The Dalai Lama escaped from Tibet to India to escape Chinese persecution, and the Zoroastrians of Persia fled to India to escape Islamic persecution. When the Jews who died at sea washed ashore on the narrow strip in northwest India called the Konkan Coast, the Jews who survived buried them adjacent to the beach, and that cemetery is still there in Navgaon, about thirty miles south of Bombay. The graves are oriented from east to west, facing Jerusalem. Since this

Poet Laureate Nissim Ezekiel, wearing white yarmulke, reading his poetry; Rabbi Marvin Tokayer is seated next to him

orientation was not customary for Hindu remains, and since it was before the start of Christianity and Islam, the orientation of the graves provides evidence that Jews once came ashore there.

The survivors settled a short distance inland, where they worked in agriculture or became oil pressers (pressing all types of seeds for oil) who did not work on the Sabbath. In the local language they were called *shanwar telis*, Sabbath oil pressers. Since no one in India observed any Sabbath on any day of the week at the time, Sabbath observance by the oil pressers on Saturday reinforces evidence that they were Jews. For nineteen hundred years, no one knew of their existence, and they had no Torah, no Jewish sacred ritual objects and no contact with other Jews. During their long isolation, they forgot Hebrew and many nuances of the Jewish rituals and traditions. They, nevertheless, continued to rest on the Sabbath, observe dietary rules and circumcise boys, and they recited one line of the Shema (Hebrew word for the call to prayer) before every religious ceremony or event.

In the middle of the eighteenth century, David Rahabi of Cochin, India (see chapter 18), five hundred miles south of Navgaon, was in the area on behalf of the Dutch East India Company. Rahabi was a very religious Jew, and when he explained his dietary and Sabbath rules (as well as other elements of Jewish observance) to the local Indians, he was surprised when they said they knew all about them. They explained that they were familiar with these rituals and traditions because they were being practiced by a small group living in the area. Of course, Rahabi was eager to meet this group. According to Nissim Ezekiel, India's former poet laureate, an expert on Bene Israel history and my friend, the meeting was quite cordial, and Rahabi was amazed as it became clear that this small group of people were, in fact, Jews.

More evidence that they were Jews were their dietary considerations as Rahabi planned his dinner with them. They told Rahabi that they could eat meat and chicken if only they could remember the proscribed way the animals had to be prepared; otherwise they abstained. They would eat fish with scales and fins, but not shell fish. When Rahabi asked what they called themselves, they responded "Bene Israel." When Rahabi asked what their ancient language was, they knew only the first line of "Shema Yisrael" (Hear O Israel).

Their recounting of their various holidays was more evidence that they were Jewish. There was one holiday, however, with which they were unfamiliar: Chanukah. They had left ancient Israel before the end of the Chanukah story occurred and, therefore, had never heard of it. Under Antiochus IV, the Jewish religion was outlawed in 168 BCE, but in 167 BCE, the Maccabee family led a successful revolt, removed the statue of Zeus from the Jerusalem Temple and freedom of religion prevailed. Chanukah is the eight-day joyous festival in late November or in December that commemorates the liberation and rededication of the Temple in Jerusalem in the second century BCE. Rahabi was certain that the Bene Israel were descendants of ancient Israel, lost for more than nineteen hundred years, and he arranged for fellow Jews to come from Cochin to fill in the gaps in their Jewish knowledge.

Nissim Ezekiel, the prominent poet laureate of India from 1988 to 2004, made a deep impression on me. Ezekiel was intellectually involved in the literary and cultural life of Bombay for more than fifty years, and he was not only a poet but also a critic, editor, teacher, political commentator and the seminal influence on Indian literature. Born in December 1924 to Moses and Diana Ezekiel in Bombay, Ezekiel was not by birth and heritage a Hindu, Muslim, Christian or Parsee; he was a Bene Israel Jew and possibly a stranger to these other religions that surrounded him as a child. In 1945 he received his bachelor of arts degree with honors in English at the University of Bombay, and two years later he received his master of arts degree in English literature and began teaching at a local university. In 1948, Ezekiel visited London and studied primarily philosophy and literature at the University of London before he returned to India in 1952. On the voyage back to India on a cargo ship, Ezekiel worked as a deck-scrubber and shoveled coal.

The same year, Ezekiel was named editor of the *Illustrated Weekly of India*, published *A Time to Change* and married Daisy Jacob Dandekar. One year later, he published *Sixty Poems*, and two years later he became founding editor of *Quest – A Bimonthly Journal of Arts and Ideas*. Ezekiel published *The Third* in 1959; in 1960 he published *The Unfinished Man*; and in 1961 he became associate editor of *Imprint*, responsible for writing the entire book review section of every issue. In 1961 Ezekiel also served as head of the English Department at

Bombay College and in 1962 he worked as art critic for the *Times of India*. In 1964 Ezekiel served as visiting professor at the University of Leeds in England; he published *The Exact Name* in 1965; and in 1966 he became founding editor of *Poetry India*. In 1967 he served as visiting professor at the University of Chicago.

In 1969 Ezekiel published three plays and rejoined the staff of the *Illustrated Weekly of India* to serve as poetry editor. In 1972 he was appointed executive editor of India's chapter of PEN (PEN is an organization that defends freedom of expression; resists censorship; and promotes reading, forums and literary awards); and in 1974 he served as editor of the Indian section of *World Poetry*. In what was a turning point of sorts, in 1974 Ezekiel was invited by the United States government to read his poetry as part of the international visitors program, and in 1976 Michigan State University's *Journal of South Asian Literature* featured Nissim Ezekiel in a special issue. Ezekiel's *Hymns in Darkness* was published in 1977, and his discussions of books and the arts were regularly featured on the radio during the 1970s.

On a trip Ezekiel took throughout Europe in 1963, he purposely traveled without any books so that he could see and hear all that was around him without being distracted. He was struck by the silence in his hotel room, compared to the constant noise in India. With the change in time zones, Ezekiel slept little and awoke too early for breakfast. With nothing to do, he picked up the Gideon Bible and started to read the Psalms. Within minutes, he had started writing his own psalms. Ezekiel's *Latter Day Psalms*, published by Oxford University Press in 1982, are a direct criticism of modern life and civilization and his argument in favor of a more humane, progressive and inclusive religion. That year Ezekiel also became professor of American literature at the University of Bombay. Ezekiel served as representative of the American Joint Distribution Committee (JDC) in India in 1986, and in 1989, Oxford University Press published his *Collected Poems, 1952–1988*. Over his lifetime, Ezekiel wrote more than five hundred essays and book reviews. In 1988 he received from the president of India the Padma Shri (great person) Award, the most prestigious honor awarded to any Indian citizen, for outstanding contributions to India.

Ezekiel was the public face of the literary and academic establishment of India. Newspaper and periodical editors were eager to publish his poetry, plays, short stories, essays, and art and book reviews. His style was described in many ways. His humor perhaps was therapeutic and a defense against the pain of the real world, and his keen intelligence, use of irony and wit and his turns of a phrase delighted the reader.

Ezekiel believed that every writer needs a national cultural identity. Without that, he said, a writer becomes a series of imitations, echoes and responses without development because there is nothing at the core to develop. His colleagues always found his poetry to be very Jewish, and although he was not sure what that meant, he said that he could not help turning to Jewish sources and themes more as he grew older.

Ezekiel's personal life was somewhat of a mystery. He believed that women were the unsung heroes of the Bene Israel community; they kept their families intact and maintained Jewish traditions while their husbands were busy with other matters, but he seldom mentioned his own wife or child. He never seemed to have much money, yet he moved easily within Bombay society. Very few people visited his home. I met with him every year when I visited Bombay (meeting with him was an attraction for me to visit India annually) and personally found him to be very courteous and generous, always trying to advance the cause of literature and the arts. One Saturday afternoon during the 1990s, I took a group of tourists, whom I was guiding, to meet with Ezekiel over tea and cookies at the Jewish Club adjacent to the Knesseth Eliyahu Synagogue, and he made an unforgettable impression on all of us. If we had not appreciated poetry before, we did after listening to him read his own poetry, which included Jewish content. We heard the alliteration, the magnificent sounds and use of words and the changes in his intonation. His writing of poetry was more than just an avocation or a profession; it was a crusade to contribute positively to India. We felt honored to be in his presence.

Every year Ezekiel encouraged me to write this book, and he even offered me his desk and promised to edit every chapter as I wrote it. In 1998, however, Ezekiel's behavior started changing, and his friends abandoned him as a result. Twelve years earlier, when Ezekiel had accepted a position with the JDC, he did not want to receive a salary for what he saw as charitable work. The JDC raises money from American Jews and uses the funds to help Jews in need all over the world, and Ezekiel had been proud to help without payment, much to his wife's dismay. Eventually, however, when Ezekiel was diagnosed and then hospitalized with Alzheimer's disease, the JDC came forward to help him. I visited him, but he was confused and living in the past. It was heartbreaking to see this great poet, teacher and friend slowly disappearing, unaware of what was happening. One day I received a message that Ezekiel had died of a lung infection. I was sad that I had not written my book, and I mourned the loss of my tea companion and friend.

Bollywood is the name of the film industry in Mumbai. Until 1920, there were no female actresses in the film industry in India because it was considered to be an inappropriate profession for respectable women. Men played female roles by shaving their facial hair and wearing saris. Eventually women did enter the profession, but not Hindu or Muslim women. Rather, Jewish women from the Bene Israel community became prominent in the film industry. Susan Solomon, Ruby Myers, Rose Ezra and Florence Ezekiel (not related to Nissim Ezekiel) were among the better known Jewish actresses. In 1947 Esther Victoria Abraham, who starred in more than thirty films, was elected India's first Miss India. Her daughter, also a film star, was named Miss India in 1967, and one of her films played for eighty-two weeks.

Other Bene Israel also were prominent in Bollywood. On March 14, 1931, *Alam Ara* (Light of the World) became the first talkie movie in India, and the screenplay and music were written by Joseph Penkar David, an eccentric Bene Israel who always wore a fur hat, even in the summer. Bunny Reuben was the classic film historian; David Herman was a prominent choreographer; and David Abraham, who also received the Padma Shri Award, starred in more than one hundred films.

The Bene Israel also distinguished themselves in the armies of the Indian states, serving in senior positions under Hindus and Muslims even before the British presence in India. Then, after service in the British East India Company armed forces, and later in the British Indian Army, the Bene Israel accomplished a major achievement. They became known for being intelligent, disciplined, loyal, brave and superb leaders, and they were given promotions and received numerous medals. In all their years in India, the Bene Israel experienced no hatred or anti-Semitism; rather, they were respected by and contributed greatly to India. This changed under British rule. Until 1870, the British Army considered the Bene Israel – and everyone else who wasn't British – as foreigners, colored or native Indians, and they described the Bene Israel as all three. In 1870, though, the Bene Israel were promoted to "preferred minority" and were finally paid European wages and rations.

Vice Admiral Benjamin Abraham Samson (1916–2008) started his career by joining the merchant navy training ship as a cadet. After completing his three-year course, he joined the Merchant Navy and rose to the rank of captain.

Without further training, he then joined the Indian Navy as an officer, went on to complete advanced naval training at the Imperial Defense College of London and served with distinction as flag officer, commanding the western fleet from an Indian aircraft carrier and from a destroyer during an India-Pakistan war. During World War II Samson saw battle on many fronts, including as a sailor on the last ship to leave Burma before it fell to the Japanese. After the war he was appointed naval attaché in London. He also held the position of chief of personnel of navy headquarters and then served as commander of two war ships of the Indian Navy. Later he served four years as commandant of the National Defense College of India. He received the Paramvir Vishita Seva Medal (peacetime military medal) from India for his brilliant contributions to the Indian Navy. This medal, referred to as the PVSM, is the highest, ultimate award for bravery, and it is given only to someone who previously has won an award for bravery.

Vice Admiral Samson was an inspiring figure – charming, polished, eloquent and courteous – with a great sense of humor. His lectures were never boring, and neighbors, vendors and shopkeepers loved to stop to chat with him. India's first prime minister, Jawarharlal Nehru, was very proud of the Indian Navy and liked to show it off to foreigners and heads of state. In April 1960 Egypt's president Abdul Gamel Nasser was invited to India, where his schedule included spending a day and night with Vice Admiral Samson, who met him in New Delhi when he landed. Someone in the air traffic control tower informed Samson that a formation of fighter jets had been sent aloft to escort President Nasser's plane. When Samson asked the name of the pilot who was leading the formation, he was told it was First Lieutenant David Solomon. Samson thought, "Here is the leader of the Arabs coming to visit the prime minister of India, spending a day and night as the guest of a Jewish vice admiral, and just a few feet away is a Jewish squadron leader and the air traffic controller is another Jewish officer! Only in India could this have happened without anyone else giving it a second thought!

Major General Jonathan Reuben Samson (1918–1995), not related to Vice Admiral Samson, was another Bene Israel held in high regard by the Indian military. He was a champion hockey player and excelled in crew. He graduated as both an electrical engineer and a mechanical engineer, joined the army in 1940 and established a reputation as a dynamic leader and developer of weapons. He created a fully modernized military using electronics, radar and the most sophisticated technology of the time. Provost Marshal Michael Samuel,

Lieutenant General Russell Mordecai and Advocate General Ellis Jhirad were also Bene Israel.

Reuben David Joseph Dandekar (1912–1989) was an internationally renowned Bene Israel Indian zoologist who created a technique that fosters the bonding between humans and animals. Throughout his life, Dandekar loved and cared for animals as if they were his children. His father was a doctor, and from observing his father's care of his patients, Dandekar learned how to nurse sick animals back to health. He was so skilled that even though he had no formal veterinary training, he was allowed to treat sick animals. He also had several patents on medications for birds and animals. The animals loved him, and he was able to tame the fiercest beasts, as illustrated in pictures of him with a tiger in his lap. The Padmashree Reuben David Natural History Museum is named for him, and there is a bust of him in the Ahmedabad Zoo. Reuben received the prestigious Tamara Patra Award (government of India award for service to the nation) and also the Padma Shri Award.

Esther David (Dandekar) Reuben (1945–), Reuben's daughter, also is a very accomplished member of the Bene Israel community. She received her university degree in the history of fine arts and sculpture, became a professor of art and served as a columnist and art critic for the *Times of India*. Esther is a well-known author of books that are based primarily on her rich Jewish heritage and upbringing. Her first book was *The Walled City* (1997); she also wrote *The Book of Esther*, *The Book of Rachel* and *My Father's Zoo*. She edited an anthology of earthquake stories and a chapter on the beautiful apparel worn in her community. Like her father, Esther has received numerous awards in India and in Europe.

Rebecca Reuben (1889–1957) had a maternal grandfather (b. 1843) who in 1871 was the first Bene Israel to earn a degree in civil engineering from the University of Bombay. One of his daughters (Rebecca's aunt) became the first Bene Israel woman to acquire a college degree in India. Rebecca was eight years old when she entered the High School for Indian Girls, one of the oldest secondary schools for women in India. Rebecca matriculated at the University of Bombay in 1905 where she was the first and only woman during the first half of the twentieth century to receive the highest grade in the matriculation exam. She was an excellent student in science, math and languages, able to speak English, Hebrew, Marathi and Sanskrit and to write in all of them except Hebrew. Rebecca always wanted to be a teacher, so she chose to major in liberal arts rather than in science, despite winning the science prize. She graduated with honors with a degree in history and later received a teaching diploma. Rebecca studied Hebrew with Dr. Israel Abrahams at Cambridge University in England. He certified that she was qualified to teach Hebrew saying, "We are all saying that if there are many like her, then the Bene Israel must be one of the finest sections of our people on the face of the earth."

After the British introduced Western-style education in India, those who received this form of education found better jobs and enjoyed a higher status in society. Seeing the results of getting a good education, the Bene Israel founded the Bene Israel Benevolent Society in 1853 to provide education with a religious base for children in their community, and in 1875 they established the Israelite School, later known as the Elly Kadoorie School (see chapter 8). It was to this school that Rebecca dedicated her life, giving up a more prestigious position as the principal of a major college for women. Speaking Marathi, the local language, Rebecca emphasized secular education and also taught English, Hebrew and Judaism, helping to bring the Bene Israel community into the modern world. In addition, Rebecca developed excellent youth activities, established a children's reading room, oversaw production of a student journal, organized student excursions and holiday celebrations, started a junior congregation for Sabbath services and created alumni groups. Girls from the Bene Israel community were educated and many became teachers; Hindu girls were married off as children and, thus, did not attend school.

Academically the school was successful, but financially it was a disaster. Fortunately, Rebecca had the skills to unite groups for a common cause and was able to convince the bankers to waive the interest on the loan they had made to the school, but, nevertheless, the school incurred a yearly deficit. In 1928 Rebecca asked Sir Elly Kadoorie to rebuild the school and provide the funds to make the school worthy of the great Bene Israel community. He agreed under three conditions: first, the school had to pay off or write off the school debt so that he could start with a clean slate; second, the community would raise funds to contribute to the construction of a new building; and third, the school would be named for him. All these conditions were accepted gladly; construction started in November 1928 and continued for eighteen months. At the point when the structure had been completed but the inside remained unfinished, Rebecca persuaded Sir Elly to increase his donation. Thanks to his support, the building was completed inside and out, and the opening ceremony took place at the end of 1930. The school remains to this very day, and Michael Kadoorie, the son of Lord Lawrence Kadoorie and Sir

Elly's grandson, recently gave a significant donation to repair the building. Rebecca was principal of the school from 1922 until her retirement in 1950. She was named honorary principal in 1950 and retained that title until the day she died in 1957.

Rebecca made significant contributions to the field of education. She wrote the most widely used textbooks to teach English in India. These books were published by Macmillan & Co. Harold Macmillan, who admired Rebecca greatly, was director of the company in India and later became prime minister of England. Rebecca started a journal for women, contributed articles in Hebrew and served on numerous government committees. She also served as a Children's Court judge and was appointed a justice of the peace. In addition, Rebecca was secretary of the Bombay Women's Council and was able to play traditional Indian musical instruments.

As was evident from her commitment to the Israelite School, Rebecca had a very strong Jewish identity. In 1925 she was an original member of the Jewish Religion Union (JRU), based on the principles of Liberal (Reform) Judaism, overcoming objections that she was principal of an Orthodox Jewish school. She served as president of the JRU and held Sabbath classes for members. The first world conference for Jewish education took place in Jerusalem in 1947, and Rebecca represented Indian Jewry and stated, "Only Jewish education has kept us alive as a people dedicated to truth and righteousness." She also wrote to Prime Minister Nehru, "We are a people of two loyalties but not divided loyalties. We have been sustained and nourished by India and Israel, and to both we owe a deep debt of gratitude."

Rebecca was one of the first generation of Indian women who chose to remain single, live simply and devote themselves to social and national causes. Her complete commitment to her community was obvious, and she earned the respect of her students and colleagues. Rebecca was a recipient of the Padma Shri Award, and during a visit to the school to which she devoted herself, B.G. Kher, the chief minister of Bombay Province, reportedly said, "If Miss Reuben wanted to, she would be elected education minister."

Every Jewish community in the world would have been proud to have Dr. Jerusha Jhirad (1890–1984) as a member. Jerusha was born in a very conservative India, where many women would rather die than be examined by a male doctor. The family was not financially well-off, and she never forgot that she was not able to attend a friend's wedding because she did not have an appropriate sari to wear. Her great-grandfather served in the British Army and was awarded the Star of India, and her maternal grandfather inculcated in her the value of an education and, with her uncle, he conducted Sabbath and High Holiday (Rosh Hashanah and Yom Kippur) services in their home. One of their valued possessions was their Torah scroll. Jerusha's mother taught her to read, write and do basic arithmetic and she also read to Jerusha from the Torah. Their home was religiously observant, and religion taught Jerusha to live with dignity and honesty. Their Sabbath always was observed with a festive meal, the lighting of the candles, and her father blessing all the children. Jerusha, who won the Sanskrit Award while in high school, was eager to learn new things and make her mother proud of her.

Jerusha always remembered how her ill sister was saved by a British doctor. She also never forgot when another family member went into labor and started bleeding profusely after the birth. A doctor was present but had to remain in another room, as no man was permitted to enter the woman's room. He gave instructions to the nurse and midwife, but the woman died. It is no surprise, therefore, that early on Jerusha dreamed of becoming a physician and managing the care of young mothers and their newborn babies in Cama Hospital in Bombay.

She wanted to help anyone in distress. "Whatever you receive is what God has given you in trust, to enable you to help your fellow human being," she said. Jerusha always was first in her class and was eager to study abroad, but the Indian government scholarship was open to men only, and she was dependent on merit scholarships to enable her to secure her higher education. Surprisingly, Jerusha became the first woman to receive a merit scholarship and attended the London School of Medicine for Women. In 1912, she graduated first in her class, won most of the awards and became the first Indian woman to be an intern and resident in a London hospital. While in London she joined the Jewish Liberal synagogue, attended Sabbath and High Holiday services and enjoyed a friendly and supportive relationship with the rabbis, even after her return to India in 1919.

In 1928 Dr. Turner Watts, the doctor who saved Jerusha's sister, retired. Through dedication and devotion Jerusha Jhirad's dream came true, and she was appointed medical officer in charge of Cama Hospital, the first woman to obtain this appointment. Once, a Muslim woman was admitted with suspicion of ectopic gestation (the fetus is developing outside the uterus). Dr. Jhirad was threatened by the woman's husband with death if she touched his wife. During the night, the woman persuaded her husband to let Dr. Jhirad operate, which she did successfully the next morning. A year later, the woman developed similar symptoms, was rushed to the hospital, and this time the woman's husband requested that Dr. Jhirad operate on his wife immediately.

Dr. Jhirad enjoyed teaching and held special sessions on weekday nights and on Sunday mornings for medical and postgraduate students, and even men respected Dr. Jhirad enough to attend. She pioneered the concept of having volunteers work at the hospital. Patients were usually alone in the hospital while their families were working, and volunteers were enthusiastic and helpful. They could talk to patients, help them write letters, teach them handiwork and bring them items they wanted or needed. Dr. Jhirad also created a postnatal clinic, well baby clinics, and a gynecological clinic. She also found time to contribute articles to the *Journal of Obstetrics and Gynecology, Obstetrics of the British Empire* and the *American Journal of Obstetrics and Gynecology.*

Dr. Jhirad's monthly salary was paid in silver rupees brought to her on a silver tray covered with a white cloth. She would send a man across the street from the hospital to her mother's house where her mother received and counted with great pleasure the fruits of her daughter's successful labor. Dr. Jhirad did not work on the Sabbath, although after attending Sabbath prayers she made her rounds to patients at the hospital. Any fees she received for work on the Sabbath, she gave to charity, and she gave 10 percent of all her earnings to charity as the Torah prescribes.

In 1936 the hospital celebrated its golden jubilee, and Dr. Jhirad saw this as an opportunity for fundraising. British, Indian, Muslim, Parsee, Christian and Jewish women worked together on the celebration, and Dr. Jhirad got to know all these women in a way that otherwise would not have been possible. They raised a large sum of money and were able to create an outpatient department, x-ray and pathology departments and housing for residents that became the first postgraduate hostel in Bombay.

At Dr. Jhirad's farewell party when she retired in 1947, the attendees manipulated a game so that she won a Schaeffer fountain pen with her name on it. The same year she was elected a fellow of the Royal College of Obstetricians and Gynecologists.

After retiring, Dr. Jhirad remained active in her field. She was a member of the medical faculties of three universities in India and was an examiner of postgraduates in gynecology in several Indian cities. Often when she went to a hospital to examine the facilities, she looked so young that she was directed to the student hall. On her eightieth birthday, the medical library at Cama Hospital was dedicated in her name.

Dr. Jhirad, a favorite of the poet laureate Nissim Ezekiel, was serious, efficient and quick-witted. She could converse affectionately and light-heartedly with young people at their picnics and concerts, and she was also understanding and patient with the elderly. She was blessed with a good brain, could learn quickly and could retain material well. Her good memory also enabled her to remember all the quotations from the poetry she read. Dr. Jhirad received the Padma Shri Award in 1966. In May 1984 Dr. Jhirad fell and suffered a fracture. After that, her health deteriorated quickly, and she passed away, a few months after her ninety-third birthday.

Dr. Jhirad played a significant role in modernizing not only medicine in India but also the Jewish community in India. She established *Stre Mandal*, a women's association which included Rebecca Reuben, where women met regularly. In 1925 she also started the Jewish Religious Union (JRU), a branch of Liberal Judaism with which Rebecca Reuben was associated from the start. Throughout her life, Dr. Jhirad always recited morning and evening prayers, which she knew by heart, and never purchased expensive clothing, jewelry or items considered to be luxuries. She lived in a simple home and ate simple foods. To Dr. Jhirad, doing otherwise would have been an abuse of the money God entrusted to her. Dr. Jhirad believed that, "There is nothing more satisfying in life than to give. It is only this and an unblemished trust in the Almighty that can give us peace of mind."

Judah Reuben, another prominent member of the Bene Israel community in India, served as a cricket umpire from 1960 until his retirement in 1977. He had a sterling reputation, was very well respected and served as a referee for ten matches, meaning a series of games played over the course of five days. There was major tension in India between Hindus and Muslims, and that tension escalated when they competed in cricket games. Both sides wanted a neutral referee, and both sides were happy when Judah Reuben was that referee.

Over the years, many other members of the Bene Israel community distinguished themselves. Dr. Abraham Solomon Erulkar was the personal physician of Mahatma Gandhi. Dr. Eliezer Best was director of medical education in India. Joshua Benjamin, my close friend, was chief architect for the government of India. David Ezra Reuben was chief justice of the High Court from 1943 to 1953; Israel Solomon was also a prominent judge; Nissim Moses, who now lives in Israel, is the contemporary historian of the Bene Israel community; Anne Solomon Killekar encouraged female Muslim education and was the principal of a pioneering and successful Muslim school; and Ruth Abraham and Sophie Pringle received Papal gold medals for excellence in teaching in a Catholic school. In 1830, Ezekiel Moses Ezekiel initiated the revival of Hebrew as a second language of study for matriculation at the University of Bombay and became Chair of Hebrew Studies there in 1870. In 1937 Dr. Elijah Moses (1873–1957), the first Bene Israel doctor, was elected mayor of Bombay by a landslide, India's first and only Bene Israel mayor. Not surprisingly, there is a street named for him in Bombay. Samuel R. Rahamin and Hanna Ezekiel were prominent Bene Israel artists.

Siona Benjamin was born in Bombay in 1960. She was raised in a Bene Israel family and attended a Zoroastrian school, all while living in a Hindu Muslim society. She is a rising star in the field of art, with the unique contribution of combining Jewish, Hindu, Mughal, Persian and Muslim themes. Her art depicts both the old and new world, and she is inspired by Jewish and Indian literature. Her themes include Indian mythology, *tikkun olam* (improving the world), and Bene Israel practices, customs, traditions and institutions. She designed and painted a Holy Ark for an American synagogue and was a Fulbright Scholar working on projects that weave Indian and Jewish narratives. In September–October 2013, a major exhibition of her work was mounted at the Prince of Wales Museum in Mumbai (formerly Bombay). A resident of New Jersey, Benjamin is also working on a series of paintings of women in the Bible.

In 1796 Samuel Ezekiel Divekar was a British soldier in the Anglo-Mysore War (1780–1784). After he survived being captured and imprisoned, he vowed to create the first Bene Israel synagogue in India, which he did in 1796, and it still stands on the street named for him, Samuel Street. In 1996 I attended the two hundredth anniversary of this synagogue, Shaar Harachamin (Gates of Mercy), and I cherish the memory.

There are now thirty-one Bene Israel synagogues in India, including Shaare Rason (est. 1840), Tifereth Israel (est. 1886), Etz Haeem (est. 1888), Maghen Hassidim (est. 1904) and Rodef Shalom (est. 1925). There also are about fifteen Bene Israel synagogues in Israel. The current world Bene Israel population is about ninety thousand, with five thousand in India and seventy thousand in Israel. An additional fifteen thousand Bene Israel live in Canada, Australia and other places. I personally have provided Torah scrolls to Shaar Hashamayim (est. 1879) in Thane (a suburb of Mumbai), Maghen Aboth (est. 1842)

Malida festive ceremony of Bene Israel community in Alibag, India

in Alibag (near Navgaon where the Bene Israel arrived twenty-two hundred years ago), and Beth Elohim (est. 1863) in Panvel (northeast of Mumbai and about two hours from Alibag). The synagogue in Panvel was destroyed in a monsoon flood, and the community decided to start rebuilding, on the theory that if they would acquire a Torah first, then the building itself would follow, which it did. I also delivered a Torah scroll to a rabbi who periodically visited isolated, remote Jewish communities in India, taking a miniature synagogue with him in his vehicle.

When I delivered the Torah scroll to the synagogue in Alibag, where the main street is named Israel Way, they held a special Malida ceremony, a happy and popular celebration which the Bene Israel believe originated in the Temple of Jerusalem. Malida, the name of both the ceremony and the food that is served, is a thanksgiving or peace offering consisting of pounded rice mixed with sugar, dried fruits, coconuts, rosewater, cinnamon and nutmeg, surrounded by five kinds of fruit, including dates. Songs and silent prayers for good health, a happy marriage, thanksgiving and other personal requests are offered to Elijah.

One can still see unique mezuzahs in India. Usually mezuzahs are miniature ritual prayer scrolls that Jews attach to the entranceways of their homes, buildings and synagogues. The unusual mezuzahs in India, however, are palm prints which are dipped in blood and placed on a piece of paper that is attached to the right side of doorposts in memory of the biblical story about God passing over the homes of the Israelites who put a drop of blood on their doorposts

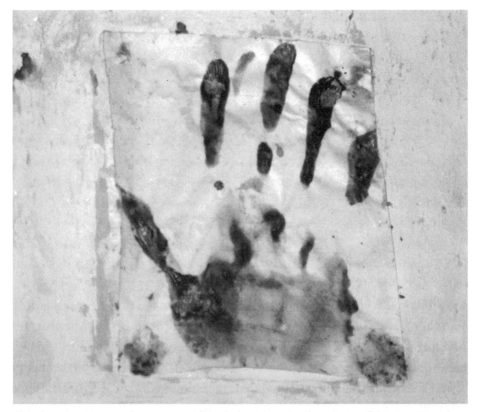

Bloody palm print used as a mezuzah and placed on the doorposts of the Bene Israel homes

in Egypt. These palm prints are changed every Passover, the seven-day biblical spring festival commemorating the exodus of Jews from slavery in Egypt.

The major emigration from India to modern Israel took place between 1950 and 1970. How nice it would be to know more about the Bene Israel community in India, as well as all the Jewish communities in the Far East. We do know that the ancient Bene Israel community was historically important, fascinating, warm and welcoming. It is also noteworthy that over all those years during which the Bene Israel were in India, missionaries made several serious attempts to convert them but never succeeded, and that is very impressive indeed.

Chapter Twenty

Forgotten by History: More Jewish Women and the Far East

Beate Sirota Gordon (see chapter 4), Laura Margolis (see chapter 9), Emily Hahn (see chapter 12), Drs. Lepishinskaya and Magdelena Robitscher-Hahn, both in Mao's circle (see chapter 13), and Rebecca Reuben, Esther David, and Dr. Jerusha Jhirad (see chapter 19) were all amazing women, but there were many other extraordinary women who have been forgotten by history or, at the very least, have not received their due, and it is a pleasure to introduce some of them to the reader now.

There was almost no opportunity for advancement in the academic world in Europe for Jewish women. Perhaps that is the reason Dr. Fanny Gisela Halpern went to China. Excellent Jewish students in Germany were advised by their professors to seek fulfilling careers in Japan and China, because there was no anti-Semitism in Asia.

Fanny Halpern was born in 1899 to Jewish parents in Krakow, Poland; her father was the surgeon general of the Austro-Hungarian Army. In 1924, Fanny was in the midst of her studies at the medical school at the University of Vienna in Austria, where in 1927 she studied with Nobel Prize winner and professor of psychiatry Julius Wagner-Jauregg. After receiving her medical degree, Dr. Halpern was invited by Yan Fuqing, the president of the National College of Shanghai, to teach psychiatry and neurology there. She accepted the invitation even though a residency or fellowship in China did not compare to one in Vienna, especially in the mental health areas. In China, the mentally ill did not receive any care beyond being restrained because the Chinese did not realize that psychiatric illness could be treated and that mentally ill patients could receive effective treatment in the hospital, as did physically ill patients.

Dr. Yan was delighted to welcome the new Dr. Halpern, whose area of expertise was neurology and psychiatry, to teach in Shanghai. Dr. Halpern held office hours at the Red Cross Hospital in Shanghai, where she served as chief of psychiatry and taught students and psychiatric nurses from the local Red Cross, universities, medical schools and major hospitals.

In 1935, Dr. Halpern was a guest lecturer at a conference in Canton (now Guangzhou) for the Chinese Medical Association during which she discussed existing problems in psychiatry in China and, more importantly, offered many solutions. Her lecture was unanimously well received and generated a substantive transformation in the approach toward psychiatric care in China. The ideas she presented led to the formation of a committee that outlined a new training system for psychiatrists, psychiatric nurses and professors of psychiatry, and also recommended the creation of mental hospitals and clinics, the promotion of good mental health, the development of treatment for mental illness and the establishment of schools for the mentally disabled. Teaching departments were created at several large and respected hospitals in Shanghai, and Dr. Yan became Dr. Halpern's first student. Dr. Halpern continued to lecture widely to scientific, educational, social and religious groups, and soon her speeches influenced public opinion to such an extent that patients began coming from all over the Far East seeking treatment in China.

In 1935, the Shanghai Mercy Hospital for Mental Diseases was created, and Dr. Halpern was appointed medical director of the new facility, which had beds for three hundred patients and ultimately became the primary teaching hospital of the National Medical College. Today this institution, now called the Center for Mental Health, consists of two hospitals with a combined capacity for twenty-five hundred patients and employs thirteen hundred people, including one thousand medical professionals, one hundred doctors and twenty professors. The center also has a research institute and a department of psychological counseling and drug rehabilitation. Dr. Halpern's lecture in 1935 – with its momentous repercussions – is considered by many to be the most important event in the history of Chinese psychiatry.

In 1939, Dr. Halpern was named dean of the faculty of neurology and medicine at St. John's University of Shanghai, an institution founded by Bishop Samuel Isaac Joseph Schereschewsky, a Jewish-born resident of China who became a Christian and later translated the Bible directly from the Hebrew and Aramaic into Chinese.

Many years later, I met some of the Chinese doctors who had been Dr.

Halpern's students, and they remembered their instructor very well. These physicians recalled how Dr. Halpern had to create her own teaching materials since no appropriate ones existed. The students took copious notes while Dr. Halpern lectured without any notes. Each of her lectures, nevertheless, was built on the preceding one in a very organized and logical manner. Dr. Halpern also did not give written exams. Instead, her exams consisted of an oral question-and-answer session at her home between her and each student.

By 1951, China was under rigid Communist control, so Dr. Halpern, who never married, left with her mother, and they settled in Canada with her younger brother. Sadly, Dr. Halpern had lived in Canada for only one year when she died of natural causes.

During her eighteen years in China, Dr. Halpern was the preeminent pioneer in China's understanding of, and advancements in, the field of psychiatry. In 1976, a delegation of Austrian scientists visited China and, together with their Chinese hosts, they paid tribute to Dr. Halpern for her great contributions to the field of psychiatry in their country. Her students went on to become the leaders in the area of mental health throughout China, and I am working toward honoring her by having a school or university department named after her so that she will never be forgotten in China.

It is hard to believe that in the 1920s, a Jewish woman from Poland wrote a best seller in Chinese, a book that sold more than five hundred thousand copies, but it is true. Stephanie Rosenthal (1885–early 1960s) moved from Poland to France in the early 1900s, and she studied biology at the Sorbonne. Her professor noticed her exceptional writing ability and encouraged her to pursue that talent as well. During this time, she became acquainted with radical Chinese students in Paris and met Hua Nangui, an architecture and railroad engineering student. They fell in love, married in 1908 and went to China in 1910, just before the establishment of the Republic of China by Dr. Sun Yat-sen.

The couple lived in Shanghai and Beijing, mingling with leading Chinese intellectuals, and Stephanie began using the name Luo Chen. Since she used other names at different times, we will refer to her as Stephanie. Her facility with languages allowed her to publish in both French and Chinese, and in 1915, under the name Luo Chen, she published a book of essays in Chinese about women scholars. Stephanie identified with the budding Chinese feminist movement, whose primary goals were to outlaw the binding of feet and arranged marriages.

Stephanie's best-selling book, *Love and Duty*, was published in 1926 and then republished in 1929, 1932 and 1934. In 1932, the book was published in French under the name *La Symphonie des Ombres Chinoises Idylle*. The Chinese version, *Lianai Yu Yiwu*, was published with Zhao Zuxin in 1939. Stephanie was listed as Ho-ro-se, and the preface was written by Cai Yuanpei, the chancellor of Beijing University. In the 1930s, a silent film, *Lianai Yu Yiwu*, was based on the book; it was received with great acclaim when it was shown again several years ago at the Hong Kong Film Festival.

The plot of the book has all the elements of a best seller, even in today's world: a Chinese woman is caught between two worlds, the traditional and the modern. When the discovery is made that she and a young man she met on the way to school have done the unthinkable and fallen in love, her parents quickly force her into a loveless marriage, and his parents send him away. Later in life, their paths cross and they become lovers again. She leaves her husband and children, but her lover is consumed by guilt, especially when his father becomes ill. A loyal son, he returns home. She bears a daughter with her lover, but then he dies, and she is left a single mother, struggling to support herself and her child. Her actions destroy her daughter's social standing so, in order to improve her daughter's future, she makes the ultimate sacrifice and commits suicide. The message to Chinese women was that until feminism was widely accepted in society, there would be consequences to a pioneering woman whose actions were influenced by an education that included Western ideas about love and a woman's right to seek love in her own way.

Stephanie also wrote about Jewish life, as reflected in elements of her 1964 book of poetry in French. One poem, "Oh Israel," is about the Holocaust, and another poem, "Israel Revived," is about the Jewish people and their suffering. This poem ends on an uplifting note, reflecting that the establishment of the Jewish state had become a reality in 1948.

Stephanie lived in both China and France and wrote about fifteen books, including compilations of her poetry. It is unclear where Stephanie lived during World War II, but in the 1950s she and her son Leon and his French wife returned to China. Her granddaughter still lives in Beijing.

Klara Blum (1904–1971), another Jewish poet, was born to a German-speaking Romanian Jewish family. Her parents often quarreled, and her father pressured her about everything, so her childhood was not very happy. After her parents divorced, she moved to Vienna with her mother where, when the war was over, she started working toward a degree in literature and psychology that she never completed. Blum was very active in the Zionist movement, writing articles for Jewish newspapers. She visited Palestine in 1929 but decided not to stay, and she sympathized with leftists and communists but never joined the Communist Party.

In 1933, when Hitler came to power in Germany, Blum won second prize for a poem she wrote in a literary competition. The prize was a two-month study trip to the Soviet Union. Blum actually stayed for eleven years, obtaining Soviet citizenship in 1935 and becoming a member of the Soviet Writers' Union.

In 1937, in Moscow, she met the Chinese drama director Zhu Xiancheng, and they fell madly in love. Scion of a wealthy Shanghai family, the smart and talented Zhu had organized a drama club in Shanghai where he would direct plays by Russian writers such as Chekhov. He also was married and the father of three children. Zhu had come to Moscow to study and work at a prestigious Russian theater, Vakhtangov, but he called Blum on April 18, 1938, to tell her that he would be returning to China to join the war effort against the Japanese invasion. Blum never heard from him again.

Blum wanted to follow her lover, but because of the war, she had to wait ten years before she finally was allowed to enter China, via Bucharest and Paris, with the support of Jewish organizations. Blum went to Shanghai to find Zhu, but his wife told Blum that she had not seen him for years and did not know where he was. Blum and Zhu's love affair had been brief, only three months, but so intense that she could not put it behind her. Blum chose to remain in China, living in the former Jewish settlement of Hongkew, hoping that she and Zhu would meet again someday.

Blum adopted the Chinese name "Zhu" and added "Bailan" (which means "white orchid," a symbol of purity). She threw herself into teaching German to ease the pain in her aching heart, lecturing at the prestigious Fudan University in Shanghai, at Nanjing University, and at Sun Yat-sen University in Guangzhou. Many of her students became noted professors of German as well as translators of German literature into Chinese.

In 1951, Blum published her autobiography as a German novel titled *Der Hirte und Die Weberin*, which told the story of a weaver and her lover, a shepherd. In the Chinese legend, the couple was separated by the Milky Way and met only once a year on the seventh night of the seventh month in the Chinese calendar. The book received critical acclaim, and in 1954, Blum received Chinese citizenship and became a member of the Chinese Writers' Association.

Unknown to both Blum and Zhu's wife, Zhu had been arrested by the

Soviets on suspicion of being a spy and had been sentenced to lifetime imprisonment in a labor camp in Siberia, the Soviet *gulag* (a forced labor camp or prison, usually for political dissidents). Decades later, after Stalin, many of these sentences were reversed, including Zhu's, but the 1990 reprieve was too late for Zhu, who had died in the labor camp in 1943. The news came too late for Blum also, as she died in 1971.

At the start of the Cultural Revolution in 1966, Blum was suspected of being a spy but never was arrested, yet she was left feeling lonely and vulnerable. She nevertheless remained enthusiastic about China's future. Blum was critical of her fellow Jews who considered themselves Caucasians and felt superior to the Chinese, but her dream of living in China as a Jew and as an insider eluded her, despite all her efforts. She no longer knew where she belonged and, sadly, fell into a deep depression and died in Guangzhou, China.

Those who knew Blum described her as a sensitive person whose life was difficult and sad, but her accomplishments are noteworthy. Not only did her students become China's educators and scholars, but also her writings are still admired. They reveal her admiration for China, a land she wrote about with love and empathy. She understood the Chinese – their smiles, their facial expressions, their traditions and their aphorisms. China to Blum – like Israel to others – held out the possibility of being paradise, a utopia where people would enjoy self-determination that would lead to a good life. Her detailed descriptions of images of Chinese scenery amazed even Chinese readers.

Despite her love of China, author Ruth Weiss (1908–2006), whom I met in Beijing in the 1990s, was considered more critical of China than her peers. She, nevertheless, was very proud to be a Chinese citizen and a member of the Chinese government.

Weiss was born in Vienna, and her father was openly anti-Soviet. In 1918, after World War I, the family moved to a crude-oil-producing region of Poland. Three years later they returned to Vienna, only to be stigmatized for being Polish Jews. Weiss started studying German and English and cultivated many other interests. She thought that her Jewish roots gave her a cosmopolitan viewpoint. For a brief time, she considered immigrating to Palestine to join a kibbutz (a collective settlement).

An exhibit of Chinese art at a museum in Vienna was Weiss's first introduction to China, and she loved the cloisonné and vases. She also was influenced by Tretyakov's dramatic play *Brulle! China* (Roar! China) and hearing Gustav Mahler's symphony *Song of the Earth*, based on six poems by Chinese poets of the Tang Dynasty, Li Bai and Wang Wei. In addition, Weiss took Chinese language courses at the Chinese embassy in Vienna and met with Chinese students and Chinese government officials who made her feel as though there was a place for her in China. In 1932, she received a PhD in languages from the Univer-

Ruth Weiss, 1908–2006

sity of Vienna and mastered several Chinese schools of thought. Weiss admired that China had remained intact for thousands of years while the borders of European countries often changed due to wars.

On a radio broadcast in January 1933 Weiss asked listeners, "What can China teach the twentieth century?" She expressed concern about how little we knew about the vast country of China. She bemoaned the fact that in popular culture the Chinese were depicted as mysterious people, hypocrites, swindlers and murderers, and she was troubled that the public believed these false conceptions. Even educated Europeans mistrusted the Chinese, Weiss said. She believed that people equate being "foreign" with being "different," and that "different" connotes "untrustworthy" to many people. In an attempt to familiarize people in the West with the Chinese, Weiss wrote about Chinese culture in several 1933 issues of a Viennese newspaper, once summarizing an interview with a Chinese pedagogue and another time penning an article on Chinese theater. For a Jewish weekly newspaper, Weiss wrote about Jews in the Far East.

In 1929, Weiss had met Mar Timo at the International Students' Club at the University of Vienna, where she was a third-year student. She played the piano, which she had begun learning at age four; he played the violin and had already earned a doctorate degree from the London School of Economics. Romance blossomed, and after weeks of dating, he asked her to marry him. Although she accepted, Mar then returned to China to start his career. They corresponded for three years while she completed her doctorate. Throughout this period, Weiss remained determined that she and Mar would marry, but this did not happen. Instead, much later Weiss fell in love with another Chinese man, Yeh Hsuan, an engineer, whom she married in China in 1943.

With Hitler rising on the scene in 1933, Europe was no place for a Jewish family, so that year Weiss boarded a ship, the *Conte Rosso*, and traveled via Trieste and Venice to Shanghai for a six-month study trip to China. Once in Shanghai, Weiss, who also was working as a freelance correspondent for Austrian newspapers, surrounded herself with other foreigners and befriended famous Chinese personalities like writer Lu Xun and Mme Sun Yat-sen. After visiting factories, Weiss was incensed by the deplorable and inhumane conditions she saw, calling the factories "infernos of exploitation," and she wrote about these issues for newspapers in Austria and for the *China Weekly Review*. Concerned about class struggle and laborers being exploited, Weiss also opposed the use of rickshaws which, she thought, made humans into beasts of burden pulling heavy loads.

Weiss, whose parents died in Germany at the hands of the Nazis around 1939, then accepted a position as a teacher at the Shanghai Jewish School. One problem she faced, however, was that she was not a practicing, observant Jew. In addition, she disagreed with both the hypocrisy of the school administrators and also with what she perceived to be their condescending attitudes toward the children. Weiss thought that the rich Sephardic Jews, who considered themselves British, were exploiting the less affluent Russian children and German refugee children.

After being dismissed by the Jewish school – which was just fine with Weiss – she accepted a position with the Chinese National Committee on Intellectual Cooperation putting together a bibliography on education, and then she taught German and English at several schools in China. In 1943, Weiss moved to Chongqing, the wartime capital of the Chinese government, and found a job she loved with the United Nations Picture News Office. After the War of Resistance against Japanese Aggression (1937–1945) ended, Weiss returned to Shanghai, where she briefly assisted Mme Sun Yat-sen in establishing the China Welfare Institute aimed at protecting women and children.

With a visa in hand, in March 1946 Weiss boarded a freighter, the *Doctor Lykes*, bound for the Gulf of Mexico, but the actual, undisclosed destination was New Orleans. In the US Weiss worked as a secretary at the United Nations. She ultimately remained with the United Nations Radio Division for five years, except for a brief return to China in the summer of 1949, while her husband remained in Cambridge, Massachusetts, working toward his doctor of science degree at the Massachusetts Institute of Technology (MIT). During her summer in China, Weiss worked as an editor for English-language and German-language Chinese journals before returning to her United Nations job in New York in September. Weiss gave birth to two sons during her years in New York, one in 1947 and one in 1949, and her oldest son was with her in the summer of 1949 when she returned to China.

In November 1951, Weiss and her two sons returned permanently to China from New York, and by December they were in Beijing, "home again," as Weiss said. Ironically, despite Weiss's attempts to convince her Chinese husband Yeh Hsuan to return to China with the family, he chose to stay in the United States, and the couple divorced around 1954. Weiss, whose Chinese name was Wei Lushi, wrote that the new China proved to be a good place for a single mother to raise her children, although when her oldest son started school, and she saw the enormous number of characters he had to learn in order to be able to read, she became concerned about the pervasive illiteracy in China. In an attempt to ameliorate the illiteracy problem, the Communists reduced and simplified the number of characters needed for basic literacy, and those changes benefitted her youngest son when he started school two years later.

Weiss, who in 1955 was one of one hundred foreigners to receive Chinese citizenship that year, considered China her homeland. She was elected as a member of the Chinese People's Political Consultative Conference in 1983. There were ten foreigners in this high government agency. Five of them were Jews and two of those five were women: Ruth Weiss, Eva Siao (see below), Israel Epstein (see chapter 13), Richard Frey and Sidney Shapiro (see chapter 13).

Weiss was one of the few foreigners who were not harassed during the Cultural Revolution (1966–1976). In fact, occasionally Mme Sun Yat-sen would send her private car to pick up Weiss and take her back to her home for a lovely visit. During the Cultural Revolution, Weiss's oldest son worked on a state farm, and her youngest son worked in a factory making spare parts for tractors. Both sons are college graduates and now live in the United States.

At first, Weiss believed that the Communist Party always told the truth, and it took her many years to see that her belief did not reflect reality. In 1999, when writing her memoir *Am Rande der Geschichte: Mein Leben in China* (In the Margins of History: My Life in China), she admitted how blind she had been and described Mao as a feudalistic dictator who did not tolerate opposition, debate or opposing views. She wrote of her belief that after Mao and the opening of China, many of the evils of the old society (including corruption and prostitution) would reemerge, but they would not be as bad as in the past because there would not be famine and death from starvation. She expressed her hope that China would achieve great success, but having spent seventy years in China and no longer a young woman, she did not expect to live long enough to see her adopted nation fulfill these expectations.

In 1979, the Chinese government published a book in English titled *Living in China*. Twenty foreign authors living in China contributed articles to this work, and Ruth Weiss was one of those authors. Weiss, who helped build bridges between China, Europe and North America, died at the age of ninety-seven. She was buried in the Soong Ching Ling (Mme Sun Yat-sen) International Cemetery in Shanghai.

Eva Sandberg Siao (1911–2001) was an excellent photographer who took wonderful photos of China, a country she loved. Her 1997 autobiography is titled *China: Mein Traum, Mein Leben* (China: My Dream, My Life). Born in November in Breslau, Germany, to a Jewish family, she wrote that China appeared in her dreams even when she was a child, and in 1940 Eva finally would travel to see the "land of her dreams."

Always referring to herself as a "German Jewess," Eva left high school before receiving her diploma because one of her teachers was a Nazi who harassed her for being Jewish. Against her mother's wishes, Eva attended synagogue with her uncle so that she could study Hebrew. Her father was a doctor, and her brother became a symphony conductor in Sweden. After Eva graduated from the State Institute for Film and Photography in Munich, she joined her brother in Sweden in 1930. There she worked in photography with a Russian Jew and met Zionists and socialists.

In 1934, at the age of twenty-three, Eva traveled to Moscow where she met the forty-one-year old poet Emi Saio, known as Xiao San, who was vacationing on the Black Sea. He and Eva fell in love, and she became a Soviet citizen in order to marry him two years later. In 1939, after the birth of their first son, Emi returned to China alone and rejoined Mao Zedong in his efforts. Emi had gone to elementary school with Mao, and they had remained good friends. In 1940 Emi sent for Eva. She left the Soviet Union and traveled via Stockholm to Yan'an in Western China to be with her husband, and they had another child.

At age forty-seven, Emi, a womanizer, became romantically involved with – and "married" – twenty-one-year-old Gua Lu, a beautiful opera singer, and eventually Eva found out. In 1943, after three years in China, Eva, angry at Emi's infidelity, returned to Russia without signing any divorce papers. Between 1944 and 1946, she lived in different parts of the Soviet Union earning a living as a photographer. In 1949, Emi traveled to Russia, which was steeped in communism, and visited Eva and their two sons. Interestingly, Eva decided to take the two boys and return to China with Emi, arriving before China was proclaimed the People's Republic of China.

When Zhou Enlai saw the four of them, he was surprised because he thought Emi and Eva were divorced. Eva explained that she refused to accept divorce papers from Chiang Kai-shek's government and never signed them. Zhou Enlai convinced Gua Lu to accept a "divorce" and found a position for her with the Chinese Opera in Shanghai. He then issued a serious warning to Emi about his messy personal life, told him to settle down and advised him and Eva to "remarry" which they did.

Eva and Emi had a third child, and the family lived in Beijing, where she worked as a photographer for *Tass*, the Soviet News Agency, and for *Xinhua*, the Chinese News Agency. In 1951, when Emi was sent as a delegate to the World Peace Council in Prague, she joined him. While there, Eva met many important writers including Thomas Mann, Arnold Zweig and Ilja Ehrenburg, the most prominent Yiddish writer in the Soviet Union. Eva also established relationships with publishing houses in East Germany, and they later published her books on China and Tibet.

Eva tried to reconcile her love for Emi and China with her longing for Europe. In her work, she attempted to describe the China she knew and loved to Europeans, and when that succeeded it gave meaning to her life and work. Eva revealed her individuality and her independence in her photographic work, which often did not fit with communist political propaganda. She was told to photograph only smiling, happy and neatly dressed workers, but she exercised her own judgment about presenting the truth in her work. Since she always wanted to reveal a person's essence in her photos, she never posed them. Instead, she attempted to document people and cultural objects, photographing the street life of China with its markets, peddlers and artisans. In China people said that Eva had a magic eye for catching the essence of the subjects in her photographs, which many described as superb.

Between 1958 and 1964, Eva was subjected to bureaucratic harassment from China for her independent thinking and her photographs that often did not present the government-approved position, as noted, and that harassment intensified after the break between China and the Soviet Union. Even though

Eva exchanged her Soviet passport for a Chinese passport in 1964, it did not help her navigate the Cultural Revolution. She and Emi were charged with being Soviet spies and spent seven years in solitary confinement in Beijing's infamous Quincheng prison until 1974 and then under house arrest for five more years. After their "rehabilitation" in 1979, Eva again secured a position with the Chinese News Agency.

When China finally opened its doors, Eva traveled back and forth across the world to accompany exhibitions of her photographs, and while traveling, she gave radio interviews about her difficult life. In some interviews, Eva said that one always remains a foreigner in China and that there were one hundred things about China she did not understand. She wrote in her autobiography, "I see China with critical eyes, but with loving critical eyes. One must have oriental patience in China. One cannot bang one's head against the wall. Despite all my criticism, I love this country just as one loves a person who is not perfect. I react to the many bad events that occur in the world with horror and locate them in world history. When something bad happens in China, I suffer."

Emi died in 1983, and Eva died in November 2001, leaving behind more than ten thousand photos of China. Her body of work over thirty years represents her declaration of love for the country that became her new homeland. Her work can be seen at the Joris Ivens Museum in Holland; at the Ludwig Musem in Cologne; and at the Moderna Musset in Stockholm.

Anna Molka Ahmed (1917–1994), born to Jewish parents in London, went on to become one of Pakistan's greatest and most honored artists. Anna's paternal grandparents were killed in a pogrom; her mother's family were Polish Jews. Anna was a difficult child, a rebel from an early age who questioned everything, including life itself, and her behavior was a problem for her father. Anna began a romance with an Indian Muslim artist who was fifteen years her senior, so every night her father would lock her in her room to prevent her from eloping. One night in 1939, however, her mother unlocked the door, and eventually Anna married the artist and moved with him to India.

Anna Ahmed was a preeminent art educator and a tireless promoter of Pakistan's art. Many of Pakistan's greatest artists, male and female, were mentored by her. She encouraged her students to develop individual ideas and become creative artists, but she was also a master teacher of techniques, including engraving, painting and design. Ahmed's own work ranges from expressive portraits to thematic works on daily life and even war in Pakistan; her goal was to document the daily life and history of Pakistan via art. The Pakistani government authorized the issuance of a postage stamp in her honor in August 2006.

Li Xiu-rong is a descendent of the Kaifeng Jewish Levite family. After graduating from Zhenghou Electric Power School in 1962, she began working for the electronics plant in Kaifeng as an engineer and became manager of the workshop responsible for the design of radio capacitors. In 1966, the Cultural Revolution began in China, and the next ten years were known as "Ten Years of Turmoil." During those years the socio-political reorganization was marked by violent sectarian conflict and "bitter intercine strife" in China, according to Li. It was a time of chaos and major instability, and the Red Guards (young, violent revolutionaries who sought to purify communism in China by eliminating whatever they deemed to be tainted from China's past) were committed to eliminating all aspects of ancient Chinese culture. Trust for one another was almost nonexistent, and people were afraid to say aloud what they were thinking.

Despite this, Li became friendly with a local Christian bishop, Zeng Youshan, who had been educated in Canada. He and his wife worked in the shop that Li supervised. After many friendly conversations, she surprised Zeng by admitting to him that she was Jewish. He was incredulous, but Li convinced him it was the truth. She told him that her parents often spoke of the great stele of the Chinese Jewish community that had been entrusted to the care of the local bishop and she asked if he had heard of it. In 1489, the Chinese Jews rebuilt their synagogue after it was destroyed by a huge flood of the Yellow River, and they designated the "Hongzhi Stele" as a historical record (see chapter 11). The "Hongzhi Stele" is the oldest remaining Jewish monument in China, and it bears an inscription with the date and details of the rebuilding of the synagogue. Zeng not only knew of the stele, he lived next door! He also expressed concern that if the Red Guards found it, they would destroy it.

Li felt a sense of urgency and suggested that they go there immediately because she had an idea. Next she found a few workers, told them the monument was hewed from quartzite, and asked them to build a brick platform and secure the monument on top. In this way she rescued the stele from potential destruction. Finally, in the 1970s, Zeng suggested to her that the monument was so important to the Chinese Jewish community that the government should have custody of it. She agreed, and they succeeded in having the stele moved to the Kaifeng Municipal Museum, where it has remained ever since. Li Xiu-rong is a contemporary Jewish heroine.

There are myriad gurus in India, each with a unique spiritual message, but only one guru was honored with a postage stamp, a city and regular visits and encouragement from Prime Minister Indira Gandhi. What is not known to either the Jewish world or in India is that this guru was a Jewish woman! And not just any Jewish woman: she was born to a very prestigious Sephardic Jewish family and was a direct descendant of Rabbi Isaac Alfassi, an eleventh-century sage who later moved from Fez in North Africa to Spain. (The name "Alfassi" means "one from Fez.") Rabbi Isaac Alfassi is well known to every serious student of the Talmud, and his commentary on the Talmud is published in every edition of this authoritative body of Jewish wisdom that was disseminated orally for centuries.

Blanche Rachel Miriam (Mirra) Alfassa (1878–1973) was born near the Opera House in the heart of Paris, the third child of Maurice Alfassa (from Turkey) and Mathilde Ismalun (from Egypt). Both parents were mathematical wizards. Her brother Matteo, who was two years older, became governor general of the French Congo (1919–1922), part of French Equatorial Africa, as well as governor of Martinique and French Sudan (1934–1935) and of French Mali (1935–1936). He was a brilliant, kind, refined and cultured man who died in August 1942 at age sixty-six. There are streets named for him in several former colonies. Like Mirra, he was a spiritual seeker.

Mirra attended an exclusive private school where she exhibited deep curiosity and joy in learning. She read most of her father's eight-hundred-volume library when she was very young, studied music, played the organ, composed music, was an impressive artist and loved tennis, all of which she continued to enjoy well into her eighties. Her grandmother frequently told her that she was born to realize the highest ideal, and she was always at the top of her class, winning the Prix d'Honneur at her high school graduation.

Mirra also experienced frequent out-of-body experiences and spontaneous trances. She remembered meditating at age four, and at age five she felt that she was "not of this world." She pictured herself in a golden robe, rising up as people gathered under her robe to be comforted and healed, and she frequently spoke of a conscious and constant union with the divine presence.

Mirra wrote that between ages eleven and thirteen, she had several psychic and spiritual experiences that she described as having revealed to her the existence of God and the possibility that humans could "unite" with God thereby producing a divine life. At age fourteen, while with her mother listening to Saint Saëns music played on the organ during a wedding in a Paris synagogue,

Mirra was gazing at a stained glass window when she suddenly experienced the sensation of a bolt of bright light coming through the window and into her open eyes, making her feel all-powerful, a feeling that lasted for four days. In 1893, while traveling with her mother in Italy, she recalled a scene she believed was from her past life in which she had been strangled and thrown into a canal.

At sixteen, Mirra, who was studying art, exhibited her paintings at a Paris salon and was associating with such famous artists as Rodin, Matisse and Monet. She met Emile Zola and wrote a novelette that sadly has been lost. Having lived through the infamous Dreyfus Affair (the persecution of a Jew named Alfred Dreyfus who in 1894 was falsely accused of being a traitor to France), Mirra witnessed the rise of anti-Semitism as well as Zola's defense of Dreyfus. The issues of truth and falsehood became important to Mirra, who yearned to live a life of truth.

In October 1897, at nineteen, Mirra married Henri Morisset, and in August 1898 she gave birth to a son, André, but little is known about either her husband or her son. Mirra dabbled in the occult and Eastern religions and traveled to North Africa for advanced study. At age twenty-six, Mirra dreamed of a dark Asian man whom she called Krishna. Krishna guided Mirra's spiritual journey through further visions in which he taught her that God was not only the Creator of mankind but also was a lover of mankind.

During 1905–1906, twenty-eight-year-old Mirra studied in Algeria with Max Theon, an Ashkenazic Jew in his mid-fifties. Born Eliezer Mordecai Bimstein, he claimed his father was a rabbi in Poland. Theon, who had long hair that he never cut, explained Mirra's childhood spontaneous experiences based on his in-depth knowledge of Kabbalah, the study of Jewish mysticism, and the Zohar, the primary text of Jewish mystical teachings. Theon's beliefs would influence Mirra throughout her entire life. In 1906, Mirra traveled to Paris, where she organized a group of spiritual seekers who would meet every week in her home.

In 1908 Mirra divorced Morisset, and in a decision about which we know little, her son was raised by her ex-husband's sisters. In Algeria, Mirra had met Paul Antoine Richard (1874–1967), a fellow student of Theon. Paul was a lawyer, political activist, author and former Christian minister who had become interested in Hinduism. The two married in May 1911 and then traveled to India. They returned to France in 1914, however, when Paul was inducted into the French Army during World War I. Paul completed his army service in 1916, but when the British denied him permission to return to India, they decided to visit Japan. Mirra and Paul set sail on the *Kamo Maru*, arriving in Yokohama in May 1916, and they remained in Japan for four years.

In Japan Mirra began practicing Zen, the Japanese form of Buddhism that emphasizes meditation. She also sketched with Nobel Prize winner Rabindranath Tagore, the renowned Bengali writer and artist, who even gave his typewriter to Mirra out of respect for her. Mirra also lectured to Japanese women on women's liberation. Her lecture, "Women and the War," was published in the Japanese press. Mirra also used meditation to assist local doctors in their medical care of patients and, in January 1919, the Japanese press reported that Mirra had used occult powers to destroy the influenza virus that caused an epidemic in Tokyo.

In 1920, Mirra and Paul returned to India, and Mirra developed a deep friendship with Sri Aurobindo, who gave up his political activities to become a philosopher, visionary, yogi and, later, Mirra's spiritual collaborator. In 1920 Paul left the marriage. Soon thereafter, by public consensus, Mirra was renamed "The Mother" and was declared a Hindu goddess. For the next fifty years she was revered as a guru.

In October 1938, The Mother wrote to her son, "Hitler is a choice instrument for anti-divine forces which want violence, upheaval and war, for they know that these things retard and hamper the action of the divine forces." The Mother believed that Hitler was the biggest obstacle in the universe and the constant negation of truth. In September 1940, The Mother and Aurobindo declared their support for the Allies in the war against the Nazis and made a large contribution to the war fund, stating, "We believe that this is a battle waged in defense of civilization, and its highest attained social, cultural and spiritual values, and the whole future of humanity." The Mother believed that she was able to defeat Hitler by "entering his mind" and telling him to start a war with Russia on the Eastern front, which, along with his lies, caused him to lose the war.

In 1969, The Mother related that the Buddha had appeared to her and said, "I see in your heart a diamond surrounded by a golden light. Learn to radiate and do not fear the storm. You carry a blessed message for those who are thirsting for compassion. Nothing can attack the diamond." The Mother reported frequent visions of this nature.

In 1968, together with Aurobindo, The Mother founded an ashram in Auroville, near Pondicherry in southwest India, as a city dedicated to human unity, with the goal of enabling mankind to progress toward a perfect world of peace, progress and harmony, above all creeds, all politics and all nationalities. The Mother believed that religion separates people, so there is no religion in the ashram. Representatives of 124 nations and 24 Indian states were present at the inauguration of the ashram, and the charter was read in 16 languages. The Mother placed soil from every country in a lotus-shaped urn inside a circular temple built in her honor. The urn is graced by a translucent globe lit by sunlight symbolizing future realization of her beliefs.

Commemorative stamp from India honoring Mirra Alfassa, known as "The Mother"

To this day the ashram has a library, an art gallery, a dining room, a playground, workshops, dairies, farms, a dispensary, guest houses, a free coeducational school, and in 1951 a university was added. Cars are banned, and there is no leader one must obey. There is a meditation chamber and a temple where The Mother is worshipped as a goddess and the divine mother.

At the ashram The Mother met with the king of Nepal, the Dalai Lama, Prime Minister Nehru, and the president of India. Woodrow Wilson's daughter spent decades of her life in the ashram. Prime Minister Indira Gandhi, a devotee of The Mother, whose advice she frequently sought, asked The Mother for an election victory of 250 seats in Parliament. The prime minister believed that her landslide victory of 356 seats resulted from The Mother's granting her the prayer she told The Mother she was offering.

The Mother's teachings are based on the Kabbalistic cosmology of *tikkun*, which means "repairing the world." The Mother dabbled in Jewish mystical teachings and stressed the concept of *shekhinah*, the divine presence in mankind and the universe. The Mother wanted to restore what she saw as the original harmony between humanity and God and between matter and the divine. Her goal was to enhance spirituality so that each person could pursue his or her own spiritual goals. She said that people are born to reach the highest level; similar ideas are also found in Hindu philosophy. The Mother preached a systematic approach to life without attachment to results or personal ego. She promoted punctuality, orderliness, cleanliness, and efficient use of energy, natural resources and money. She preached the end of hatred, bloodshed and confusion with the hope of a new reign of justice, beauty, harmony and fraternity.

Mirra Alfassa's legacy includes thirteen volumes with six thousand pages titled *Mother's Agenda*. Written by Alfassa and recorded by her students, the books document her wish to unite everyone with the divine. She struggled to bring a higher consciousness into the world and to physically transform her body into the first example of a new, higher form of human being who could "experience the world and godliness directly," rather than through the senses.

Today there are about twenty-two hundred people from thirty countries living in the ashram in Pondicherry, a model city that serves as a bridge between the past and the future. In 1966 UNESCO endorsed the ashram, and in 1999 *The New York Times* recommended that tourists visiting India should consider visiting Pondicherry. Canadian TV produced a documentary about the ashram, and in 2008 the BBC followed with a film.

Mirra Alfassa, The Mother, left her body at 7:25 p.m. on November 17, 1973. Her son André, whom she saw from time to time, was with her when she died. The Mother's four great aspects, according to her followers, were wisdom, strength, harmony and perfection. A postage stamp with her image was issued by India in February 1978. Even now, on her birthday, people line up for hours to pass through her room. They feel her presence and believe she is guiding and protecting them.

Ayya Khema, born Ilse Kussel (1923–1997), was ordained a Buddhist nun in 1979, the first Western woman to be so ordained. She established a training center for Buddhist nuns in Sri Lanka, and she traveled the world, ultimately returning to Germany, her birthplace, to create a Buddhist center near Munich.

Her life before then, however, hardly could be described as one of quiet meditation. She was born in Berlin to a prosperous Jewish family with a maid, a cook, a governess and a chauffeur, but her family became impoverished after the Nazis confiscated their assets and destroyed their twelve-room home and lifestyle in 1938. Although her father Theodore Kussel, a broker on the Berlin Stock Exchange, had been awarded an Iron Cross for bravery in World War I, it was of no help. He lost his job, and she was expelled from the school she attended; she then enrolled in a local Jewish school. The young Ilse personally witnessed Kristallnacht. Her family considered escaping to Czechoslovakia where they had relatives, but soon the Nazis invaded that country. Her uncle Leo Kestenberg, who was married to her father's sister, somehow managed to escape to Israel where he was one of the founders of the Israel Philharmonic Orchestra.

The only place that accepted Jews without a visa was the city of Shanghai, so when Ilse was fifteen her mother, (Lizzi Rosenthal) and her father – but not Ilse – became refugees in Shanghai. Ilse's mother fainted at the train station in Germany after saying goodbye to her, and Ilse became part of a *Kindertransport* (a rescue mission to take thousands of Jewish refugee children from Nazi Germany to Great Britain during the years 1938 to 1940) that went to Glasgow. There she lived unhappily with her host family; although the people who cared for her spoke Yiddish, she missed her parents who remained in Shanghai. Finally, she decided to join them when relatives provided the money for her to travel to Shanghai via a small ship with only twelve other passengers. Ilse spent the remaining war years among the refugees in the Hongkew area in Shanghai, where her family lived in one small room. She was traumatized when Hongkew was bombed in July 1945, the same year that her father had surgery for kidney stones, contracted encephalitis in the hospital and died.

Ilse, who had learned English in Glasgow, obtained a job with the arriving American forces. One day she met a fellow refugee (whom she refers to as only Johannes) seventeen years her senior and married him. In 1949, they left Shanghai on a transport ship, and at age twenty-six she became a suburban housewife in Los Angeles with a daughter and then a son. She also worked in a bank and became a US citizen. For many years, however, she struggled with an inner malaise and a feeling of incompleteness that she could not overcome. When her daughter was thirteen and her son was three, she divorced her husband. Their daughter went with him and their son stayed with her. Ilse remarried and her new husband, known by his given name Gerd, was a friend of the family and a German Jew whose family died in the Holocaust. They traveled the Amazon, visited Nepal and Kashmir, helped build a power plant in Pakistan and established Shalom (peace), the first organic farm in Australia, where she continued searching for the spiritual life. Ilse wrote to Professor Gershom G. Scholem, the world's leading scholar on Jewish mysticism, asking for his advice and guidance, but he disappointed her with a discouraging, dismissive response. Later she visited India where she met The Mother, who had an enormous influence on her and, especially, on her son.

Eventually Ilse's husband left her, and she and her son traveled to Sri Lanka. Finally, in her forties, Ilse pursued a more spiritual life with the world's leading Buddhist philosopher at the time, Sigmund Feniker, also born a German

Jew, culminating in her ordination as a Buddhist nun at the age of fifty-eight. Having her long, dark, thick hair cut off to her scalp, as part of her becoming a nun, was symbolic of her learning to let go of many things, including her ego. Her name upon ordination became Ayya Khema, meaning "venerable safety."

Ayya Khema's books about Buddhism are excellent, clear and inspiring. Although the teachings of Buddhism are profound, she wrote about the essence of Buddhism, its virtues and its path, for the ordinary person; everyone can understand her books. She provided clear, practical instructions on the fundamentals of meditation, which she believed held the key to overcoming obstacles and finding happiness. She instructed her readers on how to achieve insight, calmness, loving kindness and joy through meditation.

Whether the women in this chapter were doctors, writers, artists or teachers, and whether they remained Jewish or sought spirituality in other ways, all of them made significant contributions to their communities throughout the Far East, and they deserve recognition, admiration and a permanent place in history.

Chapter Twenty-One
Singapore: Where the First Chief Minister was Jewish

In the summer of 1969, my wife and I visited Singapore, where we were invited to the home of Mozelle Nissim (1883–1975) for dinner. Mozelle was the daughter of Sir Manasseh Meyer (1846–1930), and she lived alone in what was one of her parents' two palaces in Singapore. She was the second of seven siblings and the last to survive. Mozelle's husband Sassoon Ezra Nissim died in 1923, and she never remarried.

Mozelle's home was magnificent. The furniture was oriental, exotic and overwhelmingly beautiful. The three of us sat alone at a long table that probably could seat forty guests, and we were attended to by five to seven servants who replenished glasses with water after almost every sip and gave us new utensils after almost every bite. It seemed that since Mozelle lived alone the servants were not very busy, and our being there finally gave them something to do.

Mozelle was regal; one might describe her as "Jewish royalty." She was charming, elegant, warm, friendly, kind, well read, knowledgeable about her Jewish heritage and philanthropically generous. Despite having all those servants, she had cooked dinner by herself, and it was delicious. She prepared chicken with oranges, and after we asked for the recipe, she personally wrote it out and mailed it to us in Tokyo.

Sir Manasseh Meyer was from Calcutta, moved to Rangoon and arrived in Singapore in 1873. There he became a very successful opium trader and the largest real estate owner, owning 75 percent of the land in Singapore in 1900. Sir Meyer purchased his mansion on Oxley Rise and named it "Belle Vue." His other palatial home, named "Jeshurun," was on Meyer Road. A learned

267

Mozelle Nissim, 1883–1975, with a young David Marshall, at a synagogue school assembly in Singapore

man, he was the leader of the Jewish community in Singapore for over sixty years and served on the municipal council for seven years. Sir Meyer was a perfect gentleman by all accounts – pleasant, reliable and modest.

Sir Meyer built the Manasseh Meyer School of Science at the University of Singapore (it remains part of the university), as well as the Adelphi Hotel, the Sea View Hotel and Meyer Mansions. He also endowed the Hebrew School of Singapore, and his wax figure can be seen in the Wax Museum on Singapore's Sentosa Island. The British generally looked down on other residents of Singapore, describing them – both their physical appearance and social status – as foreigners, locals (natives) or colored. Jews were viewed as being all three. Sir Meyer, however, was considered an "honorary white" because he was rich and donated a great deal of money to many causes. Of course, the fact that he was knighted in 1929 by King George V, certainly a prestigious honor, helped as well. Mozelle pleaded with me to write her father's biography, promising that she would sit with me and provide me with all the information, documentation, photographs and recollections that I would need.

The population of Singapore is approximately 75 percent Chinese with the remaining 25 percent comprised of Malays, Hindus, Europeans, Arabs and Jews. This diversity results in a wonderful mixture of foods, dress and traditions. Mozelle spoke lovingly of the Baghdadi Jewish community and their music, food, spices and connections to Rangoon, Calcutta and Bombay. Jews were primarily traders in spices, tea, coffee, carpets and textiles, but their primary source of income was opium. Interestingly, some residents remember hearing that decades earlier, on one or two occasions, the stock exchange in Singapore was closed on the Yom Kippur holiday, despite so few Jews living there.

Calling Singapore "a small community with a large impact," Mozelle was very knowledgeable about this nation-state, which is located slightly north of the equator, at the tip of Malaya, between the Indian and Pacific Oceans. She remembered Singapore as a slum – dirty and filled with swamps – and she recalled how it evolved into a major metropolis, an evolution in which Mozelle's father played a prominent role.

Sir Thomas Stamford Raffles (1781-1826), who was British, succeeded in convincing the local Muslim sultan to enter into a treaty that resulted in the British settlement of Singapore. In 1869, with the opening of the Suez Canal, which shortened the travel between Europe and the Far East by four thousand miles (and from four months to seventeen days), Singapore was suddenly on the map. Mozelle remembered when Albert Einstein came to Singapore in November 1922. Chaim Weizmann, the leader of the Zionist movement at the time and the future first president of Israel, sent a telegram informing the Jewish community of Singapore that Einstein would be arriving, and about one half of Singapore's 625 Jewish residents greeted Einstein as he disembarked from the ship, the *Kitano Maru*. He came to raise money for the creation of the Hebrew University in Jerusalem, and the meeting took place in Mozelle's family's palace on Oxley Rise. They raised £750, a huge amount of money at that time, and Sir Meyer's contribution of £500 was the largest for many years. Other members of the Jewish community joined together and donated the additional £250. Einstein noted that Sir Meyer wore a black yarmulke (skull cap) and described the "true warmth among Jews everywhere." Einstein learned that he had received the Nobel Prize in physics one week after he left Singapore.

Mozelle, who in 1929 raised funds to build a school in Israel, also told us about the synagogues in Singapore. The first one, created in 1841, was in a very small room. In April 1878 her father purchased land on Waterloo Street to build a large, beautiful synagogue, Maghain Aboth (shield of our ancestors), which he supported. Years later, however, he was insulted at that synagogue, so he built another synagogue, Chesed El (God's grace), on his Oxley Rise property, and it was dedicated in April 1905. Sir Meyer paid Jews to attend every day to ensure that there always would be a minyan (the ten men required for services to take place). Mozelle related that these "minyan men" sued her father in court for payment in advance for their attendance, so they could use the money to start their own business, but they lost their case. The synagogue, which faces west toward Jerusalem, remains on Oxley Rise to this day. Sir Meyer is usually pictured wearing a yarmulke with a Hebrew Judaica book in his hand or nearby.

Many streets in Singapore are named after the Jewish pioneers who settled there: Solomon Street, Meyer Road, Nathan Street, Elias Road, Adis Road, Manasseh Lane and Nassim Hill. There is also Frankel Avenue, Frankel Walk, Frankel Terrace, Frankel Lane, Frankel Street, Frankel Road, Frankel Way and Frankel Drive! After the Baghdadi Jews arrived in Singapore from Calcutta in about 1830 and created their first synagogue in 1841, they named the street where the synagogue was located (now a thoroughfare in the center of Singapore) Synagogue Street, the name that remains to this day.

On the subject of synagogues, Mozelle, my wife and I debated whether it was proper to use a rickshaw on the Sabbath to travel to the synagogue if you paid for it in advance. It was, after all, a way to reach the synagogue, and the rabbis had approved of doing so. I questioned whether it is ever proper to ride in a rickshaw or whether it was inhumane to ride while another person pulled you, Sabbath or not, approved by the rabbis or not. Mozelle said she did not think anyone had ever raised that issue. In fact, Jacob Hakohen Feinstein, an emissary from Safed (a northern city in Palestine), who had visited many Jewish communities of the Far East on a few occasions, did raise the issue in 1886. In Calcutta, he published a booklet titled *Kuntres, Torat Imecha* (pamphlet about your mother's instructions) in which he mentions some unworthy customs in the Jewish communities he visited in the Far East, including Singapore, and he included the use of rickshaws as one of those "unworthy customs." Feinstein spiritually benefitted the Jewish communities he visited.

We also discussed Singapore's more recent history and how the country's Jews played an important role in its development into a modern nation. During World War II, the British believed that Singapore was invincible and they felt well prepared for a Japanese invasion by sea. There was also an escape route to Australia available to residents of Singapore, but the British considered the Jews to be second-class citizens, calling them foreigners, natives or colored, so they were prohibited from boarding the ships sailing south to Australia. The Japanese, as it turns out, did not attack by sea; they came by land from the north in Malaya, and seventy thousand soldiers quickly surrendered. The locals were very angry and disappointed when the British surrendered to the Japanese, and they began to think that the time was right for independence.

Mozelle asked me to watch in the coming years for rising stars in the Jewish community, reminding me that the first chief minister (the equivalent of the first prime minister) of Singapore was none other than the former president of the Jewish community, David Marshall (1908–1995). I met him, corresponded with him and have the utmost respect for him. His parents were devoutly Orthodox Baghdadis with some connection to Persia.

David Marshall, 1908–1995, the first chief minister of Singapore

Marshall was very smart, always studying, always first in his class from kindergarten through law school, one of the first to become an attorney and the best defense attorney in Singapore. He rarely lost a case. After the surrender of Singapore to the Japanese, Marshall became a prisoner of war and worked as a slave laborer in Japan's mines, and by the end of the war he weighed less than eighty pounds and could not have survived one more week. He eventually was repatriated and regained his strength, dignity and courage. I found him to be charming, erudite and dynamic; in short, he was a great raconteur and a magnificent orator with a clear mind, clear vision and a clear connection to his audience.

The British were not eager to leave Singapore, but Marshall was an advocate for the end of colonialism and for Singapore's independence. In 1955, during the transition from British rule to independence, Marshall ran for office in the first free elections held in Singapore. Despite an overwhelming Chinese majority, Marshall – to the surprise of everyone, especially himself – was elected the first chief minister.

As first chief minister, Marshall was invited to China, and he traveled across the vast country over a period of two weeks. Concerned that he was being watched everywhere, he was careful about what he said in public, and he wrote his "diary" in the form of letters to his brother for fear that a diary would be confiscated upon his departure. At the conclusion of his visit to China, on October 9, 1956, Marshall was invited to meet the distinguished premier and foreign minister of China, Zhou Enlai. In a friendly and productive meeting, they discussed the status of Chinese residents in Singapore. The Chinese in

China believed correctly that the British authorities viewed the Chinese residents in Singapore as foreigners, natives or colored and, thus, discouraged them from becoming citizens. The British required Chinese residents to take a literacy exam that always included unfamiliar English words and, no matter how hard they studied English, they always failed the literacy test. Marshall was as troubled by this as was Zhou Enlai, and Marshall asked him if the government of China now would encourage the Chinese of Singapore to become citizens. Zhou Enlai agreed, and both he and Marshall finally convinced the Chinese that the British no longer were in charge and could not put obstacles in their way to intentionally prevent them from becoming citizens.

Zhou Enlai asked Marshall if the Chinese residents of Singapore could return to their ancestral homeland of China as they got older if they wanted their final resting place to be China. Marshall responded that Singapore was a free country, a democracy, and the Chinese could go anywhere, anytime – an answer that surprised Zhou Enlai. He then asked Marshall, an attorney, to include in Singapore's Constitution a guarantee that any Chinese resident, at any time, would have the constitutional right to return to the People's Republic of China, the Chinese homeland. Marshall explained that it was not appropriate to put such a guarantee in his nation's constitution, which included basic rights for everyone, not just Chinese. He went on to explain that in a democracy there is no need for such a statement in the constitution, and in a totalitarian country, the statement would be meaningless. Zhou Enlai, nevertheless, requested that Marshall include language giving the Chinese living in Singapore the right to return to China whenever they wanted. Without such language in Singapore's Constitution, Zhou Enlai feared that right would not become a permanent part of the fabric of life there.

Marshall was touched by Zhou Enlai's concern for the Chinese in Singapore and told him that Jews, too, want to visit their homeland of Israel and many want to be buried there as well. Marshall went on to tell Zhou Enlai that the previous Saturday he had visited the one remaining synagogue in Shanghai where he learned that there were 543 Jews in China who wanted to go to Israel but were not permitted to leave the country. Zhou Enlai was incredulous that Jews in China were forbidden from leaving the country to go to Israel and insisted that was something China in principle would never do, but he agreed to look into the matter.

When Zhou Enlai returned to the foreign ministry and asked if what Marshall told him was true, he learned that it was. On October 24, 1956, Marshall received a letter from Reuben D. Abraham, leader of the Jewish community in Shanghai, stating that the 543 Jews now had permission to leave China. They went first to Hong Kong and from there they could go anywhere they wanted. Interestingly, Abraham's family had lived in China for 110 years, and their priceless, antique jade collection was confiscated after he refused an offer of one *yuan* ($1.30) per item. He then received a letter from the Shanghai Museum thanking him for his "enthusiastic contribution." When Marshall secured exit visas for the Jews, Abraham's family also left for Hong Kong.

A powerful speaker and a passionate defender of social justice, Marshall was tall, had bushy eyebrows and usually was seen smoking a pipe with sweet-smelling tobacco. Among his awards are the Meritorious Medal for Service to Singapore, an honorary doctorate from the National University of Singapore, and an endowed Chair of Law at the National University of Singapore. There is a chair in the middle of the synagogue of Singapore with a plaque on the back that reads: "CHAIR OF DAVID MARSHALL, PRESIDENT OF THE JEWISH COMMUNITY OF SINGAPORE, FIRST CHIEF MINISTER OF SINGAPORE."

Another prominent Jew in Singapore was Jacob Ballas (1921–2000). I read and listened to his oral history in the Singapore National Library and also met him personally. Born into a poor family, his mother supported them by baking challah bread (egg rich white bread usually eaten by Jews on the Sabbath and holidays) and cakes which she sold to the Jewish community on Fridays for the Sabbath. Ballas was humiliated by the embarrassing distribution of charity to the poor Jews in Singapore. He also was troubled about being treated by the British as a second-class citizen, as noted, and feared he would never be promoted in his job as a result of this discrimination against local Jews. Ballas, however, excelled in math; he was able to make mathematical calculations in his head without paper or pencil and even knew math tricks, some of which he taught me. In 1964, he became the first citizen of the "Asian, native or colored" social strata to head the stock exchange in Singapore.

Ballas gave significant money to charities in Singapore and Israel. Indeed, next to the synagogue on Waterloo Street where Ballas remembered taking refuge during the war is his gift to the Jewish community, the Ballas Community Center. It includes the rabbi's residence, a beautiful dining room, a kosher market, a daily prayer room and other amenities for the Jewish community. It was a true honor to have known Jacob Ballas.

I remember Dr. Yahya Cohen (1920–2003) well, and he, too, remembered suffering from colonial discrimination by the British. His father was from Aden (a British colony on the southern tip of Yemen), and his mother was from Singapore. As a Jew, under British rule he could work only as an assistant to a British doctor. He became a pioneer when, after Singapore became independent, he became a senior surgeon, and went on to train local surgeons. Dr. Cohen is considered the father of surgery in Singapore.

Among other notable Jews in Singapore: Nissim Adis built the Grand Hotel de L'Europe in Singapore. Joseph Grimberg is a successful attorney living in Singapore who represented Singapore's Prime Minister Lee Kwan Yew; Grimberg was the first Jewish Supreme Court justice in Singapore (1987–1989) and also was a justice on the International Court of Arbitration at The Hague. In addition, Grimberg led the successful fight to end discrimination against the natives, as the British called them.

To this day, sadly, Sir Meyer Manasseh's biography has not been written. Mozelle Nissim, referred to by some as "the best woman our movement should be proud to have," died at the age of ninety-two. In 1978 David Marshall was appointed ambassador to France, Spain and Portugal and served as ambassador in all three countries simultaneously. His wife Jean still lives in Singapore. And Jacob Ballas, the poor boy embarrassed by his poverty, left an estate of $300 million.

Chapter Twenty-Two
Why Did the Synagogue in Rangoon, Burma, Have 126 Torahs?

Rudyard Kipling wrote, "This is Burma and it will be quite unlike any land you know." With China to the north, Thailand to the east and the Bay of Bengal and India to the west, Burma became home to the largest Jewish community in Southeast Asia. It is best known for the city of Rangoon (now Yangon) on the Irawaddy River which is navigable for nine hundred miles. The port of Rangoon is in a strategic location for trade from interior Burma and international trade, and Burma is rich with excellent sapphires, emeralds and rubies. It is an agricultural land of rice fields, teak forests, bamboo, tropical flowers, coconuts, bananas, mangoes, papaya, betel nuts, durians (sweet, pungent-smelling fruit that many consider to be a delicacy) and cocoa. And it is graced with natural ports, huge deposits of recently found oil and gas, and Buddhist monasteries.

The Buddhist temple bells are heard everywhere, and the most famous golden Buddhist pagoda (it is believed that eight hairs of the Buddha's head are there) is in Rangoon. Shwedagon, considered the oldest pagoda in the world, is Burma's largest shrine. It has a base of 1335 feet in circumference and reaches a cone-shaped summit over 300 feet up from the base. One can climb barefoot up hundreds of stairs (there is also an elevator), and along the way vendors sell votive candles, incense and flowers. Covered with sixty tons of gold leaf from base to summit, it is topped with a seventy-six-carat diamond lotus, ten inches in diameter, and crowned with an umbrella of gold that glitters in the sun and on whose rings gold and silver bells tinkle with every breeze. The Buddha's crown is made of more than five thousand diamonds and more than two thousand rubies. In 1608, the Portuguese ruthlessly plundered this most sacred site, and in 1824 the British shamefully damaged it while using it as a fortress.

In 1755 Solomon Gabirol was commander of the king's (King Alaungpaya) army; he is the first Jew we know of in Burma. Burma is also home to the Karens, who, some believe, are one of the ten lost tribes of Israel. They are light-skinned, marry among themselves and believe in *Ywa*, an eternal God who gave them a book with their own stories of Divine Creation, the Garden of Eden, the Flood, and the Tower of Babel. Following the British annexation of Burma in 1885 as a province of India (the annexation angered the Burmese who think of themselves as independent, not as a province of India), Bene Israel Jews, and Baghdadi Jewish merchants primarily from Calcutta, 975 nautical miles away across the Bay of Bengal, came to Burma. Meeting some of the Jews who formerly were residents of Rangoon is a pleasure. They express joy and happiness in recalling their comfortable days in beautiful and hospitable Burma, which for almost two hundred years was a tolerant home for Jews.

World War II; nationalism and socialism, which led to the confiscation of private property; and Burma's independence, changed everything. Their memories of Burma are rich with images of picnics, boat parties, tennis, cricket, badminton, spectacular Burmese and Chinese weddings, theater, puppet shows, celebrations during street festivals, and hundreds of silk, paper and bamboo kites of all colors flying in the sky.

Both before and after the British annexation, Jews were making their mark in Burma. Starting in the 1850s, there was great commercial expansion in Burma, and oil was discovered by a Jewish merchant, Saul Aaron, who alerted the British to the presence of oil after he tasted traces of kerosene in the local drinking water. In 1861 the first Jewish business, E. Sassoon and Sons, was established as a water supply company, providing the British Royal Navy with water from their artesian wells as well as ice and carbonated water (seltzer). In 1964 I remember seeing a six-pointed Jewish star on the American Ice Factory Company building, which had been owned by Haskell and Ephraim Solomon since the early 1920s. There were wine and liquor stores owned by Jews, as well as coffee, fruit and antique shops. Jews also owned shops with fine, imported provisions, and some Jews were successful tailors. The first movie theater was also established by a Jew in about 1885, and in the 1930s David Sofaer, a Jew, became the mayor of Rangoon. R.A. Raphael was a Jewish mayor in the nearby city of Bassein.

As the Jews became successful financially, they became generous philanthropists and donated funds for local hospitals, libraries and schools. The Jewish school in Rangoon had more than two hundred students and included a resource room for learning-disabled students. The Sofaer family donated the iron gates at the entrance to the Rangoon Zoo, and Mordecai Isaac Cohen donated the cast iron bandstand, both of which remain to this day.

Abraham Sofaer (1896–1988) was born and raised in Rangoon and became a prominent stage actor and film and television star after first working as a schoolteacher. He had strong facial features and a resonant voice, and in 1921 he made his stage debut in London in *The Merchant of Venice*. Because of his Semitic look, he was frequently cast as a Jew, Arab, Armenian, Indian or Turk. He also appeared as Saint Paul in the 1951 film *Quo Vadis* and appeared in other films including *Dreyfus, High Finance, The Private Life of Don Juan, Rembrandt, A Matter of Life and Death, Christopher Columbus, Cairo Road* and *The Naked Jungle*. He appeared on American television in *Perry Mason, Star Trek, The Twilight Zone* and *Daniel Boone*. He is probably best known, however, for his recurring role as Hadji, master of all genies, in the television program *I Dream of Jeannie*. The father of six children, Abraham lived in Los Angeles.

Ezra Solomon (1920–2002) also was born in Rangoon and graduated from the University of Rangoon in 1940. At the beginning of World War II, Solomon fled to Calcutta, where he joined the British Royal Navy, and after the war he taught economics at the University of Chicago and then at Stanford University. His best-known book, *The Theory of Financial Management* (1963), helped shape theories of corporate finance. Under the administration of President Richard Nixon, Solomon served on the President's Council of Economic Advisers from 1971 to 1973, during which time he influenced the international financial system with his new concept of floating currencies. The author of thirteen books on economics, Solomon's obituary appeared in *The New York Times* on December 19, 2002.

Major General David Abel (1935–   ) was born to Jewish parents and became part of the military junta – at one time he was the third highest ranking member – in Burma after graduating in 1955 from the Royal Military Academy in Sandhurst, England. He served in various capacities in the military and in the civil administration. Considered the most competent economist in Burma, he was appointed minister of trade, finance and revenue and later was appointed minister of national planning and economic development. When later he served as a minister to the office of the chairman of the State Peace and Development Council, he attempted to produce a market-oriented economy, provide an influx of capital and technology and utilize Burma's natural and human resources. Major General Abel was prominent in developing twenty-four oil and gas resources in Burma both for domestic use and for exporting gas to Thailand. He pioneered a project to develop thirty-one hotels that added five thousand rooms for tourists and business travelers, and he built a golf course, beach resorts, tourist villages and an amusement park, all of which enhanced Burma's tourist industry.

The valedictorian of the 2006 graduating class at Yeshiva University, Sammy Samuels was born and raised in Rangoon, where he ranked third in the entire country on the government academic examination for high school students. Sammy, with dark hair and kind eyes, was part of the Baghdadi Jewish community in Rangoon, where his father and two sisters still live and where I have had the pleasure of visiting with them many times. Sammy, who now lives in both New York and Yangon, encourages Jewish travel to Burma; indeed, today Burma is booming with tourism as a result of the nation's more open and democratic government. *The New York Times* has characterized Sammy as the Burmese person who shoulders the burden of his community's heritage. His family takes care of the one remaining synagogue.

The Bene Israel and the Baghdadis were very proud of their vibrant Jewish community, and their synagogue was the center of their Jewish identity. The first synagogue was built in 1857, and in 1893 construction started on the Musmeah Yeshua (to bring forth salvation) Synagogue, which still stands. It was this synagogue that was once home to 126 Torah scrolls. The synagogue has a soaring ceiling, interior columns from floor to roof, magnificent chandeliers, and a Holy Ark draped with beautiful silk and velvet curtains and shaped in a semi-circle where the Torah scrolls are housed. Shops also were built on synagogue property, and rent from these stores provided a steady source of income for synagogue maintenance. In 1896, the Jewish community dedicated their new synagogue, and I have a copy of the birth, marriage and death records that were accurately kept in the synagogue over the years. Judah Ezekiel, for example, is noted as being quite prosperous, and there was

Musmeah Yeshua Synagogue in Rangoon, Burma

a Judah Ezekiel Street in Rangoon. In his will he left funds to be used for the care and cleaning of the street that bore his name.

Twice each year, on Yom Kippur and Simchat Torah (the last day of the Jewish holiday of Sukkot), all 126 Torahs, standing erect in their round wooden cases covered with silver, were displayed around the synagogue so that everyone could touch them and kiss them. It was customary for families to donate a Torah to the synagogue in honor or in memory of a loved one, and at least one family member stood next to the Torah the family had donated. The Torahs generally were read in rotation, but on the birthday or *yahrzeit* (anniversary of the death) of the honored or deceased loved one, that Torah was read. Families also donated beautiful curtains embroidered with gold or silver thread, that were placed around the synagogue, and these also were on display on the Holy Ark twice a year.

In synagogues in the United States, no one knows who donated the Torahs when they are removed from the Holy Ark and paraded around the synagogue, even though there is sometimes a name on the back in very small letters. In Burma, however, twice a year congregants had the opportunity to ask the families who were standing with their donated Torahs to talk about the person in whose honor or memory the Torah was dedicated. A family's response told of a dedicated mother or a learned grandfather, etc., giving each Torah a human face.

In Rangoon, there was an excellent coed Jewish school with a full religious and secular curriculum, and on days when a family was remembering the person in whose memory or honor they had contributed a Torah, the family brought the Torah to the school, told the person's story and competed to provide the best and most memorable lunch for the entire school of more than two hundred students. When the children arrived home, their parents asked them in whose honor or memory the Torah was dedicated. This unique custom gave each Torah a personal history that kept someone's memory alive.

No story about the Jews in Burma is complete without telling the story of the lawsuit between J.M. Ezekiel (the plaintiff) and C.S. Joseph and other trustees of the synagogue (the defendants). Remember, there were two Jewish communities in Burma, the Baghdadis and the Bene Israel. The latter had darker skin, spoke Marathi (a language spoken in the Bombay area of India) and wore Indian attire known as *saris*. The former were light-skinned and considered themselves to be British, so they were condescending towards the Bene Israel. The tensions between these two groups of Jews in Rangoon led to dissension and disagreements that finally culminated in the 1934 civil suit (Number 85) in the Supreme Court in Rangoon. In 1932, during all of the turmoil which tore the community apart, the cantor of the synagogue had chosen to side with the Bene Israel and established the Beth El Synagogue, where all Jews were treated equally. Despite the new synagogue and the fact that one of the judges was the brother of the attorney for the Baghdadis, civil suit 85 went forward.

The case revolved around a number of issues. First, the Bene Israel were upset that in the birth registry in the Rangoon synagogue the Baghdadis were listed by name only, whereas the listing for other Bombay Jews included the notation "Bene Israel." The Baghdadis wanted that differentiation because they worried that being identified with the less sophisticated Bene Israel might threaten their acceptance by the British. Second, in 1926 and again in 1929, when it was time to elect trustees of the synagogue, the Bene Israel were excluded from the list of those deemed eligible to serve as trustees. The Bene Israel asked for eligibility again before the election in 1934, but this time not only did the trustees refuse their request for eligibility to run for office, they also removed their names from the list of eligible voters and considered them as non-Jews.

The issues intensified. According to the Bene Israel's accusations, the Baghdadis stated that the Bene Israel were not allowed to vote, could not receive synagogue honors, could not be called to read the Torah or even carry it, and were not allowed to open the Holy Ark or lead the service; the Baghdadis confirmed that the accusations were true. The Baghdadis claimed that the Bene Israel were not observant and ignored some of the laws of the Torah, but the lawyer for the Bene Israel argued that not being observant did not mean that they were not Jews. Both sides also appealed to the rabbinic authorities in London, Jerusalem and Baghdad. The civil court welcomed the decisions from the rabbinic courts, but those decisions were not unanimous. The chief rabbi

Silver Torah cases in Musmeah Yeshua Synagogue in Rangoon, Burma

of the British Empire supported the Baghdadis, but the chief rabbi of Baghdad disagreed and declared that the Bene Israel were full and complete Jews.

On April 9, 1935, the Burmese Supreme Court rendered its decision. Justice Leach declared: "There will be a declaration that the plaintiffs and other Jews called Bene Israel are eligible for appointment as trustees of the Musmeah Yeshua Synagogue and are entitled to vote at the election of trustees. Defendants are not entitled to exclude from the list a Jew merely because he is a Bene Israel. I consider that the cost of this case should come out of the synagogue trust fund." On May 14, 1935, the decision was appealed, but the appeal was dismissed.

Now, to be clear, the problem between the Baghdadi and the Bene Israel Jews did not originate in Rangoon; it occurred earlier in Bombay. When the Baghdadis arrived in Bombay, at first they were cordial, albeit aloof, to the Bene Israel, but before long they tried to erect religious and physical barriers between themselves and the Bene Israel. David Sassoon (see chapter 8) tried unsuccessfully to have a partition erected in the Bombay Jewish cemetery to separate the Baghdadis from the Bene Israel. In Calcutta, where the Baghdadi Jews of Burma originated, the cemetery indeed was partitioned into sections for the Baghdadis, Bene Israel and others.

In the end, though it was not the friction among the Jews that devastated the Jewish community in Burma. While former residents' memories are happy, they also recall the rise and fall of Jewish and British fortunes in Burma. World War II, nationalism and socialism, which led to the confiscation of private property; and Burma's independence, changed everything. Residents witnessed global war, local rebellions and Japanese occupation. In addition, the Baghdadi Jews never achieved their lifelong goal of being accepted by the British (to be truly British, one had to be purely Caucasian and Christian), and the elusiveness of this goal conditioned their experience in Burma.

Sassoon Solomon was so angry about not being respected and accepted by the British that he built a palatial mansion facing the British country club (the Gymkhana Club) as a rebuke to the British for forbidding Jews from becoming members of the private, exclusive club for foreigners. There also was an unspoken agreement that Jews would not be awarded academic prizes for their achievements in school and that British military commissions would be denied to graduating Jewish and Burmese classmates, especially during wartime. The British not only showed disdain for the Jews, they also believed that the Burmese lacked human worth and dignity.

Japanese bombings of Rangoon started after Pearl Harbor in December 1941 and continued until March 1942. Rangoon was unprepared: there was no air defense warning system, no firefighters and no shelters. Rangoon's wooden buildings burned easily, looting was rampant, and casualties were in the thousands, but hospitals were bombed, too, and could not care for the injured. Chaos reigned. All hope ended with the fall of Burma on February 15, 1942. Two thousand British troops from Calcutta marched through the streets as a show of strength during the day, but they were outnumbered, so under cover of darkness at night to avoid being seen by anyone, they left for Singapore, taking Rangoon's anti-aircraft guns with them.

People began to flee to the countryside. Foreigners escaped to India, sailing 975 nautical miles across the bay to Calcutta, but Burmese natives were not permitted on the boats. Those in Burma who could not sail to Calcutta made the long march north through the jungles and then south to Calcutta. Between February and March 1942, sadly a year with an early monsoon season, 74,000 Burmese, including Baghdadis and other Jews, started to march to India without realizing how arduous the trip would be, and more than five thousand people died of cholera or exhaustion trekking through the jungle and crossing the dangerous mountains. Safe drinking water was a rare commodity, so people contracted dysentery, diarrhea and cholera. They also came down with malaria from infected mosquitoes. They walked six to eight miles each day, stopping during the noonday heat to rest or to wash in the polluted rivers, bathing which resulted in not only disease but also in leeches finding their way into every orifice and crevice of their bodies.

I remember stories Jews told of not worrying about how much rice to pack or how much water to carry, but deciding that taking a violin or an accordion made the most sense. Playing pleasant music to the tribal natives in the jungle just might get them a place to sleep and some food to eat. I remember a story about the taste of elephant's milk being sweet but, sadly, difficult to find. And I remember the story about a Jewish child who got lost on the road being found and cared for by a tribal family and then reclaimed by his biological family after the war. For those who made it to India, life started again, and children went to school and had to learn the local Indian languages.

Those who remained in Burma during and after the war years became caught up in Burmese nationalism. Burma became independent in January 1948 and was the first Asian nation to recognize Israel. In 1955 Burma's Prime Minister U Nu was the first head of state to visit Israel, after which David

Ben-Gurion reciprocated and spent two weeks in Burma. To the Burmese nationalists the Baghdadis were considered Europeans and allies of the British, the very status that originally had been denied to them by the British. When socialism came to Burma in 1962, and when businesses became nationalized in 1964, Burma became a place for only the Burmese, and foreigners, including both the Bene Israel and the Baghdadi communities, were no longer welcome. Judah Ezekiel Street was renamed Thein Byu Street, and the Solomon family home became a school where, surprisingly, the large Star of David still remains visible on the building. It was time for the Jews to leave.

The synagogue in Rangoon never was hit directly by a bomb or mortar shell during the war, and whenever a nearby fire threatened the synagogue, the Jews climbed to the roof and threw water on any embers that endangered it. The synagogue survived, and the Torah scrolls were hidden and also survived the war. Sammy Samuels's father and sisters remain the stalwart caretakers of the unique synagogue, but the 126 Torah scrolls were taken out of Burma clandestinely when the families who donated them left the country. They are now in Australia, the United States, England, Canada and Israel. In 2002, because the Jewish community is now so small in Burma, a synagogue in Hong Kong adopted the community, and its members traveled to Rangoon for the high holiday of Rosh Hashanah as a sign of solidarity and support. There is a sign on the door of the synagogue in Rangoon that says. "A tree may be alone in the field, a man alone in the world, but a Jew is never alone on his holy days." It is gratifying that in 2008 after cyclone Nargis devastated Burma, an interfaith service was held in the Rangoon synagogue.

Chapter Twenty-Three
How a Silver Cigarette Case Saved a Life and More

The Hebrew word for remember, *zakhor*, appears 269 times in the Bible. Many of the amazing people whose stories are told in these pages are unknown, and most of the people who knew them are no longer here to keep the memories alive. These heroes, artists, scholars and statesmen are Asians who helped the Jews or Jews who helped Asians and/or other Jews, and I remember them often in my prayers during *Yizkor* memorial services at synagogue.

Among those I remember are Mme Sun Yat-sen (1893–1981) who on May 13, 1933, headed a delegation that immediately conveyed a very strong protest to R.C.W. Behrend, the German consul in Shanghai, against Nazi atrocities and terror. Her husband President Sun Yat-sen (1866–1925) wrote a letter in 1920 to N.E.B. Ezra, editor and publisher of *Israel's Messenger*, the Jewish newspaper in Shanghai, showing support for the return of the Jewish people to their homeland stating, " ... wish to assure you of my sympathy for this movement which is one of the greatest movements of the present time; all lovers of democracy cannot help but support the movement to restore your wonderful and historic nation which has contributed so much to the civilization of the world and which rightly deserves an honorable place in the family of nations." Later, Sun Fo, President Sun Yat-sen's son, said, "As a lover of democracy, I fully endorse my late father's view." Sun Fo was president of the Chinese government legislative branch from 1932 to 1948, and in March 1939, when so many Jews were seeking a safe haven, he stated, "I am proposing the establishment of a Jewish settlement... in order to settle stateless Jewish people." In May his proposal was approved, and a plan to give one hundred thousand Jews refuge in China, assuring them the same rights as all Chinese citizens, was announced.

Another hero was Jacob Berglass, a banker and textile industrialist in Germany and later a refugee in Shanghai. He made contact with the Joint Distribution Committee (JDC) about another plan to bring one hundred thousand Jews to Kunming, China (a different city than the area suggested in Sun Fo's plan at about the same time), and worked out all the details. The newspapers in China expressed approval for the plan, deeming it to be advantageous for both China and the Jews. Neither Sun Fo's nor Jacob Berglass's plan was realized due to China's war with Japan and the start of the war in Europe.

Ho Feng Shan (1901–1997) was the Chinese consul in Vienna from 1938 through 1940 and is another hero. I met his daughter Manli in 2000 in the lobby of the United Nations at an exhibition featuring righteous diplomats who saved the lives of Jews during the Holocaust, and I learned from her the full story of her father's efforts on behalf of Jews. He is credited with being the first person to realize that Shanghai was a city that Jewish refugees could enter without documents such as visas and passports. Ho was a brilliant, fearless, dynamic and honorable man who named his two children for two principles of Confucius – virtue and decorum (proper conduct). Ho was seven when his father died. The family became poverty-stricken, and Ho and his three sisters lived in a sort of orphanage/asylum for the poor, yet he studied diligently and went on to earn a PhD before joining China's foreign service, eventually being stationed in Vienna.

There were more than 165,000 Jews in Vienna at the start of the Nazi era, the third largest Jewish community in Europe. A seventeen-year-old Jewish boy went from embassy to embassy and from consulate to consulate seeking a visa to escape from the Nazis, but he was unsuccessful. In 1938, as a last resort, he went to the Chinese consulate and asked for a visa. Since, finally, the response was positive, he asked for twenty more visas for his entire family, and he received them. Despite protests from the Chinese ambassador and accusations that he was taking bribes, Ho issued more than four thousand life-saving visas that permitted entry only to Shanghai, including one that went to Dr. Israel Singer, former secretary-general of the World Jewish Congress, who credits Ho with saving his life.

Ho's motto was "A great deed performed for others to see is not a true good deed," so he never sought recognition for his work to help Jews. In October

General Higuchi Kiichiro, 1880–1970

2000 Yad Vashem in Jerusalem, which honors the "righteous among the nations," honored him posthumously, and his family received the award in January 2001.

In March 1938, when German and Austrian Jews were escaping to Vladivostok en route to Shanghai via the Trans-Siberian Railroad, the train sometimes would take them to Otpur on the border of the USSR and Manchuria (a "puppet state" of Japan), and from there Jews would continue to Shanghai. No one realized that Manchuria was an independent country and, thus, a transit visa was necessary to enter. Since no one had that necessary visa, the Jewish refugees (some say there were three thousand) were stranded on the Soviet side of the border in freezing temperatures with no food. General Higuchi Kiichiro (1880–1970) was a Japanese military attaché in Europe from 1925 to 1928 and later was part of the military mission to Germany. He also was military attaché to Poland and in 1937 served in Germany with the Japanese embassy. When he learned of the stranded Jewish refugees, he requested trains that would take the innocent refugees across to the Manchurian side of the border and permit the refugees to enter the Manchurian city of Harbin, where the local Jewish community would take care of them until they could travel to Shanghai. When the German ambassador protested, General Higuchi responded that "Japan is not a vassal of Germany" and that Germany had no right to interfere with Japan's internal policies. He secured the necessary trains. The Jewish community of Harbin appreciated his efforts so much that they entered his name in the Golden Book of the Jewish National Fund.

In January 1938, at the Moderne Hotel in Harbin, Higuchi also participated in the first conference of the Jewish communities of the Far East. During the discussions, he spoke out against the Nazi persecution of Jews and also against the British prohibiting Jews from entering Palestine. In December 2009 the Israeli ambassador to Japan planted an olive sapling in front of the City Hall of Gifu City in memory of Higuchi.

In 1970 there was an obituary in the Japanese newspapers that Major

General Higuchi, a former chief of intelligence in Manchuria, had passed away, and his family called and asked me to attend his funeral. The family earnestly believed that Stalin had requested that Higuchi, considered an enemy of the Soviets, be extradited to the Soviet Union. (No evidence to support that belief ever surfaced.) Jews lobbied on Higuchi's behalf, and the Occupation did not turn him over to the Soviets. Those two reasons seem to explain why the family invited me to the funeral.

Colonel Yasue Norihiro (1888–1950) was born into a samurai family, attended army cadet school, officers' academy and then the Tokyo Foreign Language School where he was one of the first to study Russian. He was in Siberia from 1918 to 1920 as part of the Imperial Japanese Army fighting with the White Russians, Americans and the French against the Soviets. Japan had fifty thousand soldiers there, the largest contingent. While Yasue was in Siberia he read the *Protocols of the Elders of Zion* (a vicious anti-Semitic forgery claiming the existence of an international Jewish conspiracy for world domination) and the writings of Henry Ford, an American anti-Semite who promoted the *Protocols*. At the age of thirty-three, in Siberia, Yasue was assigned to General Gregori Semenov, a vehement anti-Semite who distributed the *Protocols* to every soldier fighting against the Red Army. In 1922 Yasue returned to Japan, and in 1924 he was the first to translate the *Protocols of the Elders of Zion* into Japanese.

From 1927 to 1928, representing the Japanese government, Yasue was sent to Europe and then to Palestine where he met rabbis and Zionist leaders, visited a kibbutz (a collective farm or settlement in Palestine) and found no evidence of a Jewish conspiracy. Professor Meron Medzini, the son of his guide in Palestine, by the way, is now one of the leading Israeli professors of Japanese history. Yasue also visited Paris, London and Moscow, searching for evidence of the Jewish conspiracy. In 1934, Yasue wrote that Jews control both capitalism and communism, and he became the leading authority in the Imperial Japanese Army on the subject of the Jews.

Colonel Yasue Norihiro, 1888–1950

an ear, and finally Kaspe was found brutally murdered. Upon seeing his son's mutilated body, his father shrieked uncontrollably and went insane. Although this occurred at a time when the Japanese rule in Manchuria forbade public demonstrations, Dr. Kaufman delivered a eulogy before a crowd of thousands, denouncing the kidnappers, fascists and the Manchurian government. The kidnappers were caught and convicted in court, but, because of widespread corruption, eventually they were released without punishment. The Japanese, however, replaced the corrupt officials.

Dr. Kaufman also was kidnapped in Harbin. In 1945, only days before the end of World War II, the Soviet Union, which up to then had fought on the side of the Allies in its battles on the European front, declared war on Japan and invaded Manchuria, overrunning Harbin. In August, to celebrate the end of the war, the Soviets held a formal reception to which they invited all of the community leaders of Harbin, including Dr. Kaufman, whom they then kidnapped. He was arrested by the Red Army, accused of the crime of being a Zionist, and in 1945 on Yom Kippur, he was taken over the border to the Soviet Union. Although he was never tried, never signed a confession and never was convicted of a crime, he was imprisoned in Siberia for eleven years. While in prison Dr. Kaufman put himself at risk by providing medical assistance and generally helping prisoners in any way he could.

After his release in 1956, he tried fifteen times to join his family in Israel, but all of his requests were denied. The Israeli embassy in Moscow held a passport and visa for him, but when he reached the door, Soviet soldiers refused to let him go any farther, since only Israeli citizens were permitted to enter the embassy. Dr. Kaufman wrote to Premier Nikita Khrushchev, leader of the Soviet Union, saying he had been falsely accused, deprived of a trial, did not commit nor admit to any crime, and that he wanted to join his family in Israel. Five years later, in March 1961, he finally was able to emigrate from the Soviet Union to Israel to join his family. For the remaining years of his life, Dr. Kaufman, an amazing hero, served as a physician in Israel. He wrote a book in Russian which was translated into Hebrew under the title *Rofeh Bamachaneh* (Doctor in the Camp) before his death in Tel Aviv in 1969.

After Dr. Kaufman died, there was a memorial service for him at the Jewish Center in Tokyo. The synagogue was overflowing with former residents of Harbin, Shanghai, Tientsin and all the smaller communities of Manchuria, and their crying was evidence to everyone of how much Dr. Kaufman meant to all. At the end of the service, people could not bear to leave, because being with others who also were mourning their loss provided some comfort. And comfort came, too, from the act of remembering as congregants shared their memories of Dr. Kaufman, the great-grandson of Shneur Zalman (1745–1813), the founder of Chabad (an international Hassidic outreach movement). Someone should write Dr. Abraham Kaufman's biography.

I learned of Dr. Ludwik Rajchman (1881–1965) from General Chiang Wego, son of Chiang Kai-shek, when Wego and I met in Taiwan in the early 1970s. Dr. Rajchman should be world-famous, but he remains unknown despite having improved the health and quality of life for millions of people all over the world. His many accomplishments are impressive and worthy of several pages, but here, in addition to biographical information, we will recount primarily his connections to the Far East.

Rajchman was born in Warsaw to an assimilated, intellectual and influential Jewish family. His father Alex was the founder of the Warsaw Philharmonic Orchestra and its first director. His mother Melenia was part of the Hirzfeld family, patrons of the arts, and his brother was a mathematician.

In 1902, Rajchman joined the Polish Socialist Party and began studying medicine in Krakow. He received his medical degree in 1907 and then went on to study microbiology at the Pasteur Institute in Paris, France. He continued his studies in London between 1910 and 1913 and lectured on bacteriology at the Royal Institute. From 1914 until 1918 Dr. Rajchman was chief of a laboratory in London, where he conducted research on dysentery, polio, and influenza. He returned to Poland in 1918 after World War I and became minister of health, responsible for thirty million people in Poland and Russia who were suffering from typhus, typhoid and venereal disease.

In 1919, Dr. Rajchman created the National Institute of Hygiene in Poland, and in 1921 he became director of health at the League of Nations. In 1922 he set a precedent by bringing health issues to the international stage for the first time. He knew that serious diseases could cross oceans and endeavored to bring health care professionals together from around the world to discuss prevention and find solutions. The fact that he could be persuasive in five languages was very helpful.

In 1925–1926, Dr. Rajchman was invited to Japan to study their health care system and to bring it up to date, and he also visited China, a country he loved. In 1926 Dr. Rajchman became medical adviser to, and a close friend of, Chiang Kai-shek. Dr. Rajchman was assisted in China by Dr. Victor Heisler, an American Jewish doctor with the Rockefeller Foundation. Dr.

Captain Inuzuka Koreshige and his wife Kyoko

Heisler was primarily involved with the health care system in the Philippines, and Dr. Rajchman worked with him in that country as well. Dr. Rajchman, who was anti-Hitler and anti-fascist, was forced out of the League of Nations in 1939, when the Nazis and fascists were exerting power. In December 1946, when the United Nations replaced the League of Nations, Dr. Rajchman, in his sixties, worked with former US President Herbert Hoover and New York Mayor Fiorello LaGuardia to draft a UN General Assembly resolution. They created the United Nations International Children's Emergency Fund (UNICEF), and Dr. Rajchman was its first president, serving from 1947 to 1950.

Dr. Rajchman was known as a great organizer and as being knowledgeable about sanitation, disease and nutrition, and he organized one of the first conferences on those subjects. He urged countries to develop their own supply of milk for children, rather than relying on expensive imports, and he also promoted the construction of a penicillin factory in India. In 1957, Dr. Rajchman moved to France, where he remained for the rest of his life.

I visited Inuzuka Kyoko (1909–1992) in her beautiful home in the Omori section of Tokyo many times between 1968 and 1976. Upon entering her house, guests would trace their palms and then write greetings or comments inside the palm print, remove their shoes and then sit on tatami mats sipping green tea, surrounded by hanging scrolls and beautiful flower arrangements. Kyoko cherished the life of intrigue she lived. She was a close friend of Laura Margolis (see chapter 9) and all the important Sephardic Jews of the region (see chapter 8), and her photo collection and library, documenting the Jewish experience in Shanghai (see chapter 10) until the attack on Pearl Harbor, was second to none.

Kyoko arrived in Shanghai in September 1939, and in October she attended synagogue with Navy Captain Inuzuka Koreshige (1890–1965). Kyoko was at first his secretary, next his mistress and finally his wife. Inuzuka had a checkered career, although no one seems to have known about it at the time. He was born into a samurai family on the southern island of Kyushu, attended the

Imperial Japanese Naval Academy and served on various Japanese warships. A charming man, Inuzuka could speak and write English and French, and he visited the United States (twice), England and Germany.

Inuzuka read the anti-Semitic *Protocols of the Elders of Zion*, but when he served as the military attaché in France, he claimed to have had a "kosher" kitchen there. He was known for his research, writing and lecturing about the Jewish menace and the Jewish conspiracy against Japan, putting forth all of his anti-Semitic diatribes under the pen name Utsunomiya. Yet, before the attack on Pearl Harbor, Inuzuka rejected the plan of the Shanghai municipal council to limit – and then close – Jewish immigration to Shanghai; and after the attack on Pearl Harbor, Inuzuka released to the Jews in Shanghai thousands of bags of cement intended for military use so they could build a synagogue, released Jewish funds frozen in American banks in Shanghai to the Jewish refugees and permitted the transfer of funds from Switzerland on behalf of the refugees.

Inuzuka proposed the establishment of a Jewish refuge for three hundred thousand Jews in Pudong, across the river from downtown Shanghai, and he suggested establishing a leather trade industry to bring most of the Jews in Czechoslovakia to China. He called the Jews "fellow Asians" and had read the article in the *Jewish Encyclopedia* hypothesizing that some of the lost tribes of Israel may have gone to Japan. In 1982 Laura Margolis wrote that Inuzuka could have refused to help her – an enemy national – care for the eight thousand destitute Jewish refugees she was responsible for in Shanghai, but she emphasized that she received his full cooperation even though the United States and Japan were at war.

In December 1938, Inuzuka helped organize in Tokyo the Five Minister Conference that included the prime minister, foreign minister, army minister, navy minister and interior minister. They denounced discrimination against Jews in a statement that

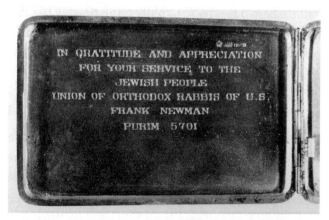

The inside of the cigarette case presented to Navy Captain Inuzuka Koreshige on Purim, 1941; this case saved his life after World War II.

became government policy. In Shanghai Inuzuka received a silver cigarette case from Frank Newman, an affluent Orthodox American Jew from Queens, New York. Newman was in Shanghai on a fact-finding mission about the city's Orthodox Jews on behalf of the Union of Orthodox Rabbis. The silver cigarette case was engraved with the following inscription: "In appreciation for your service to the Jewish people. Union of Orthodox Rabbis of America. Frank Newman. Purim 5701" (the Hebrew calendar year for 1941). Inuzuka said that as a loyal career military officer he could not accept the silver cigarette case. Newman explained that it was neither a gift nor a bribe but, rather, a gesture to celebrate the Jewish holiday of Purim (the joyous holiday commemorating the Jews' deliverance from evil in ancient Persia), which is celebrated by exchanging gifts with family and friends. With this reassurance, Inuzuka accepted the silver cigarette case.

After the war, the Occupation returned Inuzuka to Manila to stand trial for cruel war crimes while he was a commander in the Philippines. He noticed that the chief judge and chief attorney were Jewish, insisted that they had the wrong person on trial, produced the silver cigarette case with engraved praise from the rabbis and was freed within one week. That silver cigarette case saved Inuzuka's life. In 1953, Inuzuka led the Japan Israel Association.

I asked for the cigarette case to prevent it from disappearing. To me the cigarette case was one of the few important historical objects that remained from the refugee era in Shanghai, and I believed it belonged in the Yad Vashem Museum in Israel, but I did not receive it upon my request. Instead Kyoko dangled the cigarette case before my eyes for years, but when I asked for it for Yad Vashem, I received no reply until my very last day in Japan, when I rushed to her home prior to departing to the airport, and she gave it to me. In 1981, I gave the cigarette case to Yad Vashem, where it remains. In the 1960s Kyoko updated and sanitized Inuzuka's later writings.

Before the internet, I often made use of a Tokyo newspaper where one could place a free announcement to find someone. I wanted to find Shibata Mitsugu (1912–1977), for example, and availed myself of the free newspaper notice. In Shanghai, Shibata was a Japanese government official who had been present at a meeting of representatives of the Japanese consulate, the *kempetai* (secret police), the military, the director of refugee affairs and three Nazi officials, including Colonel Joseph Meisinger. They discussed the "Jewish problem." Three options were offered for consideration on how to exterminate the twenty-five thousand Jews in Shanghai. Shibata knew he had to warn the

Jews about the impending extermination that was scheduled to take place on Rosh Hashanah (the Jewish New Year) in September 1942, so he committed treason by telling them. Shibata was arrested by the Japanese and was sent to the infamous Bridge House Prison, where he was tortured and heard the tor-

Shibata Mitsugu, 1912–1977

ture and screams of the Jews he had informed about the plot who also were in the same prison. Several weeks later he was expelled from Shanghai and was warned that if he ever returned to China, he would be executed that day.

Ironically, Shibata believed that he had perpetrated a great disservice on the Jewish community by informing them of what would happen to them, thus causing their imprisonment and the torture of leaders of the Jewish community. In fact, Shibata had saved the lives of all of the Jews in Shanghai, and the Jewish community of Tokyo honored him at a Passover Seder in Tokyo in 1976. Another guest at the Seder was His Imperial Highness Prince Mikasa, Emperor Hirohito's youngest brother. At the end of the Seder Prince Mikasa broke with protocol, got up from his chair, walked over to Shibata and bowed to him. The room was silent as Shibata bowed in return. After Prince Mikasa exited, everyone stood up and applauded. Shibata died a year later.

I may be the only person to have interviewed Dr. Abraham J. Cohn (1903–1973), a tall, handsome and broad-shouldered man with black wavy hair. I met him at his home and in his medical office in Hong Kong and to my delight, when he visited Japan he stayed at my home. When I visited his home in Hong Kong, I noticed a tapestry on the wall and mentioned that it was from Nagasaki. He asked how I knew, and I responded that it was silk, with a Star of David surrounded by cherry blossoms and, combined with the 1906 date on the tapestry, I had made an informed assumption. Dr. Cohn told me that during the war in Shanghai, most of the rabbis of the Mir Yeshiva (see chapter 15) came to visit him, saw the tapestry on the wall and made no comments. He then said that since I was the first one to identify the tapestry correctly, I would inherit it after he passed away. After Dr. Cohn's death his wife Lydia, prior to returning to Scandinavia, sent the tapestry to me. It hangs on my living room wall and is one of my most precious Judaica possessions.

Cohn was born in Bukavina, Romania, came to Nagasaki as an infant and attended Japanese schools from nursery school through medical school. He was trained for his bar mitzvah in Nagasaki by a Jesuit priest who was the most knowledgeable person in Hebrew available at the time. He also won an Imperial award for writing Haiku poetry and had several black belts in the martial arts. Dr. Cohn put his knowledge of the martial arts to use unexpectedly one night when he saved the life of White Russian General Gregori Semenov, a vehement anti-Semite who was being attacked by two drunken Russians in Nagasaki. The incident, which did not change Semenov's view of Jews, would have repercussions years later. After practicing medicine in Japan, Dr. Cohn moved to China and opened a pharmaceutical factory in Hankow, moving the factory in 1939 to Shanghai, where it remained until the Communists took over.

Like Shibata, Dr. Cohn also heard about the plan to exterminate twenty-five thousand Jews in Shanghai. Dr. Cohn learned about it from bar girls, who were his patients and who had overheard German Nazis talking while they were drinking, about the Nazis' murderous plans for the Jews of Shanghai. After confirming the bar girls' report, Dr. Cohn took action. He met with Director of Refugee Affairs Kubota Tsutomu, reminding him of his (Cohn's) belief that the Jews and Japanese shared a common origin, before broaching the subject of the impending pogrom against the Jews. When Kubota said he was unsure whether he could trust him, Dr. Cohn suggested he ask Semenov, the vehement anti-Semite. Kubota informed him that the current Semenov in Shanghai was the equally anti-Semitic son of the Semenov whom Dr. Cohn knew (and whose life Dr. Cohn had saved many years earlier). Dr. Cohn said that even so, Kubota should ask the young Semenov if he could be trusted, and Semenov did, indeed, pay back the good deed Dr. Cohn provided to his father so many years earlier and confirmed that Dr. Cohn could be trusted. As Rosh Hashanah grew closer, Dr. Cohn worked with many Japanese officials to stop the impending executions. Ultimately, the Japanese did not carry out the extermination, but, instead, devised a plan to placate the Nazis. In May 1943, they relocated all the Jewish refugees in Shanghai to the Hongkew area of the city with orders that the area, the first Jewish settlement in Asia, was to be protected by the Japanese military (see chapter 10). Dr. Cohn coined the term SACRA for the Shanghai Ashkenazi Collaborating Relief Association, which governed the stateless refugees in Hongkew. Coincidentally, SACRA is a clever pun on the Japanese word "sacura," meaning "cherry blossoms," as pictured surrounding the Star of David in the tapestry I saw in Dr. Cohn's home.

After the war Dr. Cohn was trapped in Shanghai until 1957 because unrealistically he insisted that the Communist government pay him for his property and pharmaceutical factory in Shanghai, payment that would never be made. In 1957, Dr. Cohn was allowed to travel to Hong Kong, where he accepted a position as a doctor working in an office in the Peninsula building adjacent to the hotel that belonged to Lord Lawrence Kadoorie (see chapter 8). The British were very suspicious of Dr. Cohn for his wartime relationships with the Japanese and they never granted his application for citizenship. He died stateless in Hong Kong and is buried in the Jewish cemetery in the Happy Valley area of Hong Kong. I remain in touch with his grandson and great-grandchildren, with whom I recently stood at Dr. Cohn's grave, recounting how heroic he was.

Raymond Bushell (1910–1998) was a congregant of mine in Tokyo, and shortly after I arrived in 1968 we became very good friends. He was an attorney who arrived in Japan in 1948 during the Occupation after the end of World War II and did not leave until he returned to San Francisco in 1989. Almost as soon as he arrived in Japan, he began collecting miniature carved ivories, which were inexpensive and readily available at the time. Dating from 1615, these carvings, known as *netsuke*, were used as toggles on traditional male kimonos, which had no pockets. Bushell's collection of carvings range in height from one and a half to five inches and are carved in intricate detail on ivory, wood, ceramic, lacquer and glass. A generation earlier, F.M. Jonas, a Jewish resident of Kobe and also a *netsuke* collector, wrote one of the first books about these traditional carvings, but Bushell became such an expert on *netsuke* that he wrote eight books on the subject, two of which were considered so informative that they even were translated into Japanese. Bushell popularized this quintessentially Japanese art form in the United States and the West, and he continued collecting these miniatures even as the prices increased, amassing more than one thousand pieces. The collection, now worth millions of dollars, can be seen in the Raymond and Frances Bushell Netsuke Gallery in the Japanese Pavilion of the Los Angeles County Art Museum, where pieces from the collection rotate, displaying 150 at a time.

Erwin Reifler (1903–1965) must be remembered for his efforts to make the Chinese language more understandable to foreigners and perhaps also for his marriage to the daughter of the rabbi of Shanghai. He was born in Vienna, where he became an expert on the Chinese language. He spoke it so fluently that he was able to work as an interpreter for Chinese students who were studying there. Reifler was surrounded by a creative family: his father invented a snow removal machine, his brother was an artist, his cousins were Shakespearean actors and another cousin was a concert pianist. When his sister gave him a book on Japanese Haiku poetry, he became fascinated by the Japanese writing system.

Reifler eventually went to Shanghai, where he taught German at Jiatong University, taught Chinese to foreigners and created a system for understanding the etymology of Chinese characters. He also was a pioneer in the fields of computational linguistics and – in the early days of artificial intelligence – in machine translation (MT), developing a way to have mechanical translations via machine. Reifler wrote many papers about his innovative work. Eventually he became a professor of Chinese studies at the University of Shanghai, a unique position for a foreigner to hold.

Reifler had learned some basic Hebrew from his mother, an Orthodox Jew, but once he settled in Shanghai, he decided to improve his knowledge of that language. He met with the rabbi and, at the rabbi's wife's suggestion, offered to teach Chinese to their daughters Henrietta and Lilly in return for the rabbi's help with Hebrew. Reifler married Henrietta, the daughter of Mendel Brown, who served as principal of the Shanghai Jewish School in addition to his position as the rabbi of the Sephardic synagogue, Ohel Rachel.

I knew Henrietta and, whenever we met, I learned so much about Jewish life in Shanghai and about her brilliant and creative husband. I learned, for example, that Reifler studied the weights and measures of Babylonia in the ancient Near East and compared that system to China's. He found many commonalities between the two measuring systems, but the reason for their similarities remains a mystery. He studied the developmental history of Chinese ideograms (Chinese and Japanese have no alphabet; instead of letters or sounds, they have characters, sometimes also referred to as pictures or ideograms), contributing many original ideas to this area of study. He also was considered the most knowledgeable researcher in the field of comparative linguistics. In English, for example, the word *pupil* can refer to either a student or to a part of the human eye; in Chinese, the character for "pupil" meaning student is the same as the character for the human eye. The explanation for this is another mystery.

Studying Hebrew with Rev. Brown made Reifler an expert in that language as well. Japanese Navy Captain Inuzuka Koreshige, who believed that the Hebrew and Japanese languages were related, invited Reifler and his wife to tea and asked Reifler for his views on the subject. Reifler was not a politician and answered what he believed to be the truth. Reifler told Inuzuka that Hebrew and Japanese could not be compared despite some similarities such as

Lt. General Jack Jacob, the greatest living national military hero of India, currently president of the Jewish community of New Delhi

the word *you* being *anata* in Japanese, and *anta* in Aramaic and *ata* in Hebrew.

After the war Reifler, one of the finest scholars of the Chinese language, came to the United States and settled in Seattle, Washington, where he taught classical Chinese and Chinese grammar for the rest of his life. On his tombstone there are two Confucian proverbs that when translated read: "If the teacher [or Confucius] remains silent, what should the students transmit to others?" And "God does not say a word, but nature speaks on His behalf."

President Manuel Luis Quezon was another hero whose attempts to save Jews have not yet been highlighted. He offered virgin land for thirty thousand Jewish families to settle in the Philippines, but the Philippines was not independent, and the US State Department did not support President Quezon's effort. A monument to Quezon in Israel bears his quote dated April 23, 1940: "It is my hope, and indeed my expectation, that the people of the Philippines will have in the future every reason to be glad that when the time of need came, their country was willing to extend a hand of welcome."

Lieutenant General J.F.R. (Jack) Jacob (1923–) is the greatest living national military hero of India. Born to a Jewish family and raised in Calcutta, Jacob was educated in Darjeeling, where he developed a love for poetry and excelled in his studies. His family adopted a family of Jewish refugees from

Europe during the Holocaust and, horrified by their stories of the atrocities they faced, he joined the British Army. Currently he is president of the Jewish community center and synagogue of New Delhi.

Jacob was eighteen when he joined the British Army and is best known for his decisive role when what had started as a freedom fight by the eastern wing of Pakistan (now Bangladesh) against western Pakistan turned into a humanitarian crisis. Ten million Pakistanis streamed over the border into India during the humanitarian crisis, and India declared war on Pakistan. When General Jacob asked Prime Minister Indira Gandhi for a strategy and battle plan, she told him that he would figure it out.

Two weeks into the war, General A.A.K. Niazi of Pakistan invited General Jacob to lunch to discuss a cease-fire. General Jacob wrote an "instrument of surrender" which gave General Niazi a stark choice: he could surrender unconditionally and publicly and receive the protection of the Indian Army for all minorities and retreating troops, or he would face an immediate Indian onslaught. General Jacob gave him thirty minutes to decide. The threat was a bluff, and during the thirty-minute wait, he prayed to God for help. General Niazi agreed to General Jacob's terms, and the next day ninety-three thousand Pakistani soldiers surrendered. This was the answer to his prayer; General Jacob had only three thousand Indian troops. Historians agree that General Jacob's courage and strategic thinking changed the course of history and estimated that five hundred thousand to three million Pakistanis might have been massacred but for his actions.

After retiring from the military in July 1978, General Jacob was appointed governor of Goa and then governor of Punjab. When he left that office, graffiti was scrawled on the wall which read, "Without Jacob, who will feed the poor?" General Jacob's military uniform hangs in the Israeli Military Museum in Latrun, near Jerusalem.

To some, Sir Marc Aurel Stein (1862–1943) was a hero; to others, he was a thief. Born in Budapest, Hungary, to Nathan and Anna Stein, he was named after Marcus Aurelius and was known as "Aurel." Anna's brother was Dr. Ignaz Hirschler, president of the Jewish community of Hungary, a member of the upper house of the government (representing the Jews of Hungary), a well-known eye surgeon and guardian of the family. Aurel was born prior to Jews receiving political and civil rights, so he and his brother were baptized in order to gain those rights, a relatively common practice at the time. His parents, nevertheless, remained mindful Jews, educating Aurel's sister in what they viewed as the Jewish tradition: girls were to marry, care for the home and maintain Jewish tradition. Many years later when the Nazis came to power, Stein, who was in India at the time, recognized that despite their baptisms, his entire family were Hungarian Jews according to the Nazis. Thus, he helped his family and other Jews find safety outside of Nazi territory in Europe.

Educated in Budapest, Vienna, Leipzig, Tubingen and London, Stein was fluent in Hungarian, Greek, Latin, French, German, English, Farsi and Sanskrit. He attended the University of Vienna, where he studied philology and Sanskrit. At age twenty, after earning his doctorate degree in 1883, he continued his studies in England, becoming a British subject in 1904. He returned to Hungary for his military service and, fortunately, he received training in geography and surveying. He then returned to England where he studied at the British Museum. His first positions were in India as principal of the Oriental College in Lahore and as registrar of Punjab University. Despite having been baptized as a child and his major achievements as an adult – including being knighted in June 1912 and having received honorary degrees from Oxford and Cambridge – it is sad, indeed, that as a Jew Stein never was offered a position at a prestigious university in Europe.

Stein was a scholar, philologist, archeologist, explorer, geographer and cartographer. A five-foot-four inches tall sharply-dressed bachelor, he was such an intellectual heavyweight that I think his two best friends were Alexander the Great and Xuanzang, the famous Chinese Buddhist monk of the seventh century whose detailed travel diary led to amazing discoveries by archeologists and other researchers more than twelve hundred years later. Stein followed in the footsteps of his two "friends," starting with his first expedition in 1900 when, like Xuanzang, who journeyed along the Silk Road for sixteen years beginning in 629 CE, he set off from Kashmir into the Taklamakan desert (*taklamakan* means "one who enters will die and never leave") and also kept a detailed diary and wrote many books and academic articles about his explorations and what he found. In 1926 Stein walked Alexander the Great's route. Since Tibetan medicine is based on ancient Greek medicine, Stein wondered whether Alexander the Great reached Tibet, so he decided to find out for himself. Stein had seven dogs, all named Dash, and he traveled with one of them on every expedition.

A man with remarkable physical stamina, Stein led four expeditions to Central Asia that ultimately totaled more than twenty-five thousand miles: a two-year expedition from 1900 to 1902, a second expedition from 1906 to 1908, a third expedition from 1913 to 1916 and a fourth expedition in 1930. The expeditions were grueling, and Stein endured freezing temperatures, dangerous mountains, blinding sandstorms, polluted water and scarce food, debilitating sickness, wild animals, weapon-carrying bandits and inadequate shelters. He had to breathe through the sleeve of his fur coat to warm the air, carry weighty water with him to stay hydrated and suffer the loss of some of his toes as a result of frostbite. In 1903 Stein's book about his first expedition, *Sand Buried Ruins of Ancient Khotan*, was published, followed by his book titled *Ancient Khotan*.

In early 1901, when Stein was excavating among the dunes at the edge of the Taklamakan desert in Dandan Uiliq, about seventy miles northeast of the Khotan oasis, he unearthed a rich mix of traditions of East, West and South. Where the human eye saw barren land, Stein found mummies; Buddhist art and sculptures; two-thousand-year-old coins from the Han Dynasty; the earliest Indian manuscripts found anywhere; a simple guitar; rugs with elaborate Chinese and Persian designs; manuscripts, some (not written on paper) from the first century; and others (from the second century) written on paper, wood, leather and other materials in languages such as Sanskrit, Chinese, Tibetan, local languages and unknown lost languages. Stein even found a mousetrap among what others saw as simply garbage.

Oldest Hebrew (Judeo-Persian) document on paper, dated early eighth century. Found by Sir Marc Aurel Stein in Dandan Uiliq, China, in 1901, it is currently in the British Library; © The British Library Board, OR.8212 (166).

Most important, Stein found a manuscript that dates to the early eighth century. The oldest Hebrew document on paper rather than on parchment, it is written with Hebrew characters, but the language is Judeo-Persian and is the oldest example of ancient Farsi. It describes the possibly fraudulent sale of sheep. We know that the Chinese invented paper in the year 105 at the beginning of the second century and were writing on paper for centuries before the word *paper* was known in Europe and the Middle East. Imagine that the oldest Hebrew document on paper was not found in Warsaw, Frankfurt, Vilna, Jerusalem or Baghdad, but rather it was found in Dandan Uiliq on the Silk Road in far western China near Tibet!

Stein wrote that he could not open the document, which is sixteen inches long and four to eight inches wide, but he saw the Hebrew letters. It was opened in London, has thirty-seven lines, is dated around the year 718 CE and is labeled a "mutilated Persian document in Hebrew, the oldest Persian document found and the oldest Hebrew document written on paper." The discovery of this document in Hebrew confirmed that Jewish merchant pioneers known as Radanites played a prominent role on the Silk Road. Although this document revealed so much important history, its discovery received very little attention.

Sadly, no one has written an adequate translation of this ancient document, although while I was living in Tokyo, the three-volume classic study of the Chinese Jews written by Bishop William Charles White was reprinted as one very thick book, and that's where I first learned about this amazing piece of paper with Hebrew writing. In the 1980s I went to London to see this special document, which now is housed in the British Library, but the librarian was completely unaware of it. I persisted and, finally, the librarian and I found it listed in a thin Judeo-Persian catalog.

In March 1907, during Stein's second expedition, he reached Dunhuang, the crossroads of China and the Silk Road in far western China, and there he stumbled on what may be his greatest find. The area was a base for military operations and trade two thousand years ago, from 200 BCE to 200 CE of the Han Dynasty. Behind the sand dunes, there is a mile-long rock cliff located about twelve miles southeast of Dunhuang. Beginning in the fourth century CE and continuing to the fourteenth century, Buddhist priests dug sandstone caves – there were almost eight hundred – into the cliffs and decorated these caves with art. Known as "the Caves of the Thousand Buddhas" or "the Magao Grottoes," the caves were stacked on top of each other, and inside monks stored magnificent artifacts in Buddhist, Indian and Chinese styles. Travelers on the Silk Road financially supported the caves and their contents believing their contribution showed gratitude for having arrived safely and/or also to secure their successful return home. By the late tenth century, however, the Silk Road was replaced by sea routes, and travelers no longer traversed the area.

Wang Yuanlu, a Taoist priest, had become the self-appointed caretaker of the caves in the late nineteenth century. One day in 1900, Wang and other workers cleared away ten feet of sand and entered one of the caves, fifty-four feet by forty-six feet, now numbered Cave 16. Inside Wang noticed the outline of a sealed door. He pushed open the door and found a room, now numbered Cave 17, which was sealed in about the year 1000 and contained mostly rolled scrolls and textiles; the longest scroll was ninety-nine feet. Sealed for nine hundred years, most likely to protect Buddhism from Islam, it was filled with Buddhist, Taoist, Chinese and Tibetan texts. There were manuscripts on paper in more than thirty languages, with Chinese and Tibetan languages being the most dominant, and there are about 250 documents in languages that remain a mystery. "The Diamond Sutra," the world's oldest printed book, which is dated May 11, 868 (six hundred years before the Gutenberg Bible), now in the British Museum, was inside this sealed cave library, too. There were writings on palm leaves from India and "how to" texts on everything from cures for common illnesses, to why children should appreciate their mothers, to whether tea or wine is better, to a eulogy for a donkey.

The dry desert air (it rains there only about once every ten years!), darkness and sand helped preserve the scrolls in Cave 17. Wang informed local government officials about the caves and their contents, but they showed little interest and were concerned about only the expense of moving these unknown items.

Buddhist images found in Cave 45 at "The Caves of the Thousand Buddhas" (known also as the "Magao Grottoes") in Dunhuang, China; courtesy of Dunhuang Academy

No one knew where Wang found them, and no one seemed to care. In 1904, Wang resealed the library cave.

When Stein met Wang in 1907 during his second expedition, he tried to convince Wang that instead of hiding the artifacts he should give them to the world as a gift that would enlighten them, but Wang refused. Stein then tried to persuade Wang by illustrating to him that they both admired and were followers of Xuanzang, the famous seventh century pioneering Buddhist monk. Stein further explained that he literally had walked in Xuanzang's footsteps under extremely difficult conditions to be there and proposed that he and Wang now could be pioneers together. Stein also suggested that some of the items should be returned to their original source in India, and that £130 would make it possible to repair and care for the caves.

Stein's strategy succeeded, and, on May 29, 1907, Wang agreed to sell to Stein tens of thousands of artifacts, and Stein paid him in silver. Stein acquired from Wang twenty-four cases of manuscripts and four or five cases of paintings and other relics. Stein could not empty the entire cave library – there was just too much – and one of the items he left behind was an ancient Hebrew penitential prayer known as a *selichah*, dating to the early eighth century. The prayer gave thanks to God for having completed successfully the difficult journey to that remote location. In 1908, after Stein left, the prominent French sinologist Paul Pelliot found the Hebrew prayer text and brought it to Paris.

Today, there are about 490 out of the 800 caves remaining. Each one is different from the others, and they were opened to the public in 1980. Together, the caves contained the world's greatest Buddhist library and art collection – tens of thousands of artifacts dating from the years 400 CE to 1000 CE – treasures including giant Buddha statues, painted clay (there was no stone in the area) sculptures of deities, elaborate murals of Buddhist legends and thousands of tiny painted Buddha images of the time. The paintings of musicians and their instruments on some of the cave ceilings became models from which scholars could reproduce the ancient instruments. Not only the wall paintings themselves, but also the colors of the wall paintings are amazing. Some of the cave paintings were of Central Asian merchants with round blue eyes and big noses wearing funny hats – perhaps Jews. Now empty, Cave 17, the sealed cave library, once contained about fifty thousand items, forty-five thousand of which Stein removed. It is likely that the treasures Stein acquired from all his expeditions totaled more than fifty thousand.

The reaction to Stein then, throughout his lifetime, and even after his death, was mixed. He is considered by some to be the "imperialist thief," condemned in China even today for having removed precious artifacts from the caves. He is blamed for inspiring Russian, American, Japanese and French treasure hunters and explorers to plunder and damage what remained in the caves. Hundreds of soldiers from the White Russian Army lived in those caves in 1917, and the smoke from their barbecuing inside the caves damaged the art on the walls, on which the soldiers also scratched doodles. An American scholar tried to carve out a wall in Cave 328 to take a mural but destroyed part of the mural and the wall in the process. What he did take is in one of the Harvard University art museums in Cambridge, Massachusetts. Despite their resentment of Stein, the Chinese translation of his five-volume account of his expeditions was greeted with enthusiasm by Chinese scholars, and, as noted, he was even knighted by the British.

I stood in Cave 17 and placed my footprint in the empty cave library. It was the thrill of a lifetime for me, and I considered myself to be blessed to be standing at this remote historical location. I had a wonderful guide, Professor Liu, who knew everything about every inch of every cave. I explained to him and his colleagues that like Sir Marc Aurel Stein I was from Hungary. I explained that like the Chinese, Stein also had a great sense of history and like the Chinese, Stein, a Jew, also knew what it meant to be persecuted. If one thinks of Stein as a foreign devil, I continued, one is forgetting that he uncovered so much valuable history that had been lost. I reminded them that Wang Yuanlu had offered all of the treasures in the caves to the Chinese Government, but they were not interested. Thanks to Stein, I said, these treasures and the history they elucidate are now available to scholars and everyone else who appreciates their significance.

Many of the items that were taken from the caves by other explorers are no longer available. Items taken by the Germans were destroyed during bombings in World War II, and items that were kept in China have disappeared. The items Stein received from Wang, however, survived the frequent bombings in London because they were hidden below the National Library of Wales under the direction of the Hebrew scholar Jacob Leveen. Perhaps someday the treasures that reside in other countries will be returned to China, but that is a different issue from what Stein accomplished. For now, the forty-five thousand manuscripts, documents, books, folded scrolls and works of art that Stein salvaged from Cave 17 are being catalogued and protected by the British Library, where they are available for viewing by the entire world. Stein gave other items he acquired on his expeditions to the British Museum, the British Library, the Indian Museum of Calcutta, the Victoria and Albert Museum in Bombay (now Mumbai), the National Museum in New Delhi and a museum in Pakistan. Thousands of Stein's handwritten letters are housed at Oxford's Bodleian Library.

Stein introduced to the world the Silk Road and all the treasures that had been hidden there for centuries, and his use of the airplane for aerial surveys was ingenious. He was well aware of ancient China's contribution to human civilization, but he wanted to further academic research by making his finds accessible to scholars. More papers and books remain to be researched and written about the artifacts found in the caves, as well as about the Radanites. As part of an independent project, China, Japan, Korea, Russia, Germany and France are cooperating to catalogue and digitize the treasures, including the statues, clay sculptures and murals of Buddhist legends. China now is attempting to protect the caves and their contents from the weather and humans.

Sir Marc Aurel Stein died in Kabul, Afghanistan. Written on his grave are these words: "He enlarged the boundaries of knowledge." That seems to be an understatement of what Stein accomplished.

All the heroes, artists, scholars and statesmen in these pages benefitted from and/or contributed to the Far East. There may not be 269 names to remember, like the 269 times the word *zakhor* is used in the Bible, but those whose stories are in these pages – however many there are – must not be forgotten by history, and our hope is that these stories, passed on to children, grandchildren and succeeding generations, will keep them alive forever.

INDEX